UNTOUCHABLE CITIZENS

Cultural Subordination and the Dalit Challenge

Series Editors: Simon R. Charsley and G.K. Karanth

Across much of the contemporary world, culturally distinct sections of the national populations that have been the victims of systematic repression and institutionalised maltreatment are acquiring a new consciousness and developing new strategies to contest their disadvantaged condition.

Cultural Subordination and the Dalit Challenge is a series that explores—for Indian and other parts of the world—both the processes of cultural repression and the ways in which they are being overcome. It explores the different forms that repression has taken in different societies. In some, there has been a denial of recognition, of opportunities (both social and political), and of cultural autonomy. In others, it has been the ascription of a stigmatised status on various bases such as class, gender, age, race, religion and caste. This series examines the assistance which has been attempted through policies of positive discrimination, the strategies pursued by the disadvantaged themselves to transform their situation, and the opportunities and problems of the future of their societies. The coverage of the series is both historical as well as contemporary, and brings together economic, political, social and cultural studies and those that necessarily transcend these distinctions.

Cultural Subordination and the Dalit Challenge will provide an academic perspective to bring about an understanding of the real problems of the contemporary world where an informed analysis is so urgently needed.

Other Titles in this Series

Untouchable Citizens

Dalit Movements and Democratisation in Tamil Nadu

Cultural Subordination and the Dalit Challenge, Volume 4

Hugo Gorringe

SAGE Publications
New Delhi · Thousand Oaks · London

First published in 2005 by

Sage Publications India Pvt Ltd
B–42, Panchsheel Enclave
New Delhi 110 017

Sage Publications Inc
2455 Teller Road
Thousand Oaks, California 91320

Sage Publications Ltd
1 Oliver's Yard,
55 City Road, London EC1Y 1SP

Published by Tejeshwar Singh for Sage Publications India Pvt Ltd, typeset by InoSoft Systems in 10/12 Souvenir LtBt and printed at Chaman Enterprises, New Delhi.

Library of Congress Cataloging-in-Publication Data

Gorringe, Hugo, 1975–
    Untouchable citizens: Dalit movements and democratisation in Tamil Nadu/Hugo Gorringe.
        p. cm.—(Cultural subordination and the Dalit challenge; v. 4)
    Includes bibliographical references and index.
    Dalits—India—Tamil Nadu—Political activity. 2. Dalits—India—Tamil Nadu—Social conditions. 3. Democratisation—India—Tamil Nadu. I. Title. II. Series.

DS422.C3G88   305.5′688′095482—dc22   2004   2004019122

ISBN: 0–7619–3323–9 (Hb)   81–7829–453–2 (India–Hb)

Sage Production Team: Abantika Banerjee, Jai S. Prasad, Radha Dev Raj and Santosh Rawat

It is clear today, contrary to Gandhi's opinion, that the Untouch-
ables will not finally be emancipated save by themselves: the
good will of their politician superiors cannot be enough

—Louis Dumont

The innocent children playing here in the dust today, these
guileless, defenceless children should not be enslaved in future.
They should not, like us, be imprisoned in cheris. They need to
live from generation to generation with all the benefits and
freedom available to others. In order to protect their future, we
need to make sacrifices today ... As a child of your house I feel
obliged to tell you something. Instead of merely blaming others
for the problems of this village, attempt to unite amongst
yourselves forgetting your grievances, religions and differences

—Thirumavalavan (18 July 1999)

CONTENTS

LIST OF ABBREVIATIONS

ADMK	Anna Dravida Munnetra Kazhagam
AIADMK	All-India Anna Dravida Munnetra Kazhagam
AIPP	All-India Paraiyar Peravai
AMI	Ambedkar People's Movement
BC	Backward Castes
BSP	Bahujan Samaj Party
DLM	Dalit Liberation Movement
DMK	Dravida Munnetra Kazhagam
DPI	Dalit Panther Iyakkam
DPM	Dalit Panther Movement
ESRC	Economic and Social Research Council
FI	Female Infanticide
LTTE	Liberation Tigers of Tamil Eelam
MBC	Most Backward Caste
MDMK	Marumalarchi Dravida Munnetra Kazhagam
NSM	New Social Movements
PDS	Public Distribution System
PI	Penurimai Iyakkam
PMK	Paatai Makkal Katchi
PP	Paraiyar Peravai
PT	Puthiya Tamizhagam
PWG	People's War Group
RPI	Republican Party of India
SRM	Self-Respect Movement
TAYF	Tamizhaga Arundhadiar Youth Front
TDLM	Tamilaga Dalit Liberation Movement
TIP	Tiyagi Immanuel Peravai
TMC	Tamil Maanila Congress
TTS	Tamil Nadu Theological Seminary
UN	United Nations
VDS	Village Development Society
WCAR	World Conference Against Racism
WPM	Working Peasant's Movement

Series Editors' Note

The Indian elections in 2004, with all their surprises, signalled once again the conclusive presence of the Dalit movement in electoral politics. There were Dalits within parties across the wholepolitical spectrum—Dalits as a key element in the constituency of the Bahujan Samaj Party (BSP), and Dalits active in numerous other parties. Together, these make up the Dalit movement in its widest sense. The shift from protest and defence to assertion, so long in building, was strikingly evident.

Dalit concerns have also gained a major place amongst those concerned for human rights in the wider world. The well-known report published in 1999 by Human Rights Watch, 'Broken People: Caste violence against India's "Untouchables"', was a landmark in the globalisation of concern. It was followed up with a strong Dalit presence at the United Nations World Conference Against Racism (WCAR) held in Durban, South Africa, in 2001. This led in turn, through the National Campaign on Dalit Human Rights, to the presence at the 2003 Asian Social Forum in Hyderabad, Andhra Pradesh, of nearly 1,000 representatives of 25 Dalit organisations in India and 17 from overseas. Some 7,000 Dalits rallied from across that state itself, with massed drums in support. Amongst many other events, a conference on Dalits, other social groups and globalisation was held at the Asian Social Forum. In Mumbai the following year, the World Social Forum was even larger and the Dalit cause was again presented on a scale to attract wide international attention.

In parallel with all this, Dalit studies in India have been established as a major field of academic work in the social sciences, with institutions such as the Indian Institute of Dalit Studies in New Delhi and a strong presence across the range of academic institutions nationally. Many, indeed the majority, in the younger generation of those now active in the field have Dalit roots. The subject has come of age and this itself testifies again to the major and widespread achievements of the Dalit community.

A landmark was the publication in 2003 of Chinna Rao Yagati's bibliographical handbook (*Dalit Studies*, New Delhi: Kaniska Publishers 2003). This lists more than 3,500 published works and 156 theses in English alone. However, it also demonstrates that, amongst this wealth of studies, those focusing on the central phenomenon of the contemporary Dalit movement are surprisingly scarce. The movement and particularly those active in it and their interface with the wider society have rarely been addressed in a way to throw light on the realities of the human experience they involve.

Hugo Gorringe's study of the Dalit movement in Tamil Nadu, which we are pleased to be able to include as the fourth volume of our series, not only makes a new and significant contribution here; it also makes clear why it is at the same time both important and difficult to write such studies. It is important, he argues, to understand that Dalit movements 'do not pose a threat to democracy: rather the reverse'. In the state he has studied, Tamil Nadu, they have 'served to deepen the democratic process in the state by extending both the agenda and the constituency of Tamil politics'. He is able to pay particular attention to the aspirations and potential of women in the movement, though these have largely yet to be realised. He is able also to examine the important transition from a protest-oriented movement to direct involvement in the parliamentary process of electoral politics. All this is particularly valuable. By reaching beyond loaded stereotypes, the realities of action, aspirations and interaction (and the inevitable element of discord) Hugo Gorringe reveals the realities of action, aspirations and interaction, as well as the inevitable element of discord. He offers a useful and sympathetic understanding of the individual people concerned and of the significance of the movement's values in and for their lives.

Other kinds of research on the movement have been a little less scarce. Research carried out at a somewhat greater conceptual and personal distance through the study of documentary sources, by formal interviews with leaders and by surveys, is excellently exemplified in the preceding volume in our series, Sudha Pai's *Dalit Assertion and the Unfinished Democratic Revolution* (Sage, 2002). This is a study of the BSP at its heartland in Uttar Pradesh, from which it won 19 Parliamentary seats in the national elections of 2004. Only five of these were from Reserved Constituencies. Across the nation as a whole it was able to contest more seats (435) than any other party, including the mightiest of them, the Congress and the BJP. Much can be achieved by these larger-scale methods of research and Gorringe does not neglect them, but his study offers an extra dimension of insight by foregrounding first-hand experience with ordinary participants. This is the methodology which social anthropology made its own. It sought to add such experience to the special advantages of conspicuous outsider status in seeking and communicating a deeper understanding of the lives of others. The two volumes are in this way complementary, as they are indeed in representing Dalit political activity in two of its major loci—in the North and the South of India respectively. Both investigate Dalit engagement with the electoral process, though at very different stages and on different scales.

Gorringe shows the sensitivity of his methodology. It depends for its success on issues of access and rapport, here accentuated by the nature of the movement studied. Conspicuously, this is not an approach in which participants can take favourable representation for granted. What others will take to be knowledge about oneself and ones colleagues—'the facts'—cannot be a matter of careless confidence. It is a movement in which awareness of opponents interested in the possibilities of slander and exposé, even libellous misrepresentation, is bound to be strong. Such opponents in the Dalit field are not only those against whom rights are being claimed, who often include the locally powerful and therefore potentially dangerous, but also, as in politics generally, rivals within the movement itself. These are likely to be within one's own organisation as well as in others: we learn that there are more than 70 different Dalit organisations within the one state on which Gorringe is focusing. Controlling information about oneself, something that may not weigh heavily with the confident and secure, inevitably becomes an issue in such circumstances. The credentials of researchers seeking information are a matter for more than mere curiosity. Gorringe's anthropologically-inspired methods clearly cannot be used effectively in any and every situation. It is understandable that many may think it prudent not even to try.

It is therefore not difficult to see why this sensitive but crucial field of research is not more widely explored. The author has the advantage here not only of his outsider status but of resources from his personal biography to supplement his own anthropological training and judgement. He is to be complimented on using them so effectively in making this exceptional study. Being able to bring it to wider attention is timely and we as Series Editors are in debt both to our author and our publisher in enabling us to do so.

Simon Charsley
University of Glasgow, Scotland, UK

G.K. Karanth
Institute for Social and Economic Change, Bangalore,India

Acknowledgements

It is difficult to know where to begin thanking people, but first and foremost I have to record my deep gratitude to the many people who took the time and trouble to talk to me, share newspaper cuttings, protest notices and ply me with hospitality. Despite facing hardship and poverty themselves, people were always willing to spend time talking to me. They invariably provided refreshment, and often the offer of a place to stay. Such generous hospitality enabled me to travel into parts of Tamil Nadu that I could not otherwise have visited. The names of all those who contributed to this book are too many to list. If this study has managed to reflect the complexity of processes and events on the ground it is largely due to the efforts of the people who so enthusiastically cooperated and gave freely of their time, their experiences and their advice. Given the constraints of time and space, I can only thank them in this somewhat impersonal and detached way though I wish I could thank each person individually. Certain people, however, deserve particular thanks.

The Economic and Social Research Council (ESRC) provided generous funding that enabled me to embark on this study and make the necessary trips to India. The Tamil Nadu Theological Seminary (TTS) not only arranged somewhere for me to stay, but also granted me access to library and other facilities. The Dalit Resource Centre and the Social Analysis Centre staff were extremely helpful and deserve especial thanks. Gabrielle Dietrich took the time to read through my work and offer invaluable comments. She also offered encouragement and advice throughout my time in India.

Various people were instrumental in helping me achieve a more balanced picture of movements in Tamil Nadu. Isaac Kadirvelu, Rueben Santhamoorthy, Peter Paul Thomas, Jeyakaran and Ashok Kumar all took me to their homes in Cuddalore and Vellore districts. Apart from treating me like royalty, they introduced me to Dalit movements and activists in the northern parts of the state that I would otherwise have neglected. They took me to towns and villages and introduced me to people whom I could not otherwise have met.

Activists from numerous movements made time for me and cooperated enthusiastically, never once showing annoyance or disapproval when I turned up unannounced on their doorsteps. Certain people took an active interest in my research and offered comments both whilst I was in the India and after my return. Palani Kumar and his sister Dhanam are among those, as are Kamaraj and his brother Bhoomi. Daniel Gnanasekaran was always ready to answer my, sometime hostile, questions, and introduced me to the difficulties of movement activism. Jewahar, of the Tamilaga Dalit Liberation Movement (TDLM), was always ready to answer my questions and offer advice. He introduced me to cadres and opened my eyes to problems in equal measure. Inbaraj, a childhood friend, and Durairaj, his cousin, took more than a passing interest in my work and introduced me to the rural villages and villagers of Karur whilst always being there to discuss the issues that my work threw up.

Closer home, I am indebted to countless people for guiding me through the morass of my notes to a more or less coherent account. Both my Ph.D. supervisors provided encouragement and direction when it was needed during the doctoral phase and afterwards as I tried to develop this monograph. Jonathan Spencer and Roger Jeffery helped me through the process of turning rough chapters into coherent ones and had to read through prospective chapters more than once. A big 'thank you' to both of them. Once the process of writing was over I received insightful contributions from my three examiners: Tony Good, John Harriss and Mattison Mines. Their engagement with my work highlighted ways to alter it. On this score, I am indebted to the anonymous reviewer at Sage, India, for her helpful and perceptive comments on how I could improve my original manuscript. Many thanks are also due to Debjani Dutta (and later Tajeshwar Singh) for editorial encouragement and for keeping me on track and to the series editors S. Charsley and G. Karanth for agreeing to take on this book. Simon deserves especial thanks for his advice and help both before and after he assumed editorial responsibilities.

In periods when I have been struggling to find an argument or theme, or when I have been in the midst of editing, my father has been of immense assistance. He has uncomplainingly accepted each new draft and offered comments and criticisms within days despite the pressures of his own work.

Other people have commented on chapters and given me useful feedback. Mai Gorringe, Gill Haddow, Rohini Hensman, Andrew Wyatt and Martha Caddell have all read through chapters and provided me with feedback on my work. Equally as important, countless friends and long-suffering office and flatmates have kept me going, and vaguely sane, through the process of producing this book. In India, the youth of TTS welcomed me into their games of cricket, football and the like. Bas, Tambu, Adline Akka, Rajendaran Uncle, Kumbamanikam Uncle, Jeyaharan, Alex, John, Adel, Amudhan, Philip, Shiva, Dhanraj, Raja, Babu, Augusta and many others were always happy to discuss issues. I would particularly like to acknowledge my debt to Mai, Iona, my mum, Magdalen, Shivaji, Susan, Gill, Martha, Steve, Michael, Ross, Madeline, Foy, Morgan, Amy-Jo and Lou, Gerry, Juliet, Christiana, Axel, Delphine, Myriam, Karen, Richard, Kostas and Su for mutual moaning sessions and recuperating breaks. I am indebted also to Sue Renton who helped iron out countless problems particularly related to computers.

It is customary to conclude by acknowledging the lynchpin of the study in question, but no simple thanks could possibly reflect my gratitude to Edwin and his family. Edwin is a childhood friend and companion, but his selfless cooperation, interest and assistance went well beyond the call of duty. For the duration of my stay in Tamil Nadu I was made to feel like one of the family. Nesamani Akka, Shanti Akka, Danny and Athai never tired of discussing pertinent issues with me, feeding me, and keeping me alive through the year that I spent in India. Edwin was an ever-present guide, translator, companion and critic. When he left his job half way through my fieldwork he never hesitated to join me. Without him, it may truly be said, much of this book would not have happened.[1]

I wish to register my profound thanks to the NIC Tamil Nadu State Unit for their kind permission to use this map. The map is taken from the Government of Tamil Nadu website: http://tnmaps.tn.nic.in.

[1] All translations in the text are my own. I would like to thank Edwin for his tireless cooperation, and priceless support during the process of transcription and translation. Several colloquial sayings would have lost their meaning in direct translation and I have substituted the appropriate English equivalent here.

Introduction

UNTOUCHABILITY UNDONE?

Introducing the Study: Dalit Dreams and Dalit Struggles

Dhanalakshmi sighed as she looked through the photographs. The Dalit houses in Kodankipatti lay in ruins in the pictures, their tiles smashed and strewn over the floor and the skeletal wooden frames that they had rested upon casting shadows over the wreckage. 'What do you think about this', she asked, 'do you think that this is just? … We are human beings too!' Dhanalakshmi is a 20-year-old woman living in Melavassel, a Dalit Housing Estate in Madurai, the Temple City of Tamil Nadu, south India. She has been educated up to eighth standard (three years before the first significant government examination), is an excellent seamstress and is also qualified to drive an auto-rickshaw. Her father was a municipal worker, the house where they live is in his name and their occupancy depends on at least one member of the family remaining in municipal service. Her brother, who would otherwise be expected to follow in his father's footsteps, is an unpaid, full-time activist in the Liberation Panther Movement. Deprived of his income, the family lacks the resources to procure a vehicle and so Dhanalakshmi earns some extra cash by mending and making clothing on the battered old Singer sewing machine under the awning at the front of the house. With her mother she does most of the cooking for the family, collects water and looks after the livestock that they have acquired through a government scheme.

Largely confined to the house and the immediate locality, she manages to keep herself informed through the perusal of newspapers, watching television and talking to the many visitors who come to the house. As a result, she possesses a passionate sense of justice. 'I did not always feel this way, this concerned', she insisted. 'When I was in school, life was just, you know, 'jolly'. I didn't care about these sorts of things [indicating the photographs]. It was only during the riots in Subramaniapuram [a Madurai suburb] in 1996 that I began to develop a different view of life. When people from that area came here and told their pitiable stories it really made me cry and it made me angry. I felt that this was dreadfully wrong and I began to understand my elder brother's commitment to the movement'. Things are bad here, she acknowledged, surveying the children playing in the dust and dirt at the entrance of the colony. They would be at school but for economic necessity. 'They say school is free, but it never is; they hassle you for ten rupees, for the uniform, and five rupees for the books, and so on'.[1] In such a situation it would be easy to develop a sense of fatalism and to agree with those who argue that the position of the lowest castes is immutable. Dhanalakshmi, however, is convinced that 'the day will come, and not in the distant future, but soon, when we will gain our independence; our independence day, our freedom day!'

Dhanam is one of millions of ex-Untouchables, or Scheduled Castes (SCs—the constitutional term for the Untouchables), who reject the basis of their subordination and aspire towards a more equal society. In the last decades of the 20th century the SCs have become an increasingly organised and political force in Tamil Nadu. Calling themselves by the Marathi term 'Dalit', meaning 'oppressed or downtrodden', many ex-Untouchables have begun to mobilise and fight for the proper implementation of the Constitution. The term 'Dalit', as Zelliot observes, implies 'those who have been broken, ground down by those above them in a deliberate and active way. There is in the word itself an inherent denial of pollution, karma, and justified caste hierarchy' (1996: 267, emphasis in the original). Since the 1970s, the horizontal mobilisation of the oppressed has posed as much of a challenge to the dominance of the higher castes as has legislation.

Whilst the Constitution of Independent India adopted the universal franchise and proclaimed the equality cf all citizens, this book argues that it is at the local level that relations of power are challenged, negotiated and reconfigured. When villagers in Kodankipatti (south

---

[1] Shiri (1998: 26–27), Majumdar (1999: 283) and Kaul (2001:158) all illustrate the ways in which poverty constrains the educational options of Dalit households.

central Tamil Nadu) refused to perform the degrading work that was traditionally assigned to the Untouchable members of society, it was they who had to face the wrath of the dominant caste in their village and the social ostracism that resulted from their decision. Likewise, when Murugesan contested and won the seat reserved for SCs in the Melavalavu panchayat (local council) elections in 1997 it was he who had to stand against the wishes and threats of the locally-dominant Thevar caste. The legal recognition accorded to the post of panchayat president was insufficient to protect Murugesan and his followers from being massacred in broad daylight by those who could not countenance the elevation of an Untouchable to a position of responsibility.[2] It is in encounters of this nature that the caste-based hierarchies— which inform daily interaction in India—are being confronted and questioned.

To suggest that nothing has changed since Independence would be ridiculous. 'Changing formal institutions', as Putnam avers, 'can change political practice' (1993: 184). The constitution *has* undermined the legitimacy of caste and provided the oppressed with the institutional means to challenge their subordinate status. The capitalisation and liberalisation of the economy, in conjunction with the reservations system, has combined to reduce the association between occupations and caste status. Payment in cash means that contractual exchanges are divorced from connotations of purity and impurity and political legislation has guaranteed the SCs parliamentary representation. This book is about these processes of social and political change in contemporary Tamil Nadu and it raises a number of questions relating to Dalit mobilisation in the state. The history of Dravidian politics in the state renders this an ideal site for an assessment of Dalit identity and protest politics. In contrast to other

---

[2] The examples of Kodankipatti, Melavalavu and the elections in Chidambaram recur throughout this study as illustrations of caste discrimination and Dalit protest. They are detailed in specific chapters but a summary of the events may be found in the appendix. The deep-rooted nature of caste discrimination was rendered starkly apparent at the dawn of the 21st century when relief for victims of the earthquake in northern India was reportedly distributed along caste lines. The Dalits were 'grossly short-changed in this highly inequitable distribution chain', according to P. Menon (2001: 14). The deprivation of the marginalised Dalits is further highlighted by the fact that the limited relief following the disaster gave them 'the kind of access to food they would not have got in normal times'.

states in India, it is only in the past two decades that autonomous Dalit movements have emerged to systematically challenge the status quo of political establishments in Tamil Nadu.[3]

This study poses the following questions: (a) How can democracy be preserved or even enhanced under conditions of high extra-institutional mobilisation? (b) What is the current situation of Dalits in Tamil Nadu and how and why, if at all, do Dalits resort to protest? (c) How are egalitarian and democratic ideas instantiated at a local level? (d) How do the action concepts of social movements translate into the everyday lives of their members? (e) How are the demands and fears of Dalits located and played out in spatial terms? (f) Finally, what are the implications of Dalit entry into politics for the 'democratisation of democracy' in Tamil Nadu and India? In answering these questions my work addresses the literature on three main themes: caste, social movements and democratisation.

It is worth taking each of these questions in turn in order to address the main concerns of my research. The first question relates to the common assertion that democratic India suffers from a 'crisis of governability' (Kohli 1990) as a result of extra-institutional mobilisation along caste, religious and sub-nationalist lines that challenges the legitimacy of the state. In *Ethnicity and Populist Mobilisation*, however, Subramanian (1999) refutes this assertion and highlights the fact that social mobilisation is often the means by which society's tendencies to resist change have been overcome. This book similarly argues that high levels of popular participation in politics—whether institutional or non-institutional —is essential if the institutions of parliamentary democracy are to adequately incorporate and represent currently marginalised groups. My contention is that Dalit movements do not pose a threat to democracy; rather the reverse. It is only through systematic and concerted political action that Dalits have been able to expand the sphere of political participation and place their concerns on the political agenda.

This argument is supported by an analysis of the current situation of Dalit politics in Tamil Nadu. My research aims to chart the particular trajectory of Dalit activity in the state as well as point to similarities with other social movement actors. It is essential here to

[3] There have been Dalit movements in Tamil Nadu since the late 19th century. It is only in the past two decades, however, that Dalit movements have sought to enter political institutions.

provide a brief background to Tamil politics.[4] Until the 1967 elections, the Congress Party dominated institutional politics in the state. However, their vote share diminished in each successive election under challenge from the Dravida Munnetra Kazhagam (Dravidian Progressive Federation—DMK). The DMK was a regional nationalist party which played on language nationalism and espoused populist/socialist policies that were successfully mediated to the electorate through the means of cinema as well as effective party organisation. In 1967, Tamil Nadu became the first Indian state to elect a regional nationalist party to government and its accession to power was remarkable at the time.

Under its founder, Annadurai, and his successor, Karunanidhi, the DMK ruled Tamil politics until 1976. The party, however, increasingly lost its radicalism both in terms of its sub-nationalism based on anti-Hindi agitation and also with regard to its economic policies. Partly as a response to this, the DMK split in 1972 with M.G. Ramachandran (MGR), a famous film star of the Tamil screen, leading a breakaway faction called the Anna DMK (ADMK). Anna, here, was a reference to the founding father of the DMK and signalled the ADMK's claim to be closer to his ideals. The ADMK wrested power from the DMK in 1977 partly as a result of MGR's popularity and populism (as typified by his provision of free school meals for children). Since then the two parties have alternated in power although there have been signs in recent elections that the DMK's support base may be crumbling. Corruption has been a pervasive feature of Tamil government since the late 1970s as has a personalisation of politics in the personages of MGR (or his successor Jayalalitha) and Karunanidhi. Of more importance to this book, however, is the increasing de-radicalisation of the Dravidian parties.

Whilst the initial victory of the DMK was welcomed as signalling the end of Brahmin rule and the birth of a new nation of 'Tamils,' it is clear that the DMK's social radicalism was strictly curtailed. Rather than envisaging inequality in class or caste terms both the Dravidian parties played on the Brahmin/non-Brahmin divide to suggest a commitment to social change even though their leadership and core constituency were drawn from dominant, landowning Backward Castes. By stressing language rather than class the DMK

---

[4] In this brief account of Tamil politics I draw mainly on the works of Kohli (1990), Subramanian (1999) and Washbrook (1989).

(and later the ADMK) attempted to create an imagined community of Tamils and avoided acting upon its politically sensitive election pledges on land-reform, dowry and caste. Over time the DMK and ADMK moved away from their initial anti-Centre and anti-Hindi positions, softened their anti-Brahminism (to the point where a Brahmin could succeed MGR) and consistently failed to implement their more meaningful redistributive policies.

Contrary to Subramanian's (1999) account of the organisational pluralism of Dravidianism, therefore, I argue that the political map of the state is dominated by a Backward Caste élite who have become increasingly jealous of their power as evinced by their mounting hostility towards Dalit movements. Contemporary Dalit protest in Tamil Nadu is consequently only partly inspired by ideological aspirations that induce individuals to defy the very real risks of political engagement, because it is also driven by violent acts of repression. When Dalits around the state are subjected to social boycott (denied work, access to shops and to common resources), intimidated, beaten and killed simply because they come from a Scheduled Caste then it is difficult to ignore that categorical identity. Dalits, in other words, are forced into protest as much as they elect to agitate.

Dalit movements emerging out of this situation are often reactive in their approach. They are frequently reduced to voicing grievances and protesting about instances of oppression rather than campaigning proactively for social change. In their protests, petitions and roadside demonstrations, Dalit movements call upon state officials to enforce the constitution even as they seek to realise the public spaces theoretically made available in the public sphere. All of the movements, however, do have egalitarian and democratic visions of a future caste-free society. The third and fourth questions that I address are related here. In this study I sought to find out how such ideas were instantiated on the ground and how significant the ideals of the movements were for people's everyday lives. The contention here is that political rhetoric remains abstract and hollow until it is realised in the activities of movement activists. In the 1999 elections in Chidambaram, for example, the rights to self-determination and citizenship were translated into the slogan: 'We are voting for ourselves'. The abstract commitments to equal citizenship were substantialised in the physical act of voting for an autonomous Dalit candidate. Likewise, certain activists sought to act out their emphasis on education by operating tuition centres for Dalit children.

In terms of lifestyle, it was often less clear how, if at all, movement concepts influenced people's behaviour. Rhetorical avowals of women's rights, for instance, seemed to have little impact on the patriarchal basis of activists' family lives. There were also few people who had succeeded in prefiguring a caste-free society in their own modes of perceiving or expressing the world. Most activists spoke in caste terms and in terms of castes that were supposedly subsumed under the Dalit category. Yet, there were indications that allegiance to particular movements was more than superficial. Whether it was in the way that activists responded to incidences of violence, in their assertions of caste pride or their determination to reject overt forms of submission, they did incorporate elements of their political ideals into their modes of being in the world.

This was perhaps most evident in how the demands and fears of Dalits were played out in spatial terms. The continuing isolation of Dalits in separate settlements is a denial of equal citizenship and Dalit protest attempts to widen access to public space as well as create intimate arenas for interaction. Dalit movements engage in the seemingly paradoxical processes of constructing defended neighbourhoods on the one hand and carving out spaces for public engagement on the other. The first act of any movement on establishing itself in a territory is to raise the flag or emblem of that movement. In doing so a locality declares its allegiance to a particular movement and its participation in wider networks of support. Movement markers serve the dual function of communicating a locality's rejection of caste whilst reinforcing social boundaries and deterring potential aggressors. Such defended neighbourhoods provide secure areas for Dalits to form bonds of trust and friendship, but they also foster antipathy amongst those who perceive themselves to be excluded.

This leads us to a consideration of the implications of Dalit action for the democratisation of democracy in Tamil Nadu and India. In re-casting Dalit settlements as arenas of political resistance Dalit movements serve both to widen the base of political participation and exacerbate caste-based antagonisms and conflicts. In challenging the power of locally-dominant castes, the Dalit struggle has conscientised and politicised people who were marginalised by institutional politics. This process has led to the formation of independent and free-thinking Dalit parties which are contesting the hegemony of established organisations and it has also prompted the rise of Backward Caste (BC) movements. Although it is too early to tell what the eventual outcome of this process will be, I argue that Dalit movements have served to deepen the democratic process in the state by extending both the agenda and the constituency of Tamil politics. Although BC parties are often violently opposed to the extension of political institutions to Dalit actors, they increasingly have to engage (and negotiate) with Dalit parties. Given that the Dravidian parties have often held the balance of power at a national level in recent years, the introduction of radical political actors into Tamil politics could also have wider implications. If they can resist the allure of attractive alliances with established parties then these movements could serve to reinvigorate political debates in the state. In moving Tamil Nadu beyond the impasse currently represented by the alternation of similar parties in power they will have played a part in extending Indian democracy.

At the heart of my analysis is why Dalits feel the need to engage in protest movements despite the constitutional provisions that ought to ensure their equality. It is argued that many Dalits are still dependent upon dominant landlords who tend to be from higher castes. The position of rural Dalits is particularly vulnerable and the assertion of their rights can lead to them being ostracised or subjected to violence. Dalits are not necessarily able to escape caste discrimination within the urban environment, but in both, the correlation between caste and class has increasingly been subjected to challenge by the liberalisation and modernisation of the economy and the provision of affirmative action programmes.[5] Whilst Dalit activists contest the efficacy of government programmes, the emergence of an educated, professional and relatively wealthy Dalit middle class constitutes a resource base for social action. The rise of Dalit consciousness and resistance would have been much harder without alternative sources of income and increasing levels of education and self-respect.

To select one particular movement as 'typical' of the others is a meaningless exercise in a state where there are over 70 different Dalit organisations. I focus on the Liberation Panthers (DPI) because they

[5] Corbridge and Harriss (2000, Chapter 9), Karanth (1997: 324–25), Sharma (1991: 69), Subramanian (1999: 65–73) make similar claims. Sebastian (1994) has a detailed analysis of the impact of affirmative action programmes in Tamil Nadu.

are one of the largest Dalit movements in Tamil Nadu and are in the process of transforming themselves from a movement into a political party.[6] Activists from other movements disagreed with the DPI's tactics and some saw them as representing a particular caste constituency. With these disclaimers in mind, however, it is possible to distinguish some shared issues that motivate the diverse strands of Dalit mobilisation. There is, arguably, a repertoire of protest that serves not only as an opportunity for the manifold protest groups and parties, but also as a constraint that limits the degree of innovation any one organisation can attempt.[7]

By highlighting these points of similarity I hope to attain a broad picture not only of the Liberation Panthers but also of the organisational and ideological bases of Dalit protest more generally. The demands and tactics of the diverse movements may be disentangled to reveal common objectives. 'Different *dalit* movements highlight different issues related to *dalits* around different ideologies', as Shah observes. 'All of them, however, overtly or covertly assert a *dalit* identity though its meaning is not identical or precise for everyone' (Shah 1990: 317). By looking at the organisation, ideology and strategies pursued by the Liberation Panthers and the context in which they operate I hope to highlight the problems and promises of Dalit mobilisation in the state and contribute to the wider literature on democratisation processes across India.

The Field Sites

I conducted my fieldwork in the south Indian state of Tamil Nadu for 12 months between November 1998 and November 1999. Dalit

---

[6] The *Dalit Panther Iyakkam* (DPI) is so known in recognition of the radical Maharastrian Dalit Panther Movement of the 1970s. In Tamil, however, the movement is always known as the Liberation Panthers (Viduthulai Cirruthaikal). Confusion arises because the activists still refer to themselves as the DPI for short. Here, therefore, both versions will be used interchangeably. Also see Chapter 1.

[7] It is no surprise, for example, that the DPI chose to enter the electoral fray in 1999. Despite the ideological contradictions inherent in such a move, the tactic of democratic participation was seen as an imperative for movement survival. Those movements that continue to reject the parliamentary process still conform to broad patterns of acceptable and recognised protest.

movements are active in this region but, as we have seen, they developed later and have not received the recognition accorded to their counterparts elsewhere. I was based in the central city of Madurai and built upon existing contacts in the Tamil Nadu Theological Seminary (TTS), which has good links with several movements that are active in the locality. Despite this, the immediate difficulties that I encountered were those of access. Social movement participants are conscious of being part of a group and are more wary of (and used to) researchers prying into their organisation than most individuals. Each person I interviewed quizzed me first about my credentials for doing the research, the reasons why I was interested in the subject and what I hoped to achieve. Some leaders and activists were extremely defensive about their movements and were reluctant to open themselves up to criticism. Others were wary of being associated with a foreigner, for fear of accusations that they were getting outside funds. Furthermore, access to certain movements was barred by reluctance on my part. Several movements had a forbidding image and my friends portrayed them as violent organisations. Without some form of introduction it was impossible to intrude myself upon them.

Early in my fieldwork I moved into a 'Dalit colony' in the village of Kosuvangundu. The village is located 12 km outside Madurai and my intention was to live with Dalits and attune myself to their concerns. It soon became apparent that caste was a sensitive issue that people were not happy to talk about in detail. Those who got to know me were delighted to have an 'English friend', but were much less comfortable with my role as a researcher. Dalits here recurrently stated that there were no caste issues in the village because they were too strong. Untouchability, if it existed here, manifested itself in the compartmentalisation of village affairs into Dalit and non-Dalit shops. Issues surrounding the use of water had reportedly been solved, after previous disputes, by the provision of separate water pumps in various areas of the village. Occupations varied between agriculture, people working in the local dyeing industry and those who travelled into Madurai to work in construction, garments, or service industries. The predominant complaints from Dalits were about poor conditions of work and poverty.

Despite this apparent lack of caste enmity, the Dalits of Kosuvangundu were organising themselves together along the lines of a social movement. The putative form of social organisation in the village was centred round the festivities that increasingly mark 14 April as Ambedkar's birthday. Each Dalit household in the village contributed a small amount of money in order to mark the day with some food, games and speeches. The conscientisation of Kosuvangundu's Dalits owed much to the work of external activists and was not completely 'organic'. It did not, in other words, arise solely from the immediate concerns and grievances of the villagers. This was apparent in April 1999 when the villagers unveiled a flag and board not of any particular movement, but as a symbolic assertion of their independence. When I asked individuals what the point of their gesture was, however, they were united in their support for the action. 'This will show that we are not slaves', was the common sentiment (Murugan, 12 April 1999).

This example was important for two reasons. First, it highlighted people's reluctance to talk about caste issues in abstract terms—they were much more comfortable discussing a particular event. Thus it was only after the flag-raising ceremony that people were happy to open up about Dalit concerns. Second, this case brings the changing nature of caste and Dalit protest to the fore: Even those who felt secure and strong are mobilising now to articulate their political opinions. As an illustration it is unusual, however, in that the flag raised was not that of an established movement. When I pressed villagers on why they were not affiliating themselves to an active organisation, people replied that they had 'no need to belong to any particular movement just now'. Some of the younger men in the village disapproved of this stance. They insisted that just because they were doing well did not mean that they should not join the DPI or a similar outfit.[8] In 1999, some villagers had already approached the DPI to discuss 'issues and problems', but the movement had not sought to establish itself in the village. This illustrated an urban bias in movement activity and so, after a month in Kosuvangundu, I returned to the city.

The Liberation Panthers were the most significant movement in Madurai, in terms of numbers, visibility and reputation. The most visible stronghold of the DPI was in Melavassel, a housing unit

---

[8] Returning in 2002, I found that many of the villagers had been won over to the idea that they should join the DPI. This was not due to any particular incident in the village, but reflected the increasing prominence of the movement since their entry into political competition.

adjacent to the central bus stand in Madurai. The estate is populated mainly by municipal workers and the nature of their occupations—cleaning, sweeping, rubbish collection—means that the inhabitants are all Dalits. There are three entrances to Melavassel off the main road that most of the city buses travel along. The first, as one comes round the one-way system and heads into town, is fairly nondescript. The second has an archway built over it, which is painted with the emblems and name of the Tamizhaga Arundhadiar Youth Front (TAYF). The board is old and the paint somewhat faded. Driving further along the road one passed murals of the Communist Party of India, the All-India Anna Dravida Munnetra Kazhagam (AIADMK) and the DMK, each of which had a small enclosure built around them. Standing out from the compound wall on the verge of the road a tall flagpole was embedded in a concrete plinth. The red, white and blue markings of the pole showed that it did not belong to any of these organisations, even though it could be said to be encroaching on their space. It belonged to the DPI. A few yards further on, above the main entrance to the estate and located opposite the Government Tourist Board's Hotel Tamil Nadu, there was a huge, painted billboard proclaiming its allegiance to the Liberation Panthers.

Pursuing the Panthers: Gaining Access

Despite these signposts which advertised the presence of the DPI each time I went into town, gaining access to them was hampered partly by their reputation as a violent group (compounded by the reputation of Melavassel itself), and partly by a lack of contact with people in the movement. There appeared to be little interaction between members of different Dalit movements even where, as in the case of the Liberation Panthers and the Tiyagi Immanuel Peravai (Martyr Immanuel's Front—TIP), the leaders of the two organisations got on well together. Gaining access to one movement, therefore, was as likely to preclude access to another as enhance it. Though the disparate Dalit organisations have issues, ideologies and concerns in common, they can also be very protective of their own constituencies. Most of the cooperative ventures undertaken by the different Dalit groups in Tamil Nadu occur under the aegis of non-governmental organisations (NGOs) or institutions. It is telling that my initial contact with the DPI was at a National Alliance of People's Movements' meeting at the Centre for Social Analysis. The meeting was about globalisation and Monsanto and I had been asked to translate some of the discussion. Most of those present were academics or green campaigners, but one was a member of the Liberation Panthers from Muduvarpatti. Kamaraj, at the time, was an unemployed activist who had come along to the meeting out of interest rather than as a representative of the movement. It was through his intervention that I gained access to the DPI and embarked on a multi-sited ethnography.

Getting to know a member of the movement was essential as a means of establishing my credentials and gaining access to a variety of movement actors. Without the informal contact established prior to more systematic research it is unlikely that I could have collected as much detail or gained as much insight as I did. Kamaraj was instructive, both as an informant but more so as an example. Observing the way in which he interacted with friends and comrades (thozhar—the word that he used) made it abundantly clear that movement activity does not occur in a sphere separate from everyday life. Rather, the day-to-day meetings, cups of coffee and discussions constitute the ties that bind people to each other, to the leader and to the wider cause. Not all the conversations of the movement members concerned Dalits or the ideals of the DPI. Members would gather together and talk as friends on subjects as diverse as politics, cinema, the weather and the mango season. Methodological approaches that privilege formal data collection methods neglect the social ties that both hold a movement together and constitute it. Palani Kumar, the Secretary of a Madurai branch of the DPI, exemplified these informal bonds: He was frequently approached for advice on issues ranging from caste discrimination to securing loans and family matters. Not only was he literate and able to draft official documents, but his experience of dealing with such cases was recognised and valued by others. Without such informal networks the DPI did not have the administrative wherewithal to mount the public demonstrations, marches, petitions and political campaigns through which they attempted to effect social change.

My research was directed, to a great extent, by social movement activists and the events that occurred during my stay. I met many movement activists in the city and conducted most interviews and participant observation in Madurai District, but I was persuaded not to conduct a more conventional ethnography based on one particular site within the city itself. The reasons for this were manifold.

The ambiguity of social movement boundaries and a lack of formal membership precluded the isolation of a bounded field of study.[9] Activists from Madurai frequently travelled elsewhere to attend movement-related meetings, protests or functions. For me to have remained static in a 'field site', would have meant that I could not chart vital aspects of movement organisation and the costs of membership. Simply put, the movement spanned the state and many movement members travelled long distances to attend meetings or to maintain contact. Kamaraj, for instance, regularly travelled the 23 km into Madurai to liaise with comrades in Melavassel and most of my respondents had at some stage been to Chennai in order to attend a mass show of strength. They spoke of commandeering train carriages and travelling en masse so as not to have to buy train tickets.

When Thirumavalavan stood for election in Chidambaram over 50 volunteers from Madurai went to campaign on his behalf.[10]

---

[9] No movement can adopt a wholly regional perspective, because they cannot ignore the common plight of Dalits elsewhere in India. The Liberation Panthers, thus, pasted posters of protest to condemn the killing of Dalits in Bihar and Karnataka. Links were also asserted with other 'oppressed groups', thus the demolition of the Babri Masjid was condemned, as was the immolation of a Christian missionary and his sons in 1999. The internationalisation of human rights has enabled the Dalit community to appeal to a higher authority than the state, and to draw parallels with civil rights movements around the world. Mandela was frequently referred to as evidence of the power of prolonged and patient protest. More tangibly, the proliferation of the Internet and international Dalit networks have provided movements with resources for raising consciousness and support. This was perhaps best evident in the United Nations (UN) conference on racism in Durban 2001 that was attended by several Dalit organisations including the leader of the DPI. On a more sustainable basis, the Dalit Liberation Movement has forged links with groups of 'untouchables' in Japan. These connections are most significant, not for the potential of material resources, but because they are a vital source of moral support. By highlighting the worldwide concern about the Dalit struggle, such links emphasise the justice of the cause and hold up the comforting image of a vast coalition of solidarity and support networks.

[10] Kamaraj and Palani Kumar claimed that many more than 50 people had gone to campaign in the election but I was unable to verify their figure. At the very least 44 people from Madurai made the trek up to Chidambaram, since 43 of them were arrested in Neyveli (as reported in The Hindu, Dhinna Malar). Kamaraj informed me that he should have been amongst those arrested but he had left the building they were staying in shortly before the police raid.

Kamaraj and Palani Kumar (the Melavassel ward leader) routinely visited other DPI 'cells' in the city and in the outskirts. Established activists were also asked to hold 'classes' for prospective members/ wards, and to speak at regional meetings. For the duration of my fieldwork, there were also numerous occasions when movement leaders were called upon to visit the site of an atrocity, the scene of caste violence or the memorial of a fallen 'martyr'. The networks underpinning movement organisation were highlighted in personal events, turning marriages into movement gatherings and house warming parties into social rituals. Movement activists, in other words, were rarely static and had I remained so I would have missed many of the interconnecting threads of movement activity. Furthermore, since the movements are consciously directed at non-members, any sample of informants that failed to include non-movement members would have been incomplete.

As a consequence, I opted to travel around Tamil Nadu with key respondents to key sites and events in order to reflect the spread of the movement, assess the influence of locality upon the participants and better understand the organisation and the impact of the Liberation Panthers. As this discussion should indicate, by following participants to the diverse sites of movement activity I was reflecting their concerns. Although, in this attempt, I have lost some of the detail and minutiae that can emerge from long association with one particular place, my object of study was not a particular group of people in situ but the social movement itself. To have stayed in an established ward of the movement would have been to miss the critical 'rituals' and 'events' that inspire people to join a movement in the first place. This approach evolved from my engagement with the Liberation Panthers in Melavassel, which became the base upon which my research was built. Kamaraj and others impressed upon me the need to witness other places and other wards in order to get a fuller understanding of the movement.

Their argument was that the motivation behind movement action lay in the precarious and threatened conditions of rural villages or less well established urban slums. To view the Dalit community from Melavassel was to see it from a position of strength. I was introduced to other wards in the city and told different stories and trajectories of the DPI's development. In Chapter 5, I discuss in more detail the visits to Keelathurai, SMP Colony, Jansi Rani Complex and other sites in Madurai City itself. Many of the activists encountered in these diverse settings became familiar to me from subsequent movement meetings. Madurai, however, is a city in which the DPI is well established. It is also a regional centre and so numerous protests and demonstrations occur within its boundaries. This means that activists can maintain contact with other wards, give support to each other and rally round in times of trouble. The Liberation Panthers in Madurai are vibrant, active and strong. An analysis of the movement from this perspective would have neglected the diversity of perspectives and experiences of movement activity that was gained by venturing further afield.

Various respondents took me to their homes, I accompanied others when they went to places on behalf of the movement, and I also visited scenes of caste violence and prejudice. Although I did not dictate the destinations, I was not confined to 'movement models'—villages where the movement was doing well and the leader was acclaimed as a hero. The research covered a diversity of locations and experiences. Rather than being distorted by the direction of movement participants my work was given greater depth. Initially I was taken to villages within reach of the Madurai Corporation buses. I spent a week in Muduvarpatti from where I visited Vadianpatti, Kodankipatti and Lingyapatti. All four villages are on the same bus route and are about 20–30 km out of Madurai. Most of the Dalits here belong to the Paraiyar caste.[11] Many commute into the city for work though others own small plots of land or work as agricultural labourers. Mango groves line the side of the road and provide both employment and sustenance. The villages here arguably illustrate the urban bias of the Liberation Panthers. Muduvarpatti, the closest village to Madurai, has a strong and militant DPI wing partly due to the caste composition of the village, where Dalits are a significant presence, but also because several village activists regularly attend meetings in Madurai. As detailed in Chapter 5, Muduvarpatti is seen as a DPI stronghold capable of standing up for itself against casteist aggression.

Just along the road lies Vadianpatti. The DPI appears to be established here and a small open structure has been constructed as a meeting point for the movement. At one end of the room the only solid wall of the *manram* (hall) is given over to a mural of Dr Ambedkar

---

[11] There are three main Scheduled Castes in Tamil Nadu, namely the Paraiyars, the Pallars and the Chakkiliyars. See Table 1.1 in Chapter 1 for more on relations between them and relative numbers.

and a panther above which are placed photos of Thirumavalavan. This symbolic act of defiance and assertion, however, masks a shaky foundation. The people here felt abandoned as the DPI had not demonstrated against the ongoing caste disputes or the social boycott that DPI-affiliated villagers faced. Though Vadianpatti was a mere 25 minute bicycle ride away from Muduvarpatti, the lack of close informal connections with the movement leaders made the distance appear greater. Around 2–3 km along the track the Dalits of Kodankipatti had raised the flag of the DPI only to see it uprooted. Dalits here were in a minority, subject to social boycott, and came under attack from higher castes in 1999. Despite this, the Dalits had organised and stood up to caste discrimination. Some 6 km further out, in Lingyapatti, even this putative form of resistance was absent and I was told that Dalits are still prevented from wearing shoes in the village. Interviews in these villages spanned the entire spectrum of DPI activity, from success to failure. The responses elicited in the outlying villages said more about the effectiveness of the movement than could have been ascertained in the confines of the city.

The focus, thus, was on Madurai and its surrounds, but the movement extends further. I was able to accompany the Madurai Panthers to movement events in an endeavour both to track the extent of the DPI and to better understand the process by which new wards are organised and inducted into the movement. These trips took me south of Madurai, to Virudhunagar District and to the village of Srivilliputhur, and south-east to the villages of Emeneswaram, Paramakudi and Sathirakudi in Ramnathapuram. These meetings marked the extension of the movement into new territory with ardent converts. I also visited the Liberation Panther heartlands around Cuddalore, Chidambaram and Pondicherry. Here the DPI has built on the prior efforts of the Communist Party to establish itself as an organised force. Their growth has impinged upon the constituency of various factions of the Republican Party of India (RPI), and RPI leaders were united in condemning the tactics of the DPI.[12] In Chidambaram and Myaladuthurai I was able to assess the impact of the Liberation Panther's election campaign and the violence that surrounded the polls.

---

[12] The Republican Party of India was established by Ambedkar to provide a radical political platform for SCs and minorities. Whilst the party has spread across India and has offices in most states, it has failed to sink roots in Tamil politics and hence exists as a marginal political player.

Only by visiting these diverse areas could one perceive the differential impact of the incident-based approach usually adopted by the DPI and the proactive campaign mounted prior to the election. This raised issues pertaining to the movement's organisation, resources and modus operandi that would not have otherwise emerged. Later, I attended protest meetings and interviewed Thirumavalavan in Chennai, the political capital of Tamil Nadu and the place where the DPI leader resides. Seated outside his rented accommodation in K.K. Nagar, it was instructive to see people approaching Thirumavalavan for help, hangers-on devoting themselves to following their leader and to meet other leading representatives of the movement and observe the interaction between them. This study has, thus, inverted the customary top-down approach to social movement research. Instead of listening to the leaders and then assessing their impact on the people, I interviewed the participants first, gained their trust and understood their commitment before meeting the central figure around whom they seemed to revolve. This way I could put their doubts to the leader in the form of questions and engage him in debate. Finally, no analysis of the DPI would be complete without visiting Melavalavu, the 'condensed symbol' both of the reasons for protest and the costs that may attend it. Melavalavu featured in most interviews, in almost every major speech and several of the projects undertaken by the DPI during my stay.

Distinctive Demonstrators: Activist Perspectives

During the course of my research, it became apparent that the specificity of researching social movements requires the adoption of theoretical and methodological approaches that differ significantly from research into other fields. One obvious distinguishing feature of movement activists is the fact that they are already engaged in a self-reflexive analysis of society and are seeking ways to change it through action. Such consciousness is not uniform but extends along a spectrum from those who believe that they are hard done by, to movement leaders and theoreticians who have formulated an ideological critique of the system and have considered possible alternatives. Unlike other socially-conscious individuals, social movement members act as part of a group who share similar world views and aspirations.

Often, this has led researchers to analyse the movement as a unitary actor in its own right. The leader-centred nature of movements in India renders such a position attractive. The Liberation Panthers, however, had no formal mechanisms to delineate who was and was not a 'member' of the movement. People attending any given meeting, consequently encompassed various levels of commitment. Whilst those engaged in movement activity on a permanent basis display a firm grasp and understanding of the movement, its ideology and the social deprivation that they hope to eradicate, the more peripheral members tend to be less conscious of such issues. Social Movements, as Diani notes, are not 'empirical entities with clear-cut boundaries: what is and is not part of a movement is as much a matter of subjective perception as of objective criteria' (1992: 107).

Participation in movement activity is often an intermittent or transitory affair with people becoming involved in the protests over one particular issue or incident and then drifting away. Local issues would bring people out to demonstrations, but the number of core activists who turned up for almost all the meetings was minimal. A consequence of this wavering commitment is a certain ambiguity in defining a social movement. Does the definition incorporate those on the peripheries of movement action or only the activists who are aware of and committed to the ideology and principles of the movement in question?[13] This question is further complicated by the fact that people join a movement for differing reasons. Individuals may be attracted to join a movement because of its leader, due to the companionship it offers, due to the ideology it espouses or the action repertoire it adopts. Alternatively, they may join in out of moral conviction, from a personal history of suffering, due to a family

---

[13] According to some authors, social movements are networks of interaction and cannot be described as organisations at all. 'All too often', according to Oliver, 'we speak of movement strategy, tactics, leadership, membership, recruitment, division of labour, success and failure—terms which apply only to coherent decision making entities (that is organisations or groups) not to crowds, collectivities, or whole social movements' (1989: 4). I am sympathetic to the argument that a social movement is constituted by social networks of people and groups who cannot be presented as a unitary entity. I maintain, however, that the conscious acts of the movement members who choose to unite around certain goals and objectives is best reflected in referring to them as a social movement. The term, like the notion of 'collective identity', is a useful tool for analysis rather than a reality in itself.

history of activism or simply for the thrill of seeing themselves in the papers and of being part of a historical movement for change.

In order to analyse such diverse interests as part of a common programme we need some means of identifying a movement. How one defines a movement has significant implications for the research questions that are asked and the methods that are chosen to answer those questions. Whilst most sympathetic to the nuances and implications of the New Social Movement perspective, I have tried to study collective action within its social, historical and political context so as to better understand the motivations of the actors. It is often argued that New Social Movement Theory is premised on Western models of movement action and is, as such, inadequate to describe collective action elsewhere in the world. Access to resources is an over-riding concern for many movements of the South. Indeed, Oommen (1990) and Desrochers, Wielenga and Patel (1991), writing in an Indian context, insist that material deprivation is the primary motivation for movement activity.

Whilst this may be true, I concur with Rao that relative deprivation may be a necessary condition for the emergence of a movement, but it is an insufficient one (1987: 207). Whilst one must not neglect the material basis of action, therefore, 'without an understanding of identity, of the "passion of the actors" ... there is no way of explaining *why* SMs move' (Foweraker 1995: 12). This is especially the case with regard to Dalit movements. The participants in Tamil Nadu were poor, had insecure jobs or housing and were often subject to the threat of force. Ignoring the motives of the actors would have rendered much of the DPI's work inexplicable. It is naïve, however, to assume that the meaning of collective action will be the sum of its individual components. Were the diversity of Dalit voices represented in any organisation then it would be incapable of coherent action and it is important to differentiate between collective action that occurs within a social movement context and that which does not.

The key to this distinction is the question of collective identity. Identity is concerned with the self-esteem and image of a community in relation to others. It relates to questions of 'who "we" are', and 'what position "we" have in society with regard to other communities'. Dalits have long been denied a voice and have been labelled variously as Untouchables, Outcastes, *Harijans*, Backward Classes and Scheduled Castes. Dalit movements have variously been defined as caste, class, religious or people's movements. Emphasising the participants' own perceptions of Dalit mobilisation ensures that we do not neglect the agency and consciousness of the actors themselves. The extensive affirmative action programmes for the SCs have obviously had a profound influence on the emergence and practice of Dalit movements. To overemphasise the institutional influences on, or determinants of, movement organisation, however, is to underplay the radicalism and creativity of Dalit movement actors, because 'a social category is *not* a behavioural entity' (Foss and Larkin 1986: 131, emphasis in the original). Rather, such categories have to be created, recreated and lived if they are to be meaningful.

As Rudolph and Rudolph observed, the caste *association* assumed the characteristics of a voluntary organisation. 'Membership in caste associations is *not* purely ascriptive, this is a necessary but not sufficient condition. One must also "join" through some conscious act involving varying degrees of identification' (1967: 33). Without an approach that takes cognisance of this process of movement formation, key aspects of Dalit movements, evinced in their adoption of the term 'Dalit' would be downplayed. This point is especially pertinent here, where caste blocks *are* often taken for granted and perceived to act as coherent units—as in widespread calculations about 'vote-banks'. So as not to conceive of caste ties and structures as necessarily 'pre-given' or even pre-eminent, we require alternative approaches to questions of identity formation and assertion, organisation and mobilisation undertaken in the name of that category. The explanatory potential and methodological implications of a New Social Movement (NSM) framework have been used here to raise searching questions about the processes and practices observed.

Social Movements: Actors, Identities and Analysis

A social movement can be described as people united in a common belief or issue, who operate democratic organisations (in a loose sense of the term) of their own in posing an extra-institutional challenge to the prevailing order (Foweraker 1995: 12, Oommen 1990: 30). Although a recurrent question in this book is whether the DPI is a *Dalit* or a *caste* movement, I have chosen to speak here in terms of a social movement rather than caste-based collective for several reasons. First, it serves to emphasise the radical objectives of the movement which aims to *eradicate* caste, rather than simply better its own position in the social hierarchy. Second, the DPI consists of members from different castes. Even if we were to dub the DPI a caste-based organisation due to its preponderantly Paraiyar constituency, it is only a small proportion of that group who have joined the movement. Many seek alternative means to improve their lot, many are not prepared to engage in risk-related actions and some members of the social category express disapproval of the DPI. Movements, therefore, depend upon members *choosing* to participate, even if most of those who become involved belong to a particular caste. Third, whilst the DPI does not fully conform to the definition of a 'New Social Movement', the epithet 'new' highlights the contemporary nature of this manifestation of caste.

Part of the problem with much of NSM theory is that it has been developed within the specific context of Western Europe. Wignaraja (1993) and contributors, therefore, suggest the terms 'people's' or 'poor people's' movements to describe movements of the South. These epithets strike me as inadequate here, because the DPI and other Dalit movements in Tamil Nadu have yet to shed their caste basis completely. The experience in the 1999 and 2001 elections, as we shall see, demonstrated the fact that they cannot as yet claim to represent the mass of people in the state. Neither is the term 'poor people's movement' satisfactory given that some of the supporters of the Dalit movements are well to do. Haynes (1997) offers the term 'action group' as a means of circumventing these problems, but this fails to capture the day-to-day interaction that forms the basis of Dalit movement activity in the state. I have chosen, therefore, to use the (admittedly problematic) language of social movement theory. When speaking of the DPI as a movement I refer to the loose collection of people who identify themselves with its leadership and objectives and turn out (at least occasionally) to support it in protest meetings.

Social movement actors are neither homogeneous nor necessarily united. The social category of the SCs is cross-cut by divisions on the basis of religion, caste, region, class position, gender, age and language. Research into Dalit movements, therefore, has to tease out the contesting aspects of signification evinced in the many movements that work with and for the Dalits. The areas of interest to emerge from this relate to the processes of conscientisation and identity formation, relations between movement organisers and the participants and how deep the ideologies and discourses of the movement as a whole have penetrated to its individual members. In other words: how do the action concepts of the social movement translate into the everyday lives of the actors involved? Rather than decide *a priori* that members of a group must subscribe to the views propounded by its leaders, I adopted a methodological assumption of ignorance in order to assess the meanings and relevance of the movement for the agents themselves. This was especially useful in the aftermath of the DPI's decision to contest the elections. Speaking to members who were unaware of, or unconvinced by, the change in policy, I was able to tap into the contradictions between the leaders and the participants.

Any focus upon individual participants and life histories within a movement that is far from homogeneous raises important methodological issues. It is necessary to establish a relationship of trust and reciprocity with anyone before they are willing to answer questions openly (Patwardhan 1979: 153), but this process is compounded when talking to movement leaders or activists. They were all too ready to talk and express their views, but they often followed an established pattern of movement stories. This problematic lies at the heart of any fieldwork experience, but it is further complicated in this instance by the collective nature of the phenomena observed. Whilst all individuals develop stock responses to common questions, the regurgitation of movement narratives by activists serves to obscure the differences of opinion that fissure any collective actor. One means of overcoming this problem is to engage with the respondents on a day-to-day basis, both to win their trust and in order to ask searching questions that disrupt the pre-rehearsed narratives.

Counter-intuitively, I also attempted to follow researchers into this field who have shown a preference for group-based, collective interviews (Melucci 1992; Omvedt 1979; Touraine 1981). The significance of this emphasis is that it reasserts the *social* component of movement activity that might be obscured by perspectives that take the individual as the primary unit of analysis. Several interviews that I conducted culminated in a group discussing the matter amongst themselves and debating what should happen next. In this process they were forced to move beyond the formulaic responses that they could have fallen back upon as individuals. In Vadianpatti, for example, I interviewed local members of the DPI in the 'hall' of the movement (20 March 1999). Despite the impressive nature of this construction and the ubiquity of movement symbols and photographs of the leader, the villagers insisted that the DPI had not done enough to help them.

Kamaraj accompanied me from the neighbouring village and he rejected their claims asking what more the movement could be expected to do. For 10 minutes he argued and discussed their situation whilst I remained an interested spectator. Ultimately it was agreed that a delegation from the village would meet local leaders of the movement to air their grievances.[14] Another example of such action-oriented discussion came during my interview with Pandiammal, a Women's Wing leader in Madurai (28 March 1999). Several local women sat in on the interview and when I asked them about caste discrimination they were unanimous in citing the problems they faced at the ration shop. They maintained that they were constantly under-served and frequently made to queue for hours. Their complaints led to a consideration of how this could be overcome and it was agreed that a poster would be printed to protest against this discrimination. This poster was later printed, but it is unlikely that it had any effect on its own.

Guided discussions, or collective interviews, should facilitate and stimulate the flow of discussion rather than following a fixed sequence or set phraseology. Such interviews, as we have seen, often assume an internal dynamic of their own. I feel that this process should be encouraged. 'That the "collective interview" should fade into the "organising meeting"', as Omvedt holds, 'is not inappropriate'. 'An "organising meeting" is after all a fully developed form of this: the "respondents" are presented with new values, new aims which are explained and elaborated as fully as possible and then asked not simply to express feelings during the meeting ... but to act after that' (Omvedt 1979: 384). Through group discussions, thus, I have attempted to chart the diversity of movement voices, analyses of action and sentiments to assess how far members are attuned to the concerns of the movement as a whole and what motivates their participation, without isolating them from the field of action.

Group Work: Studying Collective Actors

In the event most of the interviews I conducted prompted group discussions. Even when I made appointments to see individuals, it was very rare that I would find them alone. The problems with this are obvious. Movement leaders being interviewed in front of their

---

[14] The Vadianpatti members remained sceptical that anything would be achieved and I was unable to follow up on what occurred in this instance.

followers may be tempted to reiterate the movement position and avoid talking about themselves personally (cf. Della Porta 1992: 182). The interview could become a staged performance in which all questions would be answered and the interviewer convinced. Where I met people in their houses, there were usually activists waiting to see them and so these conditions often arose. The group discussions could often be turned to my advantage, however, particularly where I was introduced by acquaintances. Inevitably they would join in the interview themselves and as they were always informed and engaged I encouraged this process.

The answers elicited from such exchanges were more detailed and frank than those proffered to me, or to an uncritical audience of movement participants, since both sides could speak from experience and ask pertinent and probing questions. Such meetings also offered the chance to observe how power negotiations and questions were tackled within movement organisations. In Vadianpatti, as we saw, I was told that the Liberation Panthers existed only in name. Had I been there on my own the assertion would have rested unanswered, though I might have later put it to a movement activist. I was accompanied by a DPI activist who refuted the suggestion, entered into a lively debate and then arranged a meeting. Although I had not planned it as such, I was able to witness the group dynamics that arise in organisational settings in a way that would have been impossible otherwise.

A considerable amount of the research was conducted through informal conversations during which I not only listened to my 'informants', but also expressed my own thoughts. Conversations would range over innumerable subjects not necessarily relevant to this research. The exchange of views, however, resulted in an atmosphere where we could talk openly about subjects. I would frequently voice my ideas about Dalit movements and, as Templeman (1996: 9) found in his study of the Nadar caste, such engagement often led to instructive critiques of putative analysis. In a politically charged atmosphere it would not have been surprising had people refused interviews, but showing understanding and commitment over time rendered people more willing to answer difficult questions.[15] Getting

---

[15] For much of my fieldwork the political environment was highly charged. There were massacres and riots, villages were ransacked, people were murdered and communities subjected to debilitating social boycott. This not only

involved may have influenced my perspective, but it also gave me far greater access to the networks of affiliation that constitute a movement.[16] For example, when I asked the leader of the Dalit Liberation Movement (DLM) how he could possibly support the DMK–BJP combine in one constituency, but back the Tamil Maanila Congress (Tamil State Congress—TMC) elsewhere, he initially refused to answer. When I put it to him that I was being called upon to justify this by others, however, he was more willing to explain the reasoning behind his actions.

The fact that Dalit movements are embedded in, and emerge out of, a specific political culture should caution one against too easy an acceptance of movement claims. The rhetorical commitment to the rights of women, for example, rarely translated into the everyday lives of the individual members. In the attempt to analyse the veracity of a movement's assertions, the use of participant observation assumes great significance. 'Hanging out' with activists informally in their home environments allowed me to assess the influence of the movement in people's daily lives. I also attended DPI meetings in order to observe the movement 'in action'. It is clear that protest meetings in themselves are valuable sources of information and interaction and members often frame their opinions by listening to the speeches of the leaders.

Participant observation enabled me to note the relational patterns between participants—followers and leaders, men and women—and between peripheral members and activists—rather than privileging the speeches of the leaders. Participant observation renders movements and meetings a novelty that may be absent from the perspectives of those accustomed to its mode of operation. Issues of class, sub-caste and gender within the leadership or group structure and

---

hampered my movements it also enforced an exaggerated sense of solidarity on the movements and meant that their ideological objectives were often muted by the need to respond to the actions of others. In times of peaceful, but persistent, protest it is probable that a greater number of dissenting voices would have made themselves heard. Studying movements at a time of political conflict, furthermore, rendered contact with opposition groups extremely difficult.

[16] 'As long as I remained uninvolved', Bellwinkel noted in a similar situation, 'I did not get the information I wanted, being condemned to the surface of events. This changed completely when I became personally involved' (1979: 150).

questions relating to the levels of democratic participation in meetings and policy decisions may be observed by the researcher, whereas the members may wish to play down their significance. Such observation was crucial to an understanding of the hierarchical structures of the DPI and the way in which the movement recruits new members.

Allied to this is the fact that for social movements 'protest is their most important medium and decisive for their existence, identity and outcome. ... The study of SM protest can tell us a lot about features such as the concerns of the people protesting, their capacities for mobilisation, their forms of action, the social characteristics of activists, the spatial and temporal distribution of protest, etc' (Rucht and Ohlemacher 1992: 77). As we have seen, it was only by tracking DPI participants that I was able to understand the scope of the movement. I follow Melucci, therefore, in stating that collective 'action itself (not structure or opinions) should be a meaningful subject for research' (Melucci 1992: 247). The meetings are vital to the construction of a 'we-feeling', a sense of being part of a wider movement and the activists will talk for weeks about a particularly brilliant speech or turn out. These speeches and rallies can be viewed as a means of 'persuasive communication' that convince people that the movement is appropriate and necessary.

Hunt argues that 'producing revolutionary talk is as much a part of the revolution as the barricades.... For without new vocabularies and rhetoric, new fields of interpretation, new symbols and signs, the revolutionary interpretations would not have been as easily made' (Hunt quoted in Johnston and Klandermans 1995a: 13). The 'strong cultural' implications of this assertion are flawed in the Indian context where movement rhetoric often echoes existing legislation, but it is certainly true that symbols and speeches help to constitute a movement and define its aspirations. Collective identity is constantly constructed and negotiated through ritual means of interaction and an organisation mostly 'maintains its identity and continuity through its symbolic representations' (Kertzer 1988: 18). As noted earlier (see also, Chapter 5), symbols and emblems attain great importance in the establishment of a move-ment. The high point of most movement meetings is the speech of the leader. In this peroration the leader outlines the position of the movement and comes to symbolise the movement in his/her person. By analysing the content of these speeches it is possible to ascertain what issues are deemed to be important and how these differ from views on the ground. Such observations are difficult to obtain in interviews.

The problems and methodology outlined here relate to issues of researching social movements and of Dalit movements in particular. There were also issues that are more specific to my own relation to the field. My relationship with the interviewees was crucial to the sort of narrative that was produced. Often I was the subject of questioning myself. I encouraged such exchanges and felt that they improved the quality of the subsequent interview. People were happier speaking to me when they knew who I was and where I was coming from. My age and my status as a single man also acted to offset the traditional imbalance of power between the researcher and the researched. I was addressed as *thambi* (younger brother) and frequently asked if I would be prepared to marry a Dalit girl. Such initial exchanges helped to establish rapport. The interviews were conducted in Tamil so I did not need to work through an interpreter and could clarify issues on the spot. This fact was essential to the interviews that I was able to conduct in the remoter villages.

The nature of the groups being interviewed meant that it was necessary to gain access through the mediation of activists, or 'gate-keepers'. This initially took the form of a snowball sample, as the people I got to know introduced me to others and so on. The self-selecting nature of these studies, as we have seen, has possibly given my work a movement perspective, but I have tried to correct this bias both by interviewing members from several areas and movements and by interviewing Dalits not involved with the movement. Many of the people who acted as 'gate-keepers' for me knew my family from the seven years we spent in the country between 1979 and 1986. My father worked in the Tamil Nadu Theological Seminary and I met many of my informants through Church contacts. This had the advantage of explaining my interest in the subject and rendering me less strange to people, but it may have influenced the type of people I got to meet and the sort of answers that I received. I have tried to overcome this through extensive interviews in rural and urban areas but the possibility of some bias cannot be ignored. The absence in my work of a BC perspective is conspicuous and I can only highlight the need to conduct research amongst the increasingly prominent BC movements. My close association with movement members, however, gave me better insight into the DPI than would have been possible had I insisted on interviewing their opponents as well.

Conclusion: Beyond the Rhetoric

The methodology adopted enabled me to analyse the movement in all its guises and forms. This diversity of contact was especially important because social movement activists are very conscious of the power of the written word and follow all the media coverage of their organisation. They were very keen, therefore, to ensure that I received a positive impression of the movement in question. As we shall see, this often led activists to play down the shortcomings or violence of a movement on tape. Rather, they focused on the 'successes' of the movement, of protests that achieved their objectives, well attended rallies and the sense of security which they derived from participation. The distortion that this can lead to was most obvious in the comments of a union facilitator. Whilst we were waiting for a bus, chatting informally, he insisted on the need for violence to secure the liberation of the Dalit people. After some time, however, he said; 'I am not talking like a responsible movement leader now! We should meet at another point when you can interview me' (20 April 1999).

By studying Dalit protest in terms of the material conditions from which it arises, the identities and ideologies that are constructed and the subjective experiences of participants, I hope to have acquired a better picture of the concerns of the DPI and, by extension, other Dalit movements in the state. What Rajni Kothari terms 'grassroots thinking' 'is an effort to redefine the scope and range of politics and to open up new spaces for the articulation of protest. It is here, at the convergence of social activists and the poor but conscious and restless people, that a new arena for "counter-action" or "counter-cultural movements" is emerging and challenging existing hegemonies of thought' (Kothari quoted in Mageli 1997: 24). It is this process of social criticism and creation that I have attempted to chart. In doing so I hope to have provided an understanding of the Dalit movements, the conditions of their emergence, their real grievances and demands, the difficulties they face and the world they wish to see.

Chapters

Although Dalits are increasingly becoming assertive and aware of their rights, the majority of them continue to live in conditions of poverty. The road to democratic equality and citizenship in India has been confused, complex and often contradictory. The structure of this book, therefore, is *thematic* rather than linear. The absence of a chronological narrative highlights the fact that there is no *one* story to tell, but many overlapping events and experiences. The chapters on the elections are placed at the end because they bring together many of the issues that are raised elsewhere and not to suggest a culmination of DPI activity. By highlighting related and interconnected themes I seek partly to examine and problematise the diverse aspects of the Dalit struggle but especially to reflect the concerns of my respondents.

The first section places the movement within a wider social and political context. In the first chapter I introduce the Liberation Panthers and outline their history, their mode of organisation and sphere of operation. Although I interviewed both activists and non-participants, I have chosen to focus upon active members of the DPI who are at the forefront of the struggle for social change. The contention is not that they are representative of the Dalit population as a whole, but that their actions and words have a much wider impact than might be supposed from the numbers who take part in roadside demonstrations. Little has been written about Dalit movements in Tamil Nadu. The second chapter, therefore, provides a political overview of the specific context of this book as well as applying the insights of social movement theory to an analysis of democracy and discontent in the state. It is argued that political movements follow recognised patterns of action and that they do not, for the most part, threaten the existence of the state and often enter the political process themselves. This does not mean that they do not demand structural changes but that they recognise the possibility to effect reform from within the current system and are pragmatic about the avoidance of repression.

Chapter 3 argues that the repressive aspects of the caste system have often been downplayed by the assertion that Dalits live 'in consensus' with the caste system. This chapter places Dalit activism in its *social* context, highlighting the fact that not everyone is in a position to rebel and that those Dalits who do not join social movements are not necessarily in agreement with the values of the caste system. The risks of Dalit assertion are real and apparent to most participants. Movements, therefore, face great difficulties in mobilising individuals into action. Despite this, countless examples of local resistance highlight the fact that many Dalit communities, not only those engaged in movement activism, are no longer prepared to tolerate their subordination. Where there is resistance there is power, as Abu-Lughod (1990) insists, and Dalit assertion has often prompted violent counter-movements. In face of the dangers of activism the 'free rider' problematic might be expected to apply. In other words the majority of Dalits might be expected to remain inactive and risk averse, whilst hoping to benefit from the protests of the vociferous minority. Movement leaders, however, employ powerful discourses of heroism and honour to create a sense of solidarity.

The next section assesses the material context of Dalit action and seeks to analyse the economic and social setting of movement activity. The Liberation Panthers do not operate in a vacuum but respond to specific features of their social world. Chapter 4 focuses on the economic considerations and alterations that hamper or enable protest. I argue that despite huge improvements, ties of dependency persist in contemporary India. The chapter discusses the importance of protest movements in making states accountable to their citizens and follows Kohli (1987) and Sen (1997) in questioning the capacity of the liberal state to effect social change. It is argued that poverty is not solely an economic condition and that the Dalit struggle cannot be explained purely in material terms since economic success for Dalits has rarely been attended by an increase in their social status. Dalit movements often arise in response to local issues, but these concerns are reflected in the conditions that Dalits live in across India. Chapter 5, therefore, considers the spatial context of Dalit action.

An examination of the social places from which movements such as the DPI emerge and of how they attempt to reconfigure social relations across and through space will emphasise the caste-based nature of much social interaction. It is argued that the public sphere is a universal, abstract realm within which citizens can meet 'others' and exchange opinions and values. Fifty years after the creation of a democratic state this sphere largely continues to be a 'virtual' entity. Caste continues to determine levels of access to, and recognition within, 'public spaces'. It will be argued that the struggle over and in space represents an attempt to forge a more open and equal society in which the views of all sectors can be represented. The egalitarian promise of such struggles, however, is often undermined by a tendency to organise along caste lines in a manner that accentuates divisions rather than allowing for cooperation across them. Highlighting the problems associated with mobilisation on the basis of caste is not to insist that all Dalits share the same experiences. Rather, the community is divided along generational, regional, caste, religious, gender, class and language lines.

The third part of the book problematises important aspects of the Dalit struggle and seeks to assess their practices and rhetoric in their own terms. If the Liberation Panthers wish to 'democratise democracy' in India, then they need to critically examine their own modes of organisation. Focusing on the key issues of gender and leadership, the chapters in this section analyse both the promises and the practices of the movement in question. Often the most salient social divide is that of gender. Chapter 6 considers the role of Dalit women, questioning how they interact with Dalit movements, challenge the patriarchal nature of movements and activists and seek to make themselves heard in predominantly male space. Although the role of women is raised in many chapters, a separate analysis of Dalit women is justified since they suffer from cumulative oppression: by caste, by a patriarchal society, by capitalism and often by their men within the home as well. Despite the large number of women who take part in movement meetings and protests, women are under-represented at the leadership level and it is argued that this imbalance in power needs to be addressed since it constitutes a contradiction of the movement ideals.

In Chapter 7 I turn to a consideration of leadership. Dalit movements often revolve around the central figure of a leader who is cast as a spokesman, a hero and a protector. Given the participatory emphasis of movement demands, such modes of organisation appear to be contradictory. The emphasis on the leader, therefore, needs to be questioned. The prominence of a central individual may make the concept of charisma attractive, but —contrary to appearances—the DPI incorporates a number of mechanisms that serve to limit the absolute power of the leader and render him accountable to the members. The notion of charisma cannot capture the social relationships that underpin leadership and ignores the agency of the individual members. There are also several alternative visions of leadership, which pose a challenge to this mode of organisation and seek to prefigure a more participatory society in their own movements. This concern highlights the fact that movements are pre-eminently about moral vision and social change.

During the course of my research, in 1998 and 1999, movements moved away from extra-institutional protest as a means of change and began to adopt the weapons of parliamentary democracy. Chapters 8 and 9, in the fourth section, present an analysis of this process and an examination of the movement's first foray into electoral competition. There are powerful incentives to adopt the path of democratic contention, but the pitfalls, of which the movements were initially wary, have not disappeared. Entering the political arena can lead to cooption, compromise and corruption, each of which could alienate movement activists and lead them either to apathy or radicalism. The two chapters on the election comprehend over-lapping terrain, but they are examined separately here to emphasise the importance of the shift from extra-institutional protest to parlia-mentary participation.

Chapter 8 discusses the DPI's transition from a movement to a party and the difficulties and debates involved in this process of transition. Here I analyse the process with reference to Offe's (1990) theory of institutional self-transformation. Whilst Offe's stage model is useful in the Tamil context, I highlight several significant differences that characterise the DPI's experience. Chapter 9 builds upon these issues in an examination of the Lok Sabha elections of 1999. Focusing on questions of representation and recruitment, I examine the political context of the Liberation Panther's entry into party politics. The election campaign highlighted the continuing salience of caste conflict and the exclusion of the Dalit community. It also emphasised the significance of 'events' in reconfiguring political opportunities. I argue that this election has helped to redraw the map of Tamil politics and extended the political process to hitherto excluded citizens.

The concluding chapter seeks to sum up the issues and ideologies that inform Dalit protest. It highlights the objectives and aspirations of Dalit activists before concluding with a critical appraisal of their impact in terms of Tamil society and politics. It is argued that the DPI, and Dalit movements more generally, are helping to reconstitute civil society and democracy in India. Often working at great risk to themselves, Dalit activists have sought to raise the plight of the downtrodden and fight for a just and equal society. They do not always live up to the ideals that they espouse and they are not always effective at defending their members from attack or in securing justice. They do, however, serve as witnesses to continuing oppression and violence against those who continue to be associated with Untouchability and are still among the lowest and poorest sectors of India's society. It is to their work and courage that this book is dedicated.

1

MAPPING THE MOVEMENT: INTRODUCING THE LIBERATION PANTHERS

The organisation of the Liberation Panthers ... is a movement aimed at the well-being of the general population. It seeks to promote better understanding between castes. It is a democratic movement which gives voice to the people at the bottom rung of society (Thirumavalavan, 18 July 1999).

The Dalit Panther Movement

The Dalit Panther Movement (DPM), probably the best known and most discussed Dalit movement in India, was formed in Maharashtra in the late 1970s by a young group of Dalits who were disillusioned with the existing SC parties and leaders. Their frustration found an expression in militant literature, poetry, painting and theatre as well as political agitation. They drew their inspiration, and title, from the Black Panther Movement in the United States (Joshi 1986: 87; Morkhandikar 1990: 586). Today, the initial aggression and militancy of the DPM has waned, the movement has split into several camps and most of the leaders are now in the Republican Party of India (RPI). They have, however, inspired mobilisation across India. In 1982, in Madurai, a group of disaffected Dalits led by M. Malaichami formed the Dalit Panther Iyakkam (Movement) (DPI) (also known as the Liberation Panthers). Following the death of Malaichami in 1990, a former government official, R. Thirumavalavan, succeeded him as the DPI leader. The movement was intended to be a radical alternative to existing Dalit groups. As with their counterparts in the north, the DPI both built upon and expressed frustration with the work of those who preceded them.

One of these political precursors to the DPI in Tamil Nadu was the Ambedkar People's Movement (AMI). Formed in the late 1970s and early 1980s, it was most active in challenging the social practices of untouchability. The AMI was acknowledged to have raised awareness about the issue of untouchability and taken the fight against caste discrimination onto the streets (as discussed in Chapter 7), but it was increasingly depicted as being too close to established political parties. As Guruvijay Paraiyar, of the Paraiyar Peravai (Paraiyar Front) put it: 'the old movements have become political brokers or agents. Y Balasundaram (the leader of the AMI) and Ellayaperumal (who founded a human rights organisation) are respected Dalit figures but they are not leaders, they have not brought about social change. The best they can do is to secure government loans' (interview, 10 October 1999). This judgement is harsh on the elder Dalit statesmen, but it reflects the increasing frustration with the slow pace of change.

Another tributary that led into DPI activism came in the form of radical class-based movements. For instance, a number of DPI cadres, notably the then General Secretary 'Tada' Periyasami, had been active in radical Communist Party groups that organised against class and caste in Thanjavur. Over time, however, Dalit activists had come to question the commitment of the Communists to the caste struggle. Sankar, now an accountant in a handicraft shop in Madurai, related an instance in which he visited the district offices of the Communist Party of India (CPI) in the 1970s:

> The leader was sitting in his office speaking to a deputation through the window when I came in. After the visitor had left I enquired who it was, and was informed that it was the head of the Scavengers' Trade Union. 'So, he is also a comrade', I said, 'why didn't he come into the office?' 'How can that be?' was the response, 'he is a scavenger' (interview, 5 December 1993).

Sankar, and many like him, came to the conclusion that the caste struggle needed to be resolved before a class struggle was possible.[1] Though the DPI was founded as a non-violent consciousness-raising

---

[1] 'Things like fraternity (sakhotharar unnarchi) and equality (samunilai) are central to the Dalit struggle' Kamaraj insisted, when I asked him whether he was attracted by the Communist Party. 'But the communists don't *do* anything about that whereas we try to' (interview, 18 March 1999).

organisation, its appeal has always hinged on its aggressive rhetoric and resistance to upper-caste dominance. Whilst the Liberation Panthers did stage demonstrations against the closure of textile mills and the unemployment of the workforce between 1998 and 2002, their focus was upon caste discrimination and conflict.

The Liberation Panthers are perhaps best described as *issue based*, in that they articulate a coherent set of principles and demands, but *incident sensitive*, in that they react to the aggression of others more often than campaigning on issues. This is not necessarily a criticism, since the highlighting of abuses is a crucial part of the search for justice. Violence can, however, restrict movements to a narrow agenda and may force them back upon their own caste or community because it reinforces divisions between categories of people and sets them in opposition to each other. Pre-existing networks of kinship and neighbourhood facilitate the process of organisation, but I should stress at this point that castes are *not* homogeneous categories and are divided by gender, class, generation and region. People within caste categories need to be convinced that they have interests in common and that the similarities between them override their points of difference. The problems of mobilising people around caste are exacerbated when activists seek to unite all the castes that are categorised as 'Dalit' or, more ambitiously, all those who are termed as Backward, Most Backward or Scheduled Castes.[2] The political mobilisation of one group has often fostered counter-mobilisation by others. As Dalit movements have increased in strength and profile and have come into conflict with various 'clean caste' organisations. Consequently, whilst the DPI has tried to build on the cross-caste work of the early Communist groups, it has struggled to escape categorisation in terms of caste.

The Liberation Panthers cover a large swathe of the state, stretching from Chennai down to Virudhunagar and from Cuddalore across to Perambalur and Dindugal (see Figure 1.1). They appeal mostly to Paraiyars, but the determination to resist being branded as a caste movement has meant that significant numbers of Chakkiliyars and Pallars have been drawn into the organisation. In order to understand why some castes are more or less likely to be

---

[2] The Maharashtrian Dalit Panthers of India's definition of 'Dalit' included all the oppressed sectors of society regardless of their caste status (Manifesto in Joshi 1986), but such unity has never been realised.

Figure 1.1 Map of Tamil Nadu

Note: This map is not to scale. It shows the district boundaries in Tamil Nadu. In terms of key sites mentioned in the book, Madurai and Tirunelveli are marked. Chidambaram is located on the coast in the south west of Cuddalore District. Melavalavu is located in the north west of Madurai District.

attracted to the DPI we need to consider the caste context in which the DPI operates. As detailed in Table 1.1 the Pallars, Paraiyars and Chakkiliyars are the three most numerous SCs in Tamil Nadu. Table 1.1 provides estimates of caste population, but the caste categories listed are contested and political. Adi-Dravidar, for example, literally means 'original Dravidian' and was adopted by Untouchable groups in the late 19th and early 20th centuries (primarily by the Paraiyar castes) as a means of improving their standing in society. Likewise, the terms Chakkiliyar, Arundhadiar and Madari are often used interchangeably, as are Pallar and Devendra Kula Vellallar. These figures are further complicated since the last census which enumerated all caste communities was in 1931, so these are only approximations and extrapolations on the basis of their population proportions then and partial enumerations in later censuses.

Although all three main Dalit castes are represented throughout the state, their distribution broadly speaking is mirrored by that of the Dalit organisations. The DPI is strongest in the northern districts of the state where the Paraiyars are preponderant; The Puthiya Tamizhagam (PT) is strongest where the Pallars are most numerous (in the south and west, up from Thirunelveli to Coimbatore). The Arundhadiars or Chakkiliyars in Dindugal, Erode, Dharmapuri and Karur have yet to establish a comparable political movement. It should be stressed here that the Pallars, Paraiyars and Chakkiliyars are caste categories rather than castes in their own right. Each of the three are sub-divided into sub-castes and split along numerous lines including language and occupation. The use of the terms here is a political one and emphasises the creation of pan-Tamil caste links and movements. The tripartite division also rides roughshod over the complexities of caste constituencies, movement allegiances and sub-caste differences, but they present a general idea of the map of Dalit politics. Furthermore, these perceptions shape actions on the ground and respondents frequently repeated this stereotypical portrait.

Activists likewise operated with a crude analysis of the relations between the main Dalit caste categories. Thus, it was constantly asserted that the Pallars were the most organised Dalit caste, partly by virtue of superior land-holdings. They were said to look down upon the other Dalit castes and to perceive themselves as superior. This perception was given credence and substance by movements such as the PT—the first Dalit movement to organise into a coherent political force in Tamil Nadu—claiming to represent the Devendra Kula Vellalars, rather than the Pallars. The Sanskritisation of the name suggests an attempt to distance themselves from other Dalit communities. The Paraiyars, by contrast, make no pretensions of being a 'clean caste' and several movements have inverted the stigma attached to the name by according it a certain cachet. A number of activists—such as Guruvijay Paraiyar—have renamed themselves so as to emphasise their Paraiyar origins and organisations such as

Table 1.1: A Brief Account of Key Caste Groups

Caste	Description	Location
Paraiyar	The name Paraiyar is said to derive from the Tamil word for drum and indicates their traditional occupation as musicians as well as settled cultivators and agricultural labourers. They are the most populous SC in Tamil Nadu. There is some confusion about their number because many Paraiyars have adopted the term Adi-Dravidar (original Dravidian). Including both categories there are approximately 4.5 million Paraiyars in Tamil Nadu according to estimates based on the 1991 Census.	The Paraiyars are found throughout Tamil Nadu but their primary concentration is in the northern districts of the state.
Pallar	One of the three main SCs in Tamil Nadu. Estimates based on the 1981 Census place their numbers at around 1.3 million inhabitants in the state. Traditionally they worked as plantation labourers, skilled labourers and in animal husbandry. They are seen as being higher up the caste hierarchy than other untouchable castes, and as better organised than the other SCs. They are also known as Devendra Kula Vellalar.	These are mainly based in districts around Coimbatore, Ramnathpuram, Tirunelveli and Madurai.
Chakkiliyar	Chakkiliyars are the lowest of the three main SCs in the state. They are traditionally landless and work with leather. The community is also known by the terms Arundhadiar and Madari. Approximations based on the 1981 Census place their number at around 1 million. Many of the community speak Telegu.	They are distributed all over Tamil Nadu but they are primarily concentrated in the central and western districts of Tamil Nadu.

Caste	Description	Location
Paraiyar, Pallar, Chakkiliyar	Taken together these three caste categories comprise around 17% of the Tamil population. Given that the SCs combined make up 18% of the population one gets a sense of their significance.	
Vanniyar	Traditionally most Vanniyars were agricultural labourers particularly engaged in oil pressing and about 50% of them still are. Increasingly, however, they are benefiting from political influence and organisation and they now own about 50% of the lands of the traditional landowners. The Vanniyars were classified as a Most Backward Caste and were granted extra state benefits after successful agitation in the 1980s. Vanniyars, according to Radhakrishnan (2002) are the largest single community in the state and account for approximately 12% of its population, corresponding to about 6.5 million people.	Vanniyars are concentrated in the northern districts of Tamil Nadu.
Thevar	Often lumped together with Mukkulathor, Kallar, Maravar and Agamudiyar, Thevar itself is a title that literally means God. They are said to have been a martial community that ruled in Tamil Nadu. They have a distinct and developed caste identity and a high degree of caste pride. They are a Backward Caste whose educational and economic achievements have been negligible. Substantial numbers of Thevars, who are a major land-owning caste in south Tamil Nadu, are small or marginal farmers or agricultural labourers. Very	The Thevars are predominantly located in the southern districts of Tamil Nadu.

Caste	Description	Location
	approximate figures based on the 1931 Census estimate that there are nearly 1 million Mukkulathors, though whether this includes all of the Thevar castes is unclear.	
Kounder or Gounder	They are mainly a landowning community who were traditionally involved in settled cultivation and animal husbandry. Now, however, they have diversified into government service and self employment.	They are concentrated in the adjoining areas of Madurai District.

Source: Extracted from Sebastian (1994) and Singh (1993).

the Paraiyar Peravai tap into this sentiment. When the DPI split in 2002, the breakaway faction dubbed itself the Paraiyar *Viduthalai* (Liberation) Peravai.

Several DPI interviewees asserted that the Pallars discriminated against lower-caste Dalits in areas where they held land and power, and they emphasised the mainly Paraiyar constituency of the DPI as a source of pride. Indeed, the orator of the Liberation Panthers, 'firebrand' Murugan referred to Thirumavalavan as a 'Paraiyar Ambedkar' or 'Paraiyar leader' on numerous occasions. It was often noted as a cause for concern that the Chakkiliyars had not organised themselves in a similar manner. They were regarded as the least organised of the Dalit categories, the most oppressed and lowliest in caste terms. Although organisations such as the Tamilaga Arundhadiar Youth Front, the Tamilaga Dalit Liberation Movement and the Dalit Liberation Movement (see Table 1.2) campaigned with them, none of these has yet emerged as a significant movement. This partly seems to be due to geographical factors and the fact that the Chakkiliyars are often in a dependent minority. In an attempt to comprehend this absence of significant movement activity, I travelled to villages in Karur, Dindugal and Erode. Despite the lack of organisations, it was evident that attitudes were changing and that Dalits were resisting the imposition of caste-based work. Several young men whom I interviewed in this area spoke of the DPI as the organisation which they empathised most with.

Table 1.2: Commonly Cited Political Parties and Dalit **Movements**

Party or Movement	Description
Dravida Kazhagam (DK)	The Dravidian Federation was established by the radical Tamil leader E.V. Ramasamy Naicker (popularly known as EVR or Periyar). It posited an imagined community of Tamils and sought to free them from the Brahmin, or northern, yoke. Influenced by socialist and Soviet ideas, the party envisaged a caste free, classless and egalitarian society which it tried to prefigure through the promotion of rational ideas and non-ritual weddings. The party emblem is a black and red flag.
Dravida Munnetra Kazhagam (DMK)	Meaning the Dravidian Progressive Federation or the federation for the advancement of Dravidians. One of two hegemonic political parties in Tamil Nadu. The DMK wrested power from the Congress Party in 1967 and has held office periodically since then. In recent decades, the DMK was the party in power between 1989 and 1991 and from 1996 till 2001. The DMK's symbol is the rising sun. The leader of the party is K. Karunanidhi.
All-India Anna Dravida Munnetra Kazhagam (AIADMK)	When the DMK split in 1972 the faction led by the film-star M.G. Ramachandran (MGR) called itself the Anna DMK. Anna refers to Annadurai, the founder of the DMK, and suggests that the ADMK is closer to his ideals. When MGR died Jayalalitha took over as the party leader. Under her leadership the ADMK moved further away from its non-Brahmin, Tamil nationalism. This was symbolised in the extension of the party name to the All-India ADMK. The party emblem is two leaves. The ADMK and AIADMK have enjoyed long periods in office, most recently between 1991 and 1996. They also won a landslide in the 2001 elections.
Paatali Makkal Katchi (PMK)	The Toiling People's Party emerged in the mid-1990s and built on the successful mobilisation of the Vanniyar Union. The Vanniyars are a peasant caste mostly based in the northern districts of Tamil Nadu. They fought for and won the benefits that accrue to groups categorised as Most Backward Castes. The PMK initially tried to unite

Party or Movement	Description
	the 'working classes' and worked on Dalit issues in tandem with various Dalit movements. As their political power-base has been challenged, however, the PMK has been increasingly identified as a caste-based organisation. The party leader is Dr Ramdoss and the party's symbol is a mango.
Bharatiya Janata Party (BJP)	The Indian People's Party formed the national government from 1998 until 2004. It is a Hindu nationalist party. The party emblem is a lotus flower and it is led by the former Prime Minister A.B. Vajpayee.
Congress Party	The Indian National Congress (INC), grew out of the anti-colonial nationalist movement. It assumed power in 1947 and dominated Indian politics until the late 1970s. The Congress was ousted from power in Tamil Nadu in 1967 by the DMK and has never regained power in the state though it has been part of successful coalitions. The Congress symbol is a white hand and is led by Sonia Gandhi.
Tamil Maanila Congress (TMC)	In 1996, the state wing of the Congress party split off from its parent body in protest against the INC's decision to ally itself to the AIADMK. The TMC did very well in its first elections in alliance with the DMK but could not emulate its success thereafter. It was led by G.K. Moopanar from its inception until his death in 2001, when he was succeeded by G.K. Vasan. The TMC and Congress merged once more in August 2002. The party symbol is a cycle.
Dalit Panther Iyyakkam (DPI) or Liberation Panthers	The Dalit Panther Movement are known by two names, partly because they only introduced the second epithet in 1998–99. They are still widely known as the DPI. From the late 1990s they have been the largest Dalit movement in the state and were seen as radical political actors. The movement leader is Thirumavalavan and the symbol of the movement is a 'panther' (though leopards and other wild cats are often used).
Puthiya Tamizhagam (PT)	New Tamil Society/State rivalled the DPI as the second largest Dalit movement. The PT attained prominence and high profile in the mid-1990s

Party or Movement	Description
	when its leader, Dr Krishnasamy, was elected to the Legislative Assembly. The symbol of the movement is a bullock cart.
Tiyagi Immanuel Peravai (TIP)	Martyr Immanuel's Front is named after a Dalit activist who was killed during riots in the central districts of Tamil Nadu. It is a fairly local movement and is primarily confined to Ramnad District. The TIP still boycotts elections and has a fairly low profile. Its leader is Chandra Bose.
Tamil Nadu Arundhadiar Youth Front (TAYF)	TAYF is one of several parties that are seeking to organise the Chakkiliyar or Arundhadiar caste. In the late 1990s it secured an understanding with the Bahujan Samaj Party (a successful Dalit party in north India). It is led by Kalyani Sunder.
Ambedkar Makkal Iyyakkam (AMI)	The Ambedkar People's Movement could be termed the first 'second wave' Dalit movement in Tamil Nadu. It emerged in the late 1970s and early 1980s and sought to realise the rights and freedoms opened up by the Constitution. AMI members walked down caste streets, smashed up tea-shops that still served Dalits in separate glasses and demanded entry to temples and common lands. It is led by Y. Balasundaram, who used to be the mayor of Chennai. In recent years it has declined in popularity.
Dalit Liberation Movement (DLM)	The DLM began as an attempt to unite the diverse movements in the state. This endeavour failed and the movement has continued on its own. It is led by Daniel Gnanasekharan and mostly works in the western districts of Tamil Nadu amongst the Chakkiliyars.
Tamilaga DLM (TDLM)	The Tamil DLM split off from the DLM due to concerns with its leadership style. It is a fairly localised movement around Ottanchattram in the western-central districts of the state and it is led by a leadership committee of five people.
Penurimai Iyyakkam (PI)	Women's Right's Movement. A strong state-wide but city-based movement that campaigns on women's rights issues that has collaborated with Dalit movements on a number of issues. There is no central leader figure.

Source: Extracted from fieldnotes, Subramanian (1999).

Across the state, relations between the caste categories were strained and there was little by way of daily interaction and communion between them. Amongst most of my informants, the schism between the Paraiyars and the Chakkiliyars was perceived to be the least problematic. Residents on Dalit estates in Madurai frequently asserted that there were inter-caste marriages amongst the two. Such unions were admittedly not the rule, but neither were they so uncommon or frowned upon as to be forbidden and hushed up. The unity fostered by urban proximity and interaction, however, was less evident in rural areas. In the villages of Vadianpati, Kodankipatti and the villages around Cuddalore, Vellore and Erode, Dalits were more evidently divided. The poorer and less established castes still tended to perform caste work even after other groups had abandoned such practices. Consequently, caste barriers have proved harder to overcome in these areas.

Isaac, a rural Paraiyar student studying to become a pastor, admitted that he had to battle against his 'instincts' in order to interact freely with lower Dalit castes. The 'structures of the mind' were proving to be resistant to change (interview, 23 February 1999). In such circumstances, the Liberation Panther's caste neutral terminology is essential, both to avoid violence (discussed in Chapter 5) and to foster a greater sense of unity. When asked whether the Pallars, Paraiyars and Chakkiliyars were united in Vandiyur, for example, Nagaraj of the DPI replied:

> There aren't any Pallars here. Let me tell you, when I say 'our lot' or 'us', then I mean that we are Dalit people: Paraiyar, Pallar, Kothari Vannar or Vallavoor ... all these castes—since we have been in the Liberation Panthers we have been united.... There are Pallars here, one of them is a leader in the movement (interview, 26 March 1999).

Nagaraj, in other words, was trying to create a political community of *Dalits* in which people's individual caste backgrounds did not matter. He also asserts that such an imagining has only become possible in the advent of DPI mobilisation, but it is telling that he could still identify individuals in terms of their caste origin. What is clear is that people's 'structures of the mind' were coloured by movement activism and participation, and that activists attempt to draw a line between their lives before the movement and their subsequent positions.

What's in a Name?

Despite using the movement as a key point in his own chronology, Nagaraj, like most of my interviewees, placed an overriding emphasis on the active movement rather than its past. This partly relates to the fact that most members had joined the movement under the present leader, but also emphasises the transformation of the DPI under Thirumavalavan. For example, Perumal—a municipal worker in Madurai—insisted that earlier he used to be arrested and harassed by the police but that now he is respected. 'The main cause for this transformation is one man. I have his photo here—our leader Thirumavalavan—all this is his doing ... he is a saviour for us, a deity' (interview, 8 March 1999). As highlighted in Chapter 7, Perumal is by no means alone in such hero-worship but it is telling that any sense of the early movement is absent from his account. Likewise, when inaugurating a new branch of the DPI in Reitingpatti, Virudhunagar District, Thirumavalavan provided a potted version of the movement's emergence and his rise to its leadership. Having mentioned the DPM he continued, 'this movement came to Madurai in 1982 under Malaichami. I came to Madurai and got to know him. In January 1990 unfortunate circumstances led me to take up the leadership of the movement and since then we have met fierce repression' (speech, 7 August 1999). The past is considered briefly as a prelude, but the present is very much the focus, as if to erase the memory of times when the movement was not so well established.

The transformation in the movement is emphasised in that, under Thirumavalavan, the DPI has also come to be known as the Liberation Panthers (Viduthulai Ciraithukkal). The name is instructive on two counts. On the one hand, it is an obvious reference to the Liberation Tigers of Tamil Eelam (LTTE) in Sri Lanka. Several of the DPI activists carried small photos of Prabhakaran, the LTTE leader, and the conflict in Sri Lanka was occasionally referred to as an indication of the violence that could occur if their demands were not met.[3] On the other hand, the name points to problems associated

---

[3] During my fieldwork there were no systematic references made to the LTTE and none of my respondents (either DPI or not) said that there were any links between the organisations. It appeared to be more of a symbolic gesture than a meaningful comparison of issues/strategies. It is also worth noting that the most overtly

with the term 'Dalit'.[4] At a flag-raising ceremony in July 1999, Thirumavalavan appeared to reject the term, maintaining that 'today we have given ourselves a new name: The Liberation Panthers' (speech, 18 July 1999). According to Thirumavalavan, the attempt to escape the Dalit tag occurred for three reasons: First 'everyone now is using the name "Dalit"', and so it is seen to have lost the radicalism that was associated with it and has become an ascribed rather than a chosen epithet. Second, there was a suggestion that the word Dalit was becoming a caste term in Tamil Nadu where it was used as a code word for Paraiyar. Third, as the DPI grew in strength in Tamil Nadu they felt the need to distance themselves from the increasingly divided Maharashtrian Dalit Panthers.

The first and last reasons are the best founded, since Dalit *has* become a ubiquitous term of reference that *categorises* people rather than reflects their own self-definitions. By coining a new name, therefore, the DPI is attempting to recapture the revolutionary import of the original Dalit Panthers in Maharashtra. Despite this I have described the DPI as a Dalit movement, partly to facilitate comparison with other studies, but also to reflect the continuing use of the acronym 'DPI' alongside the name Liberation Panthers, and their continuing campaigns on 'Dalit' platforms and conferences. The alteration in name, thus, is more significant in its assertion of autonomy and radicalism than as heralding a shift in world view or practice.

---

pro-LTTE political party in Tamil Nadu was the Paatali Makkal Katchi which is opposed to the DPI. Lipsky (1970: 186), however, notes the advantages, for movement leaders, of suggesting that they have a 'large group of passionate followers willing to take risks'.

[4] There is a trend for movements to discard any pretensions towards Dalit unity and organise on the basis of their immediate community. Movements, such as the Paraiyar Peravai (Paraiyar Front) or the Arundathiar Nalla Iyyakkam (Arundathiar Welfare Movement) have, thus, confined their demands to the particular interests of their own caste. Guru (1993), Suresh (1996) and Duncan (1999), in different contexts, note the attraction of organising along caste rather than Dalit lines. Whilst the DPI has maintained the term 'Dalit', many participants and opponents regard it as primarily a Paraiyar organisation. One of the underlying issues considered in the text relates to whether the DPI should be seen as a caste movement or not. These criticisms, however, apply equally to established political parties.

The new name also emphasises the influence of the present leader, but despite the importance of the alteration in leadership, I could find little information about the process of succession. Whilst Palani Kumar, a ward leader in Madurai, spoke about elections, the movement decidedly lacks internal democracy and there are no transparent procedures for the election of its leaders. Local-level activists work their way up the movement hierarchy by engaging in organising activity and making best use of opportunities to address demonstrations and make contacts. It is instructive that Thirumavalavan got to know Malaichami because he went to law college with the former leader's brother. Thirumavalavan gained popularity through his unquestioned abilities as an orator and the aggressive content of his speeches. Given that the defining feature of the DPI for over a decade was its boycott of elections (as detailed in Chapter 8), he was the obvious choice to act as the spokesperson and figurehead of the movement. Under his leadership the DPI has become one of the two foremost Dalit organisations in the state. The lack of transparency and accountability in the choice of a leader, however, is evident in the entire operation of the movement.

Movement Organisation

On the face of it the DPI is highly structured and well organised. There is a 'convenor' Thirumavalavan—and two 'general secretaries'—'Tada' Periyasami and Cinthanai Selvam—all of whom travel around the state meeting different movement branches. At the local level, there are a number of 'assistant general secretaries' who are responsible for setting up meetings and keeping abreast of issues and events in their area. Sakhtivel, for instance, was in charge of Madurai and Melur districts. He was responsible for organising meetings and addressing problems in this area as well as more high-profile occasions such as the commemoration of the Melavalavu massacre.[5] The 'high command' was backed by several district secretaries and coordinators who, in turn, kept in touch with city representatives, women's wing leaders and prominent activists.

[5] See Introduction or the note in Appendix A for a brief account of the massacre which is referred to repeatedly in this book.

This skeletal structure served to keep the movement from disbanding altogether and meant that there was almost always someone senior and experienced to seek help from. It was, however, unclear what the precise relations of power between these senior positions were. The pre-eminent focus on the leader often detracted from the contribution of others. These offices did not correspond to a transparent hierarchy of command, either, apart from providing a rough sense of who did what in a locality. For instance, Nagaraj, a construction worker living on the outskirts of Madurai in Vandiyur, recounted how Dalits in his area sought to join the DPI. They had received *pattas* (deeds) for land that they were unable to claim. The Vandiyur group resolved to take the matter to Thirumavalavan and approached the Madurai area secretary, Mohan, for an introduction:

> Mohan Annan said 'do not go and see him [Thirumavalavan]' and we asked 'why'? 'You are concerned about land here are you not? Then it is Baikiam and Kannadasan [Madurai leaders] who will look into that' (interview, 26 March 1999).

Frequently, local activists took decisions of their own accord and only referred to senior leaders if problems arose. It is worth noting that the chain of command was stronger and more apparent in urban centres, but despite this few of the local activists knew who was responsible for issues related to land. Indeed, the initial approach of the Vandiyur group was typical in its valorisation of the 'big man' over and above local leaders.

A putative hierarchy did exist nonetheless, and in 1999 there were several meetings of a 72-member strong 'organising committee' which comprised the high command, regional and local leaders. Such meetings were infrequent at best, as the usual mode of communication was through top–down contact between Thirumavalavan and the various localities. In 1999, these meetings were occasioned by the sea-change in movement policy and the disputed decision to enter the elections. The autonomy of regional representatives was evident in the heated discussions that took place on this issue, and it is clear that the frequency of such meetings will have to increase if the diverse sections of the DPI are to be kept informed. As the movement has grown there have been increasing calls for a formalisation of the structures of power. The DPI began work on a handbook to this end towards the end of 1999. Movement expansion has fostered a need for greater accountability and clarity of roles.

Although a 72-person steering committee suggests that the DPI had extensive organisational structures, beyond the central figures I found that both positions in the movement and ties between participants were purely informal. This 'organic' form of organisation was evident in Madurai. The DPI extends into 40 'wards' of Madurai City. A movement 'ward' is marked by the presence of a flagpole, painted board (or both) with the colours (sky blue, red and white) and the emblem of the DPI (a panther), an obligatory portrait of Dr Ambedkar and usually a depiction of the movement leader. Each ward has its own committee which is 'elected locally', according to Palani Kumar, which handles local issues. Informal contact is maintained through occasional (by no means regular) visits, notices of forthcoming events and discussions at meetings as and when they occur.

> I asked if there were meetings on a monthly basis or some such mechanism to meet up. Palani Kumar replied: 'No, nothing like that ... but we should.' When I asked how he contacted those outside his immediate neighbourhood he asserted that 'when there are problems or difficulties, then they come to us.[6]

The fact that my visit to various wards in Madurai provided an opportunity for the local-level organisers to catch up with what was happening reveals the claims of local elections to be more an aspiration than an accurate portrayal of practice. As an organisation the DPI lacked the records and details of members to ensure that such an election could take place, or if it did that it would be representative. The meetings to discuss the move into political competition, for example, were constituted of those key activists who had the time and money to attend the meetings rather than elected representatives. Although DPI activists spoke of the probability that they would develop membership cards and dues, there was no evidence of such administration in 1999. In many villages around Madurai and in the city itself the DPI's board or flagpole often appeared to be the only evidence of movement activity.

In sum, from 1998–2001, the DPI was based around core cells in the Dalit populated areas of cities such as Madurai and Cuddalore.

---

[6] Taken from my field notes, 26 March 1999.

Each cell was more or less connected to the district organiser through a network of informal contacts. There was no systematic structure to bring the local bodies and the main organisation together. Consequently, the further afield from the cities one went the looser the links became. In the villages which were located over an hour's drive away from Madurai, these connections were delicately maintained by threads of trust, family networks, informal visits by the regional organisers to villages and city wards and posted notices about impending events. Given this there was some ambiguity as to how to define the movement. There were, however, recurrent 'rituals' and events that gave the DPI coherence and distinguished the movement from others.[7] These constituted the informal 'rules of the game' that applied not only to the Liberation Panthers but were discernible in other organisations across the state. First, an area or group of people had to mark their association to a movement by erecting a flag or painted board with the colours and emblems of the movement in question emblazoned across them. Movement membership, thus, was an act of public affirmation. Such flag-raising events made a public statement and reinforced the sense of unity upon which the movement depended.

New groups or members were usually the ones who initiated contact with a movement. They approached movement activists having heard of the movement or having suffered caste discrimination. As Palani Kumar suggested, it was rare for the movement itself to actively campaign for new members.[8] Once they had contacted the DPI several prominent activists in the vicinity were assigned to visit the new area, tell them about their work and help organise an inaugural meeting. In this period activists offered legal advice if required, organised protest meetings to pressurise authorities to take action and answered questions about the movement. The flag-raising symbolised the inauguration of a new ward of the DPI. Ideally the leader would be in attendance to hoist the flag or unveil the board, meet people in the locality and then make a speech. Membership

---

[7] My use of 'ritual' here draws on the work of social movement theorists. Taylor and Whittier (1995: 176), for example, define rituals as: 'Symbolic expressive events that communicate something about social relations in a relatively dramatic way'.

[8] As shown in Chapters 8 and 9, when the DPI contested the election in 1999 they were forced to reassess this mode of operation.

in the movement afforded local areas a sense that they were part of a wider, stronger group and it was seen as a deterrent to other competing groups or to state officials. As Sekhar, a young man from Jansi Rani Complex—a pavement-based community in the heart of Madurai—put it: The DPI murals on the wall by their ramshackle settlement 'are there as a security measure to guard against people or against police raids who come at night to drag us away' (interview, 11 March 1999).

Movement imagery fosters a sense of being part of the Dalit struggle for 'liberation' and equality. The movement gets exposure, a larger pool of people becomes available to raise funds from and there is a sense that the movement is growing. Beyond that, the relation between the movement and the ward varied according to circumstance and key individuals. Notices of impending events were sent to the contact person in each ward. They were expected to inform their neighbourhood and, for particularly prestigious events, they were pressured to provide a contingent of people to make up numbers. This latter task relied upon social rather than formal pressure and attendance at demonstrations fluctuated widely.[9]

The Issues in Question

The lack of a proselytising campaign and the fact that an area usually had to approach a movement, rather than *vice versa*, begs the question: Why join the DPI as opposed to the many other movements in the state? Members and participants intimated that the DPI was so successful because it was aggressive, spoke of fighting back and had an articulate leader with an attractive public image. The two most quoted aspects that typified this radicalism were the 10-year election boycott and the slogan promising to return 'a blow for a blow'. Previous Tamil Dalit movements, like the AMI, had cam-

---

[9] Attendance at DPI demonstrations in 1998–99 varied between 75 people clustered round a microphone to the 2,000 or so in Melavalavu. This latter figure is misleading, however, in that many movements were involved in the memorial at Melevalavu. The average attendance was around 250–350, but the crowds drawn for election meetings were much higher. Members and non-members alike said that the DPI had held vast demonstrations in Madras, but I did not witness any of these.

paigned against untouchability through legal means and were often innovative and *socially* revolutionary, but they did not challenge the political establishment. The DPI, by contrast, rejected the parliamentary process as a sham and called for more radical change. When even the poorest Dalits articulate a sense of injustice and demand their dignity, as shown in Chapter 3, it is not surprising that the more militant movements are seen as more popular. Through its boycott of the elections, the DPI effectively equated the inefficiency and corruption of established politics with the perpetuation of caste discrimination. It followed, therefore, that Dalits should take the law into their own hands. As Perumal, from Melavassel, put it: 'The main cause of our problems is the police. Police first and upper castes second. They are turning us into guerrillas' (interview, 8 March 1999).

The percentage of Dalits engaged in protest is not high, but, as Perumal's reference to police repression suggests, the risks that they run are disproportionate to any tangible gains that they can reasonably expect. To ignore the issues that inspire participation and hold out the prospect of a different society, therefore, would be a mistake. When asked why they had decided to join a given movement, most members would cite the leader as the main cause. But when asked why they chose to protest at all, people spoke of an abiding sense of injustice. Cinnathambi from Vadianpatti was typical in articulating these sentiments:

> We are still suppressed. We have not been liberated or granted our independence yet. However high we rise up, when we go there [into the main village] we are slaves! ... Gandhi got everyone independence but he didn't give any to us. It has been 50 years since Indian Independence but we still don't know what it means (interview, 20 March 1999).

Activists, in other words, have an articulated and coherent account of *why* they choose to protest. This means that whilst the leaders may be idolised they are never beyond reproach if they are seen to betray the cause.[10] Movement action should educate people as much as make a point and activists were remarkably well-informed about core issues and current affairs. Without an understanding of these

---

[10] The validity of this assertion was seen in 2002 when the DPI split into two opposing factions.

demands it is impossible to fully appreciate movement strategies or gauge how 'successful' they have been. The importance accorded to each issue varied over time and campaigns on one particular issue did not necessarily reflect the pre-eminence of that cause. Political convenience can be as important for the timing of a campaign as ideology. The demand for a 'share of power', for example, is fundamental to the Dalit movements' attempts to fashion a different society and yet only the DPI voiced it with any conviction when the opportunity to enter the polls arose. Likewise, the stress on human rights in 1999 was not inconsistent with prior concerns, but its prominence owed more to the 50th anniversary of the Universal Declaration of Human Rights than any internal decision, as could be seen in a number of joint meetings of Dalit movements sponsored by human rights organisations.

Dalit movements have consistently struggled for social inclusion. The exclusion of Dalits from the main body of society is symbolised on many fronts. Physically the *cheris* are located outside the main village; semantically they are referred to as 'Untouchable'; spiritually, Dalits are denied access to temples, told that they are impure, and village processions refuse to enter the Dalit areas. Materially, Dalits are alienated from resources and land, culturally their skills are demeaned and socially they are served in different receptacles at restaurants. One of the defining issues confronting the DPI, therefore, is the demand for equality of access to the social sphere. Bound up with this struggle for social respect and recognition, is the call for *self-respect*. DPI activists portray many educated and well-off Dalits as lackeys because they do not actively support the rest of their community. S. Martine, an advocate and co-founder of the Village Community Development Society, insisted on the need for self-respect and self-reliance. 'Why do shops established by Dalits fail?' he asks. His answer is that the higher castes boycott such institutions and members of their own community do not support them. Social attitudes depicting Dalits as dirty still pertain and these need to be challenged within the Dalit community as well as the rest of society (S. Martine, interview, 18 January 1999). The emphasis upon honour and dignity in the speeches of movement leaders indicates the psychological significance of the DPI. The Dalit struggle, thus, is as much about building the self-esteem of the community as combating material oppression.

Self-esteem, however, is not divorced from the perceptions and actions of others. The esteem of Dalit groups and movements is intricately bound up with issues of social status. In contemporary Tamil Nadu, the politicisation of caste has rendered such questions matters of party-political import. The demand for social inclusion, therefore, *is* fundamentally bound up with the struggle against political and economic exclusion; it is a demand for equal citizenship. The nationalist struggle, according to this perspective, remains incomplete whilst certain citizens are demeaned simply because of who they are. On the face of it the demand for social inclusion would appear to be met by the positive discrimination measures of the Indian Constitution. The DPI, however, points out that the façade of the reservation system is more impressive than the substance. They insist that it is not functioning efficiently or fairly and that it has failed to filter down to most SCs even if we discount the fact that Muslim and Christian Dalits are not entitled to reservations. Political reservations are obviously more visible and it would be impossible for any party not to field a Dalit candidate in a reserved seat. Politically speaking, therefore, Dalits *are* equal members of the polity. Reservation has now been extended to cover panchayat councils, so in theory Dalits have a voice in every level of government in India. In many areas and states, such decentralisation programmes have led to remarkable social alterations. The Liberation Panthers are obviously cognisant of this and press for the adequate representation of Dalits on such bodies, but disillusionment with established parties has led to the establishment of autonomous parties.

Whilst parliamentary politics are, of necessity, mediated, the injunction on a Dalit leader to be one of the people renders them much more aware of the needs and desires of their community than career politicians are likely to be. The requirement for Dalit leaders to visit villages and meet people during flag-raising ceremonies means that their political manifestos and promises must reflect the concerns of their constituents in a way that established parties have failed to do. When the Liberation Panthers contested the Lok Sabha elections in 1999, their demand for a 'share of power' rather than an alliance reflected the ideological commitment to *self-determination*, which entails both access to common properties and a place in decision-making bodies (S. Martine, interview, 18 January 1999).

Having said this, autonomous movements are not free from the constraints imposed by the institutions which they aspire to enter. The DPI's continual demand for separate electorates, for example, reflects the fact that few constituencies have sufficient Dalit voters

to enable movements to win in open competition.[11] The independence of Dalit movements, thus, is often compromised by the need
to secure electoral alliances with others. Aside from the problems
associated with the first past the post system of politics, the partial
successes of autonomous Dalit political parties must be placed in the
context of Dalit poverty. 'Rather than thinking about the paradise
of tomorrow', as Chandra Bose put it, 'they want an end to today's
hunger' (interview, 23 February 1999).[12] The land reforms of the
1950s and 1960s have been largely ineffective, and the majority of
Dalits in the state still do not own any land. This renders them
dependent upon others for employment and makes them vulnerable
to social boycott. It is not surprising, therefore, that land rather than
political participation remains the core concern for most Dalit
movements.

Movements and Institutions: Dalits and the NGOs

Lack of funds dictates an over-reliance on volunteers. This fosters
feelings of sacrifice and self-denial amongst activists that strengthen
internal bonds but alienate them from others in society. Movement
activists confided that they face constant pressures to settle down,
get married and get a steady job so as to contribute towards their
family. There is a perennial tension in such situations between NGOs,
many of which have overseas funding, and protest movements.

---

[11] 'A joint electorate for a small minority and a vast majority is bound to result
in a disaster to the minority. A candidate put up by the minority cannot be
successful even if the whole of the minority were solidly behind him.... Even if
a seat is reserved for a minority, a majority can always pick up a person
belonging to the minority and ... get him elected.... The result is that the
representative of the minority elected to the reserved seat instead of being a
champion of the minority is really a slave of the majority' (Dr. Ambedkar Writings
and Speeches, Vol. 5, p. 347).
[12] Shri Rangan Prakash of the RPI (Tamil Nadu) stressed that the BSP policy
of 'one rupee, one vote' (meaning that each member should pay one rupee per
month) was not feasible in Tamil Nadu. It was not that the sums were beyond
most people, but that it was difficult enough to motivate people to protest, let
alone to ask for money on top of that.

Karunakaran, an activist from Andhra Pradesh, insisted that the proliferation of NGOs had had a debilitating effect on the people's movements in that state (interview, 13 January 1999). 'NGOs' he maintained, 'are not grassroots organisations, they are merely funding bodies with a grassroots façade. They are not people-based, spontaneous movements. The Dalit Movements here had people's support'. He blamed NGOs for raising expectations and for producing activists who are motivated by cash rather than ideology.

The situation described by Karunakaran has yet to emerge in Tamil Nadu where NGOs and movements work in concert on many issues. As far as NGO activity in Tamil Nadu is concerned, the publication of well-researched and systematic reports by the better-equipped NGOs provides the information with which movements can castigate the government.[13] Such reports also add an air of objectivity to the subjective outbursts of the protest groups. Since they are not in direct competition with any of the rival organisations, NGOs can also provide forums for issue-based debate and interaction. The DPI activists occasionally voiced resentment that NGOs profited from the cause that they were devoting their lives to and wished that the funds obtained by such institutions were spread out more evenly; yet it is these organisations that have been able to organise the unorganised sectors of the employment market. Rickshaw drivers, domestic workers, municipal workers and tri-cycle workers have all been unionised largely to the efforts of such organisations.[14]

[13] On the 1 December 1999, for example, Thirumavalavan and other Dalit leaders from Tamil Nadu addressed the National Campaign for Dalit Human Rights' Conference at the Madras School of Social Work. He praised the organisation for releasing a 'Black Paper' on reservations in the state and said that it provided an answer to the question of how movements and institutions could profit from allying together. 'You can conduct research on behalf of movements', he told the panel.

[14] The more detached perspective of NGOs, churches and national political parties means that they can also engage in activities that have a less immediate impact, but which are consistent with the ideological objectives of the movement. The Dalit Resource Centre, thus, sponsors an annual Dalit Arts Festival (*Kalai Vizha*), maintaining that; 'The Cultural Revolution is a part of the struggle'. By emphasising the value of traditionally despised art forms, such programmes not only assert the dignity and skill of the artists, they also challenge the notion that Dalits do not have a distinct cultural heritage. Access to funds, staff and infrastructure enables these bodies to engage in organisational activity and this should be seen as a resource rather than a threat.

The links between movements, NGOs and similar organisations are informal and reciprocal. There are no steady funds from organisations to the DPI and prior to the elections in 1999 movement leaders were forced to approach various institutions for contributions. The relationships as they stand tend to consist of little more than mutual publicity pacts. Institutions and NGOs call upon the movements to address meetings on Dalit issues, cooperate with people compiling reports and lend weight to their campaigns—publicly signing petitions for the fulfilment of the UNDHR, for example. In return, movements receive publicity, credibility and institutional networks of support. They also gain access to lawyers and academics when required, have the benefit of institutional advertising for the meetings that they sponsor and establish a network of institutions who can be approached for monetary contributions. There were some indications of NGO-sponsored attempts to foster unity amongst the diverse Dalit-based movements, but the main institutional sources of funding and support remained the political parties in Tamil Nadu.

Dalit movements thus turn to political parties both for electoral alliances and funding. Potential solidarity with many organisations, however, is jeopardised by political rhetoric that is hardly suited to the subtleties of inter-caste understanding. In speeches, for instance, caste names are used to castigate whole communities, thus reinforcing the boundaries of mistrust and antipathy. The Paatali Makkal Katchi (Toiler's Party—PMK), for example, is denounced alternately by name and by reference to the Vanniyars who constitute its main constituency. Whilst the PMK is a Vanniyar-based party, lumping all members of a caste together merely reinforces divisions between caste categories and alienates non-PMK Vanniyars and other Backwards Castes. Although the DPI campaign in the 1999 elections was aimed at minority groups of all castes, they found it impossible to escape their categorisation as a radical *Dalit* organisation. Caste-based polarisation has not, however, served to unite all SCs. Tellingly, both newspapers and people on the ground portrayed the DPI as Dalit in relation to established parties, but as *Paraiyar* when comparing them to the mostly Pallar Puthiya Tamizhagam. Consequently, issue or incident based link-ups between Dalit movements have only had short-term success.[15]

[15] This is not just an issue for Dalit movements. Speaking of social movements across India, Sethi notes that: 'So long as the issue is live and important, groups

The various leaders of Dalit movements are not averse to sharing platforms with each other and frequently address meeting from the same podium. Rarely, however, do they do so simultaneously. Whilst leaders themselves may be prepared to co-operate, their followers are less likely to do so. The 1999 memorial meeting in Melavalavu, for example, was an exquisitely choreographed illustration of this. Sufficient space was enforced between each speech to allow leaders and followers to drive in and out of the village before the next party arrived. It is plausible that such synchronised events reflect police concerns about large gatherings of Dalit activists and the trouble that could arise. The leader-centred nature of most movements, however, means that movement cadres place inordinate emphasis upon their own chosen leader to the detriment of others. Indeed, when Dr Krishnasamy of the Puthiya Tamizhagam and Thirumavalavan sat side by side to condemn the atrocity in Tirunelveli, DPI activists showed me photographs which displayed 'the superior deportment and sensitivity' of their own convenor. Such views constitute a microcosm of the rivalry that exists between the two organisations. The members of each rarely interact on a daily basis and on the few occasions when they held joint demonstrations the respective camps kept well apart.

In other words, the diverse Dalit movements pursue separate agendas and only unite in the wake of (admittedly numerous) well-documented cases of atrocities against the Dalits. Many of these atrocities have been perpetrated by the police and DPI activists regard such acts as state policy—trying to stem the rise of a radical and autonomous Dalit party. It is as likely that the police force merely reflects its own caste constituency. The police in India are not divorced from the communities of their birth and they do not leave their prejudices behind them when they enter the force. The DPI has come into increasing conflict with the state apparatus, however, as it has assumed overtly political positions. Increasing levels of political awareness have soured the relationship between Dalits and the state. Dalits are no longer content to be the recipients of state-sponsored programmes but are demanding an active role in politics and a share of power. This brings Dalits into conflict with those in office, as it

---

can disregard differences of ideology and approach, but as soon as it loses force, the alliance breaks down' (Sethi 1993: 242).

mounts a challenge to their interests and deprives them of electoral support. Hitherto, Dalits have tended to be seen as voters who could be bought off at election time with promises and hand-outs.

Given the increasingly organised nature of the community, such measures are now perceived to be out-moded. Most political parties, therefore, seek alliances with Dalit organisations and all display images of Ambedkar on their campaign material. As yet, however, Dalit movements are neither established nor strong enough to contest the elections independently and so they are in a fairly weak position when it comes to negotiating alliances. It was for these reasons that the DPI initially embarked on a boycott of the elections. This boycott was immensely popular with activists who trumpeted their position as an indication of their radicalism. Rejecting the parliamentary process, however, allowed them to be cast as undemocratic. Once branded as a threat to society existing laws were employed to clamp down on them and alienate them from the masses. During 1998 and 1999, over 50 DPI activists were remanded under various national security and anti-terrorism Acts, apart from the countless 'preventative arrests'.

Such arrests both deterred members from engaging in civil disobedience and also constructed the DPI as a threat to peace, thus deterring others from joining the movement. This reputation made it more difficult for the DPI to secure police permission for political protests, demonstrations and rallies. Deprived of these means of reaching the public and articulating their grievances on a wider stage, the movement was faced by the choice of an escalation of radicalism or a reappraisal of their approach. The DPI opted to participate in the processes of established politics; they entered into negotiations with various electoral coalitions and ultimately decided to contest the 1999 elections under the banner of the TMC. State suppression, thus, fuelled the gradual institutionalisation of the Liberation Panthers. They sought to form an autonomous Dalit party that better represented the interests of their community, but the logistics of electoral competition induced the movement to seek alliances with established parties.

The DPI's links with political parties are ties of convenience rather than those of conviction and remain decidedly fragile. The alliances forged are electoral pacts and do not involve convergences in terms of policy. Of late, the DPI has allied itself to parties which have antithetical objectives, such as the Hindu nationalist party, the BJP, because that coalition offered the movement more seats and was opposed to the PMK. In other words, such alliances are based on 'realpolitik' rather than ideology. As a consequence, negotiations and agreements occur between leaders and are subsequently communicated to the rank and file. The partial nature of such communication was evident in the run up to the 1999 and 2001 elections when even 'Firebrand' Murugan (one of the main rhetoricians of the DPI) was uncertain about the movement's political alliances. At a local level, the divisions between camps are manifold and run along the faultlines of caste, leadership, organisation and ideology, with the first and last being most prominent. In the 2001 elections, for instance, many DMK affiliates simply stayed away from the polls rather than supporting the DPI candidates who stood on their ticket. Likewise, DPI cadre turned out in droves to canvass for their own candidates but were subdued in areas where DMK politicians were contesting the elections.

Against N. Subramanian (1999), therefore, I argue that the Dravidian parties have failed to create an open, democratic and plural society, and that the proliferation of Dalit and other caste parties is, in part, an attempt to extend the scope of Tamil politics.[16] The egalitarian emphasis of Dravidian rhetoric has not translated into social practice and the incorporation of Dalits into a system of state patronage does not equate to an extension of democratic participation. In *Frontline*, T. Subramanian highlights how ironic it is 'that such a large number of caste parties should sprout in Tamil Nadu, the cradle of the Dravidian movement' (2 March 2001). But it is precisely because the interests of excluded social groups were not served by established politics that they have mobilised for a share of political power. As Subramani, a DPI activist in Cuddalore, insisted, 'without protest we cannot achieve anything. One cannot claim anything from the government without protest. Only if we protest is there an opportunity for our community to do anything' (interview, 27 April 1999).

---

[16] This does not set out to be a critique of Subramanian's (1999) otherwise excellent book. In many ways it can be read as an extension of his study into the present day. Many of the trends that are apparent now were not in evidence 10 years or so ago. It is only in the past decade or so that there has been a concerted effort by Dalit and minority caste groups to form autonomous organisations of their own in order to gain better representation at the state level.

As Pandian rightly notes, Dalits in Tamil Nadu today treat the DMK 'as a sign of betrayal. Their hostility is so complete that a number of Adi Dravidar political groups active in the state willingly let the gleeful Brahmin off the hook while projecting the DMK as the sole villain' (1994: 221). The one caveat to Pandian's analysis is that the AIADMK has similarly fallen out of favour. The betrayal of Dravidian ideals is a frequent topic in Dalit speeches and interviews, and activists often cited their own movements as the true heirs of Periyar. Speaking at a marriage function on the outskirts of Madurai, for example, Thirumavalavan made the following observations:

> Dravidian parties have shown their true colours. The people have become disillusioned with them and they can no longer hide their real face. In Father Periyar's time he said 'forget God and think of Mankind'. But what the DMK repeated was 'one society, one God'. They asserted the existence of God and thus removed their first mask and lost their critical humanism. Next they insisted that 'we will have a Dravidian land or else a cemetery'. Then, they aban-doned this demand for separation despite insisting that the reasons for the original demand remained in place. Thus, they lost the mask of Dravidianism. They said: 'If you see a snake and a Brahmin together, then leave the snake and hit the Brahmin'. But then, Periyar said 'we are not against Brahmins or Brahminism'—so saying, the DMK removed the mask of anti-Brahminism.... 'We cannot implement Tamil medium education even if Tamil scholars threaten to go on hunger strike' quoth Karunanidhi. 'I will ask the opinion of all English medium nursery school heads before making any decision'. With this he removed his mask of Tamil language nationalism. Finally, from Khaider Mhilat's time he has claimed to have good relations with Muslims, but the alliance with the BJP has shattered the mask of protecting Muslims. Karunanidhi has been revealed as the typical caste Hindu: Not a Tamil, not a humanist, not an anti-Brahmin, not a defender of Islam—a typical, real, caste Hindu! (Thirumavalavan, 16 June 1999).[17]

The fact that Dravidian parties have presided over a period in which the materially better off sections of the non-Brahmin community has prospered at the expense of others is compounded by the fact that both parties have now forged links with the BJP. 'Those who fought so hard to overthrow the domination of the Brahmins', as Ravichandran

---

[17] All speeches were tape recorded and translated by the author.

of the Marutham Network put it, 'have taken on board the caste scriptures and structure in their turn' (interview, 27 September 1999). In the run up to the 1999 elections, the DPI found common cause with Muslims, Christians and tribals in an indictment of Dravidian 'misrule'. Particular opprobrium was heaped on K. Karunanidhi, the chief minister at the time, as in this speech:

> The Karunanidhi who used to sport a black shawl today wears a saffron one. The Karunanidhi who used to sing the praises of Periyar is today singing the praises of Vajpayee. Have you seen? Have you noticed what is happening to the DMK's image? The history of the Dravidian Movement is going to end with Karunanidhi. After Karunanidhi the DMK will not be able to raise its head—it is on its last legs. Backward Classes, MBCs, Dalits, Muslims and other minorities whom Karunanidhi used to champion have been excluded by him today when he says: 'the majority Hindu people are sufficient for us' …. He has made a big mistake in history, he has slipped up. This is an unforgiveable fault (Thirumavalavan, 13 July 1999).

The castigation of the DMK, however, did not signal a complete rapprochement with the AIADMK. Under both regimes, I was frequently told, atrocities against Dalits had occurred and gone unpunished. A common metaphor was the assertion that the mask of Dravidianism had slipped to reveal the 'true', casteist faces of the Dravidian parties.

Despite this, in successive elections, the DPI has allied with both Dravidian organisations. Thirumavalavan entered the Legislative Assembly in 2001 under the DMK's symbol of the rising sun, despite the DMK's alliance with the BJP. Subsequent to his election he has continued to criticise both Dravidian parties. What this signals, thus, is not the manifestation of ideological confusion, much less the evidence of common ground. Rather, the DPI has been forced to respond to the pragmatic realities of Tamil politics. Despite the rise of countless autonomous, caste-based parties over the past decade, the Dravidian parties remain the hegemonic influences in the state. To have a realistic chance of success in the polls the DPI required an alliance. Having taken the decision to contest elections, therefore, pragmatism dictated a loose agreement with one or other of the main parties. This process of adopting contradictory alliances led to a crisis of identity for the DPI and ultimately resulted in the movement splitting into two different camps in 2001 when the General Secretary, 'Tada' Periyasami, left the movement accusing it of becoming a personal vehicle for Thirumavalavan's ambition.

The departure of one of the movement's key figures was traumatic and received a lot of publicity at the time. It carried to a logical conclusion trends that had been evident for a long while. During my fieldwork it was apparent that the lesser leaders were, if not jealous, aggrieved at the attention heaped upon Thirumavalavan and the perceived lack of recognition for their own work. Thirumavalavan was likened to MGR (the film-star turned politician who founded the AIADMK) for his demagogic speeches and popularity. When I returned to Tamil Nadu in 2002, on the surface it seemed that nothing had changed since the split. Activists in Madurai described the events as a blip and asserted that very few members had followed Periyasami. They also seized the moral high ground by pointing out that his new movement had adopted a caste-based name and had swiftly vanished from the public eye. Certainly the DPI did not appear to be much weakened by the schism. It did, however, highlight that forging an alliance with a political party and entering the parliamentary process had challenged the identity upon which the movement was built by accepting the system that it had hitherto portrayed as corrupt and corrupting. Movements entering parliamentary politics and wishing to win will probably have to abandon some demands and principles since they will be the junior party in any alliance. This, as much as anything, contributed to the departure of Periyasami.

In the short-term, however, strategic political pacts resolved issues of funding and offered a path out of the problems posed by exclusive rhetoric. Identity-based politics can lead to the creation of defensive enclaves and reinforce communal divisions, but where it is used as a vehicle to political participation it contains the seeds of its own diffusion. Because the Dalits cannot win elections on their own, entering the political process requires them to negotiate with other groups. Protest movements often get carried away with their revolutionary character to the extent that they neglect the painstaking processes of negotiation and lobbying.[18] As Dietrich observes, how-

---

[18] 'In failing to recognise that all politics operates in the arena of compromises and deals and addresses itself to what is potentially realisable, revolutionary purism ends up painting State structures and processes in fortress-like terms that are amenable only to assault and smashing' (S. Kothari 1990: 12).

ever, it is often the persistent chasing up of officials and harrying of bureaucrats that produces results, rather than the grand demonstration that disrupts traffic for a day and gives the cadres a sense of power (personal communication, 25 October 1999).

This is not to say that Dalit movements should abandon the objective of radical structural change. Far from it, for 'without affecting the well-being of the dominant caste', as Chandra Bose puts it, 'how will the lowest caste get a solution?' (interview, 23 February 1999). The question rather, regards the best means to achieve that end. In the current political climate it is arguable that more can be achieved by acting as the radical conscience of the democratic system than by allowing the militant tag to stick. When I arrived in India, in 1998, the DPI was vehemently opposed to participating in the 'flawed structures of government'. A combination of shifts in the political opportunity structure, state and caste repression, and the will of the Dalit people forced them to reassess that position. During my research I observed the process of its transition from a radical movement to a junior partner in a coalition. This process was instructive not only as an indication of the political opportunity structure, but also as an insight into the mechanisms through which movement policy is debated and decided. In 2002, the DPI was still negotiating its way around the corridors of mainstream politics. Further research, therefore, is required to assess the extent to which this move will result in the institutionalisation of the DPI and whether it will be able to retain its reputation for radicalism.

The DPI's involvement in the political machinations attending the state elections in 2001 has certainly been a source of disillusionment for many observers. If political participation results in 'more of the same', they argue, then the objectives of the movement will have been betrayed. In this book I argue that despite the compromises engendered by electoral calculations, the Liberation Panthers and movements like them have constituted a meaningful force for socio-political change in the state. In this sense they are helping to 'democratise democracy' in India. Before beginning my analysis of contemporary Dalit movements, however, it is necessary to have an understanding of the historical context. The next chapter, therefore, provides a brief survey of the socio-political backdrop to social movement action in Tamil Nadu.

2
DEMOCRACY, DEMONSTRATIONS AND DISORDER: SOCIAL MOBILISATION AND SOCIO-POLITICAL CHANGE

The political and industrial revolutions were (earlier in the city and later in the village) transforming old institutions, uprooting the old society, changing old habits and modes of thinking, and imposing new techniques ... such breaks with the past could not fail to leave their mark on the form and content of the crowd's activities (G. Rudé 1995: 5).

Introduction: Democracy and Disorder

At the stroke of midnight, on 15 August 1947, India became an Independent Republic. The Constitution of the nascent state, agreed upon in 1950, proclaimed India to be a democratic country with socialist tendencies. The commitment to affirmative action programmes, health and schooling for all and a programme of national industrialisation heralded the dawn of a new era. The mass movement of the people, which had rendered the victory of the nationalist cause inevitable, similarly demanded the adoption of more open modes of government and social interaction. The inclusive emphasis of the new state was reinforced not only by the directive principles and legislative changes of the Constitution itself, but by the selection of Dr Ambedkar as the chairman of the Drafting Committee. The new state promised a nation of equal citizens, where none need fear discrimination on account of who they were, and instituted the legislative measures to ensure such an end. The participatory emphasis of the state suggested that people's demands would be heard without their recourse to extra-institutional protest. If Dalits were oppressed, if women were molested or if Muslims were discriminated against on the basis of religion, they now had the legal entitlement to enlist the state apparatus as an ally in their quest for justice.

Fifty years after Independence, however, extra-institutional protest—much of it directed against the state—continues to the point where several commentators have argued that India suffers from a 'crisis of governability' (Kohli 1990: ix).[1] In retrospect it was never going to be easy to erase centuries of social inequality by legal means, and the introduction of the franchise offered more tangible avenues to power than had been available before. Forms of protest found to be effective in the nationalist struggle also established a whole array of methods to draw upon. India's transition from a conglomeration of segmented kingdoms to a centralised democratic political order raises significant questions about the organisational forms and implications of political protest. This chapter will focus on the proliferation of extra-institutional mobilisation that has accompanied this socio-political transformation. I shall consider the forms in which protest has been, and is, manifested; how collective action relates to political institutions; and whether mobilisation of this nature is a challenge to the legitimacy of the state or a possible path to political participation.

In the scholarly literature on this subject, a majority view highlights a correlation between democratic institutions and the increase in social mobilisation and conflict. 'As democracy is introduced and competing elites undertake political mobilisation', Kohli asserts, 'old identities are rekindled and reforged. Modern technology hastens the process ... and the collision of mobilised identities with each other or with the state ought not to be totally surprising' (Kohli: 1998: 9). This outcome is presented as an ineluctable result of the 'profoundly subversive power of the democratic discourse, which ... allows the spread of equality and liberty into increasingly wider domains, and therefore acts as a fermenting agent upon the different forms of struggle against subordination' (Laclau and Mouffe 1985: 155). An

---

[1] Although they do not use the same phraseology, Saberwal (1986), Adas (1991) and Mitra (1992) also raise questions about the political stability of India. This chapter deals with only the political issues that are said to have contributed to India's 'crisis of governability', thus reflecting Kohli's assertion that the factors behind this crisis are 'more political than socio-economic' (Kohli 1990: ix).

leg warm up on back

jama

(a)een Riders
Tue 7.12 nos?

£45 1oclass

£660 - 5pm.

OUT OF EDEN

Tel: 01768 372 939
Fax: 01768 372 636
Email: sales@outofeden.co.uk
www.outofeden.co.uk

unsettling conclusion that one can reach from such analysis 'is that India's democracy has itself contributed to the over-politicisation of the Indian polity' (Kohli 1990: 20). This perspective risks presenting events that are particular to a specific country and time as merely a part of the 'great democratic revolution' (de Tocqueville 1994a [1835]: 3). It is insufficient as an explanation because it cannot explain *why* certain groups or individuals mobilise whereas others do not, why certain mobilisations result in violence whilst others are assimilated into the mainstream and how the language and institutions of democracy filter down to the grass-roots level. Furthermore, as Mitra (1999) observes, the notion of over-politicisation appears to take minimal liberal democracy as the norm and any deviation from this is presented as excess. In short, it is in danger of obscuring the specificity of the movements themselves, as well as a sense of change over time.[2]

Colonisation and Conflict: Indian Society and British Rule

Historical analyses of India frequently highlight a perceived opposition between the karmic passivity of the 'traditional' inhabitants—living in social harmony due to the 'perfect integration' of the caste and village systems—and the political mobilisation that has caused increasing levels of instability today.[3] The images of people starving

---

[2] Foucault argues that power is 'never localised' and that individuals 'are always in the position of simultaneously undergoing and exercising power' (Foucault 1980: 98). Rather than read people's actions as the consequences of 'higher' discourses and power relations, therefore, he calls for 'an *ascending* analysis of power starting ... from its infinitesimal mechanisms' (Foucault 1980: 99).

[3] Bonner's (1990: 1–2) is perhaps the most simplistic articulation of this view. He sees contemporary social movements as enabling 'the poor' to escape their belief in *karma*. Adas (1991: 296) observes that revisionist historians have correctly challenged the image of the passive peasantry but warns against the creation of a counter-'myth'. The impact of everyday resistance, as he notes, should not be overstated. Although 'India was never easy to govern' (Kohli 1990: 3–4), Mitra notes that collective conflict in democratic India 'indicates the growing assertiveness on the part of previously powerless groups' (1992: 141). Where 'tradition' ends and 'modernity' begins, however, is not so clear cut. Here

to death outside granaries during the Bengal famine (Thompson 1991: 349) and of Dalits accepting their subordination (Moffatt 1979; Racine 1998) reinforce this dichotomy. According to this construction, current unrest is possibly due to 'a lack of fit between the principles which have gone into the designing of these institutions over many long centuries in Europe, and those informal institutions to which we in India have traditionally been heir: family, caste, village' (Saberwal 1986: 2). The consequence of this disjunction, Inden argues, 'is a nation-state that remains ontologically and politically inaccessible to its own citizens' (1990: 197). The current 'crisis' of legitimacy may then be explained by the fact that the socio-political institutions of the 'developed' world were precipitously introduced to India before it was 'ready'. Such terminology, Casteñeda insists in a Latin American context, 'is of delicate usage: it signifies simply that natural, historical processes are being "rushed" by the extension of the products of modernity to societies that have not generated them' (1993: 337).

An alternative view, proffered by Weiner, 'is that violence among caste, linguistic, and religious groups is endemic in India's variegated social structure, and that there is no reason to believe that the situation is worse now than in the past' (1997: 241). The work of James Scott (1985) and the 'Subalternists' has gone a long way towards challenging the historical image of a fatalistic or passive peasantry. The absence of overt conflict did not mean that people accepted the prevailing order or that they were not engaged in 'everyday acts of resistance' that enabled them to ameliorate their condition. Adas (1991) and Prakash (1990) note the historical significance of 'avoidance' protest, such as the flight of peasants, withdrawal into religious sectarianism like the *Bhakti* cults, or the shift from one patron to another. Increasing centralisation under colonial rule enabled landlords to demand the return of labourers who had fled to neighbouring states, but it also rendered migration or emigration easier and allowed many labourers to escape from exploitative labour relations. Better communications and transport systems also

---

an arbitrary break in the modes of protest can be posited to exist between the Indian mutiny of 1857 and the rise of the Indian National Congress (INC) in 1885. Where the mutiny was an uprising in defence of religious values, the INC was a deliberate attempt to wrest power from the British.

enabled horizontal mobilisation on a larger scale thereby facilitating more confrontational modes of protest.

The opposition drawn between passive peasants and contentious citizens may be somewhat overstated, but the significance of social and economic change to the behaviour of 'crowds' cannot be denied. In his seminal work, *The Crowd in History* (1995 [1964]), George Rudé charts the transformations in politics, society and the economy that were wrought by the political and industrial revolutions of the 18th century in England and France. 'Such breaks with the past', he observes, 'could not fail to leave their mark on the form and content of the crowd's activities' (1995: 5). It would be puzzling had the introduction of British rule, and the social, economic and political transformations that attended it, not had a comparable influence on protest in India. Prior to the Raj, India had experienced centralising drives by ambitious military monarchs, yet it remained (particularly in the south) compartmentalised into the territorial frameworks of 'little kingdoms' (Dumont 1997). As Saberwal argues, 'confining persons into their segmental spaces may indeed be taken as the principal, if unintended, theme of the caste order' (1997: 125). In other words, the inhabitants of 'traditional' India were not able to conceptualise collective protest on a large scale (Kaviraj 1997: 147).

In south India, caste and kinship could be equated with locality and only recently has the endogamous community extended far beyond the boundaries of the village. Drawing upon his fieldwork in Tamil Nadu, Mines insists that the paradigm of society was that 'of *constituencies*, which form around dominant individuals and their patronage' (1994: 112). Towards the end of the 19th and the beginning of the 20th centuries, the British were forced to confront and interact with these prominent individuals (Washbrook 1976: 109). So long as these 'big men' remained the focus of social interaction, the strength of vertical ties of obligation and patronage militated against the possibility of group action on the basis of horizontal solidarity. If a magnate considered it to be personally advantageous, Washbrook (1976) notes, he could dictate social and political alliances for his followers, which they would usually regard as ritually polluting or economically counter-productive.

Positions of great economic power and status were maintained through patron–client ties and the use of force (ibid.: 151). Pace Pandian (1995), it is important to stress the subaltern politics that existed beyond the limited public sphere of colonial India and the limits to political power. Even allowing for dissenting voices, however, resisting the compulsions of economically dominant patrons was (at best) impractical because agricultural production was dictated by adherence to caste practices and roles. Each person was assigned their place in the system and resistance to the landlords resulted in social ostracism or violence. 'Before the development of a substantial non-agrarian economy', therefore, 'it was impossible to break free of its economic logic' (N.K. Bose, in Kaviraj 1997a: 6). When colonial rule laid the basis for a centralised, commercial economy it assimilated the traditional compartments into a larger whole, thus enabling each dispersed caste to unite across a much wider territorial area.

In the face of this process of social transformation, the preeminence of the caste headman soon disappeared. Despite the retention of private armies, the authority of the headman largely rested upon consensus, 'whose area of influence was limited to the locale. That consensus was abruptly withdrawn when western style education expanded possibilities of occupational and physical mobility' (Mines 1994: 112). Communities bound by marriage, kinship and locality were gradually replaced by statewide caste associations bound as much by political affiliation as by blood ties. To view this change as a purely political shift would be mistaken. This extension of the basis of caste organisation, according to Barnett, 'revolves around the meanings assigned by South Indians to the symbol of blood *purity*. A stress on blood as embodying a caste-wide code for conduct replaces caste hierarchy; a stress on blood as embodying natural substance opens the ideological field to other identity choices' (1977: 396–97). This transition from a hierarchy of interdependent social categories to a universe of 'essentially identical' competing blocs is what Dumont terms the 'substantialisation' of caste (1980: 222). The formation of statewide caste associations and the extension of marriage boundaries, he notes, facilitate mobilisation so that castes now appear as collective individuals (ibid.).

Arguably Dumont's primary emphasis on hierarchy and interdependence results in his downplaying the fluidity of the pre-colonial caste system. Competition and substantialisation were 'traditional' elements of the system (Dumont 1980: 417).[4] It is clear, however,

---

[4] Rao (1987: 5) observes that the 'traditional caste system was relatively open and upward mobility occurred in two ways': First, through military prowess, and second, through new religious sects. Rudolph and Rudolph (1967: 29) and

that the processes of social change set in train by the British offered the lower castes greater scope for mobility. The proliferation of caste associations in the late 19th century must, therefore, be examined in the light of structural alterations that enabled individuals to exercise more choice in their lives. In other words, rather than casting the emergent forms of caste mobilisation and consciousness as the instrumental outcome of power struggles between the colonial state and an Indian elite, one needs to chart the agency, ideas and actions of the actors involved. 'By projecting an entirely different worldview', as Ramashray Roy observes, 'British rule not only made the creation of new opportunities of physical and social mobility possible but also changed, even if gradually, the consciousness of the socio-economically deprived by making them aware that there was nothing immutable about the system' (Roy 1990: 41).

Even before the introduction of democratic modes of government, therefore, social processes were in train without which the mobilisation of communities as political actors would have been impossible. Similar processes of change were underway in the economic sphere. Commercialisation meant not just the increase in the use of money in the economy, but also 'the use of objective monetary values to express social relationships' (Bayly 1988: 11). The decline in payment in kind and the universal validity of cash-based salaries gradually opened up the possibility of occupational mobility. The opportunity to change cannot, of course, explain the decision to do so (Constable 2000), but the importance of analysing processes of democratisation in terms of social as well as political practices should be apparent. New opportunities for employment (in the government, industry and service sector) and the importance of an education in English led to a physical transition of élites to the centre of government adminis- tration. Motivated by the new possibilities available to them, indi- viduals and their families eschewed the local endogamous units in favour of families within the same caste category, but with a similar outlook and education, thus reinforcing statewide caste communities (Rudolph and Rudolph 1967: 33). Less privileged caste groups similarly seized the opportunity to escape from relations of depen-

---

Washbrook (1989: 237) make similar points. Srinivas, however, argues that social mobility in pre-modern India was individualistic: 'The need as well as the facilities for "corporate mobility" did not exist' (Srinivas 1991: 315).

dency and bondage. The accelerated growth of urban areas reflects a desire for change and independence.

Colonial Classification and Community Politics

This socio-economic transformation opened up new fields of identity choices and simultaneous advances in technology facilitated the formation of group associations. Transport and communications infrastructure made members of widely dispersed groups more accessible to each other. 'The effect of a newspaper', as de Tocqueville noted, 'is not only to suggest the same purpose to a great number of persons, but to furnish the means for executing in common the designs which they may have singly conceived' (1994b [1840]: 111, cf. Anderson 1991). The potential of such publications was immediately apparent to political aspirants in India. Educated Dalits, such as Ayothidas Pandithar in the early 20th century, 'used his weekly (*Oru Paisa*) *Tamizhan* to spread his ideas and theories' (Rajadurai and Geetha 1993: 2092). The impetus that such media can afford to mobilising groups was even more apparent in the example of the non-Brahmin movement (Irschick 1969: 48). Railways, the press and the weakening of patron–client ties contributed to widening the scope of group action, but it was the political opportunity structure that influenced the course that this would take.[5]

Confronted by an alien society and systems of social stratification that they could not easily comprehend, the British administrators sought neat and comprehensible categories. The exercise of power creates knowledge, as Foucault (1980) observes and the by-product of exercises such as the census and the communal Government Orders, was an unintended 'production of the Indian people'.[6] The census was one of the new mechanisms of power and forms of control introduced by the colonial state. Whereas previous rulers had established centralised kingdoms, their power was never continuous or

---

[5] See also Anderson (1991) and Price (1996), for the way in which public discourse was shaped by the emergence of new court procedures and legal reports. These allowed the development of alternative notions of community, identity and mobilisation among 19th century south Indians.

[6] Cohn (1990), Dirks (1989, 1992, 1997), Hansen (1999) and Smith (2000) present similar arguments.

widely dispersed. Colonial power, by contrast, ceased to be concentrated in the person of the king and was systematically diffused. Through the imposition, and regular collection, of income tax, control of the productive processes in the country and the gradual development of legal and political institutions, the government became increasingly prominent as a controller of people and resources (Baker 1976: 16).[7]

The increasing intrusion of the state into the lives of its citizens required not only new forms of knowledge about society, but also the exercise of new forms of control and the production of disciplined and receptive political subjects. 'Political order was to be achieved not through the intermittent use of coercion but through continuous instruction, inspection and control' (Mitchell 1988: xi). The significance of the census to this process lay not only in the illusion it gave of 'knowing the people' (Cohn 1990), but also in the modes of observation and classification which it introduced. The conception of caste as a distinct entity, thus, enabled caste-based enumeration. By asserting that each caste conformed to certain characteristics and that everyone belonged to a caste, administrators avoided, and arguably precluded, the painstaking problems of differentiating between individuals (Smith 2000).[8] The desire for neat labels, according to the 1921 Census Superintendent, Mr Middleton, did not simply permit officials to understand their Indian subjects, it 'led to the crystallisation of the caste system' (in Dirks 1996: 266). Each caste was defined, counted and ranked in a manner that allowed for no anomalies or fluidity. Indeed, census officials refused to accept certain caste names and insisted upon establishing the 'true' caste of each person (Cohn 1990: 244).

This claim to certainty and truth is one of the primary features of the disciplinary world (Mitchell 1988: xi). Power works in a chain (Foucault 1980: 98), however, and the British attempt to impose order upon an alien social world led to increasing interaction with the people, and this exchange profoundly affected the nature of the

[7] Mitchell's (1988) book on Egypt provides a parallel account of the impact of colonialism in that country.

[8] There were other possible modes of categorisation and census taking, as Smith points out, such as the registration of births and deaths. 'That, however, would have been to deal with the population as individuals, not as members of some social or territorial collectivity' (Smith 2000: 33).

classificatory enterprise. In the process of mapping society, colonial powers unwittingly assumed the royal prerogative of deciding upon the hierarchical position of castes within their jurisdiction (Dirks 1987: 8). Petitions demanding a change in caste rank, thus, were now submitted to the census commissioner rather than the sovereign and the potential to renegotiate one's caste position led to a 'livening up of the caste spirit' (Ghurye 1932 quoted in Cohn 1990: 241).

It is arguable, therefore, that 'colonialism in India produced new forms of civil society which have been presented as traditional forms' (Dirks 1989: 43). To describe caste as a classificatory 'trope' (Dirks 1992), ignores its social and political significance, but government classifications certainly encouraged the formation of political groups which bore little resemblance to the categories that gave rise to them. 'The conversion of the Madras Government to the policies of active communal discrimination', as Washbrook notes, 'was the prime factor in the development of communal politics' (1976: 273). Whilst Pandian (1995) rightly critiques the denial of agency in the Cambridge School, the introduction of quotas based on communal categories meant that Indians had to adapt to British ideas in order to take advantage of the British system.[9]

Even nationalists, who remained beyond the emerging institutions of self-rule, were forced to confront the social categories of the British when challenged by representatives of Untouchable, non-Brahmin or Dravidian groups. The introduction of a limited franchise in the 1920s and 1930s offered new channels to power and influence, and its increasing prominence in the everyday lives of its citizens rendered government office an attractive objective. The appeal to communal sentiment was found to be a powerful mobilising tool for what Ramaswami Mudaliar defined as a 'jobocracy' (Irschick 1969: 262). Confronted by a state with increasing powers of patronage, new organisational forms sought to secure economic benefits, jobs or special concessions (Rudolph and Rudolph 1967). The non-Brahmin movement, thus, exploited British unease over the preponderance of Brahmins in office (Rajendran 1994: 53), but also drew on more widespread resentment of Brahmin domination and 'arrogance' for political ends (Baker 1976: 28; Irschick 1986: 82). It banded 98 per

---

[9] Baker (1976: 322), Hardgrave (1979: 16), Irshick (1986: 5), Ramaswamy (1997: 247) and Smith (2000: 2) likewise observe how indigenous groups had to refashion themselves in order to meet British expectations.

cent of the population together solely because they were not Brahmins. This category was so diverse as to have no sustainable social basis, but it 'gratified British expectations' (Baker 1976: 322). It was also confined to the Madras Presidency, itself an administrative construction of the British.

This should not be read as denying the consciousness and sentiments of the actors involved. Colonial classifications were not passively accepted; they were appropriated and inhabited by indigenous groups, often in wholly unpredictable ways.[10] By 1920, for instance, it had become immaterial whether the category of non-Brahmin had any actual basis in Tamil or Hindu society, as Irschick notes, 'by that time the term 'non-Brahmin' had powerful political meaning' (1986: 27). Though described as an élite protest that by no means represented or mobilised the majority of non-Brahmins, the rhetoric and ideological visions inspired many subsequent protests. The movement also helped to form the shape of future Indian politics, in that one of its abiding legacies was the early institution of affirmative action programmes for deprived castes which set a template for others to follow.

Important though the introduction of electoral competition was, the social and political shifts noted here cannot be reduced to the process of democratisation alone. Countless developing countries even today show that there is no inevitable correlation between the transformations associated with 'modernity' and political democracy. Although the gradual breakdown of traditional authority and the opening up of the political and economic spheres may loosely be seen as a process of 'democratisation', a distinction must be drawn between the social and political senses of the term. From this perspective we can follow Kaviraj in observing that 'modernity changes fundamentally what people are, what they think they are,

---

[10] Several authors note the process of negotiation through which indigenous groups rework colonial labels. For example, Ludden (1989: 190) notes how court battles helped shape access to public space. Irschick (1994: 7–8) and O'Toole (1996: 242) observe how the alien concepts of the British were appropriated in the construction of new meanings and ways of being. Ramaswamy (1997: 247) points out that Tamil language nationalism 'was fashioned into a weapon to contend with both British colonialism and Indian nationalism', and Hansen (1999: 35) observes how colonial rule served to reinforce caste identities. For more on the Dravidian and self-respect movements in this regard see Pandian (1995).

and more fundamentally and elusively, their way of being what they are' (1997a: 25). As the horizons of segmented communities were expanded by the growth of a cash-based economy, a centralising state and the introduction of the limited franchise, not only were 'old' identities challenged, but a whole raft of other identities became available. We may thus accept Lefort's suggestion that democratisation entails the gradual 'dissolution of the markers of certainty' that made existing hierarchies seem natural and pre-determined (1988: 19, after Hansen 1999).

Hansen describes the history of Indian democracy as a 'circum-scribed questioning of hierarchies and authority, spreading from the political field' (1999: 8). It is clear that the 'political field' is inseparable from the social and economic ones and that social transformation in these spheres was a prerequisite of political mobilisation. What Hansen highlights is the predominant role that politics has come to assume in this process of social reordering. Thus the Nadars increased their status through social organisation (such as educational and employment associations) and economic im-provement, but contemporary SC and BC movements seek mobility primarily through party political action. The non-Brahmin movement is instructive of the gradual process by which the 'British adminis-trators and the Indians who interacted with them began to develop what was in effect a common understanding about appropriate techniques for political expression' (Irschick 1986: 115).

The processes of structural, social and discursive transformation 'associated with democracy', Hansen observes, 'profoundly modify and transform a society's imagination of itself' (1999: 9). The significance of the Justice Party victory in the 1920 Legislative Assembly polls in Madras, thus, lies less in the replacement of one clique by another rather than in the manner of this reorganisation. 'After 1920', as Washbrook observes, 'channels of political commu-nication were joined and largely replaced by those of election' (1976: 326). Henceforth, political demands were arguably formulated as much to influence official policy as to attract a following. The non-Brahmin movement exemplified the increasingly secular orientation of the new organisational forms of caste and religion and a significant legacy of the movement was the implicit assertion that social and ritual hierarchies could be challenged and renegotiated through political and electoral mobilisation. Once a few parties had estab-lished the efficacy of such mobilisation, as Philips indicates, 'the exigencies of competition require that the others do not lag too far behind' (Philips 1991: 81).

Group Identity and Social Mobilisation

This proposition has frequently been taken to establish a correlation between the increase in democratic institutions and the rise in social mobilisation. Whilst acknowledging the importance of reservations to the strength of communal appeals, Gallanter maintains that the 'franchise itself, with its invitation to mobilise support by appeal to existing loyalties' has been most responsible for this outcome (Gallanter 1997: 197).[11] The argument is obvious: As power is opened up to electoral competition political leaders in search of votes draw upon existing identities and community feeling. These social categories make 'available to the leadership structural and ideological bases for political mobilisation, providing it with both a segmental system and an identification system on which support could be crystallised' (Kothari 1997: 64). This argument undoubtedly contributes to an explanation of the continuing salience of social categories in Indian politics, but expressed in such terms it is overly simplistic and cannot elucidate the complex processes involved. I shall highlight two fundamental weaknesses of this approach. First, it throws no light upon the processes by which communal identities are constructed and made to 'stick', nor can it explain the impulse to organise collectively. Second, a facile correlation between democracy and mobilisation cannot by itself explain the prevalence of extra-institutional, especially violent, protest, except insofar as it is geared towards political participation of the mobilising group.

The classic electoral maxim of 'one member, one vote', presupposes a trend towards individualism. This was the danger that de Tocqueville was most apprehensive about in the 19th century: That each individual would be so confined by his (sic) domestic affections and attachments that he would be thrown back 'forever upon himself alone' (1994b: 99). The willingness of people to engage in movements

---

[11] Rudolph and Rudolph (1987), Gould (1988), Kohli (1990), Mitra (1994), Mitra and Lewis (1996), Basu and Kohli (1998) and Hansen (1999) have all remarked upon this correlation.

that place their lives at risk, by contrast, suggests a stronger affinity with the group than the individual (cf. Kakar 1996). On the face of it, the objection that the establishment of democracy cannot explain the continuing impulse towards collective action would appear to be misplaced in India. The democratic state, in its commitment to social justice, itself recognises certain categories of society as the beneficiaries of affirmative action programmes (Beteille 1991b). Dumont (1980) attempts to explain the continuing salience of caste by depicting substantialised castes as 'collective individuals' in that the interests of individual members are seen as those of the entire group. Horizontal collective action thus becomes a natural means for securing concessions, rights and justice for the whole.

These concessions, however, as Roy observes, 'have to be individually utilised' (1990: 46). Reservations can equally be perceived as a means of individual mobility, as is evinced by the creation of a 'harijan elite' who 'tend to disassociate themselves from the degraded state of their community and orbit in an entirely new sphere' (ibid.: 47).[12] The identities that have so much political relevance today, according to this argument, retain little resemblance to those that they have replaced. To see the contemporary salience of communal sentiment as a continuation of tradition seems misguided. Another answer to this problematic is to stress the different conceptions of individualism that pertain in India. Although community identity is declining, the continuing significance of 'big men'—as evinced by the popularity and significance of cinema-star fan clubs and populist charismatic leadership—may help to explain the per-

---

[12] Reservations, in this light, function to effect what Foucault terms a 'reversal of the political axis of individualisation' (1977: 192). In modern societies, it is argued, reputations and community decline in importance with regard to the common individual, whereas individualisation was greatest at the summit of society under feudal systems. 'Habermas characterises the transition as a whole as one from "role-identity" to "ego-identity", understanding by the latter a form of personal identity which is no longer determined by contents unreflectively inherited from cultural tradition, but is defined by the mastery of procedures of critical examination and argumentative grounding employed in the acquisition of cognitive and moral beliefs' (Dews 1984: 82). In the *History of Sexuality* (1981), Foucault similarly observes the dissolution of the forms of group identity characteristic of traditional societies. The question then becomes how and why identities that were present in traditional society have retained, if not increased, their saliency in democratic India.

sistence of collective action (Mines 1994: 40–41). Ties of loyalty, patronage and friendship serve to bind people to leaders, who are expected to fight on their behalf. The followers bathe in the reflected glory of their leader and hope to achieve individual prominence by working for the 'big man' (Dickey 1993a: 349). De Tocqueville's argument, however, is that democratic contest and government encourages the sort of self-centred rationalisation that is the hallmark of an individualistic society.[13]

The adoption of a democratic mode of government ought to give rise to the inclusion of hitherto excluded people by extending to them the institutional means to voice their grievances. The prevalence of collective or extra-institutional protest, therefore, may reflect a failure of the institutions of interest mediation. To posit a correlation between democracy and mobilisation in this instance is to insist upon the social implications of democratic practice. In addressing these themes many authors draw attention to the 'instrumentalist' manipulation of 'primordial' sentiments. 'Ethnic conflicts', as Kohli insists, 'are not inevitable expressions of deep-rooted differences.' 'The process of identity formation and ethnic conflict', he continues, 'is also not so indeterminate as to defy a causal analysis' (Kohli 1998: 30). That is to say that the role of identity as it is currently conceived, cannot be presented merely as a primordial attachment.[14] Such identities cannot be taken as ascribed but must be seen as complex constructs that both draw upon primordial categories and differ from them.

Social movement theory has, as we have seen, been instrumental in mapping this terrain, and explaining how identities are produced and made the basis of meaningful action. Since political struggles may appear to be abstract, and divorced from everyday life, a key means by which this is achieved is through what Della Porta and Diani

[13] This certainly appears to be Dumont's (1980 [1966]) interpretation when he argues that in an egalitarian system, *Homo Major*—man as a collective being— gives way to *Homo Minor*, or man as an individual.
[14] Caste today, as Mitra observes, 'is a resource that political actors use in order to negotiate their status, wealth, power and identity' (1999: 114). Mitra cites the existence of caste out—with Hinduism as evidence for this. Christian Dalits, for example, mobilise as Dalits rather than as Christians in order to secure state concessions. Brass (1996), Ramaswamy (1997) and Parikh (1998) similarly show how seemingly 'primordial' identities need to be constructed and inhabited in the present.

(1999) term 'identification rituals'. 'Ritual', here, refers to an analytical category that may be defined as 'symbolic behaviour that is socially standardised and repetitive' (Kerzer 1988: 9). Commonly these rituals take the form of meetings of the group in question. A series of 'identifiers', such as flags, posters, banners and even style of clothing or behaviour enable the group to be recognised by others and reinforce a sense of unity (Kerzer 1988). Although caste is portrayed as an ascribed condition that individuals are born into rather than choose, it increasingly functions like ethnicity.[15] This enables the formation of caste organisations, movements and parties that claim to speak on behalf of the entire group. In this process of transformation, ascribed affinity gives way to political identity. Identity is never simply 'given', but the move from locally-based endogamous connections to statewide socio-political alliances has rendered the construction of caste identity more of a conscious enterprise. Furthermore, individuals can potentially seek alternative sources of identity and ways of being.

Collective protest is not just about identity, however. It is 'preeminently about moral vision, for participants make claims about how the world should be, but is not' (Jasper 1997: 135). Too restrictive a focus on the concept of identity can lead one to neglect the material basis of social mobilisation. Communal identities in India are not merely empty shells to be filled by the rhetoric of self-seeking populists (cf. Pandian 1995). They frequently have a real basis in the physical segregation of communities, in differences of occupation, in the food people eat or in ties (if only fictitious) of kinship. It is uncommon for close friendships to be made, or to persist, across these divides and though inter-caste marriages are now recognised as occurring, they are still frowned upon. 'Caste', as James Manor puts it, 'possesses material substance' (1997: 266). This 'substance' is most visible in the lingering practices of untouchability, in endogamous marriage groups and the continuing isolation of Dalits in *cheris* or specific urban neighbourhoods (see Chapter 5). 'The members of social movements', as Desroches, Wielenga and

---

[15] Gould (1988: 11), Searle-Chatterjee and Sharma (1994: 20), Fuller (1996: 25), Subramanian (1999: 2–3) and Corbridge and Harriss (2000: 176) have all remarked on the 'ethnicisation' of caste. That is to say, the local, close-kinship basis of caste networks is increasingly being rendered obsolete by transformations in communications and transport technology.

Patel observe, 'do not simply want to imitate the life style and customs of privileged groups, but rather ... they seek to remove their relative deprivation' (Desroches et al. 1991: 17).

Collective action is often motivated by a sense of deprivation or insecurity. For marginalised or excluded groups, extra-institutional collective action may be the only means of political participation on their own terms, but the more oppressed sections of society have found it most difficult to overcome the legacy of their dependency, powerlessness and segmentation.[16] This is compounded by the fact that communal identities often draw upon 'everyday forms of mutual mis-recognition and suspicion that characterise the co-existence of Hindus and Muslims, as well as caste groups, in so many places in contemporary India' (Hansen 1999: 203). This highlights the significance of 'naming' in the construction of political realities. 'The labels we apply constitute our understanding of the world: they direct concern, outrage, and sympathy; they allocate blame, praise and trust' (Jasper 1997: 85).

If naming one's own group is a significant aspect of the construction of an identity, then naming one's opponents is equally, if not more so. 'The ability to impose negative and stigmatised definitions of the identity of other groups', as Della Porta and Diani remind us, 'constitutes, effectively, a fundamental mechanism of social domination' (1999: 92). The forms of mobilisation inspired by such discourses are an indication of the new field of identity choices that are available to Indian citizens, but they also increase the risk and the occurrence of new forms of violence and disorder. Collective mobilisations may encourage and 'empower' members, but they frequently give rise to counter mobilisations. Attacks on Dalits by Backward Castes have increased in intensity and number, in part because they fear that the Dalits are becoming their equals (Vincentnathan 1996: 494).

---

[16] It is only through organising themselves that such groups can force their demands onto the agenda. Organisational pluralism may mean that such mobilisation has a better chance of being accommodated, but it does not in itself encourage direct action. Rather, it is the radical ideology/practice of Untouchable protest, Constable (2000) argues, that led to the re-formation of cultural identities.

Protest Norms: Legitimising Notions and Action Repertoires

'Crowd theorists' constructed an image of collective actors as 'mobs' of desperate people acting in 'irrational' ways (Rudé 1995: 8–9). The scale of violence perpetrated against Dalits and Muslims, and the self-immolation of upper-caste protestors against the implementation of the Mandal Commission, appear to support such analysis. The communal riots in Bombay, the breakdown of law and order in Bihar, the atrocities allegedly perpetrated by the People's War Group (PWG) in Andhra Pradesh and the conflicts in Assam, Kashmir and Sri Lanka serve as ever-present reminders of where an escalation of conflict can culminate. In Orientalist depictions, as Mitra (1999: 259) shows, the Indian mind is presented as incapable of individual rationality, since even individual preferences and opinions are seen as conditioned by the family, caste or tribe to which they belong. As Weiner notes, however, in India there is 'a deep and justifiable fear of uncontrollable violence among religious caste and linguistic groups' (1997: 250).

At the village or panchayat level, this violence is rooted in the conflicts between dominant, land-owning and rich middle peasant castes and landless labourers/SCs who have few resources but an increasing consciousness of their rights (cf. Pai 2000). In the urban conglomerates such antipathy is nurtured in residential segregation and mutual stereotypes.[17] The prevalence of such sources of enmity means that they are seen as endemic, or 'normal', parts of the social and political imaginary. It becomes critical then for us to achieve a better understanding of how this 'normal' state becomes a patho-logical one. Alternatively, why, given the ubiquity of fault lines in society, is violence not a more customary feature of politics? The answer, in part, lies in the fact that actors are not as irrational or despairing as many would lead us to believe. Even that most impetuous of the crowd's activities—riot—has been shown by Thompson to constitute 'a rational response, that takes place, not

---

[17] Hansen identifies certain areas of 'condensed' conflict, or 'trouble spots', where 'communal violence and enmities are regular features of their social and political organisation' (1999: 205). Ali Asghar Engineer, similarly, highlights areas where there is what he terms an 'arithmetic of violence' (Engineer in Austin 1994: 45).

among helpless or hopeless people, but among those groups who sense that they have a little power to help themselves' (Thompson 1991: 265, cf. Tambaiah 1996: 216).

The image of India as a land of non-violence and passivity that acquired a certain currency through idealised depictions of Gandhi and the victims of the Bengal famine, may be dismissed as a chimera. The portrayal that often replaces it—of a country suffused by political disorder and lacking in legitimacy—is equally exaggerated. Except in a few instances in certain areas, democratic India has not witnessed widespread and sustained violence. Violent conflict along caste, communal or ethnic lines *has* been endemic, but this has tended to occur on a local level and has usually been contained through a mixture of state repression, compromise and cooptation. For the most part, the legitimacy of the federal state has not been subject to question. Comprehensive studies of these issues have appeared recently and a more detailed examination may be found in their pages.[18] A few of the salient points and arguments will be referred to here, however, and an attempt to answer the questions posed here will be made through recourse to social movement theory and the work of social historians.

It is my contention that the absence of prolonged conflict, the continuing legitimacy of the state and the prevalence of extra-institutional mobilisation as a means of interest articulation, may fruitfully be analysed in terms of 'repertoires' of action. Social movements have to take into account the forms of organisation and action that are recognised as acceptable to the wider community. In the absence of such 'legitimising notions', collective actors lay themselves open to the risk of state repression and alienation from popular support. People's legitimisation of protest, Thompson argues, is 'grounded upon a consistent traditional view of social norms and economic functions of several parties within the community, which, taken together, can be said to constitute the moral economy of the poor' (1991: 188). This concept of the 'moral economy', like that of Scott's (1985) 'hidden transcript', helps to explain the underlying understandings that participants in social protest draw

---

[18] See for example: Rudolph and Rudolph (1987), Kohli (1990), Roy and Sisson (1990), Mitra (1992), Mitra and Lewis (1996), Kaviraj (1997), Mitra and Rothermund (1997), Basu and Kohli (1998), Nandy (1998), Hansen (1999), Mitra (1999) and Subramanian (1999).

upon. This is why protest movements tend only to innovate within certain parameters or during times of great political upheaval. In circumstances of rapid social change these understandings can be substantially altered or even wholly overthrown within a very short space of time.

The moral assumptions of the contemporary Dalit community, such as the demand for access to temples, wells and common land, draw upon the constitutional provisions of democratic India in challenging the more 'traditional view of social norms' that the Backward and Upper castes continue to enforce. These concepts emphasise the general belief amongst protestors that they are supported by a wider consensus. Over time, a collective memory or repertoire of forms of action, modes of organisation, indeed the 'whole set of means (a group) has for making claims of different types' is evolved (Tilly 1986: 2). Using standard forms of protest is a means of claiming legitimacy by following in the footsteps of past political movements. The history of the nationalist, non-Brahmin and sub-nationalist movements has provided a diverse palette of organisational possibilities for collective actors to select from. 'The existing repertoire', however, also 'constrains collective action' (Tilly 1986: 390). The AIADMK activists who set fire to three college buses in Dharaupuri early in 2000 were met with widespread condemnation. This outcry was not prompted by the act of vehicular arson, for the targeting of government buses has become a standard form of protest across Tamil Nadu. Rather, it was the tragic deaths of three college students who were unable to escape the inferno that transgressed the bounds of public tolerance.[19]

People do not simply 'act collectively'. Rather, they conform to culturally-conditioned repertoires of action. 'No less than in the case of religious rituals or civic celebrations, contentious politics is not born in the organizer's heads but is culturally inscribed and socially communicated. The learned conventions of contention are a part of society's public culture' (Tarrow 1998: 20). There is, in other words, a culturally-recognised and accepted gamut of forms of protest that

[19] In 'Violence as Protest', Fogel (1968) makes a similar point with regard to political violence in the West. Urban riots in 18th-century Europe, he argues, 'were articulate not only because the elites understood them, but also because in view of the mob's potential for disorder *the violence was restrained*' (1968: 38, emphasis added).

have been tried, tested and introduced into the public arena. 'Situated between the institutional and radical alternatives is a range of methods of uncertain legality such as *gherao, dharna, boycott,* and protest movements like *satyagraha, rasta-roko, jail bhoro, hartal, bandh* and *morcha* whose ubiquitous presence has made them an integral part of Indian political discourse' (Mitra 1992: 9). In contemporary Western democracies, such methods occasionally bring an element of unpredictability into the everyday routines of institutional politics, but in Tamil Nadu they constitute a routinised aspect of life.[20]

The prevalence of extra-institutional politics is often expected to result in a loss of legitimacy but, as Mitra suggests, institutional participation and radical protest, may be 'perceived as complementary forms of action' (ibid.: 210). Demonstrations, rallies, hunger strikes and protest meetings frequently culminate in lobbying the Legislative Assembly, in the presentation of a petition to the governor or in the speech of a supportive Member of the Legislative Assembly (MLA) or Member of Parliament (MP). Although extra-institutional protest implicitly or explicitly challenges the legitimacy of institutions of interest mediation, political parties perceive protestors as potential constituents. Collective protest emerges out of the disjunction between the demands raised by mobilised groups and those that get onto the government agenda. Since the legitimacy of the democratic state rests upon the recognition and representation of diverse interests, the assimilation of emerging demands into the political mainstream may enhance institutional legitimacy (cf. Zashin 1972).

Power Negotiations: Direct Action and Institutions

The role of the government and the state are vital in this process of power negotiation. Whether the state is tolerant of, or tries to repress,

---

[20] The temporality of this statement is evident from a perusal of *Urban Riots* (Connery 1968). In that volume Smith notes that violence is ever-present in Western democracies, and is 'employed in a self-conscious fashion to achieve political ends (Smith 1968: 116).

any particular group is crucial to the group's sustainability. Along the wide spectrum ranging from outright repression to accommodation lies a multitude of possible state responses. By choosing to turn a blind eye to local disputes, for example, the police can inordinately increase the levels of oppression that subordinated groups are subjected to. Equally, when such groups attempt to protest, the authorities can render or deny permission for gatherings, make preventative arrests or provide protection, disrupt or enhance the organisation of a movement and concede or deny the demands of the protestors. Electoral instability increases the propensity to support protest, according to Della Porta and Diani (1999), since it heightens the requirement for new sources of electoral support. A weak government, however, is just as likely to resort to repression for fear of being toppled.

This equation is also rendered more problematic by the fact that social movements need to show their popularity before established political parties recognise the expediency of forging an electoral alliance with them. Such an alliance does not necessarily benefit the collective actors as much as the party, however, since they are rarely in a position of strength when negotiating terms with an established institution. The PMK is a prime example of this problematic. Initially branded as extremists, the party has subsequently done well in the polls and forged alliances with both the major parties in the state. The PMK is not yet seen as an equal partner, however, as is evinced by continued political wrangling between them and their allies. The PMK is portrayed by turns as an ally in the ruling coalition and a threat to the security of the state. Similarly, the imprisonment of the Marumalarchi Dravida Munnetra Kazhagam (MDMK) leader Vaiko in 2002 for 'extremist' views highlights the precarious position of smaller parties who do not abide by the established 'rules of the game'.

'The time worn response to dissent', as Nandy asserts, 'is to neutralise it by absorbing it into the mainstream' (1998: 51). Such cooption, as the examples discussed earlier show, is not always possible nor is it complete. As will be seen in chapters 8 and 9, movements profit from political instability by wresting greater concessions from established parties. In 2001, for instance, the PMK and the Liberation Panthers swapped coalitions (to the AIADMK and DMK camps respectively) in the belief that the alternative offered them greater potential to influence policy.[21] Cooption also, would only appear to be feasible when the collective actors are not seeking to establish an alternative power structure. Kohli's study of ethnic nationalism points to a different conclusion, however. 'Given a well established central authority and firm but compromising leaders', he notes, 'self-determination movements typically follow the shape of an inverse U-curve' (Kohli 1998: 8). He argues that group mobilisation is encouraged under democratic processes. As these collectives coalesce they enter into a protracted phase of conflict and negotiation with the state. In this phase 'some leaders are repressed, others are co-opted and a modicum of genuine power sharing and mutual accommodation ... is reached' (Kohli 1998: 8). Although this pattern was diagnosed by reference to sub-national movements, it may be extended to other forms of communal mobilisation.

In Tamil Nadu at least, the successive stages of mobilisation, confrontation and accommodation could almost come out of a textbook of collective action. From the non-Brahmin movement in the 1920s to the Dalit and Backward Caste movements today, mobilisation has tended to follow a broadly similar pattern. The Vanniyars in northern Tamil Nadu, for example, are an organised force. 'Throughout Tamil Nadu, and especially in the South Arcot district with its large Vanniyar population, the Vanniyars damaged government and private property, businesses, busses, lorries, and trains and caused extensive inconvenience to the public during 1988' (Vincentnathan 1996: 500). The culmination of this extra-legal mobilisation was the political assimilation of the PMK into the mainstream which serves to validate the expression of concerns through extra-institutional agitation. As Illangelian, a homeopathic doctor from Chidambaram District put it:

[21] In the aftermath of the 2001 Assembly Elections, Muralidharan observed that 'the particular exigencies of coalition politics today ensure that there are no permanent friends or adversaries in national and State politics' (2001: 13). Whilst he notes that the institutionalised opposition between the two main Dravidian parties eludes this generalisation, it is apparent that there has been an erosion of political loyalty among the smaller parties. This uncertainty constitutes both an opportunity and a constraint for the smaller, emergent groups. It is an opportunity in the sense that the major parties have to seek out and recognise smaller parties, but it acts as a constraint in the sense that their importance can diminish overnight. The importance of the DPI to both the TMC and the AIADMK, for example, was negligible when the opportunity to ally with the PMK became available.

> Now there is the PMK—a Vanniyar party. In the beginning there
> was no violence that they did not engage in. They blocked roads,
> chopped down trees—Ramdoss used to be called 'Tree-Feller
> Ramdoss—Now he says 'I only like planting trees'. What connec-
> tion is there between his words and his deeds? None at all! So what
> it seems like is that one can only become a political party by taking
> part in violence first, now that is the route we must follow it seems
> (interview, 29 September 1999).

When the PMK and, later, the PT activists felled trees, blocked roads
and led violent agitation across the state, they were echoing the past
struggles of the self-respect movement and the Dravidian parties'
anti-Hindi protests. That the two main parties in Tamil Nadu rode
to power on the back of direct action has created a repertoire in which
violence and extra-institutional action are recognised as having a
degree of legitimacy. Recurrent forms of collective behaviour are not
accidents of circumstance. Rather, as the interview with Illangelian
evinces, they are conscious echoes of past struggles and may, thus,
be said to constitute a type of collective memory about the limits
and possibilities of protest.

Such protest is not necessarily inimical to political engagement
and may actually encourage it. Where structural factors perpetuate
the conditions of the conflict, however, a solution may require
alterations in land-holdings and agrarian relations that would prompt
violent counter-mobilisation by those whose interests are attacked.
Similarly, when a group's identity is based in part upon the caricature
of an evil 'other', accommodating them into rival political parties
could merely provide an institutional basis for their antagonism and
render the exercise of the franchise a period for violent recriminations.
'Dispersal of power', as Della Porta and Diani observe, 'increases the
chances of access not just for social movements but for *all* political
actors, including counter-movements' (1999: 200). The nature of
democratic governance is such that a degree of institutionalised
conflict is unavoidable, but channelling such competition through
institutions arguably forces political opponents to address the concerns of their adversaries. 'In the abstract', therefore, as Basu
concludes, 'it would seem that an accommodating, conciliatory state
would be highly desirable in India' (1998: 248).

In this light Swamy is justified in the assertion that a significant
alternation of parties in office can 'affect the conditions under which
parties might turn to violence' (1998: 109). Swamy contends that

this suggestion is 'contingent upon the accuracy of the claim ... that parties are indeed responsible for instigating and co-ordinating certain kinds of violence' (ibid.: 109). The waves of violence attending the Dravidian parties' accession to power and the violence unleashed by the PMK before gaining office and now when that office is threatened, seems to corroborate the suggestion. This may well account for the fact that despite evincing all the conditions that are generally thought to be conducive to political violence, Tamil Nadu remains remarkably stable politically. The alteration of the two major parties in power appears to be able to accommodate the periodic cycles of violence that arise. Visible alterations of power affirm the efficacy of the franchise and engender at worst 'illusions of reform and participation' (Casteñeda 1993: 335) and potentially an avenue through which collective actors can channel their concerns. Much of the violence today is the product of as yet excluded groups seeking to establish themselves and of the vested interests that seek to maintain their isolation.

The current upsurge in radical Dalit politics, thus, is arguably merely a continuation of the process of normal politics. In this light, extra-institutional protest does not presage escalating cycles of violence. Rather, it constitutes a demand for greater representation, for human rights and for better access to and share of resources. The path that they are treading now is not an uncharted one, but the well-worn route to political influence that the Dravidian and Backward Caste parties have trodden before. Rudolph and Rudolph (1987) describe this as 'demand politics', but, following Subramanian (1999), we could equally describe it as *mobilisational pluralism*. Already we can trace the faint outlines of a predictable solution as the Liberation Panthers and the PT ally themselves to alternate Dravidian parties rather than rejecting their overtures. In this perspective, Tamil politics can be presented as part of a much wider pattern of political protest and negotiation. The increase in contentious politics, as Tarrow observed elsewhere, has largely been confined to forms of protest associated with 'the conventional repertoire' (1998: 206).

Indeed, it is the threatened forces of caste dominance and privilege that are more prone to violent breaches of the accepted norms than Dalit movements. Dalit movements, according to this depiction, represent the forces of continuity as much as those of change. What is 'new' and radical about current Dalit protest, thus, is not so much the strategies that they adopt, as the structural position of the protestors. The political awakening that started with the Brahmin monopolisation of provincial politics in the 1910s and 1920s can be seen to have worked its way through the ranks to the very lowest members of society. Tamil democracy, we can conclude, is working and ever more sectors of society are being incorporated into the mainstream. Such analysis is attractive, but it is only partly sustainable. To posit the status quo as the object of Dalit protest would be to minimise its significance. The increasing political profile of Dalit mobilisation has not been reflected in alterations to the structure of the agrarian economy. If anything, the immediate position of the rural Dalits has been worsened by their political success. Counter mobilisation of BC groups has led to violent attacks on Dalit villages and the imposition of debilitating social boycotts.

Increasing frustration with the empty promises of Dravidian rhetoric and the perceived betrayal of Dravidian ideals has turned Dalit movements away from the DMK and AIADMK. In 1994, Pandian identified a crisis in the DMK, which was haemorrhaging Dalit supporters. Since then the rift has been widened and the AIADMK has also come under fire. Anti-Dalit atrocities have gone unpunished under both regimes and anti-terrorist legislation has been used to crack down on autonomous Dalit protest. From this perspective it is hard to credit the Dravidian parties with fostering social pluralism. Rather, the independent action of assertive, and sometimes violent, Dalit movements has struggled to carve out a right to public space and representation. The methods adopted and the ideology espoused casts them firmly in the mould of Tamil politics. The appeals to Periyar's vision and the claims of having inherited his legacy are an attempt to legitimise their protest by placing it squarely within the accepted gamut of political activity in the state. This helps to explain why the 'extremist' DPI has been welcomed into established coalitions rather than isolated. From hereon the DPI will be able to lobby for change from within political institutions.

Conclusion

This chapter has focused on the dialectical relationship between demonstrations and democratisation. The exigencies of electoral competition certainly broaden the arena of political contest and encourage the mobilisation of new constituencies. It is also evident that self-interested politicians may attempt to re-forge traditional identities and play upon communal sentiments to construct a meaningful vote-bank. To reduce collective action to the demands of electoral competition, however, is a gross oversimplification that denies what Jasper (1997) terms: the 'art' of political protest. Extra-institutional protest consists of complex processes of identity forma-tion, ritual action and protest, which draw on established norms. The concept of a collective memory bank of 'repertoires of action' is a useful analytical tool that can contribute to our understanding of social mobilisation.

It is, perhaps, most significant in casting light on the ways by which radical protest can be seen as complementary to 'normal' politics and in explaining the continuing stability of Tamil democracy. The history of social mobilisation arguably underpins the resilience and strength of relatively new institutions like the PMK, PT and the DPI and we may tentatively echo the conclusions of Alexis de Tocqueville. 'Freedom of association in political matters is not so dangerous to public tranquillity as may be supposed, and possibly, after having agitated society for some time, it may strengthen that state in the end' (1994b: 118). Equally, however, unless the status quo is altered, the disillusioned and disenfranchised mass of deprived citizens may threaten the very state itself. The social and material conditions of protest, in other words, cannot be ignored or downplayed. It is these issues that are discussed in the following chapters.

3

Victimisation, Violence and Valour: The Context of Dalit Activism in Tamil Nadu

Suppressed has been the slave instinct,
What has broken and dispersed it,
Is the Dalit Movement
(Popular movement song, translated from the Tamil by the author).

Introduction

Across Tamil Nadu, statues, portraits, posters and nameplates bearing the image of Dr Ambedkar proliferate. Halls, schools and colleges named after him abound and even his ideological opponents feel obliged to reproduce his picture and lay claim to his legacy. This obviously indicates the rise of Ambedkar as a pan-Indian figure, but the importance here is what it signifies about Dalit politics. Ambedkar may have chaired the Drafting Committee of the Constitution, but he is primarily identified as a symbol of *Dalit* assertion. 'Ambedkarisation' in Tamil Nadu, thus reflects the increasing prominence of Dalit movements. The mobilisation of the Dalit community, however, has been neither easy nor pre-ordained. This chapter examines the social context of movement work to evaluate the problems of mobilisation and the risks associated with activism. Moffatt (1979) argued that Untouchables in Tamil Nadu live in consensus with the caste system and try to replicate the structures from which they are excluded rather than challenge them. I question the validity of this as Dalits are able to critique the caste system on its own terms and articulate alternative, more egalitarian, conceptions of the self and of society. The chapter points to the continuing importance of repression in maintaining the subordination, and then considers the rise of assertive movements and the rhetorical devices used to unite, and overcome the fears of, Dalit activists.

Somankottai, a small village in the south west of Tamil Nadu, on the main road between the two regional centres of Mulanoor and Dharapuram in Erode district, is a good place to start such an examination. Alighting from the bus, two friends and I stopped to have a 'cuppa' at the tea-stall-cum-general store immediately opposite the bus stand. As is usual, the owner brewed the tea made with milk and plenty of sugar and then poured it into our steel cups and back into the pot several times to stir the sugar in and to make it frothy on top. He then passed the cups over to us and we stood aside to enjoy the drink. As we did so, one of a group of men gathered nearby strolled over to the counter and helped himself to one of the glass cups on the side of the bar. He rinsed it out thoroughly at the tap in front of the shop, gargled a few times and then placed the cup on the counter. Having ordered a cup of tea he wandered away. The owner prepared the tea in the usual way, but then just poured it into the glass as it stood on the counter without touching it. When he called out that the tea was ready, the other man returned, picked up his cup and walked nonchalantly away. We drank more slowly and waited for him to return. Eventually he did. Casually he leant down to the outside tap and washed the glass, less rigorously this time, before placing it back from whence he had taken it. Calling for the owner to 'put it on account', he left the shop. Not once in the transaction had the owner handled the glass. My friends and I handed back our cups, paid and left. We were not expected to wash up after ourselves.

The two friends, Edwin and Inba, are both Dalits. Both, however, have been raised in the more egalitarian environment of urban Tamil Nadu. Neither of them had seen the 'two-glass' system, as it is known, practiced so blatantly before. The 'two-glass' system refers to the once prevalent custom of serving Untouchables in a receptacle separate from everyone elses, because they were seen as dirty and impure. Traditionally, the 'glass' would have been a half-coconut shell and would have hung on a hook outside the stall. Much has changed in the past 50 years and the example given here is, if not exceptional, no longer the norm.[1] It does, however, point to the

---

[1] It is more common for tea-shops to continue this discrimination in a concealed manner. So people from all castes will be served as normal, but there are different

persistence of social inequality and domination that has not been eradicated by legislation, and highlights the need to examine the material bases of Dalit movement activity. Edwin was appalled. 'I could not live like that', he said, shaking his head, 'I would rather die than lead such an existence'.

His view reflects the feelings of many Dalit activists who see their struggle as vital to establishing their dignity as human beings. This often takes the form of a 'Dalit standpoint perspective', maintaining that society as a whole can only be liberated (can only find its true humanity) if Dalits are first regarded as equal. In this sense the Dalit struggle is that of the entire community. Inba, however, took a different stand. He has more experience in village life and has trained as a pastor in rural Tamil Nadu. Villagers here lack the easy assumption, and assertion, of equality that their urban counterparts are achieving. When one depends upon dominant castes for food, shelter, work and security, it is harder to raise one's voice in protest. 'They don't see it as a big deal', Inba explained, 'they just wash the glass. At least that way you know that it is clean'. For such co-operation, we should not forget, they get tea on account, the local landlords provide them with work and they are able to use the common resources of the village.

Willing Victims? The Internalisation Debate

Cooperative attitudes and practices have been interpreted to mean that the Untouchables live in consensus with the established social order. The Untouchables, as Weber put it, have 'internalised' the Hindu order (1958: 41). A perennial debate is the extent to which they share the values of the hierarchical system that oppresses them. Authors such as Weber have pointed to the absence of overt rebellion as indicative of cultural consensus. This assertion, however, has been challenged by 'subalternist' historians and social anthropologists such as Deliège (1997), who have highlighted a 'hidden history' of protest and repression. Dumont's (1980 [1966]) and Moffatt's (1979)

---

cups that are reserved for Dalits and are not used by others. At first sight, therefore, it seems that all customers are equal but the slight is evident to, and keenly felt by, local Dalits.

structural analyses, however, led them to conclude that the values of hierarchy pervade the whole of caste society. In a highly controversial study, Moffatt claims to have gone beyond the explicit and superficial manifestations of domination and resistance to reveal the implicit and unarticulated structures of cultural life (1979: 290). At this 'deeper level' of Indian village life, he maintains, 'Untouchables and higher-caste actors hold virtually identical cultural constructs ... they are in nearly total conceptual and evaluative consensus with one another' (Moffatt 1979: 291).

. He bases this claim on the finding that the Untouchables of Endavur 'recreate among themselves virtually every relation and institution from which they have been excluded for reason of their untouchability' (ibid.: 89). An obvious criticism of Moffatt's structural analysis is that it ignores the changes that have occurred in the caste system over time, and which are evident in his own work. Other empirical studies have challenged the assertion that the caste system rested upon shared values. Moffatt's thesis has inspired criticism and debate on the issue of normative consensus. The view from the bottom, as Berreman (1963) and Mencher (1991) observe, is very different from that at the top, and they highlight a distinction between rhetoric and practice amongst the lower castes. What a Paraiyar displays in asserting that he will not accept water from a lower caste, therefore, is merely that they are cognisant of the *ideological* opposition between the pure and the impure or of the hierarchical pecking order in their locality. In fact, as Deliège (1992: 162, 1997: 114) argues, such distinctions are rarely made in *practice*.

Furthermore, several authors have noted the egalitarian emphasis of Dalit communities in intra-caste relationships.[2] Even if this does not translate into inter-caste interaction, it shows that hierarchy does not pervade *every level* of social relationships and it provides a basis from which to critique hierarchical practices. Whilst Dalit castes may engage in the same touch-me-not-ism displayed towards them with regard to other low castes, this cannot be read as belief in the notions of *ritual* status.[3] That it is primarily a claim for higher *social* status

[2] Gough (1981), Vincentnathan (1993), Kapadia (1995), Deliège (1997) and Charsley and Karanth (1998) provide ethnographic studies which illustrate the more egalitarian basis of relationships *within* Dalit castes.

[3] Vincentnathan (1993: 53) argues that Untouchable's 'concepts of person and society, differ from those of caste Hindus'. Mosse (1994: 68) insists that

may be seen in a rejection of their own inferiority in relation to those castes that are above them in the hierarchy. In his study of Dalit Christians in Tamil Nadu, Mosse (1994) suggests the possibility of a middle path between the extremes of cultural consensus and rejection. He insists that 'social protest need not be premised upon disjunction' and that cultural consensus need not rule out political activism (Mosse 1994: 99). Certainly those castes which have succeeded in mobilising against their subordination often seek to confirm their status through the adoption of distinctive titles, such as the Pallar movements' adoption of the Sanskritised term 'Devendra Kula Vellalar' (loosely translated this means the 'exalted group of Vellalas').

Sharma (1999) attempts to resolve the debate by suggesting that members of the lower castes are ambivalent about their status. Certainly, different contexts elicit differing reactions from Dalits about their place in caste *society*, but I would contest the assertion that Dalits are 'deeply ambivalent about the *values* of caste' (Sharma 1999: 57, emphasis added). Both Sharma (1999) and Racine (1998) insist that differences in analysis owe as much to methodological problems as to empirical observation. 'If we hear only those who articulate their anger, protest or expectation, what about those who remain silent?' (Racine 1998: 3). In their studies of Paraiyars in Tamil Nadu, Racine (1998) and Racine and Racine (1998) draw upon the narrative of an illiterate Dalit woman whom they call Viramma. Viramma is said to share 'the consensus that places the Dalits at the bottom of the caste hierarchy and accepts the rationale of a system based on 'purity'' (Racine and Racine 1998: 7). She also 'accepts the concepts of Karma and dharma' (ibid.).

The Racines' work is important because they do not attempt to construct a timeless model of structural consensus, as Moffatt does. Rather, they base their account upon life histories and interviews and they are fully aware of contemporary developments. They imply, however, that Dalit movements are radical innovations; the product of a younger generation that has been exposed to egalitarian

---

'structuralist interpretations of Harijan society have underestimated the tensions and conflicts which underlie apparent consensus'. Kapadia (1995: 3) notes how Tamil Dalits have the counter-cultural ideologies of the Dravidian and Self-Respect movements with which to critique the Brahmin model.

ideologies.) 'While Viramma takes pride in adhering to the Pariah's dharma, her son, exposed to modern reformist discourses, wishes to uphold his self-respect' (ibid.: 7). In sum, the Racines draw upon empirical observation to reinforce the idea that the Untouchables, the older ones at least, are the willing accomplices of their subordination. Research findings are profoundly influenced by the area and period of study, the nature of the respondents and the questions posed by the researcher. In Tamil Nadu it is possible to find many 'Virammas' who are afraid of the militancy of young people. Although Gough (1960: 44) found that ex-Untouchables displayed a 'fanatical passion for equality', such passion has never been echoed by all Dalits, least of all with regard to sexual equality. Many Dalits today are still dependent upon the upper castes for labour and they are wary of engaging in social or political action.)

Indeed, as the example from Somankottai shows, many Dalits still acquiesce to overt forms of submission. My contention is not that all Dalits resist or are egalitarian, but that they do not live in consensus with a hierarchical system based on purity and pollution. A history of conversion to Buddhism, Sikhism, Islam and Christianity, migration and flight both within and out of India and the attempt to Sanskritise caste practices all testify to the numerous 'weapons of the weak' (Scott 1985) which have been employed against the dominant values of society. Many authors have also noted the prevalence of Untouchable myths of origin, which explain the low standing of Dalits today in terms that implicitly or explicitly reject the impurity ascribed to them.[4] The Racines (1998) themselves note the prevalence of the critical *Bhakti* tradition in south India which dates back to the 8th century. Although they observe that *Bhakti* cults were soon assimilated into mainstream Hinduism and did not aim to 'dismantle the caste system' (Racine and Racine 1998: 8), they stress that the socio-cultural world of the Dalits is distinct from the Brahminical model—especially in the relative autonomy that it accords to women (ibid.: 7). Having acknowledged the existence of such forms of proto-protest to, and disjunction from, the dominant social values, however, Racine and Racine fail to explore their implications.

---

[4] See, for example, Rudolph and Rudolph (1967), Lynch (1969), Zelliot (1996) and Pai (2001).

These forms of resistance exhibit the ability of Dalits to interpret their own lives and identities in ways that differ markedly from the upper-caste constructions. In contra-distinction to Mosse (1994), I would argue that cultural disjunction does not always preclude political conservatism. There are many reasons for people to work within the hierarchy of purity and pollution and even to practice the rules prescribed by it. These range from a fear of demons and the inertial authority of habit to a desire for personal or group advancement or the fear of violence and the requirements of subsistence. Authors who insist that Dalits live(d) in agreement with the system have arguably underestimated the levels of repression employed against them and the absence of economic resources or alternatives.[5] Years of subordination cannot but have left their impress upon the oppressed. The Commissioner for the SCs and STs, B.D. Sharma, observes that the Dalits have been reduced to the 'psychological state of accepting deprivation and destitution as justified and proper' (1990: iv).[6]

Indeed, resistance only exists as part of a binary opposition the obverse of which is domination. Whilst the dominant conceptions of the world cannot prescribe the worldview of subordinate classes they do have the power to naturalise the social order (Hall 1988; Foucault 1980). The material basis of the caste system condemns Dalits to a life of servility that threatens their own sense of self-respect and worth. Compliance with this system, however, should not be taken as consensus, for people may both participate in a culture and resist it at the same time. In responding to the position assigned to them, 'they have to find ways of knowing themselves that neutralises the way they are defined as social persons in terms of their caste identities' (Parish 1996: 102). Such ways of knowing are arguably found in the *Bhakti* cults of south India or the alternative lifestyles of the lower castes that are so easily dismissed by the Racines. The assertion that all are equal in the eyes of God, which underpinned the *Bhakti* tradition, is a subversive rejection of the values that underlie the hierarchical order (cf. Zelliot 1996: 26).

[5] Wade (1988), Delièges (1997) and Karanth (1998) also highlight the continuing repression of Dalits in southern India.
[6] Fanon, Cesaire and the Indian National Congress have made similar claims about the psychological effect of colonisation, which infused its subjects with 'fear, inferiority complexes, trepidation, servility, despair, abasement' (Fanon in Caute 1970: 7).

Such statements are echoed in the everyday conversations of contemporary Dalits who insist that 'we are all human beings' or who assert that they are not 'Hindus' because they worship in different ways (Appavoo 1986). Time and again they assert their common humanity: 'If we are cut do we not bleed? Is our blood not as red as yours?' Old ladies, such as Viramma, would pose these questions in an indignant rejection of their innate inferiority and seek ways of getting round caste rules. Athai, is an 83-year-old woman who now lives in Madurai but spent most of her life in rural areas. She earns an income from selling home-made pickles and idli powder. In the following conversation with her niece, Nesamani, and I many of these themes emerged:

> Author (H.G.): We went to a village this afternoon where Dalits are supposed to take their shoes off before getting off the bus and walking home.
> Nesamani (N): Yes dear (*aamma pa*), that's how it is—when I was younger my aunt used to tell me to take my shoes off before going past the temple because of God, but I always used to wonder if it was due to *Sami* (God) or *Jadi* (caste)! Which is it Athai?
> Athai (A): That was partly due to the deity—it is that sort of figure. I mean, I don't take my slippers off but I walk as far away from the temple walls as possible. But when I used to go to market near Virudhunagar to buy tamarind, chilli powder and other things, I would be told to take my shoes off, but I never did. I can't walk without my chappals! So I walked along the market street with my chappals on and asked for chilli powder. The shop keeper said 'What are you?' I asked: 'Does who or what I am affect the colour of my money?' Then they said 'you are not supposed to wear slippers on this road', so I said; 'I'm a Puliyamma (a Backward Caste in Tamil Nadu). I can wear them, are you going to serve me or do I have to return to the bus?'
> N: Ah, but you had to lie about your caste didn't you. You couldn't say 'I am a Paraiyar'.
> H.G.: Also, you did not live there, you would be there for ten minutes and then go away....
> N: Say that again (*appadi sollu*), they don't worry so much about outsiders.
> A: Oh but it is all a nonsense—if you prick me, and if we prick you then the same blood runs out of the wound doesn't it? (discussion, 21 March 1999).

This conversation and countless others in a similar vein served to capture the ambivalence of peoples' *actions* in comparison to the assurance of their values and beliefs. Athai, thus, would tell her niece to take of her shoes, or would lie about her caste background in a manner that, superficially at least, suggested conformity with the caste system. At the same time, however, the intent and effect of her actions was to avoid complying with injunctions that she clearly disagreed with. Dalits reject the dichotomy between purity and pollution like this and in the frequent assertions that such concerns have never been significant enough to prevent the upper castes from raping Dalit women, beating Dalit men or (more recently) approaching rich and powerful Dalit individuals for aid.[7] People are shaped by the culture into which they are born and their perceptions are influenced by it, but they are not merely passive receptacles of the hegemonic value system.[8] Individuals are not only the inert or consenting targets of hegemonic power, as Foucault insists, 'they are always also the elements of its articulation' (1980: 98).

Their actions may not be revolutionary but they do register protests against their position in society and seek to improve both their standing within it and their own self-worth. Even Viramma has not absorbed the notions of *karma* and *dharma* to the extent of denying her son an education, although 'the Pariah's dharma' has not traditionally permitted such advancement (Racine and Racine 1998; Viramma et al. 1997). She may fear the consequences of his radicalism and may feel obliged to, and dependent upon, her landlord, but she is not a slave. She has perhaps sought to find some value in her caste identity by reference to cultural norms, with a view to a better life in the future. Her actions, however, constitute a denial of the dominant caste belief that the Untouchables are incapable of change. The phrase 'Pariah's dharma' is misleading, therefore, since Viramma clearly believes in an individual's capacity to affect their own destiny and not that of their caste (Viramma, Racine and Racine 1997: 71, 104, 121). Her son, like the vast majority of India's Dalit population today, seeks self-respect and dignity within his own lifetime. 'Cultural consciousness is equivocal, is ambivalent' (Parish 1996: 204). The appearance of total accep-

---

[7] Freeman (1986: 169) asserts that there is evidence to show that Dalits have desired freedom from oppression for the past 2,000 years, but they have lacked the means to express their discontent.

[8] See Foucault (1980: 98), Guha (1988: 41), Hirsch and Black (1994a: 7–8) and Scott (1990: 45).

tance or consensus, therefore, would appear to be a methodological artefact (ibid.).

Deliège insists that there 'is no reason to be proud of one's origins and this shame certainly represents a problem of cultural identity for the Harijans' (1997: 127). This statement is in part self-evidently true, but the decision by Dalit élites to hide their origins cannot wholly be put down to 'shame'. There are practical, political pressures that require Dalits to hide their caste background in order to get ahead or to obtain good housing and social regard. There has also been a concerted effort by movement and NGO activists to resurrect the proud history of Dalit activism, which date back to the petitions of 1799 at least, and the distinctive cultural characteristics of the community such as music and dance. The visions of the past which I refer to here, are not the ambiguous 'myths of origin' in which Dalits explain the means by which they came to be degraded, rather, they are much more political and assertive. In a state that continues to be governed by Dravidian parties, I am surprised at the prominence that Deliège's respondents accord to stories which relate to how particular castes came to be seen as Untouchable. The 'histories' that were retailed to me are every bit as mythical as tales of origin, but they are far more explicit in their rejection of the caste system and of the position of Dalits within it. The anti-Brahmin movement first popularised the Ayran/Dravidian divide, but Dalits in Tamil Nadu have appropriated this rhetoric to insist that they were the original 'sons-of-the-soil' in the south before the invasion of the Aryans.

'When a caste rises socially', Deliège notes, 'the myths used are more grandiose' (1997: 135). The differences in our findings may perhaps be said to be those between two communities. The villagers of Valghira Manikam are struggling to subsist and to antagonise the dominant Kallar caste in this situation would jeopardise their security, land tenure and livelihood. The more assertive Dalits featured in my account are active in social movements. Mosse's study of 'Harijan' strategies of social mobility found that they do not 'generate a new discourse. They are not counter-cultural and do not signify withdrawal from dominant cultural idioms' (1994: 99). Such a statement can only claim some validity today if we see the writings of Periyar as contributing to the dominant cultural idioms of the state. Even before the rise of radical, contemporary movements, however, old and new myths of origin shared an ontology that presented all castes as equal and perceived inequalities as culturally constructed rather than biologically determined.[9] Whilst Dalit values and beliefs may reflect hegemonic norms in some respects, as Vincentnathan concludes, 'their concepts of person and society differ from those of caste Hindus in areas that relate to untouchability and the caste system' (1993: 79).

Caste in Stone: Misleading Terminology

Given the broad generalisations employed about Dalits as opposed to upper-caste Hindus, a brief word on terminology is required especially in light of Pandian's probing question: 'how far can we employ the categories of backward castes and Dalits as large collectivities explaining caste conflicts?' (2000: 514). It is misleading to group the 'upper castes' or 'caste Hindus' together as a coherent and unified social category. There is some justification in doing so because it reflects the perception and diction of the Dalits whom I interviewed but, at the local level, most Dalits were exceptionally nuanced in their social analysis and usually differentiated between specific castes and sub-castes. The 'higher caste' (mel jadi, aadhika jaadi) tag was, in fact, predominantly employed with reference to repressive groups. As such, it most frequently referred to a Backward or Most Backward Caste, rather than the upper castes per se. The dominant castes in Tamil Nadu tend to emanate from these social groupings partly as a result of the non-Brahmin movement, but also due to the absence of a Kshastriya representative caste in the state.

The immediate opponents of the Dalits in Tamil Nadu were the Backward Caste (BC) Thevars (especially the Marava clan) and Kounders, and the Most Backward Caste (MBC) Vanniyars. The Thevars and Vanniyars have formed political associations to protect and advance the interests of their communities and they are the ones who feel most threatened by the social, political and economic advance of the Dalits. They have responded to this 'threat', as Pandian (2000) notes, by uniting behind a heightened sense of caste pride and superiority. To paint members of these castes as

---

[9] As Parish points out, 'dreams of possible worlds'—articulated through myths of origin, songs and narratives that reject the caste hierarchy—'imply possible futures' (1996: 224).

homogeneous, however, would be mistaken. In areas where they are a minority such castes also suffer from exploitation and many members of these castes are poor or even destitute. Communist Party and NGO attempts to forge a class coalition amongst the SCs and BCs persist although most of my informants felt that they did not adequately reflect the caste concerns of the Dalits. Also, many BC individuals are committed to a more egalitarian society and were involved in NGOs and other institutions working for the uplift of the Dalits (cf. Beteille 1986). The boundaries of caste, however, are rarely transgressed.

Marriages between castes do happen and are increasingly recognised but they are still frowned upon, may face violent dissent from the higher castes (cf. Chowdhry 1998) and always meet with social disapproval. Even where marriages are eventually accepted, it often takes the arrival of grandchildren before the parents of the cross-caste couple can be induced to interact with them again. Caste remains the dominant idiom of social organisation in India, even though its parameters have been significantly altered. As seen in Chapter 2, a steady process of substantialisation has expanded the local basis of the community and transformed the internal organisation of each caste so that it functions more like ethnicity than the traditional system of stratification. Indeed, the polar opposition between the 'pure' Brahmins and the 'impure' Untouchables has lost much of its salience.[10] Brahmins remain influential but they are seldom in direct competition with the Dalits and so there is little enmity between the two communities. Other landed castes resent calls for land reform and higher wages, but Brahmins are often absentee landlords and so any contact is mediated through the intermediate castes. The (M)BC/SC divide, therefore, has become the prime fault-line of caste conflict in Tamil Nadu.

The separation between the categories, however, is not hermetic and neither of the opposing blocs represents a homogeneous entity. There is, therefore, room for manoeuvre and negotiation at a local

[10] In 'Crisis in the DMK', Pandian (1994) suggests that Brahmin groups retain significant dominance when he states that the Dalit focus on BCs, lets 'the gleeful Brahmin off the hook'. A recurrent feature of Dalit movement conversations and speeches, however, was that the Brahmins were 'not bad' in comparison to the BCs. The Brahmins are 'let off the hook', therefore, but in an intentional and conscious manner rather than by default.

level. In Kodankipatti (discussed later), for instance, the Dalits entered into a political alliance with Naidus and other BCs in an attempt to unseat the Kounder panchayat president in one election. Conversely, the Chakkiliyars of Vadianpatti sided with their landlords against the Paraiyar community. The term 'higher caste', therefore, may obscure the complexity of social organisation on the ground and the specificity of caste-based mobilisation, but it is used here to highlight the antagonism felt by the Dalits towards those who perpetuate their subordination.

In answer to Pandian, therefore, it is clear that these broad categories are insufficient to explain caste conflicts on a local level. Other factors and local power negotiations must always be considered. Having said that, many of the clashes between caste blocks today result from the fact that Dalits are organising as a group and demanding equal rights. Conflicts across the state are informed and influenced by the wider processes of social change that have led Dalits to join social movements and BCs to form assertive political parties. The Dalits I interviewed seldom distinguished between castes that carry out an atrocity and those that merely stand by. All the 'upper castes', they would aver, benefit from their suppression. In like manner, the heightened caste spirit and pride that is projected by BC organisations is directed against Dalits of all castes. During the elections in Chidambaram, for instance, the faces of all the Dalit leaders were daubed with cow dung, rather than just those who were contesting locally. Those desecrating the election poster were not indiscriminate in their actions either, since the non-Dalit faces in the photo were untouched.

Domination, Dependence and Resistance

'Harijan identity', as Mosse puts it, 'is itself principally *defined* by dependence and service' (1994: 73, emphasis in the original). The move from being a 'class in themselves' to a 'class for themselves', therefore, is beset by difficulties. 'The majority of Dalits living primarily in rural areas', as Nandu Ram says, 'have perhaps lacked, since early times, a tradition of well organised and regulated protests or protest movements due to obvious reasons' (1998: 107). These 'obvious reasons' relate to a poverty of resources, economic dependence and the repression of the social system—reasons that are too often downplayed. Time and again, during the course of my fieldwork, violence was unleashed against those who challenged the dominance of the land-owning castes through words, deeds or gestures. They were murdered, beaten, their houses were burnt, Dalit women were raped or they were simply subjected to social 'boycott'; they were not provided with jobs, not served in the local shops and not given access to common resources. There is no reason to consider that the reaction would have been any less repressive in the past, especially as there were no liberal urban centres to flee to, nor were there legal guarantees of their rights. The second aspect in the continuing submissiveness of Dalits is their economic dependence.

As the example of Somankottai highlights, the localised nature of caste as a 'lived' system rendered the Untouchables dependent upon the locally-dominant caste for work, food, shelter and patronage. Speaking to villagers in the rural districts to the west of Dindugal, one is initially struck by an acute sense of fatalism. With no land of their own they have either to work for the local landlords, walk further to work at the risk of physical harassment or find employment in the garment industry. With little prospect of change they are *resigned* to the system, as the following exchange illustrates:

> Thangamma: I work for coolie in the Kounder's fields, if I want water then they pour it into my hands, like this... (cupping her hands she indicated that the water was poured into her palms from on high).
> Author: What? Even today?
> Thangamma: Yes today—now. This is happening in many villages.
> Edwin: Can you not take water with you, in a bottle or something?
> Thangamma: We have to walk 2–3 km to work, if we are carrying spades and everything, then we have to choose between water and a tiffin carrier. If you take a cup or a pot, then they will pour water into it—but you are not allowed to touch their vessels. But if we get angry then what do we do? We will have to go 5–6 km to work. They sometimes let us take spinach and other vegetables home with us—we would lose all that as well. (Discussion in Sakaravalasu, 19 October 1999).

Thangamma is in her mid-fifties. Both she and her husband have been agricultural labourers all of their lives, but the resignation evident in the discussion quoted here is somewhat deceptive. Despite continuing to till the fields, they have built a relatively large home for themselves and educated their children through school and college. It is not poverty of ambition that they suffer from, but lack of resources. 'They have all the land, what can we do?' was a frequent complaint. The logic is compelling. In this area, it has meant that many of the Dalits continue to perform the demeaning jobs demanded of their caste. These tasks are called *adimai thozhil* in Tamil. It is an instructive phrase literally meaning 'slave work'. Drawing upon Bharadwaj (1974) and Bhaduri (1983), Corbridge and Harriss observe that the poor 'are frequently "compulsively involved" in markets in circumstances of "forced commerce"' (2000: 84). Performing such work out of compulsion should not be mistaken for showing that the Untouchables are in consensus with the values of the hierarchical system.

Even in the situation discussed here, Dalits whom I spoke to were keen to maintain their dignity. 'Slave tasks' were now performed for cash, albeit less than an outside group would get, which is deemed to be less polluting (Mosse 1994: 86) and certainly less undignified. Other initiatives also indicated the desire to be treated as human beings. Anandraj had opened a small shop in the front room of his house. The store had very little by way of stock in it, but it served a symbolic purpose more than an economic one. 'I opened a small shop here', he explained, 'because the Chettiar shop near the bus stop would not serve our children properly. If they asked for sweets, they would be poured into their hands from a distance so that half of them fell on the floor' (interview, 19 October 1999). Anandraj had managed to set up the shop from the income he earned working in a local power loom; others were not able to escape dependency so easily. Indeed, Anandraj himself said that pressure was being put on the mill owners to sack him because he had 'two jobs'. Even such localised and insignificant a piece of 'resistance' is sufficient to challenge the hegemony of the dominant caste and to let it go unpunished would be to set a dangerous precedent. In Robinson's telling phrase: 'What the landlords most fear is a population without fear' (1988: 259).

Such insignificant challenges to the dominant system, as Scott (1985, 1990) has so admirably shown, constitute the shared understandings that are drawn upon in times of more overt struggle. 'The hidden nature of much resistance', Scott points out, 'is conditioned by fear and coercion. Lacking any realistic possibility, for the time being, of directly and collectively redressing their situation, the village poor have little choice but to adjust' (1985: 246). From this perspective, the democratic state in India has extended the autonomous spaces and rights to subordinate groups that have enabled them to communicate and coordinate their common grievances and plans for action. The villagers of Sakaravalasu, as well as those of Deliège's study, remain subject to structures of caste dominance in ways that preclude joint action. The higher castes in such areas control much of the power and resources that are available and are more organised as a group than the Dalit community. Even where Dalits have ceased to be economically dependent upon the higher castes by virtue of a job in a nearby town or by investing in a handloom, they are constantly brought up against the power of the dominant castes.

Backward Castes tend to be better placed in administrative authorities, local politics and the police. Whether they want to apply for a government loan or scheme, to set up a shop in the village, to gain a recommendation for admission to college or to install electric lights and paved roads in their part of a village, therefore, the Dalits are forced to turn to them. As one of the young boys from Melavalavu put it: 'If you go for a pee anywhere round here it is on higher caste lands'. The context was a discussion in which movement activists from Madurai were berating the village youth for their 'cowardice' in not avenging the victims of the massacre there. 'It is easy for you to say that', they responded, 'you can come and go as you like. But we live here'. Implicit in this statement is a recognition that higher castes do not necessarily differentiate between 'innocent' and 'guilty' Dalits. Often the whole *cheri* is made to suffer for the 'effrontery' of one or more of its members and people are beaten or huts set ablaze to teach them 'their place'. 'If you come and stay here for two days, you too will acquire a slave instinct', one of the boys insisted, 'how can one change character immediately?'[11]

Shanti, a Dalit woman from Kodankipatti, explained the necessity of being on good terms with the higher castes. 'I can't even pawn my gold to get some money when I am in debt', she said. 'We have to go to … places where they ask a thousand questions about who I am and so on' (interview, 22 March 1999). A recurrent complaint of Dalits anywhere is of the corruption and extortion of the locally-dominant castes. The predominance of the higher castes in the offices

---

[11] Discussion, 25 March 1999. I was largely an interested spectator in this exchange between village youth and Liberation Panther activists.

of administrative authority grants them influence over the distribution of public resources and finances. The Dalits of Vadianpatti (discussed next) accuse the higher castes of bribing officials not to give the Dalits the title deeds to their land, because 'if they have a good life they will cease to respect us' (interview, 20 March 1999). In SMP Colony, a Dalit housing board in Madurai, the young people recall how high-caste money-lenders used to 'come to reclaim debts in the husbands' absence and try and force themselves on the wives' (interview, 23 March 1999). More frequent complaints refered to the corruption of those high-caste officials or educated people who act as mediators between the Dalits and the state.

Poorly educated or illiterate Dalits often turn to a big man or patron for assistance in obtaining a government loan or securing compensation (cf. de Wit 1996: 17). In doing so they place great trust in 'benefactors', but this trust is often betrayed. The story of Pandiamma is typical. She is a widow from Sivarakottai Village situated 40 km to the south east of Madurai:

> Pandiamma: My husband's name was Alagar. He passed away. I have four or five children. I have to provide them food by labouring. There is no other work, no other way or amenity. It has been three years since he died and I have spent Rs 1000 trying to collect a pension. ... I went to the panchayat office where the money was supposed to have gone. There was a form there with my photograph and all. They got me to sign it, and that was it....
> Vairamani: When you went to the panchayat office, did you not take anyone with you, an educated person?
> Pandiamma: No.
> Vairamani: Right, well that's it. They will have eaten your money. You have given your signature to say that you have received the money and they will have shared it out (interview, 3 April 1999).[12]

More commonly, the officials are said to have siphoned off a considerable 'commission' from any loan or grant that they receive. The poorer BCs in rural areas proffered similar complaints about the

[12] Vairamani is a member of the dominant Thevar caste in Sivarakottai. He agreed to accompany me and introduce me to the Dalits in the village due to his own particular history. He fell in love with and married a Dalit girl from a nearby village. The abuse and threats that he has subsequently received have made him more sympathetic to the plight of the Dalits in his home village.

corruption of officials (interviews in *Lingyapatti*, 21 March 1999). Lack of education is often a hindrance for the poor. As in the case of Pandiamma, many people are unaware of what they are signing exactly and are eager to get their hands on the much-needed source of income. The preponderant influence of the higher castes in such offices certainly makes it more difficult for Dalits to stand up for their dues. There is also a widespread perception that Dalits are ignorant, disorganised and gullible, therefore easy to defraud. Movements provide a useful service in providing the services of educated members who can fill in documents, read the small print and chase up an application. Corruption and bureaucratic red tape are merely an extension of more prevalent and persistent indignities.

The ration shop, bus stop and tea stalls are usually located in the main *oor*. These conveniences are also staffed and run by higher-caste people. 'There is a ration shop in our area', the women of Keelathurai (a residential area in central Madurai) complained to me, 'but they (the higher castes) distribute kerosene to their lot first'. Furthermore, there is a rule that 'coolie workers are supposed to get 10 litres of kerosene, but they only give them seven litres and sell off the rest to others' (28 March 1999). Such irritants are ongoing aspects of life, but it would be false to present them as problems specific to the Dalit community.[13] Where one community is pitted against another, however, or in villages where Dalits have traditionally been dependent upon the higher castes, such minor problems can easily escalate into conflict.

Vadianpatti is a small village located 20 km to the south west of Madurai. The Paraiyars in this village have been subject to a social boycott since they established a Liberation Panther association here and built a meeting hall for the organisation. The boycott has meant that the men are unable to find employment in the vicinity and have to travel elsewhere for work, they are also prevented from using the village square and have been unable to get their hair cut in the area. The local leaders of the DPI were away in another district harvesting sugar cane. Those present, therefore, were peripheral to the movement and at times critical of it. Most of them were daily labourers

---

[13] Anecdotal evidence for the prevalence of such forms of pilfering and official obstructionism was highlighted towards the end of 1999, when the hit film *Muthalvan* (The Premier) featured a tale in which a social activist becomes the chief minister and puts such problems to rights.

in Madurai where they were predominantly employed as construction workers. 'In this village', Guru stated, 'with all this hassle we have yet to gain independence'. Chandran agreed with this assessment. 'We can't wear shoes in the village or go anywhere with peace of mind. If we wear shoes they say "look at him, he thinks he is a big man now". They call us "Pallan" or "Paraiyan"'.[14] 'There is a bench at the bus stop, but if we go to sit down there they will not let us. If we sit down despite this, then they beat us. Be slaves, or be hit (adimai illaate adi) there is no other option' (interview, 20 March 1999).

The price of protest is high for these villagers, but they are no longer prepared to accept subordination. Not everyone can afford to travel further and further afield to find work, however, or sever ties with the higher castes. Bonds of debt, tradition and inertia still connect some Dalits to the higher castes. Consequently, not all the Dalits in Vadianpatti are deprived of employment. Several families from the Chakkiliyar community continue to work in the village and to corroborate the higher caste accounts in legal disputes.

When asked why they had not registered a case under the Protection of Civil Rights Act, the Dalits replied that several members of their community would come forward to testify that: 'What these people is doing is wrong and false', and that 'only what aiya (sir) is doing is correct'. 'People like them', Chandran says, 'they call for work, but people like us they refuse to employ'. For the 'losers' of Scott's (1985) study, for 'those who call out thalaivar, aiya, sami with bowed heads, those who take their towels off their shoulders and tie it round their waists to say Vanakum aiya—there is work available' (interview, 20 March 1999).[15] The villagers affiliated to the DPI refer to such people as 'traitors' to their community, but the compulsions of poverty, a lack of resources and physical fear should not be underestimated. 'The Harijans', according to Deliège, 'are afraid. They will never fight back in case of problems with the high castes' (1997: 158). It is doubtful whether this statement was ever wholly

---

[14] The suffix '-an', rather than '-ar' in the names Pallar or Paraiyar is a more derogatory and disrespectful usage and would never be used between equals.
[15] Chandran continues; 'If you say the Dalits should remain as slaves then they will call you a hundred times. Then you have to go and stand behind their house if they call you, you must not go to the front of the house. Even if they have sent someone to call for you, you have to stand behind them and call out "Aiya" after them' (interview, 20 March 1999).

true, and it is patently false today, but it serves to highlight the very real perils of Dalit assertion.

Social exclusion from the *oor* or from the temple (see Chapter 5) and the imposition of a social boycott are the most frequent sanctions imposed on resistant Dalits. Lest the Dalits of Vadianpatti become too bold or gain ideas 'above their station', however, there are always examples of more severe retribution. Kodankipatti is a village 6 km down the road from Vadianpatti. For 10 years, the Dalits here have been refused employment because they stopped doing the 'slave tasks' that were demanded of them. The example of Kodankipatti highlights the extreme vulnerability of *cheris*. Dalits here are an impoverished minority. The dominant castes are not only dominant in terms of land and finances, but they control access to vital resources such as the common lands, the village shops and the open square. The houses of rural Dalits rarely have bathroom or toilet facilities and they depend upon access to the common lands (*poramboke*) around the village and the local pond (*kanmai*) for these purposes. 'If we womenfolk go there they tease and taunt us', Puliyammal said. 'We are left with only this colony'.

Ten years ago, this friction translated into violence. The higher castes of the village burst into the *cheri*, beat the men, women and children and set fire to their huts. 'Run you [*Wodu de*: *De* is the impolite, vulgar form of "you"]', they are reported to have said, 'we will drive you out. This is our place and we will rule it'. Several of the Dalits bore scars of injuries that they had sustained in their frantic flight. The government at the time had conducted peace meetings, rebuilt the houses with tiled roofs and persuaded the Dalits to return, but the peace was fragile. When I visited them they were terrified of further violence, due to a confrontation over the right to common space in the village. 'Recently what happened was that we worshipped the God (*Sami*)', Lakshmi recounted. 'Having anointed the God we thought, "OK, we will all of us together show a film in the common square (pothu manthai)". So we collected and saved up cash amongst the 10 of us to screen this film. But when we screened the film they said "Oi! This place is not open to you, your area is the colony", and they chased us off' (interview, 20 March 1999).

The police, when they arrived, upheld the complaint of the upper castes by insisting that the Dalits should have sought permission to screen a film in the common area. The next week, the Dalits complained about the weekly market saying that they had not been consulted. When they threatened to disrupt the market stalls 'about a hundred police came here'. 'SC peoples', Shanti sardonically observed, 'do not even have the value of vegetables'. Like most rural Dalits, those at Kodankipatti accuse the higher castes of appropriating the produce and income from the common village lands to create a 'village fund'. 'They use this money to make their own laws (*kattu padu*)', Shanti continued. 'That is not government. They keep it for themselves. In this way even if they killed one of us downtrodden (*tazhtapattoor*) ones, they would use that money to save themselves' (interview, 20 March 1999). The panchayat president of Kodankipatti dismisses such talk as nonsense. 'They have some sort of inferiority complex', he said, 'they think of themselves as depressed. Now if we are going to worship God, then any money raised is used for this' (interview, 21 March 1999). As seen in Chapter 1, however, the temple funds are not collected from Dalits who are subsequently excluded from decisions made about the money. When confronted with Murugan's responses, Laxmanan, who works as a forest ranger, laughed and said: 'he is running a little kingdom of his own' (interview, 21 March 1999).

The fears of the Dalits in Kodankipatti were prescient. Early on the morning of 20 June, three months after the interview discussed here, the higher-caste residents of the village stormed into the Dalit colony and ransacked their houses as the Dalits fled in terror. Twenty-four houses were smashed up or set alight, belongings and tiles lay strewn across the floors. The Dalit inhabitants walked down the road and took asylum 6 km away in the DPI stronghold of Muduvarpatti. Here they were crowded into a half-constructed marriage hall in cramped and dirty conditions. 'We can never return' they said, and they pressed the government to provide them with alternative accommodation closer to the village where they now reside (cf. *Dinakaran*, 21 June 1999, *The Hindu*, 7 July 1999). 'We only want to live', Balasundaram said, 'but they do not see us as human there' (interview, 13 July 1999). The point that rankled most was the persistent inaction of the law enforcement authorities. 'We have been to see every official', they told me, 'now we are looking to you for help' (interview, 9 July 1999). Thirumavalavan called on the chief minister to resign. 'Why did the higher castes set light to their houses? The downtrodden want rights to walk on common paths, they want rights to common assets, they want rights to the lands which are leased out every year. Because they asked for these rights 10 years ago, 40 houses were razed to ashes. Had Karunanidhi taken proper, orderly, thorough action then, would this attack have taken place today?' (speech, 13 July 1999).

Violence, Valour and Counter-Violence

'The major kind of violence today', according to Mendelsohn and Vicziany, 'is visited on the Dalits due to their resistance to subordination and claims to social respect, high wages and land' (School of Oriental and Asian Studies [SOAS] Seminar, London, 1 December 1999). They see this violence as qualitatively different from that of the past. What have come to be known as 'Harijan atrocities' are incidences of high caste retaliation against the perceived insolence of Dalit individuals. They 'often follow a line of extravagant revenge out of all proportion to the initial incident' (Mendelsohn and Vicziany 1998: 53). Events in Tamil Nadu, such as those in Kodankipatti, have often followed this pattern of escalation. Dalits have been beaten, raped and killed for petty 'misdemeanours' such as wearing shoes or trousers through the *oor*, for brushing against a high-caste person in the cinema or for demanding a share of the common resources of the village. Given the *ever-present* threat of violence and the regularity with which that threat is violently visited upon the bodies and belongings of the Dalits in Tamil Nadu, we can perhaps understand Gough's insistence that the Pallars of Tanjore show a 'fanatical insistence on equality' (1960: 44).

'If we thought that mere existence was more important than honour (*maanam*)', the Dalits in Vadianpatti observed, 'then we would have joined the higher-caste side as well …. If we live but for a day it should be with honour' (interview, 20 March 1999). The sentiment is surprising from a community that is living from day to day on subsistence wages and in constant fear of alienating the higher castes. The temptation is to dismiss it as a rhetorical flourish. 'The DPI talk boldly' a Dalit academic told me, 'but they won't *do* anything'. In a social environment where non-compliance has rendered the Dalits of Kodankipatti refugees within their own land, however, *not doing* what is expected of you requires equal courage. My contribution to this debate is, needless to say, coloured both by the contemporary social context and by the fact that I was working with social movements. What I hope to have shown in these examples, however, is that despite social changes, Dalit activism is by no means easy or safe. Challenging hierarchies and flouting caste rules continue to render activists extremely vulnerable to retaliation. We still, therefore, face the question of what makes people protest.

It is my contention that part of the answer lies in the Dalit movements' adoption of discourses of valour and honour that tap into deeply held cultural values. 'What you need is resistance', as Palani Kumar of the DPI told the Dalits of Kodankipatti, 'the strength to resist. One must resolve not to live in fear but to fight back even if that means dying' (speech, 21 March 1999). This rhetoric of honour and heroism taps into wider cultural norms and values. As we shall see in Chapter 7, heroic figures in Tamil Nadu are portrayed as altruistic and virtuous, seeking to benefit others rather than themselves and there is a depth of devotion felt towards leaders who play such roles. The archetypal hero figure in recent Tamil politics has been M.G. Ramachandran (MGR), the AIADMK chief and chief minister of Tamil Nadu for 10 years between 1977 and 1987. Through his film career, and carefully orchestrated acts of state and personal charity, MGR cultivated an image of a heroic figure and was almost seen as a deity.[16] There is great value attached to notions of heroism, courage, bravery and honour in Tamil culture. Popular cinema is replete with such notions and, in this it mirrors the concerns of society. Great respect and worth is ascribed, for instance, to women who take their own lives rather than lose their virtue. Integrity and honour are accorded such status that screen heroes frequently suffer misfortune—go to prison, become servants or accept a beating—rather than sacrifice their good name.

The Dalits of Deliège's (1997) study emphasise their subordination by having no pride in their origin and seeking to shroud their antecedents. Increasingly, however, Dalit movement activists are proud to call themselves by their caste names and emphasise the cultural differences between them and the caste Hindus. It is perhaps the recognition that some Dalits are ashamed, however, that has led the Dalit movement to emphasise the heroism of past leaders and martyrs to the cause. This process has been attended by simultaneous attempts from Dalit institutions and NGOs to 'rediscover' the wealth

[16] See Pandian (1992) and Dickey (1993b) for more detail on the politics of film in Tamil Nadu.

of Dalit arts and culture. This process is a direct rebuttal of the common assertion that Dalits do not have a separate sub-culture. The focus of the socio-political movements, however, has been upon the heroism of leaders rather than the distinctive aspects of Dalit culture. By praising the selfless heroism of those who have given their lives, the movements seek to recast the very real fears of their potential constituents and persuade people to take part in protest action.

'Social movements are not only a set of beliefs, actions and actors', as Fine insists, 'but also a "bundle of stories". Movement allegiance depends upon personal accounts showing similar experiences and feelings' (Fine 1995: 134). The 'story' of Melavalavu is known to all Tamil Dalit activists, for whom it has become a 'chosen trauma'; an event which encapsulates their grievances and demands (Kakar 1996: 50).[17] The premeditated massacre of panchayat president, Murugesan, and five of his followers would, in 'rational actor' terms, be expected to deter potential members from joining. The murders, however, served to convince many of the need to protest against such injustice and also added glory those who did so. Melavalavu has become a 'condensed symbol' (Turner 1967: 29) of the necessity to struggle and the importance of honour in life or death. In the memorial rites that take place each year on the anniversary of the six men who were massacred, Murugesan is depicted as a heroic

---

[17] The term 'chosen trauma' is particularly apt in this instance where the movements have so many cases of higher caste aggression to highlight. 'Chosen traumas' do not only emphasise the significance of an event, they also reflect the concerns of the movement in question. In Tamil Nadu, the massacre of 44 labourers in the village of Kilvenmani in 1969, is articulated by movements to evoke a sense of strength and the capacity for retaliation. When the main accused in that case was released from prison 14 years later he was waylaid by Marxist-Leninists and hacked into 44 pieces. The massacre at Melavalavu has become especially pertinent now as it points out the way that Dalits are prevented from participating as equals in the democratic process. As the Dalit Panthers have entered the political arena, Melavalavu has encapsulated the Dalit struggle for a more democratic society. The term 'chosen trauma' is also apposite in the sense that different movements can highlight different incidents. On the anniversary of the Nellai massacre in 2001, therefore, PT activists processed to the banks of the river Tamiriparani and laid wreaths and made speeches. They called for the construction of a memorial on the site and raised the Manjolai dispute into the public arena again (*The Hindu*: 'PT Threatens Militant Struggle', Syed Muthahar, 30 July 2001). See Appendix and later chapters for details of the Nellai massacre.

figure who should be emulated. This comes out clearly in the rousing speech given by the Liberation Panther leader on the occasion of the second anniversary in 1999:

> One thing all of you need to remember is that Melavalavu panchayat is a reserved seat for the downtrodden. Only a downtrodden person may compete for it. Hearing this news the high caste fanatics asked: 'Can a Paraiyan sit on the seat of our panchayat office? There may be a Paraiyan as the President of this Republic, but we will not permit a Paraiyan to become our panchayat president.' So saying the fanatics held a panchayat meeting where they called on all candidates to fall at the feet of the leaders and vow not to compete. 'If you do compete we will behead you', they threatened. Even after such threats and scare-mongering for the sole objective of protecting the government-given rights to reservation and to make them a reality Murugesan did not bow to the pressure or the threats. 'Even if my head rolls, we will protect these political rights' he said and competed in the government elections. That alone is true bravery! He did not compete unawares or in ignorance, he knew what would happen.... There can be no Dalit, politician or one studying about the Dalits who has not heard about Murugesan and his brave comrades. Does anyone know about those who murdered him? Will applause for Murugesan's killers have flown around the world? Apart from accounts of their cowardice, none can speak of them as heroic figures. Therefore there is no need for great distress or tears, in this land caste fanatics have murdered people without number. ... No matter how many places have witnessed murders, bloodshed or decapitation, until our rights have been attained, until we gain our liberation, this race will continue fighting, this downtrodden race (Thirumavalavan, 30 June 1999).[18]

The themes of honour, courage and the ultimate triumph of heroic virtue over evil are inescapable. Which Dalits who listened to such

[18] The word that I have translated as race here *inam*, is an ambiguous one. In various contexts it can mean race, caste or ethnicity. I have used race here since caste is clearly too inadequate a term to encapsulate all those incorporated in the term 'downtrodden'. Race has been preferred to 'ethnicity' in part because of the history of Dravidianism in Tamil Nadu which often emphasised the racial differences between the 'Aryan' Brahmins and the 'Dravidian' Tamils. I do not intend to suggest that the Dalits constitute a separate race from other castes and nor would most movement members. It is a rhetorical flourish, rather than a descriptive or analytical category.

sentiments could remain unstirred? The fallen heroes, it is asserted, will have honour in death, whereas the cowardly villains will be erased from history. 'Those with no interest in people's liberty leave no trace after their death', Cinthanai Selvam, the assistant general secretary of the DPI, emphasised. 'Liberation Panthers have no fear of this, if we die in the cause of our people we will remain in the hearts of our comrades' (interview, 30 June 1999). History awaits those who can lose their chains, people were told and there is also a reassurance that their efforts will not go unmarked. The construction of a collective and heroic 'we' serves to lend courage to the villagers who are on the front line of this struggle as was evident in an interview with the youths of Melavalavu. Accused of being lily-livered they retorted that they were more than prepared to exact revenge for the killings if they received encouragement and support from the movement (discussion, 25 March 1999).

Whilst people may be moved by such sentiments, intangible benefits are probably insufficient to induce most people to adopt similar courses of action. 'It's all very well saying "attack them, attack them"', as one of the young men put it, 'but we need resources and money to execute such a task' (ibid.). The existence of official paths for individual mobility also serves to cast activism as an unnecessary and risky business. Most of the speeches, as a consequence, devoted time to demand government compensation for the bereaved and security for the current panchayat president. It would, however, be wrong to underestimate the powerful sentiments unleashed in the praise of martyrs and heroes. It places the individuals facing potential violence into a historical perspective. These great leaders fought and died for the liberation of the Dalit people, we are told. 'Even if we do not have freedom', the 'Martyr' Immanuel Sekhar is reported to have said, 'we should stand up with valour for our rights' (Chandra Bose, interview, 23 February 1999).

The emotive content of such perorations, and the glorification of fallen heroes, has been seen by some as too effective a tool of mobilisation. Both Dalits and the state blame the passion and barely muted aggression of the speeches for inciting violence and for alienating the institutions of interest mediation. Shri Rangan Prakash, the state leader of an RPI faction, blames the incendiary speeches of the Liberation Panthers for inciting frustrated Dalit youth into acts of violent protest that transgress the laws of the land. Murugan, an agricultural labourer who used to be a DPI member, highlighted the

↓ government benefits due to resistance

difficulties associated with this sort of extra-legal protest. 'I was a member of that movement', he recounted, 'I cannot now receive any government benefits or assistance, because I am an offender' (interview, 27 April 1999). Those with criminal convictions are not entitled to the government provisions that are earmarked for the SCs. If this trend was to continue, according to Shri Rangan Prakash, 'then in 10 years or so many of our youth will suffer, they will all become terrorists' (interview, 27 April 1999). The focus of the Dalit movements should be upon the economic and educational uplift of the community, according to these two analysts. Any form of protest that hinders the social advance of the community is to be rejected.

Many leaders adopt this moderate line and stress the need to remain within the law. They argue that Dalits are the real losers in any escalation of violence. Other caste communities and the state are better organised and have access to more resources and means of oppression. Not only would Dalits lose out on the benefits offered by the liberal state, they would also constitute most of the victims. Those living in glass houses, as the state secretary (SC/ST) of the BJP, Palinivelu Swamy, asserted, should not be the first to throw stones. 'If we hit back at them', he continued, 'we do not have the finances, we do not have educated lawyers or money to get bail' (interview, 10 April 1999). The veracity of this statement was made evident when I accompanied members of the DLM to a bail hearing. The leader and 12 activists had to attend a court in the town where they had been apprehended during a demonstration. For most of them this meant a bus journey of a few hours, a day off work and the prospect of a fine or prison sentence at the end. The hearing itself was a farce. The group waited around for several hours before confirming their names and being asked to return on another occasion.

Shri Rangan Prakash directed my attention to the numbers of Dalit youth in jail. It is the responsibility of the movement to stand by them and get them out, he insisted. The DPI recognises this responsibility and frequently campaigns for the release of their cadres, but the reputation of the organisation for violence has made it increasingly difficult for it to negotiate with the authorities. 'The police are running scared of a Dalit organisation for the first time', is their proud boast, but this has led to rising levels of repression targeting movement members. Moderate leaders perceive the DPI to be at least partly responsible for this state of affairs. They highlight how the violence of the movement's rhetoric and of some of its protests are used to legitimise the institution of draconian laws and preventative arrests. Rather than engage in a futile conflict with the state, such leaders urged, the DPI should organise a political force to raise the concerns of their members in the Assembly.[19]

The spaces for reform and protest offered by the democratic state make such an argument difficult to ignore. The Indian state not only allows for the free formation of associations and political parties, but also provides reservations, quotas and welfare schemes to the Dalit community. Engaging in violence, therefore, is seen as unnecessary, costly and counter-productive. Simultaneously, however, no Dalit leader can afford to ignore the real frustration and anger of the Dalit youth who are not prepared to tolerate the incredibly slow changes in their social position. The benefits are welcome, but they are perceived to be a façade for continuing inaction. The government, by persistently refusing to publish the findings of a White Paper on the reservations situation, merely fuels speculation that many of the schemes do not reach their intended targets (cf. Sebastian 1994: 209). Reservation quotas are constantly attacked by upper castes who demand that merit be the sole criterion of any appointments. Though the reality on the ground is that many of the places supposedly set aside for the Dalits remain unfilled, the *perception* that the state is pandering to the Dalits, has been sufficient to increase the numbers of atrocities.

The state general secretary of the RPI (Gawai) N.V. Jayaseelan, is a Buddhist who insists on the need for a non-violent approach. Yet when he was pressed on the rising levels of violence against Dalits he was adamant that 'we are not like Jesus Christ who said if they hit you on the one cheek than you should turn the other. ... How many blows can I remain patient for? If I do not hit back, will the people behind me give me any respect?' (interview, 26 April 1999). Dalit movements argue that they are anxious to remain within the law, but that the state and the higher-caste communities do not want to see the Constitution enforced. Every demonstration contains a demand that the state enforce the law—be it the Prevention of Atrocities Act, the Untouchability Offences Act, the Protection of

---

[19] 'The place to raise our grievances and opinions', according to Shri Rangan Prakash, 'is the Parliament or the Assembly' (interview, 27 April 1999). This was three months before the DPI entered the polls.

Civil Rights Act, or even the standard Criminal Justice Act. 'I do not wish for rivers of blood to flow', Balasundaram, the moderate Dalit statesman, warned the state authorities at Melavalavu, 'but you are creating a situation where violence against our people goes unpunished' (speech, 30 June 1999).

Such assertions serve the dual purpose of legitimising the protests of the Dalit movements whilst inciting people to engage in extra-institutional action. Movement activity is justified by the claim that it is merely seeking to enforce the constitution. There is a strong element of irony and humour in such appeals, with movement speeches frequently expressing mock surprise that those who seek to enforce the law are perceived to be on the wrong side of it. Demands of this nature also help to reinforce group solidarity and inspire protest, because the cause is seen as just and the relevant authorities are perceived to be either inadequate or caste-biased. In such a scenario the impulse is to assume responsibility for the law. In 1999, the desire to engage in radical protest merged with increasing disillusionment to create a volatile situation. 'Many people are asking us why we have not revenged these killings', 'Tada' (a nickname derived from his imprisonment under the Terrorism and Disruptive Activities (Prevention) Act [TADA]) Periyasami of the DPI admitted (interview, 30 June 1999).

There is a half-hearted assertion of the belief that violence can act as the 'midwife' of liberty. Caste, to paraphrase Fanon, 'is violence, political, military, cultural and psychic; only a counter violence operating in the same spheres can eradicate it' (Caute 1970: 81).[20] 'It is only because people are prepared and ready to hit back', as D'Souza of the Tamilian Republican Party asserts, 'that we have

---

[20] The comparison with colonialism is not perhaps as inapt as it might seem. It is often asserted that India may be independent but that the Dalits have yet to gain their liberty. The Dalit movements also frequently made reference to the example of South Africa. At a flag-raising ceremony in Emmeneswaram, Thirumavalavan assured the gathered activists: 'I am prepared to spend however many years in jail for the sake of these people. Nelson Mandela, for the people of South Africa, for the Black people's freedom, spent 26 years in prison. Yet he emerged with the same courage, with increased valour to gain the freedom of the people and to seize the reins of power. Having seen and experienced this the prison cells can hold no fear for us anymore. A cell; the den where a Panther takes rest' (speech, 18 July 1999).

attained a degree of respect and dignity' (interview, 17 January 1999). 'At the level of individuals', as Fanon observed, 'violence is a cleansing force. It frees the native from his inferiority complex and from his despair and inaction' (1967: 74). The aggression implicit in the popular slogan of 'a hit for a hit', however, has been seen as responsible for much of the escalation in anti-Dalit violence. In areas of high caste domination and oppression, the very slogan can cause resentment because it asserts the Dalit demand to be seen as equals.

Mathivanan of the Working Peasant's Movement disapproved of the Liberation Panther's tactics, but he denied that they were violent. 'That is', he explained, 'they are hitting me and I am defending myself. Do I not even have such human rights? Do I have rights to defend myself from attacks or not?' (interview, 28 September 1999). The inaction of the state authorities is the most commonly cited reason for the turn to violent protest. If the government did its job, they argue, then there would be no need for these movements to exist at all. The state's propensity to turn a blind eye to acts of higher-caste aggression is believed to be one of the main causes for the continuing incidences of caste violence. A familiar rhetorical trope was to point out that if those setting light to a *cheri*, or the perpetrators of innumerable massacres were tried, sentenced and imprisoned, then they would not be able commit an offence again.

An unintended offshoot of the rise in social tension has been an increase in Dalit consciousness. Those who would normally be unwilling to see themselves as part of a community, are being defined and targeted as such by others. 'If another hundred or so people die, if another 1,000 huts are razed to the ground—well let them', Ravichandran of the Marutham Network insisted. 'Due to this our people are starting to think about who our friends and enemies are, they are starting to identify themselves are they not? … In every village now, people have started to resist' (interview, 27 September 1999). In Chapter 2, I referred briefly to the urban bias of the movement. This is never more apparent than in quotes such as that of Ravichandran's. The easy assumption that increased violence will result in consciousness—and an onward march to freedom—ignores the palpable sense of vulnerability and fear that is evident throughout rural Tamil Nadu. The popularity of the Liberation Panthers, according to Ravichandran, rests on their ability to fight back and to protect people from caste-based violence. While there is evidence for and against this assertion, it is clear that the rhetoric of the movement is highly popular and that they are seen as a deterrent.

When the villagers of Kodankipatti fled in fear of the higher caste mob, for example, they were able to take refuge in the DPI stronghold of Muduvarpatti. When this village was in turn subjected to attack by the local higher castes they were repelled by men and women who refused to run. In such situations, the impact of the violence extends beyond the immediate tally of the number of people who have died, the cost of damaged goods or the extent of the injuries on both sides. The riots in Ramnathapuram during October 1998 saw scores of houses burned to the ground, hundreds of people rendered homeless and 11 people killed. S.Viswanathan (1998: 36) described it as a 'black day' for the people, but many Dalits cast it in a different light. They cited the fact that five of the victims were from the BCs as an indication that the Dalits would no longer give in to violence.

'We are no longer slaves', Professor Gnanasekaran, a social historian from Neyveli University, told a meeting to recall the Dalit martyr Immanuel Sekhar (Dalit Resource Centre Seminar, TTS, 17 September 1999).[21] The assertion is that the BCs will think twice before attacking a Dalit community in the future. The claim rings hollow, however, since 'all the victims were from among the economically weaker sections' as Viswanathan notes. He suggests that political machinations lie at the roots of the disturbances (*Frontline* 1998: 36). For Viswanathan and other Dalit leaders, this highlights the weakness of a strategy of violence. The primary victims of violent caste conflict are the marginalised poor. Fighting back, they aver, cannot put food in the stomachs of the hungry, or provide work for the unemployed unless it is merely one part of a concerted programme. Whilst this is self-evidently true, in some ways it misses the point. What Dalit assertion can achieve is to enhance the dignity of the oppressed and redeem the pride of a stigmatised community. This objective is evident in the testimonies of movement members, in the

[21] Dr S. Kambamanikam of the TTS has studied psychology as well as theology. An element of violence is necessary to raise the consciousness of the oppressed he asserts. For it is only through such assertion that they can realise their humanity. Such action, he states, cannot really be seen as violence: 'A hit for a hit, an eye for an eye, is the slogan. But is this violence or justice? For so long the oppressed have tried peaceful means, this is a very last resort' (interview, 1 October 1999).

speeches of leaders and also in the denials that the DPI is a violent organisation:

> Were we perpetrators of violence? How many days would it have taken us to counter attack in Kodankipatti? Are we unable to muster 500 people? Can we not march to Kodankipatti? Could we not attack the caste fanatics? Could we not wipe out their assets? Of course! But, we do not believe in violence. Time and again we have placed our faith in this government; we have asked them to process our demands. This displays the faith that we still have in this Republic (Thirumavalavan, 13 July 1999).

This quote is typical of countless references to the Dalits as a 'restrained force'. Whilst many people questioned why the DPI did not act as violently as its rhetoric promised, it is arguable that assertions like this stand in for action. If we recognise the demand for self-esteem and honour as central to Dalit struggle then we can analyse the speech-acts of various leaders as effective in their own right. What is suggested in such rhetoric is that the Dalits are so far from being subordinate that they can exercise moral restraint.

Conclusion: Educate, Agitate, Organise

'Tell a slave that he is a slave and he will revolt', Dalit movements often quote Ambedkar as saying. The rising consciousness and assertion of Dalit movements in Tamil Nadu marks a determination to resist the indignities that they have suffered for so long. The Dalits on their own cannot transform society through violent struggle, as we have seen in the villages of Somankottai and Sakaravalasu, where they are a dependent minority. The inequality of these social structures cannot be altered overnight, or by returning a hit for a hit. The Dalit movements recognise the need to campaign on issues other than the immediate security of their members. The need for land, education and financial security are paramount, but in the process of achieving greater equality in these fields it is likely that the caste Hindu oppression will become even more severe. Under threat of violence or the withdrawal of caste Hindu support we have seen that the fissiparous Dalit community may be even further sub-divided and set against themselves. 'Violence on a national scale liquidates tribalism and regionalism, while binding the community together and committing each individual in the eyes of themselves and of others', according to Fanon (Caute 1970: 84). If this were the case then the occasional and limited resort to violence, by Dalit movements trying to assert their humanity, might be said to advance a search for justice. As shown in Chapter 5, however, violence has rarely united the various Dalit movements and has often divided them.

Dalit activists insist that hitting back against the upper castes in word and deed affirms that they too are human beings. Violence is never an unproblematic solution though and often causes a backlash. It also alienates the state, which casts movements as militants or terrorists. Ambedkar exhorted his followers to 'educate, agitate, organise'. Dalit movements have often been guilty of organising themselves in order to agitate rather than to provide coherent support networks for marginalised Dalits.[22] This chapter has sought to place Dalit activism in context and to chart the problems that beset protest. The threat of violence, as we have seen, is ever present and its manifestation is too frequent to ignore. In these circumstances the risks of mobilisation and assertion are so great that the temptation is either to 'free ride' on the efforts of others, or to engage in counter acts of violence. As we have seen, the Dalits are often dependent labourers who are too scared of violence or hunger to resist. We have seen how movements mobilise powerful discourses of honour, valour and pride in order to inspire activists to protest and to overcome the fears of waverers. Pride and honour alone, however, are insufficient to mount a sustained campaign. The next chapter, therefore, discusses the economic context of Dalit action and the material and

---

[22] It should also be noted that Ambedkar closed his speech in Nagpur in 1957 urging his followers to 'educate, organise, agitate' (Michael 1999a: 34). The emphasis, however, has to be on organisation if any agitation is to be meaningful. Ambedkar's commitment to democracy would also have prevented him from calling on all Dalits to become mere agitators with no means of gaining power. The importance of organisation is emphasised in a recent *Frontline* article on the situation in Uttar Pradesh. T.K Rajalakshmi shows that 'despite all the rhetoric on Dalit mobilisation, Dalits continue to be killed in the absence of organised political resistance' (2001: 38). The rhetoric inspires a BC backlash that an unorganised community is unable to rebuff. The emphasis must be on the strength of the solidarity shown in Muduvarpatti rather than the helplessness of the Kodankipatti Dalits.

structural alterations that have accorded the Dalits the means with which to organise on a sustained basis. 'Tada' Periyasami was jailed for five years under the Prevention of Terrorism Act, which might have been expected to fuel his radicalism. Rather, it seems to have convinced him of the opposite. 'Mustering four people and exacting revenge upon the killers of Murugesan is no big deal', he states, but to secure a lasting solution to the problems of the Dalit community there is only one way to proceed:

> Countless martyrs have died at the hands of the dominant castes (*aadhika jadi*). To gain a final solution and combat a thousand years of oppression we need to organise. Our community is often referred to as a flock of crows. With crows there is no need actually to throw stones, if you merely bend down they will scatter. But who can throw stones at a swarm of wasps? You cannot. If you throw stones at the wasps they will turn around and sting you. We need to become a swarm of wasps. It is our first duty to build an organisational strength capable of protesting against our opponents' (Periyasami, 30 June 1999).

4

COSTS, COERCION AND CASTE: THE MATERIAL CONTEXT OF DALIT PROTEST

They harvest the paddy, tie up the sheaves and put them in sacks, they winnow it and lay it out to dry. Then they break the husks and extract the rice. Then they grind it on stones for flour. They put all the good rice in sacks for the houses of the dominant and the remainder with stones and chaff, which is not rice, but some sort of diseased rice, they boil up and eat after it has fermented over three days (Thirumavalavan, National Campaign for Dalit Human Rights, 1 December 1999).

Introduction

The levels of dependency highlighted in Chapter 3 raise the question of why people accept the very serious risks and costs of protest. Part of the answer is that 'it is wrong to think that the poor perceive deprivation only, or even mainly, in terms of material conditions' (Oommen 1990: 57). As we have seen, the intangible benefits of honour, dignity and self-esteem are every bit as significant as cost–benefit analyses in inspiring protest. Social movement activity requires resources, however, and it is arguable that differentiation in class terms has *enabled* Dalit movement activity. Indeed, Backward Caste groups maintain that Dalits have only become 'uppity' since the introduction of new economic opportunities and value systems. Such assertions perpetuate the image of the integrative and harmonious 'traditional' caste system,[1] but, as we have seen, the ideological

---

[1] Interestingly, the latest National Curriculum Framework for School Education in India describes the traditional agrarian system in the country as emphasising

nature of this idealisation is evident in Buddhist and *Bhakti* critiques and conversions to more egalitarian religions.[2] Here it is argued that the emergence of a market economy and the gradual disbanding of the village as the organisational basis of production have been crucial in expanding the actions of social movements.

Whereas Untouchable protest was marginal and geographically contained before, as shown in Chapter 2, contemporary Dalit movements potentially have the resources and infrastructure to mount a sustained challenge to caste hegemony. Lack of means rather than will remains the principal hindrance to protest. It is fair to say that the persistence of caste discrimination owes much to the inequalities that render many Dalits dependent upon higher-caste landlords or employers. There continues to be 'a definite correlation between economic and social status' (Mukherjee 1978: 287).[3] From this perspective the rise in Dalit protest could be said to result from the increasing disjunction between the aspirations fostered by democratisation and the continuing marginality of the Dalit community.[4] This chapter charts the material bases of Dalit protest and argues that the majority of Dalits continue to be poor and that this serves to reinforce the position of movements even as it jeopardises their attempts at sustained mobilisation. Poverty, as Sen (1997) has shown, cannot be measured according to purely

---

'self-sufficiency, contentment and operational autonomy for each village' (Rajalakshmi, T.K, 'A Biased Agenda', *Frontline*, 22 December 2000: pp 92–93). The persistence and proselytising of such opinions renders it even more necessary to question their historical accuracy.

[2] 'Bhakti or devotional cults', as Omvedt notes, 'rebelled against caste hierarchy and Brahmin domination. Many of these in turn developed into religious traditions that consider themselves explicitly non-Hindu' (1995: 8, cf. Rajadurai and Geetha 1993: 2096). 'In the final analysis', according to Sugirtharaj, 'although Bhakti movements became popular among Dalits, insofar as they did not change their socio-economic status, the equality professed by them remained a myth' (1990: 23). Even where the authors of *Bhakti* songs and hymns lived in harmony with the prevalent system, however, the lyrics registered social protests and indicated alternative worldviews (Vincentnathan 1996; Zelliot 1996).

[3] For more up to date analyses of the link between caste and class see the work of Robb (1993a), Mendelsohn and Vicziany (1998), Jeffrey (2000), Chattopadhyay (2001), Omvedt (2001) and Pai (2001).

[4] A situation aptly described by Hardgrave and Kochanek (1986), as a 'revolution of rising expectations'.

economic criteria but must incorporate various social indicators as well. This not only helps to explain the willingness of Dalits to engage in costly protest activities, but also has implications for Dalit movement programmes.

The Historical Status of Untouchables

Beteille's assertion that the Dalits' 'fundamental problem' is an economic one, remains persuasive. 'It is a problem of landlessness, poverty and unemployment' (Beteille 1967: 117). Poverty levels are such that agricultural labourers in Tamil Nadu regret the decline of attached or bonded labour, because such a system at least guaranteed job security (Kapadia 1995: 221). To suggest that Dalits were 'better-off' under a system of caste based specialisation ignores the fact that such retrospective assertions almost inevitably contain an element of nostalgia for a mythical 'better' era.[5] It also neglects the socio-economic transformations in train from the mid-19th century, which opened up new modes of political expression (as seen in Chapter 2) and offered new economic possibilities that reduced (though they have yet to eradicate) the absolute dependency of the lower castes. The introduction of a capitalist mode of peasant farming was highly significant in this process because, as Mosse observes, 'relationships are no longer hereditary and are devoid of extreme expressions of subordination' (1994: 86). The transition from payment in kind to cash transactions allowed subordinate castes to escape the ritual and social stigma of being bound to one employer. The process, however, was slow and beset by frequent setbacks.

[5] Dalits in the past were almost certainly worse-off and were frequently held as slaves in Tamil Nadu (Karashima 1997). There is some controversy over whether slavery here is comparable with servitude elsewhere (Washbrook 1993a). The caste system marginalised the lowest castes, but it also accorded them certain obligations. The most important of these 'rights' was that land-owners had an obligation to employ serfs born on the land. In this sense, according to Kumar (1965), the labourers were not 'landless'. Hjejle, however, rejects the thesis that bondage in India was mitigated by the existence of codes of reciprocity and shows that Untouchables—whether they were serfs or indentured slaves—were barely paid enough to subsist upon (1967: 93).

Indeed, the expansion in cash crop agriculture and the industrial processing of cotton initially served to reinforce the dependency of agricultural labourers (Cederlöf 1997: 91). Furthermore, conditions of bondage and the practice of payment in kind still persist in parts of the state.[6] *Coolie irrundar thaan Kanji* (only if we get work can we eat) is a common saying and we have seen how some rural Dalits are prepared to accept forms of subordination in return for a living. Employers continue to demand exaggerated respect from their employees and dissenters are threatened with eviction or violence. Pre-capitalist constraints on labour relations, in other words, have been transmitted to the capitalist sector through social norms and through corruptions of the labour-contractor system that tie indebted labourers to their employers (Cederlöf 1997: 98; Robb 1993b: 48). Payment in kind has declined but it continues to persist in the agrarian sector where it is used to supplement wages.

In the 21st century, the recurrent complaint of movement members is still a lack of resources. It is this continuing shortage of funds which enables a nostalgic re-imagining of the security provided by the *jajmani* system. Poor Dalits, especially women, frequently suffer from malnutrition and many live in makeshift shelters for lack of a proper home.[7] In urban areas, such as Melavassel, a municipal estate in the heart of Madurai, self-help networks and schemes abound out of necessity. Many of the residents supplement the household income through rag-picking and the recycling of discarded paper, plastic and cloth. The surplus food from hotels is routinely distributed and many older women set up informal stalls hawking cheap, home-made food. At the more entrepreneurial end of this spectrum, young men with mobile phones plaster city buses with advertisements offering to clean drains and unclog sewage tanks.

---

[6] In Madras Presidency in 1951, Kumar (1965) reports, nearly one-sixth of the agricultural workforce were still tied labourers in some sense, mostly due to debt bondage. The Bonded Labour System (Abolition) Act, 1976 rendered all agreements serving to perpetuate human bondage illegal. In a recent *Frontline* report, however, Sharma highlighted the case of five Dalits in Karnataka who had chains riveted to their legs to prevent them escaping from the quarry where they worked as stone crushers (Sharma 2000: 45-6). Human Rights Watch estimates that 'forty million people in India, among them 15 million children, are bonded labourers' (1999: 139).

[7] 'While people do not die of hunger', as Deliége asserts, 'they do die of malnutrition' (1997: 65).

Making ends meet was a permanent preoccupation for most Dalits and it should come as no surprise that activists were put under constant pressure to do a 'real job' by their families. The time requirements of movement activity and the uncertain timing and location of meetings and events, however, rendered it very difficult for committed activists to hold down permanent positions. In general, the central figures in any movement tended to be parasitic upon their families, friends and networks of support. Even those who had part-time jobs, such as 'Firebrand' Murugan, were dependent on the goodwill of others in order to participate fully. Activists in cities were usually better off than coolies and labourers for whom work is often irregular and seasonal. It is largely as a consequence of this that Dalit movements display an urban bias. Even in the urban arena, however, families resented the loss of income and the depletion of household resources. Most of the activists in Madurai lived in council housing or in impromptu mud and thatch dwellings and struggled to make ends meet before any expenditure on movement business.

Employment Opportunities

Given the significance of such issues for a movement's success it is worth considering the occupational status of Dalits in Tamil Nadu. The precarious position of most rural Dalits meant that activists tended to derive from families involved in the 'modern' sector. Approximately 17 per cent of Dalit main and marginal workers are employed in this area, of whom roughly 6 per cent have secured work as government employees (predominantly as municipal workers, and also as electricians, drivers, teachers, clerks, etc.) or manage their own businesses. It would be premature, however, to see this as the 'sector of the future since, whilst the number of Dalits employed in this sector has increased substantially, around 6.4 per cent work as unskilled, manual labourers engaged in brick-making, construction, manufacturing and coolie work.[8] Young Dalits aspire towards professional careers, especially government jobs. However, whilst the demand for manual work is high, skilled occupations remain limited

[8] Data extracted from the Tamil Nadu Government's *Statistical Handbook 2002*. cf. Nagaraj (1999: 74).

especially in rural areas. This means that educated youth either have to revise their expectations or migrate elsewhere. Where jobs do exist caste links are influential in determining their distribution. The Dalits in Kodankipatti, thus, insist that there is a pressing need for government enterprises to provide caste-neutral jobs. 'In the higher caste milk societies and dairies', they say 'there is no work for Dalits' (interview, 18 March 1999).

Opportunities are also limited in urban areas partly due to continuing discrimination against Dalits as employees (cf. Harriss 1982). Despite legislation rendering discrimination a punishable offence, caste is still of vital importance in institutionalising labour arrangements. Recruitment to the permanent labour force is, at the very least, assumed to be carried out through networks of kin and caste.[9] Dalit workers in Madurai frequently asserted this and many felt the need to shroud their social origins in order to advance or were deterred from applying for certain positions. Furthermore, castes tend to monopolise jobs that approximate to their traditional specialities (Kolenda 1978: 145). Thus, Nirmala—the coordinator of the Municipal Workers Union—observes that 90 per cent of its members are Dalits and 10 per cent are poor non-Dalits for whom considerations of impurity and social status are of less importance than the rates of pay (informal interview, 12 December 1998).[10] Balasubramanium from Kodankipatti works in an insurance firm but he insists that most Dalits have not been able to escape caste stereotypes: 'Why is it only Chakkiliyars who stitch shoes?', he asks rhetorically, 'and why is it only upper caste people in suits who sell them?' (interview, 20 March 1999).

[9] Also see: Rudolphs (1967: 132), Holmström (1984: 246), Gould (1988: 14, 167), Harriss-White (1996: 250, 313), Omvedt 2001 (hyperlink given in bibliography). Beteille (1991a: 10, 22) argues that caste ties are being steadily eroded in modern India and that family ties, as distinct from caste ones, are more important to the reproduction of inequality. As family ties and informal connections are still largely dictated by caste, however, the process of erosion still has far to go.

[10] Many informants suggested that caste Hindus would increasingly take up cleaning and drainage work if technological advances made the work less 'hands on'. Given the sentiments of caste pride and honour discussed in the last chapter, however, it is probable that only an alteration in the social significance of such work would result in a marked increase of non-Dalits in these occupations.

In explaining such discrimination away employers often resort to 'transference', arguing that 'Harijans would like to work for us but feel themselves to be unclean' (Harriss-White 1996: 250). The sophistry involved in such assertions is revealed in the fact that Dalits find it difficult to secure regular wage work, let alone set up in trade. Speaking of this difficulty for Dalit entrepreneurs, Chandra Bose argued:

> In the name of caste many economic opportunities are denied to them.... In general today they are unable to practice a trade, run a hotel, engage in someone else's [another caste's] work in the common spaces. I mean, they [BCs] will not tell you that you cannot set up a hotel there, but if you do then, they will not eat there, neither will their social organisation. So it becomes a loss-making business. This too is a form of untouchability (interview, 23 February 1999).

In 'Challenging Untouchability' (Charsley and Karanth 1998), there are numerous examples of SC groups overcoming caste barriers and establishing themselves. Despite the success stories, however, the fragility of Dalit assertion is evident. Even in Ashok Kumar's study of dominant Samagars in Karnataka, he notes that the benefits accruing to this (marginally untouchable) community have not extended to the *'Harijan'* groups in the village. Furthermore, even the dominant Samagars have not felt able to insist on temple entry. Where the *'Harijans'* have profited in this example, it is as wage labourers for other communities.

The case discussed here is not an isolated one. Indeed the continual association between Dalits and manual labour led Mendelsohn and Vicziany (1998), in their study on untouchability, to posit the rise of a 'new Indian proletariat' engaged in unskilled, manual labour in demeaning conditions. In 1996, Guru raised the prospect of caste finally being eroded as economic liberalisation swept away the networks of patronage and politics associated with caste and compensatory discrimination. When freed from the state requirement to set aside quotas, however, most employers will probably opt for a caste Hindu over a SC candidate. Whilst the caste system may be said to have 'modernised', the modernist assumption that caste would disintegrate in the face of economic change, urbanisation and increasing industrialisation has proved to be unfounded. In the 21st century 'the barrier to entry into the secure labour force is not geographical but social' (Harriss-White 1996: 249).

Given the constraints that Dalits face in the employment market, the reservation of places for the SCs in the public sector assumes added importance. The reservations system has been crucial in beginning to de-link caste and occupation and in establishing a layer of well-educated and prosperous Dalits. Movements, however, point out that government quotas for the SCs remain unfilled and that Dalits are preponderantly employed in the lower echelons of government service (cf. Gallanter 1991; Radhakrishnan 1999; Sebastian 1994). According to the Tamil Nadu Government's statistical handbook for 2002, only 31.6 per cent of vacancies for SCs notified to the employment exchanges were filled. A recurrent demand of Tamil activists was for the publication of a white paper on reservations. In the absence of such a document, Dalit institutions conducted their own research and released a 'Black Paper' in December 1999 that castigated the performance of the Tamil Nadu Government.

Several less partisan studies also conclude that reservations have not filtered down to the lowest strata of society. In 1974, according to the 1986–87 Report of the Commissioner for SCs and STs, the representation of SCs in public sector enterprises varied significantly according to the class of employment in question. The SCs constituted just over 1 per cent of Class I jobs (the highest in the administrative and managerial services), 3 per cent of Class II posts (lower administrative and managerial positions), 10 per cent of Class III posts (clerical cadre) and 25 per cent of Class IV posts (peons, attendants, drivers and so on). There is an inverse ratio between the desirability of a job and the number of Dalits employed in those positions. It is telling that in the category of sweepers the SCs made up 81 per cent of the workforce. In total Dalits made up 18 per cent of the workforce in accordance with quotas set by the government, but the disproportionate numbers of Dalits in the most menial positions somewhat tempers the significance of this (Sebastian 1994: 78–79). Even these levels of representation are not met in the private sector.

Over the years there has been an incremental rise in the number of Dalits in the higher classes of jobs but they are still disproportionately represented in the Class IV and sweeper jobs. Furthermore, 'like all remedial redistributions compensatory discrimination imposes its own arbitrariness and unfairness' (Gallanter 1991: 547). The emergence of a privileged SC elite and the failure to extend similar provisions to Muslim and Christian Dalits and the poor among the higher castes are examples of this lack of parity. Even where quotas are filled they are not straightforward. Housing schemes, loans and food subsidies have rendered it much easier for Dalits to embark on entrepreneurial ventures, but the numbers involved are extremely low. Widespread corruption and the need for contacts limit the impact of such schemes.[11] As Chandra Bose of the TIP puts it: 'There are some benefits for him (the ordinary Dalit), enough to prevent him from continually protesting. The government, thus, keeps him oppressed. It neither lets him live, nor will it let him die' (interview, 23 February 1999).

Working the Land: Rural Dalits and the Agrarian Sector

It is also important to note that such employment only affects a minority of working Dalits. Nearly 80 per cent of Tamil Dalits in the employment market work in the agrarian sector and 64 per cent work as agricultural labourers.[12] Manual agricultural tasks were traditionally reserved for lower castes since ploughing the land was deemed to be demeaning and because various leather implements were used. Just over 14 per cent of Dalits cultivate their own land, but most are either landless or marginal landholders (Rath and Konlade Statistics 2000: 705–12). Of the operational holdings owned by SCs, 95.8 per

[11] Ashok Kumar (1998: 257) shows the bind that SC entrepreneurs are caught in: They need capital to start a business but without surety or contacts they are unable to receive them. Both in this chapter and other volumes in this series, there are indications that it is only a tiny élite within the SC category that are able to access bank loans and government schemes.

[12] These figures are for 1991. This information is taken from the Statistical Supplements to the Special Issues of the *Journal of Indian School of Political Economy* on the SCs (July–December 2000: 616). The supplements were compiled by N. Rath and S. Konlade and draw on information from the Indian Census (1961–91), the Fourth and the Sixth All-India Educational Surveys and the various rounds of the National Sample Survey from 1978 onwards. Hereafter the supplements will be referred to as Rath and Konlade Statistics 2000. In 2002, the Tamil Nadu Government Statistical Handbook estimated that 63 per cent of Dalits were employed as agricultural labourers.

cent were classified as either marginal (84.6 per cent) or small, that is, under 2 acres (Tamil Nadu Department of Economics and Statistics 2002). The inadequacy of landholdings is highlighted in the fact that the number of Dalits engaged as cultivators fell by 4 per cent between 1981 and 1991, whilst the percentage of agricultural labourers increased marginally (ibid.: 616)—a finding that ties into Mendelsohn and Vicziany's conclusions pertaining to the deskilling and impoverishment of Dalits.

'We are not educated', as Kannima from Kodankipatti observed, 'we can only do coolie work' (interview, 20 March 1999). Coolie work refers to daily wage labour. This is usually agricultural work but can involve odd jobs such as mending fences, loading lorries or carrying bricks. Most Dalits work in nearby fields in return for a daily wage of between Rs 28 and Rs 60 (£ 0.45 and £0.90 at the 2002 exchange rate). The women are usually paid just over half of what the men receive due to a legal wage differential, but the amount of work they do is often comparable. The work is seasonal in nature and highly erratic. 'When it is wet we have work, when it is dry we go hungry and the coolie rate goes down', Durairaj, an elderly agricultural labourer from Karur District explained (interview, 19 October 1999). In dry seasons, the wage was said to drop far below the minimum coolie rate, but 'the recommended wage is never given' according to Jayseelan of the RPI (interview, 26 April 1999).

Whilst movements fight to raise the levels of pay and to standardise the income of male and female workers, labourers themselves are often resigned. 'Going hungry is not unusual for us', Kameswari, an agricultural labourer in Myaladuthurai insisted. Landless, rural Dalits lived in thatched mud huts with little space, rarely any electricity and no piped water. Water was available from nearby hand-pumps though its quality was variable.[13] Women usually squatted outside the houses to cook on wood or kerosene stoves because it was too hot and dark inside.[14] Lentils, vegetables and meat are scarce, however, and

---

[13] In the Myaladuthurai area prawn farms had caused salination and villagers had to walk further and further afield to find potable water. The provision of drinking water and electricity was a major theme of the 2001 Assembly Election campaign.

[14] As a result of popular state government schemes increasing numbers of Dalits live in *pucca* (brick and mortar) houses and have electricity connections. On average, more households in rural Tamil Nadu have access to electricity, piped

people commonly eat rice steeped in water (*kanji*) which is livened up with pickle, raw mango or dried fish (*karuvaad*). This insecurity is exacerbated because agricultural wages are deflated and plummet in slack seasons when people have no option but to work. During the long-running labour dispute at the Manjolai Tea Estate, the PT called for a 'living wage' of Rs 150 a day. As the estate owners noted, however, their offer of Rs 63.9 for an 8-hour day was relatively generous (*The Hindu*, 2 July 1999). The vulnerability of agricultural labourers is highlighted by the fact that the estates were arbitrarily able to dock wages by accusing the workers of adopting 'go-slow' tactics. Across the state, Dalits who I interviewed accepted as little as Rs 20–40 a day in barren months. Minimum wages, as the Rudolphs noted, 'are observed more in breach than practice' (Rudolph and Rudolph 1987: 266).

Caste, Land and Uneven Development

In other words, even where there are legislative provisions to improve the well-being of Dalit labourers there are few guarantees that these will be implemented. It is arguable, however, that in the main post-Independence economic policies have served to strengthen the main proprietary classes (the industrial and agrarian bourgeoisie) and they have benefited most from state policies.[15] Indeed, Herring argues that the dominant local castes and the state are enmeshed to the extent where it is not possible to separate them from each other (in Lerche 1998: A29). Whilst not going so far, the Rudolphs' (1987) research in Tamil Nadu argued that agriculturist associations and interest groups became the arbiters of policy in the state. Thus, whilst Tanner (1995)

---

water and the Public Distribution System (PDS) than in India as a whole (Shariff 1999). The PDS gives poor households access to subsidised rice, kerosene and other products, but the quality is poor and there are frequent complaints of bias in the process of distribution. Much of the rice cooked in rural Dalit households is obtained from their place of work and helps to supplement their income. 63 per cent of households in rural Tamil Nadu use electricity, 50 per cent have piped water and 82 per cent make use of the PDS (Shariff 1999). This compares favourably to a national average of 43 per cent, 25 per cent and 33 per cent respectively.

[15] On this subject see Bardhan (1988, 1998) and Eswaran and Kotwal (1994).

notes how land reforms and elections eroded traditional patron–client ties in Karnataka, Kapadia (1995) and Gough (1991) recount that proposed legislation to give land to the tiller in Tamil Nadu in 1969 actually backfired because worried landlords reclaimed the land habitually worked by Dalit labourers. Alternatively, having registered the land in the names of their dependants, landowners continued as if nothing had altered. The issue, as Agarwal notes, 'is not just one of property ownership; it is also that of property control' (1994: xv).

It is apparent that the failure to implement effective land reform programmes has curtailed the decision-making capacity of Dalit communities by rendering them dependent upon others for work. In was a recognition of this that led the British to pass a Government Ordinance in 1892 that assigned available forest and wastelands—called Panchami land—to Dalits.[16] Likewise, other Indian governments have instituted land reform programmes with varying success. Citing successful reforms in West Bengal, Kohli (1987) states that a well organised, left-of-centre regime is required to initiate redistributive programmes. Since land continues to be the basis of economic advancement in rural communities, he argues that where landholdings have remained static landless households and marginal landholders should be targeted as the beneficiaries of the emerging non-agricultural sector. In the absence of concerted political will, however, it has often proved impossible to realise parliamentary reforms. In Vandiyur, an outer suburb of Madurai, for example, land set aside by the Adi Dravida Welfare Department was encroached by people from other castes, who had influence. Reporting the land-grabs to the police was apparently ineffective and the residents turned to the DPI to intercede and claim land back on their behalf (interview, 26 March 1999).

---

[16] Designated as Panchami (Depressed Class) land, the acreage was ceded under certain conditions of tenure: The land could not be sold, given, mortgaged or leased for the first 10 years and after this it could only be transferred to another Dalit (Kadirvelu 1998). The Act rendered any transactions that transgressed these conditions legally untenable. As Pandiyan observes, however, uneducated Dalits failed to realise the significance of Panchami land and of the conditions attached to it. Dalits who emigrated due to poverty or famine were conned into selling it prior to their departure. Coercion, forgery and deception were employed to obtain the land, which 'is how the dominant castes come to be in possession of Panchami land' (Pandiyan 1999: 38–39).

Given the number of Dalits employed as landless labourers it should come as little surprise that land remains one of the Dalit movements' principle demands.[17] This is manifested in calls for land reform programmes or in efforts to redeem Panchami land, but 'as far as the untouchable landless and near-landless are concerned, such political will has never been exerted on their behalf by any government' (Kapadia 1995: 197). The most prominent Tamil land struggle took place in 1994 in Karanai, Chengleput District. When campaigns to reclaim alienated Panchami land failed, Dalit movements proceeded to occupy the contested plot. They marked their presence symbolically with the erection of a statue of Ambedkar and staged protests demanding legal recognition of their tenancy.[18] The desecration of this statue led to violent protests during which two leading activists—John Thomas and Ezhilmalai—were killed in police firing (Kadirvelu 1998; Moses 1995; Pandiyan 1999; Fr. Yesumarian 1995).

'These two deaths', as D'Souza of the Republican Party, who was present at the shooting, recalls, 'led to a concerted struggle, and highlighted the issue of Panchami land in the state' (interview, 17 January 1999). Subsequent to this struggle the subject has been raised recurrently, but rarely with such cohesion. The prime importance

---

[17] Sudha Pai (2000) and Bardhan (1998) suggest that education offers the quickest route for upward mobility. Given the intractability of land-holdings this may be true, but land remains critically important as a basis for mobility and/or the perpetuation of structural inequalities. Dalit activists see education as crucial, but they generally lack the resources to mount literacy campaigns. Land-grab protests are more high profile (in media terms), offer the prospect of a short-term solution and resonate with the immediate grievances of movement members. Pai, controvertially, argues that the 'traditional structures of rural dominance based on land and social status are undergoing change, and that ownership of land is not as important a source of power and prestige as in the past' (2000: 192). This may reflect the influence of the Bahujan Samaj Party (BSP) Government in Uttar Pradesh where her study is based. Jeffery, Jeffery and Jeffrey (2001), however, suggest that Dalits largely remain dependent on the local landowners for their subsistence and that change is slow (Social and Political Dominance in Western UP: A Draft Response to Sudha Pai). Interestingly, in a more recent article, Pai (2001) asserts that 'land and ritual status, remain the main source of … socio-economic dominance in village affairs' (2001: 648).

[18] See Anandhi (2000) for the significance of these symbols of Dalit consciousness for the land struggles.

of land in Dalit campaigns emphasises their imperfect integration into the modern economy. In a detailed study of caste and poverty in rural India, Gang, Sen and Yun (2002: 10) suggested that households depending upon labourers were worse off than those who were self-employed (whether in agriculture or not) and they further suggested that SC agricultural labourers were poorer than their counterparts. Landless Dalits remain impoverished because alternative sources of income are unavailable, partly due to caste discrimination. Somandam, an assistant regional leader of the Working Peasants' Movement, emphasised how access to land could alleviate this situation: 'Now we are working for a daily coolie wage of Rs 20–30. If we had our own land to work on, we, who are hungry 10 days in every month, would at least have *kanji* to eat. One acre per person would be sufficient for this purpose' (interview, 29 September 1999). The demand for land, however, extends beyond economics. The interplay between resources, values and self-image is captured by Father Yesumarian's assertion that: 'For us Dalits, land is a crucial issue, a self-dignity issue and a very survival issue' (1995: 20).

Landownership, however, continues to be highly concentrated. The Human Development Report survey (Shariff 1999), suggests that Tamil Nadu has one of the highest concentrations of rural land ownership in India. Those Dalits who do own land, fall into the category of marginal landowners and their land is seldom irrigated (Shariff 1999). Land is the prime asset in rural areas and is instrumental in determining both the living standard of the occupants and their social status. 'The negative relation between the risk of rural poverty and land access', as Agarwal insists, 'is well established. Apart from the direct production advantages through growing crops, fodder or trees, land titles increase access to credit, enhance bargaining power with employers, help push up aggregate real wage rates, and serve as mortgageable or saleable assets in crises' (1998: A4).

A consequence of the Dalit's continuing landlessness and dependence on landlords for work is that elements of the tied labour system persist today. Although Dalits are theoretically free to seek work elsewhere there are often few alternatives available to them. A pattern has emerged whereby the villagers who agree to perform the caste tasks associated with untouchability, such as bearing news of a death and beating drums, are employed whilst those who refuse are ostracised. Such discrimination was evident in Kappalur, a satellite village of Madurai where the primary form of employment is in the local cotton mill. Interviews with Dalits in the village painted a picture of poverty that was largely devoid of caste connotations. I was told that there were no caste problems in the village, but on the outskirts of Kappalur, Alagar Sami—a DPI activist—presented a different account:

> (A.S): Over the past 15 to 20 years we have faced attacks and problems which became court cases and were decided in our favour. 'We' refers to us Paraiyars. That is why we face certain social restrictions and tasks.... If they die then we must beat the drum and prepare the body. We must also beat drums at the temple for eight days. Only for such things are we allowed to enter the 'oor'.
> Author (H.G): Do they pay you for this?
> A.S: Salary? A salary that doesn't pay ... but if we refuse then they will not let us in to the temple or anywhere near the temple. It is 20 years since we went in to the temple to worship God.
> H.G: Is this all Dalits?
> A.S: We are some 15 houses.... They don't let us into the temple because we don't do any of this work.... They let others in, because they beat the drums and so on (interview, 29 March 1999).

Dalits are usually paid for such tasks now and contracts are often negotiated before the work is undertaken, but in villages across Tamil Nadu Dalits who reject such roles are subject to social boycott. Gough (1978) and Ramachandran (1990) report a decline in the number of attached labourers since Independence, but labour in this sense *is dependent* upon compliance. 'We could refuse', as Durairaj explained, 'but that would create bad blood between us, and we depend upon the higher castes for coolie work' (interview, 19 October 1999). In Kodankipatti and Vadianpatti, Dalits had to seek employment outside the village since they were not given work locally. 'Everyone is migrating to towns now, where caste is hidden to an extent and one can use one's skill to obtain employment', according to Valentine, a women's wing leader of the Communist Party. 'But we cannot all go!' (speech, 25 October 1999).

The mechanisation of agriculture is further reducing the demand for labour and the bargaining power of landless labourers.[19] The

---

[19] Karunakaran, a social worker and activist in Andhra Pradesh, insists that technical modernisation will gradually eliminate the more arduous and degrading aspects of agricultural work, but it will also result in increasing unemploy-

scaling back of opportunities does not affect all workers evenly, however, as caste and gender mediate the impact. This shortfall is likely to hit the Dalits hardest, because they lack the connections or capital to set up on their own. As Ashok Kumar (1998) shows, this situation has led to the revival of contracts that are thinly veiled forms of tied labour. As we saw earlier, the number of Dalits employed as agricultural labourers rose slightly during the 1980s, but given the overall decline in agriculture many of these workers have had to seek work in other sectors. Both the World Bank (1997) and Repetto (1994), suggest that the non-farm economy is pushing up real wages and providing employment. But Harriss-White and Janakarajan deny that the non-agricultural sector can offset the poverty of the most disadvantaged, since such employment is 'biased against women, against the lowest castes and the poorest classes' (1997: 1476).

The increasing engagement in non-farm activities may, therefore, mirror the increasing casualisation of labour. Indeed, the new wave of capitalist development that has revitalised the rural economy in Tamil Nadu has largely been unskilled, small-scale commodity production.[20] The Dalit communities that I visited, particularly in Karur district, were heavily involved in weaving and textile home industries. As seen earlier, however, this proletarianisation of the rural workforce has not necessarily heralded a new era of opportunity predicated on free market contracts. Members of the Dalit Liberation Movement, for example, insisted that children were still employed in home industries, often being withdrawn from school for this purpose. Semi-autonomous, sub-contracted householders utilise family members as cheap or unremunerated labourers in weaving, fireworks, *beedi* and other industries (discussion, 14 December 1998). Nihila's

---

ment. 'Even today our coolies and agricultural labourers sit hungrily by while their jobs are replaced by machines. This is a very dangerous trend that will reduce employment opportunities, and cause the take-over of more land. Before it used to take four people to plough a field, now the jobs of hundreds of people are performed by one machine' (interview, 13 October 1999). Such views are not a conservative defence of the prevailing agrarian structures and Dalit and Women's movements actively seek better employment conditions for manual and unskilled labourers, as well as campaigning for the proper implementation of policies of positive discrimination.

[20] See also Harriss-White and Janakarajan (1997: 1475) and the Women's Section in *Economic and Political Weekly* 34 (16 and 17).

study, of tanning industries in western Tamil Nadu, also suggests that whilst the prospects for employment may be rising, 'the quality of the employment has deteriorated' (1999: WS-26).

Given the limited opportunities at home, increasing numbers of Dalits (and others) are seeking jobs in the Gulf states or the Asian tiger economies, to improve their financial position. Emigration has a long history in India, often as a response to unemployment or famine and has been seen as a path to social mobility (Carter 1996; Kazi 1989). Conflicting experiences portray such jobs either as 'dreams come true' or as exploitative. Families usually borrow substantial amounts to finance the initial journey. This means that there is pressure on the migrant to succeed, but this money often ends up in the pockets of unscrupulous middlemen and scams purporting to ease passage to the Gulf are legion. Where applicants are successful, however, remittances from abroad accord the families of such workers a degree of financial stability and even affluence. Venkatraghavan, a middle-class Dalit student in Vellore, linked such mobility with Dalit assertion, stating that: 'Dalits have begun to rise up now, and they are conscious of their position. Many of them have jobs abroad in the Gulf, Singapore and Dubai so they have money and are dominant in the villages' (interview, 20 January 1999).

As Kazi (1989) points out, few migrants return to the jobs they had prior to their departure and about a third of them attempt to start up new businesses. The 'new-found wealth and access to consumption may dramatically alter their status and their relation-ships with others', the Osellas note, 'and offer them the chance to forge new identities' (Osella and Osella 2000: 119). Despite this, successful migrants have found that working abroad does not exempt them from caste considerations. In several areas, the Dalit's new-found prosperity has led to increased tensions because BCs feel that their status is challenged. This resentment has fuelled a BC backlash that erupted into violence in Kodiyankulam in the south of Tamil Nadu. 'Kodiyankulam has at least one graduate per house and Gulf workers' (Viswanathan 1995: 40–41). On 26 July 1995, a statue of a Thevar (BC) leader was desecrated leading to intense Dalit/Marava (a Thevar caste) clashes. The residents of Kodiyankulam were not involved in these clashes, but police entered the village in force, ostensibly in search of trouble-makers and proceeded to destroy property worth hundreds of thousands of rupees (Human Rights

Watch 2000).[21] Dalits who experience mobility in class terms, thus, may face exacerbated forms of caste discrimination.

Poverty Issues: The Incidence and Intensity of Poverty

The accusation levelled at affluent Dalits is that they bankroll Dalit agitation, but there is little evidence to support such a view. The majority of Dalits who devote themselves to movement activity are poor.[22] None of the activists in Dalit movements were paid for their work and their families frequently sought to tie movement members down by marrying them off or finding them a job. Informal solidarity networks of friends, neighbours and family are drawn upon by those who wish to devote themselves to 'the cause'. The 'orator' of the Liberation Panthers, for example, had to rely upon other, ordinary members of the movement to fund his travel. 'Firebrand' Murugan turned up at Melavassel on a couple of occasions seeking bus fares to attend meetings. A problem that arises here, as women's movements in Madras found, is that it is difficult to agitate for rights when

---

[21] The police are alleged to have specifically targeted consumer durables and the passports and testimonials of educated Dalit youth, as well as poisoning the main drinking water well. The police insisted that the raid was justified in its attempts to capture Dalits allegedly involved in the murder of three Thevars. Indeed, the Justice P. Gomathinayagam Commission of Enquiry into the incidents, published in November 1999, stated that there was 'no excess' in the police action (*The Hindu*, 25 November 2000). Movement leaders across the state—who burnt copies of the report—and journalists suspect that it was 'the relative affluence of the Dalits that attracted the attention of the uniformed men. The idea, it appears, was to destroy their economic base, because the police feel the Kodiyankulam Dalits provide moral and material support to the miscreants in surrounding areas' (Mani, *The Sunday Times of India*, 3 December 1995).

[22] Based on estimates from Madurai it is a tiny percentage of the Dalit population that is devoted to social movement activity. Rounding up the number of Dalits in the city to 200,000 it is clear that only about 0.01 per cent of Dalits were active on a regular basis. Demonstrations rarely had more than 2,000 people in attendance. This tiny segment of the population, however, has a disproportionate impact. The Dalits of Kodankipatti and Vadianpatti, for example, were persuaded to renounce the caste jobs assigned to them partly because of the work of these activists.

basic needs are not being met (Mageli 1997: 48). Dalit movement leaders frequently complained about the difficulty of mobilising protestors and funding their campaigns. Chandra Bose of the TIP noted that, 'rather than thinking about the paradise of tomorrow, people wish to end today's hunger' (interview, 23 February 1999).

Given this background, the main question is *why* people protest at all. The answer partly lies in the fact that it is mistaken to define 'poverty' in purely economic terms. The scale of poverty in a given society is usually calculated through an analysis of household income. According to Rajuladevi, this is 'the best indicator of economic and social position, because annual income represents the net outcome of household productive capabilities and resources' (2000: 475). A focus on income is unnecessarily limiting, however, since poverty is not only determined by the impoverished state in which an individual lives, but also in the foreclosure of opportunities. This is especially the case where caste considerations operate in tandem with class. Dreze and Sen's (1995: 11) concept of 'capability' is essentially about the degree of autonomy a person has in deciding what kind of life they want to lead. Equality-related capabilities such as self-esteem, protection from violence and the ability to participate in society and politics are valuable to people even if they remain poor (Drèze and Sen 1995: 13). This was never more apparent than in the protests that followed violence which erupted during the 1999 elections. Kannima, an agricultural labourer, addressed a group of over 500 people who had gathered outside a police station in Cuddalore:

> I can only feed the family by working. Coming here today means that I have lost a day's salary. The schools are still closed [following the violence] so even the free midday meal is not available for the children....If we travel anywhere we are cross-questioned and harassed. That is the situation we are facing TODAY! That is why we are here (speech, 25 October 1999).

Significantly, the speaker had a clear conception of a future society in which her immediate needs could be transcended and to that end immediate material issues were presented as secondary to caste-based discrimination. Whilst economic inequality obviously curtails Dalits' access to assets, this should not obscure the significance of *socio*-structural inequalities. As we have seen, equality-related capabilities are often denied to Dalits even if they are rich and successful.

Inequalities build on each other (Drèze and Sen 1997b: ix) and Dalits may thus be said to suffer from 'cumulative deprivation' (Oommen 1990: 255).

One who is economically poor but has influential connections, a good education and physical well-being, in other words, has more opportunities to better himself than someone without these attributes. It is clear, therefore, that poverty does not impact on all individuals equally. 'The poor among the forward castes—who are undoubtedly numerous—have one advantage which the dalits [sic] do not have, viz., the use of caste links with the rich to obtain a small job or a petty loan', according to Balagopal. He concedes that not all of them will be successful in this endeavour, 'but the possibility is undeniably present' (1990: 2232–33). Edwin pointed out that many of his indigent BC friends had the option of hosting a family ritual—piercing a child's ears, shaving an infant's hair and so on—at which all in attendance would contribute money.

We need, therefore, to differentiate between the *incidence* of poverty—referring to the numbers of people subsisting under the poverty line—and the *intensity* of poverty, which refers to the cumulative aspects of inequality (Shariff 1999: 38). It is clear that 'the relevant dimensions of inequality include not only income (or expenditure) but also health achievements, literacy rates, self-esteem and other aspects of well-being' (Drèze and Sen 1995: 96). Dalits feature prominently among the poor according to both the incidence and intensity of poverty and the two can be reinforcing. Many Dalit women and children, thus, forfeit an education either to save expense or because their income generating capacity is required.

Inequalities in education not only reflect social disparities, as Sen (1997: 14) notes, they are instrumental in *sustaining* them. Illiteracy not only denies people access to alternative means of subsistence, but also hinders access to available opportunities. Corrupt officials, for example, exploit poor education to defraud Dalits of loans and compensation claims. An increase in awareness and literacy enables people to take a more active role in politics and local decision making and increases their capability levels. Despite this, Drèze and Sen argue that, 'the social value of *basic education* has been neglected not only by government authorities but also in social and political movements' (1995: 137, emphasis in the original). Certainly, the literacy rate for Dalits is persistently lower than that of the population as a whole. In 1991, the literacy rate for SC men stood at 58 per cent compared to the 74 per cent figure for Tamil males in general. Women are less literate than the men across India, and only 35 per cent of SC women were literate as opposed to 51 per cent of all Tamil women. Contrary to Drèze and Sen's assertion, however, education is one of the primary themes of Dalit movements.

Kamaraj—a manual labourer who has studied till ninth grade (the penultimate year before the government examinations)—is a member of the DPI. 'Education is most important for our development' he maintains, 'that is why the higher castes do not want us to study. If we did we would leave for other jobs and then who would clean the toilets?' (interview, 13 March 1999). 'Literacy tends to bestow multiple benefits on its practitioners', as Mendelsohn and Vicziany observe, 'but above all it lends confidence and expands mental horizons. It leads to a more assertive, less compliant, community' (1998: 35). In recognition of this, many movements have been instrumental in setting up tuition centres in *cheris* and in helping poorer members to buy notebooks and uniforms. Urban literacy figures are much higher partly as a response to this, but it would be a mistake to see such schemes as hugely significant. The focus for political movements has consistently been conscientisation rather than education due to the perception that 'those who have studied run off and do not seek to develop the people' (Anandan, DPI activist, interview, 23 March 1999).

Dalit movements in Tamil Nadu, thus, are caught in a double bind: Poverty is both an inspiration for, and a hindrance to, political participation. To mobilise support and secure the active participation of large numbers they need supporters who can afford sustained campaigns. Affluent Dalits, however, are often removed from the causes of protest and may continue to distance themselves from it. In other words, Dalit mobilisation is mediated by class and Dickey (1993b) is correct to assert that poverty is one of the most salient aspects of identity in the slums and housing estates of urban India. Equally, it is apparent that the experience of poverty is filtered through caste. In using absolutist language and mobilising around essentialised identity categories, Dalit movements attempt to secure the support of the wealthy and educated Dalit élite. Appeals to human rights or a distinctive culture have enabled approaches to NGO's and other institutions, but such support tends to be short term and project based rather than sustainable. One of the prime motivations underpinning the entry into political participation, therefore, has been the need for resources. Whether confronting modes of inequality or seeking to maximise support, Dalit movements are confronted by the weak economic position of the majority of their constituents. This encapsulates the central problematic of the Dalit struggle.

'The problem', as Beteille rightly notes, 'is not simply why inequalities come into being, but why, despite efforts of many kinds, they refuse to disappear' (Beteille 1991a: 20). An analysis of Dalit life in contemporary Tamil Nadu must address the question of why affirmative action programmes and economic liberalisation have failed to create an equal society. 'Untouchability' is still practised and the ritual, economic and asset poverty of the Dalits looks set to perpetuate their subordination, but it is this continuing exploitation that has fostered awareness amongst Dalits (especially women) of their shared interests. The emancipatory potential of this development is fuelling Dalit mobilisation and yet it is mitigated by a 'striking localisation of identity' and increasing intra-caste differentiation which divides better off Untouchables from their caste-fellows living in less developed streets (Kapadia 1995: 239). Increasing differentiation *within* castes and the formation of solidarity networks *across* caste, thus, are countering the processes of caste substantialisation.

Conclusion: Contemporary Experiences of Caste

The Dalit category, in other words, has increasingly been fissured by class differences as many Dalits have made use of the economic opportunities offered by the market and the state to advance. The provision of education for all and the weapon of the franchise has enabled Dalits to escape conditions of servitude but the liberatory potential of literacy still evades the majority and should be a prime concern of movements. Whilst many educated individuals are denounced for distancing themselves and attempting to shroud their social origins, the leaders of Dalit movements emerge from this class of people as seen in Chapter 7. Their example is also crucial in persuading other Dalits to aspire towards better positions. The majority of Tamil Dalits, however, are poor and struggle to make ends meet. As B. Scharma, the Commissioner for SCs and STs notes, 'the life of the vast majority of our people is linked with three elements, viz., the right over resources, the right over means of production, and the entitlement for labour' (1990: ii). Crucially, the proliferation of new opportunities has allowed most Dalits to escape from a position of dependency on one caste or landlord. Whilst some Dalits in rural areas are still tied to local landlords and coerced into the performance of humiliating 'caste work', such practices are increasingly subject to challenge. At the least, such assertion is evident in the demand for wages in recompense for their labour.

Writing in 1973, Epstein noted that 'this progressive emancipation is, to be sure, not yet finished, but it is a "clear tendency" which can be observed in rural India' (1973: 140). Chapter 5 examines this progressive emancipation as it is played out in public space. We shall see that the material conditions of untouchability are not only economic but also spatial. As we have seen in this chapter, the liberal state is unable to address the structural conditions of the Untouchables. Those who have freed themselves from servitude, as Epstein noted, do not always improve their own economic position (ibid.). Thirty years on the situation has not altered considerably from this assessment and it would be scant comfort for the Dalits if social liberation were to be 'attended by perpetual poverty' (Mendelsohn and Vicziany 1998: 270). The increased freedom and opportunities open to the community have, however, increased Dalit participation in social and political life. Such public attention and activism not only increases the confidence and self-esteem of individual Dalits, as Drèze and Sen (1997b) note, it may be the ultimate guarantee of governmental initiative.

5

IDENTITY, SPACE AND POWER: THE SPATIAL BASES AND PRACTICES OF THE DPI

The cultural geography of the Indian village is carefully laid out to assign to Dalit dwellings the lowliest and least desirable areas—the southern outskirts believed to be the abode of Yama, the God of death; the tail end of the irrigation systems; close to the most polluting areas; or on the fringes of deserts (P. Sainath in Devi 2000: 50).

Setting the Scene

Above the main entrance to the Melavassel Housing Unit, in Madurai, stood a makeshift archway atop two poles painted in light blue, red and white stripes. The board forming the arch displayed the striking images of a roaring leopard and the face of a man cross-cut by bolts of lightning. In between the two images bold lettering pronounced this to be a stronghold of the DPI. The face staring insolently out at Hotel Tamil Nadu, across the road, was that of Thirumavalavan, the leader of the movement. On either side of the gateway the compound wall had been turned into a series of political meeting points. The slogans and images of the DMK, the AIADMK, the Communists, and the Liberation Panthers vied with Hindu shrines for wall space. Several parties had constructed ramshackle shelters in front of murals depicting their leaders and symbols. These 'halls' (*manram*), as they were grandiosely referred to, served little material function and adherents of the organisations in question tended to congregate elsewhere. The booths only came into their own during moments of political import such as elections, when canvassers gathered with their supporters. They mostly stood deserted save for stray chickens or pigs rooting around for rubbish. The bright colours and vivid portraits of leaders and symbols competed for attention with the hoardings featuring movie posters or advertisements.

It was when I was visiting people in the house nearest the estate entrance that the significance of these symbols became apparent. Two Dalit men approached us in search of assistance. The manager of the hotel where they were working had abused them in caste terms and was making life unbearable for them. They had recently arrived from the countryside and had no relatives or friends to turn to. Having noticed the board above the entrance, therefore, they had resolved to approach the DPI. In this sense the flags, posters and billboards of various social or political organisations establish a 'cartography' of political affiliation. Movement and party emblems function as political signposts that indicate which organisations are represented in a given area, and they served, in this sense, to establish a claim to the territory. No hamlet is too remote to have an array of flag-poles, and these often function as indicators of popularity as well, for the taller the flagpole and the better maintained it is, the stronger a movement or party is in the area. Conversely, the flagpoles of discredited parties may be uprooted and cast aside in the symbolic rejection of their ideals.

The first move of any organisation, on establishing itself in a locality, is to haul up its flag on a painted pole or tree stump. More permanent constructions may follow—the flag poles are often made taller or given a concrete plinth with a plaque embedded within it, statues, billboards and buildings may also be erected—but the immediate impulse is to identify the area with the party or movement in question. The flag-raising ceremony not only provides the social glue that binds a locality to a movement, it also constitutes a public assertion of political allegiance. Less permanently, such concerns are reflected in the actions of protestors who attempt to lay claim to public space. Coconut matting or canvas *pandals* (marquees) are put up to provide some shelter for the demonstrators, and their emblems and posters publicise their organisation and the cause that they espouse. This concern with marking territory highlights the significance of space to Dalit movements.

Identity, Space and Power: The Importance of Space

In this chapter I wish to explore the significance of public space to Dalit identity and to the functioning of Dalit movements, as a means of examining the social concepts that underlie much movement action. The notions of 'space' and 'spatiality' are not often verbalised in this context, and yet conflicts over and for space are central to the movements and for the production of identity in general.[1] Recently several theorists have argued that space is as much a social construct as a physical entity, and this construction is significant to the processes of inclusion and exclusion. Thus, Lefebvre (1991) argued that each society's versions of space, as manifest in the built environment, exposed a particular ideology or view of the world. Social space, in other words, is enmeshed in relations of power. The oppression of the Dalits is materially manifested in the physical isolation of Dalit *cheris* (quarters). The notion of space, thus, is a central social idiom of the Dalit struggle. Dalit movements flourish in the impoverished conditions of rural *cheris* and urban slums, where they can draw upon pre-existing networks of affiliation and family ties. They emerge out of local issues and problems and yet the conditions they are fighting against are familiar across India: land-lessness, poverty, low social status, poor working conditions, lack of amenities and poor housing conditions.[2]

   Considerations of place and space have long been important in Tamil Nadu. 'What is your native place (*sontha oor*)', is one of the most frequently asked questions in introductions. Answering that one comes from Madurai, or some other urban conglomeration, is rarely perceived as an adequate response and the questioner will probe deeper: 'No, but originally (by which they mean the native village of the parents) where are you from?' Alternatively: 'which part of Madurai do you live in?' By thus mapping the background of their new acquaintances, people build up a sense of the person's identity. Even today, networks of relatives and friends tend to be localised

---

[1] See D. Massey (1994), Hetherington (1998) and Escobar (2001) for a more theoretical account of this relationship between social movements and social space.

[2] Many of the grievances raised are local ones and relate to specific incidents, but they are accorded a wider currency due to the universality of *cheri* conditions. 'The economic network of caste-based institutions', as Fernandes and Bhatkal note, 'is awesome. A huge number of hospitals, schools, colleges, co-operative banks and other "modern" institutions are controlled by a thinly veiled caste institutions' (1999: 5). Dalits feel excluded by this network of caste interests and bemoan their own community's lack of organisation.

around one's place of settlement. Over time these spatial divisions have come to be associated with strong cultural identities through processes of local negotiation and in interaction with the British colonialists.[3] Four factors, as Mines observes, contribute to the overriding significance of locality to communities and individuals: '1. Locality based marriage rules, 2. The roles that personalised trust and connections (including kinship ties) continue to play as determinants of social and economic success, 3. The community-making roles that big-men play, and 4. The presence of "charitable" community institutions' such as temples and schools (Mines 1994: 119).

Dalits were, and in some cases still are, further tied to a locality through bonds of patronage and the threat of violence. Although British 'emancipation laws' (1843 and 1860) legally permitted workers to carry their labour wherever they chose, 'once the state ceased to be segmentary, peasants could no longer engage in rituals of flight' (Irschick 1994: 193). The sedentary nature of Dalit groups, therefore, had more to do with the economic and social compulsions of the *jajmani* system than any real exercise of choice, but the writings of British missionaries and administrators enabled them to place a different gloss on their immobility. As early as in 1818, F.W. Ellis of the Indian Administrative Service noted that the Paraiyars of Tondaimandalam 'affect to consider themselves as the real proprietors of the soil' (in Irschick 1994: 182). The claim to be the 'original' inhabitants of the land has a deep-rooted appeal that finds an echo in the speeches of movement activists today. The poor conditions of Dalit settlements are magnified when contrasted with the supposed 'golden age' when Dalits tilled their own land and were their own masters.

This sense of grievance is most apparent in the struggle to reclaim the land ceded to Dalits by the British.[4] *Panchama nilam* (Dalit land)

---

[3] Each of the various caste and community groups in Tamil Nadu, as Irschick notes, 'claimed a special (often "original") site in the landscape and fashioned a cultural representation of the area that flowed from this construction' (1994: 67). Tamil Nadu is said to consist of five socio-emotive regions, or 'tinais', (mountains, forest or pasture, countryside, seashore and wasteland) each of which had its own character (Irschick 1994: 67; Ram 1991: 4; Subramanian 1999: 18).

[4] The significance of the fact that the Dalits were largely landless was not lost on the British administrators such as Sub-Collector Mullally. In his report of 1889 he notes that a lack of land 'renders these unfortunates nothing more than the

was supposed to be the inalienable 'possession of the habitually dispossessed', and a means of alleviating the poverty of the SCs. The initial act in 1891 prohibited the sale, gift or transfer of this land into non-Dalit hands but little is occupied by Dalits today, and that little has been the subject of fierce struggles and bloodshed. Land ownership is a politically charged issue in the struggle over space.[5] So long as Dalits are denied land ownership in rural settings they are likely to remain dependent upon the other castes for work (cf. Chapters 3 and 4). Where Dalits do own land their economic and educational position has risen accordingly and they are given greater social respect. 'The Dalit's struggle for land and water', as Kadirvelu points out, 'is integral to the struggle for liberation from all forms of oppression in the caste society. This struggle for common resources should not only be viewed from an economic perspective, it also has a social dimension' (1998: 3).

Important as it is, land is merely one aspect of the wider struggle for recognition as equal citizens and unfettered access to public space. Material space is extremely important in the everyday lives of Indian villagers. The inferiority of the Dalit community is high-lighted in their exclusion from common areas in the village and in the (higher caste) village committee's refusal to collect taxes from them for village festivals. The sub-division of space, into sacred and profane areas, further serves to separate the Dalits from the rest of the community by denying them access to temples. In a historical study of social mobility amongst the low-caste Nadars during the 1890s, Good (1999) charts the conflicts over access to public space. Whereas temple authorities claimed that they owned the surrounding streets and could prohibit impure groups from using them, the Nadars challenged this assertion in the British courts by insisting that the streets in question were public roads which people of all castes could use. The ownership or control of land and public resources, it is clear, affords power and status to the occupant. Consequently, important

---

slaves of the *mirasidars* who exact from them labour for nothing or at a much lower than market rates' (in Irschick 1994: 171). See Chapter 4 for a discussion of these themes.

[5] 'Is this land not ours?' as Thirumavalavan demanded at one demonstration. 'The downtrodden want the right to walk on common paths, they want rights to common assets, and they want rights to the lands that are given out for lease' (Interview Madurai, 13 July 1999).

villagers receive special indications of their significance. The image of the village God will stop at their houses when it is being chaired round the village for example; or they will be accorded prominent places near the front at any community event. Space, thus, is a very important symbol in Hindu life.

Lowliness and wrongdoing is similarly marked in spatial terms. Disobeying moral codes or the demands of the village committee may lead to social exclusion and ultimately exile. Couples who break the caste taboo may be allowed to live in peace, but they are rarely allowed to remain in the village. Transgressors are removed from the boundaries of the village lest their example should prove to be contagious. Individual Dalits who challenge the power of the village council, such as the panchayat presidents in Melavalavu and Maruthankudi, may be hounded out of the village, threatened, beaten or killed.[6] In considering the importance of spatiality, space and power, therefore, we need to address several issues. First, we must recognise how multiple elements of individual identity are manifested in various spaces. One can, for example, be a Dalit, a council worker, a woman and a mother. These multiple identities influence the way one behaves or is treated in different settings and at different times. Second, we need to examine the social relations (and relations of production) which shape the course of people's protest and the spaces

---

[6] On 19 July 2000, *The Hindu* reported the case of the Dalit president of Maruthankudi panchayat in Madurai District. The traditionally Thevar panchayat was brought under the 'reserved list' in 1996. This meant that only a Dalit candidate could stand for election. Having forced the cancellation and postponement of previous elections through force, the village committee finally issued a dictat that everybody should vote for V. Nagar. Nagar was duly elected with Thevar support, but he was immediately forced to tender his resignation with a plea to the state government to strike the village off the reserved list. The dispute dragged on and the council was unable to function, but Nagar was prevailed upon to sign some forms authorising the payment of panchayat employees. As soon as the committee came to know of his actions they 'called Nagar a cheat and accused him of misusing the money'. 'When the threats increased', the article continues, 'Nagar fled the village with his family. "It is better for him and for us if he keeps away from the village," said a villager'. Two other villages in the same district face similar problems, and it was just such a dispute that culminated in the massacre at Melavalavu. Source: http://www.the-hindu.com/2000/07/19/stories/04192234.htm. See Pai (2001) for an analysis of panchayat elections and problems in Uttar Pradesh.

within which such protest occurs. Dalits in small rural communities, for instance, are less likely to challenge the status quo or refuse to accept the daily indignities they suffer since they are dependent on higher castes for work. In conclusion we can consider whether the rise in consciousness indicates a reordering of power relations. This focus, of necessity, requires an analysis of power relations on both a social *and* political level.

The stress on locality, however, should not blind us to the fact that locally-constructed identities are 'also constructed in relation to processes of classification or categorisation by the state and other social groups' (Aitken 1999: 19). The oppression of Dalits by certain BC communities in Tamil Nadu, for example, has fostered a fragile sense of Dalit unity that transcends the narrow boundaries of each SC community. The constitutionally created category of 'SC', similarly, enables solidarity between Dalits of differing regions, languages and cultures. Paradoxically, the very government programmes designed to alleviate SC poverty and provide better conditions for them have often culminated in the reproduction of marginality. A rhetoric of 'meritocracy' denies due recognition to the academic and employment achievements of Dalit youth, and the rows of small, single-room, concrete government constructions are as sure a sign of a Dalit settlement as any that existed previously. The communities derived from such 'colonies', in Appadurai's terms, 'are context-produced' as much as they are 'context-generative' (1995: 217).

These means of controlling and coordinating Dalit life offer what Foucault (1980: 72) terms a micro-physical power, which works in part by reordering material space. The attempt to eliminate the disorder and dirt of the crowded *cheris* and to impose structural order upon them, however, has not always worked. Dalit movements are increasingly questioning their marginality and demanding recognition as citizens. There is a paradox here, since it is arguable that the identification of a given locality with one particular movement results in the privatisation of that space and serves to create an enclave cut off from the rest of society. Social and political action, however, 'militates in the long run against separatism because it assumes an orientation that is *publicist*. In so far as these arenas are *publics* they are by definition not enclaves—which is not to say that they are not often involuntarily enclaved' (Mitchell 1995: 124).

When Dalit movements raise their flags above the entrance to an urban housing block or unveil a painted board in the heart of a *cheri*, therefore, they are raising fundamental questions about the nature of public space and social interaction.[7] Dalits, movement activists often asserted, have been 'confined in *cheris*' for too long. Isolated, excluded and ostracised they constituted a 'non-people' who were not accepted as being members of the 'Hindu public', but were perceived as 'outcastes' on the fringes of civilised society.[8] By struggling over and within the social spaces from which they have traditionally been excluded, Dalit movements are engaged in a negotiation of both their own identity and the limits and possibilities of civil society in India. Examining the Dalit movements in spatial terms, therefore, provides an indication of the state of democracy in Tamil Nadu.

Protest in Public Space and Public Sphere

At issue in the Dalit struggle are questions concerning the nature of both 'public space' and the 'public sphere', and the position of Dalits within them. The emergence of the public sphere is depicted as an offshoot of the process of modernisation and the transformation of feudal societies into modern, capitalist nation states (Habermas 1994, 1996; Mitchell 1995; Price 1996). The 'public sphere' is described as the 'realm' in which communication occurs: 'a network for communicating information and points of view' (Habermas 1996: 360). The term indicates a transition from traditional authority to a new form of social relationship and mode of organisation based upon consensual authority. Under the monarchical system 'state' and 'society' interpenetrated each other to such an extent as to preclude the emergence of a 'public' (Price 1996: 132–33). Colonial rule resulted in the spread of a new political order, which inscribed the social world with new conceptions of space, new forms of social

---

[7] See Pandian's (1995) excellent critique of the Cambridge School for a spatial analysis of the Dravidian movement.

[8] In his history of the peasantry in south India, Ludden notes that the British administration bought into the idea that the Untouchables were lesser citizens: 'When roads needed to be built, public works officers justified their coercion of Pallas [sic] by citing the *public right to Palla manpower*, a right which they extrapolated from village to government (1989: 174, emphasis added). Also see Price (1996: 133–34).

relation and new forms of person-hood.[9] Under the British, formal monarchical rule was gradually disbanded and standardised laws were introduced that, theoretically at least, treated everyone as equals.

Democracy, in complex societies, according to Melucci, is predicated upon the 'creation of conditions which allow social actors to recognise themselves and be recognised for what they are or what they want to be' (1996: 219). Habermas (1996) recognised the difficulty of transferring from one mode of governance to another, and foresaw an incremental transition of the public from its initial condition as a 'collective subject' into the position where it could constitute the conscious collective sovereign of itself. The public sphere, according to such formulations, is a universal, abstract realm (Mitchell 1995: 117). It comprises the constitutional rights to freedom of association and expression, the right to protest, the courts, the media and public institutions that all provide a metaphorical space for representation, recognition and communication. It is mistaken, however, to infer the existence of an open and politically-active civil society from the number of civil institutions present as liberal political theory does. This ignores the fact that subordinate groups lack the material means to guarantee equal access to, and equal participation in, the public sphere (Chandhoke 2001: 10). In actually existing democracies some groups are always excluded. It was an admission of this inequality that led the authors of India's Constitution to create a system of opportunities aimed at incorporating the most excluded of its citizens into the body of society.

Despite these provisions, as we have seen, many Dalits are still marginalised. They are discriminated against in the hindrances they face on free passage through a village, at teashops (where they are sometimes served in different glasses) and in the unequal distribution of proceeds from common resources such as mango groves. 'These

---

[9] With reference to an incident in which the higher castes of a village objected to the passage of an Untouchable's corpse through their streets, Ludden notes that the government saw it as 'a matter of principle that the state should define rules concerning the use of public space' (1989: 188). As a result of local disputes such as this the collective control of elites over the use of space was eroded to produce 'truly public space' (Ludden 1989: 190). For more on the links between colonialism and the production of new forms of social relations see: Mitchell (1988: ix), Ludden (1989: 190), Price (1996: 41–42) and Kaviraj (1997a: 25).

restrictions are extended to the use of public properties. The Dalits are forbidden to draw water if there is only one well meant for drinking. They are not allowed to sit at the *chavadi* (meeting place), but have to squat on the ground' (Jeyaharan 1992: 44). Despite an ideology of citizenship in India, to paraphrase Shklar (1991), the history of citizenship has been one of exclusion. Hundreds of Dalits were prevented from voting in the 1999 elections in Tamil Nadu, and many Dalit politicians at the panchayat level have been prevented from carrying out their duties (*see* Chapter 9 and footnote 6, this chapter). This demonstrates the difficulty of translating the spaces theoretically made available in the public sphere into material spaces where marginalised groups can speak and be recognised as citizens. Whereas the public *sphere* is abstract, in other words, public *space* is material; 'It constitutes an actual site, a place, a ground within and from which political activity flows' (Mitchell 1995: 117).

It is somewhat unclear, however, what public space actually is. It may refer to the concrete, physical spaces of the built environment or the experiential space of social relations (Weintraub 1995: 281). 'Is it, as the US Supreme Court recognises, simply those spaces in cities (and elsewhere) that are publicly owned and have 'always' been used by citizens to gather and communicate political ideas' (Mitchell 1996a: 127)? If so, then few areas in India constitute public space in any meaningful sense since space has usually been hierarchically patterned. To what extent can villages in Tamil Nadu be regarded as public spaces, considering the social exclusion of Dalits from these areas? According to D. Massey's (1994) notion of 'power geometry' 'a place is made unique by its own particular "constellation of relations" ... that is, the unique combination of economic, political, and social links with other places' (Cope 1996: 180). The positioning of Dalit *cheris* is significant, because in most rural areas they are located on the edges of villages and are placed in a position of dependence upon higher castes for work, water and other amenities. The question 'what is public space', therefore, ultimately derives its significance from the culturally-determined boundaries between the public and the private.

In 'Filth and the Public Sphere', Kaviraj (1997c) challenges the applicability of the public/private dichotomy to India. 'The idea of the public', as he asserts, 'is a particular configuration of common-ness that emerged in the capitalist-democratic West in the course of the 18th Century' (1997a: 86). The idea of universal access was not present in traditional India, where one's social attributes determined one's level of access to 'hierarchical space'. Drawing upon Tagore, Kaviraj suggests that a more apt differentiation would be between 'Home and the World', the inside and the outside.

Reference to the 'world' and the 'outside' avoids the problematic connotations of 'public space'. In replacing the term 'private' with that of the 'home' Kaviraj's contention is that the collective nature of Indian households renders them very much the reverse of 'private', because they are not driven by the desire of individuals to be accorded their own space.

There is, however, a gendered differentiation of space within the home. It is often argued that Dalit women experience greater autonomy than their higher-caste counterparts due to their earning potential. The secreting of women in the home, as Kaviraj notes, is very much a middle class and middle caste way of life. Dalit women suffer less from such social restrictions than their caste Hindu counterparts, but this does not exempt them from the general notions of propriety and good conduct which largely restrict women to the home. It is, as Sharma observes, 'difficult for a woman to engage in public, political or economic processes which involve contact with unrelated men since it is her business to withdraw from such situations' (1980: 213). Dalit women may work, shop and collect fuel and water but they are not permitted to linger unnecessarily in the public streets or frequent tea-stalls. Thus, as Mitchell (1988: 50), observes, space itself is polarised between the female domestic realm and the public, male world of the market place.

Like Kaviraj, Sharma problematises the notion of public space. She does so by drawing a distinction between the *bazaar*, which constitutes public space within the village, and the *jungle*, which represents the public spaces and wastelands beyond the village boundaries (1980: 220). *Cheris,* from this perspective are equated with the 'jungle' on the peripheries of public space. Dalit women assert their right to enter public space fleetingly in their daily lives and, more significantly, through their participation in rallies and demonstrations, and yet they simultaneously embody the persistent division between the public and the private spheres. When higher castes want to 'get even' with assertive Dalits they frequently abuse or rape Dalit women. When women enter public spaces, therefore, they are often responsible to their families for their reputation and honour, and fear for their reputations (Sharma 1980: 218). Public space is thus cast as dangerous for women and opposed to domestic or private space, which is seen as the secure province of women, despite the frequency of domestic violence (Subadra 1999: WS28). Even the home, as Sharma notes, is 'zoned into private, semi-private and semi-public areas', with the women largely confined to the kitchen. This represents the epitome of domestic space to which access is restricted (1980: 227).[10]

Movement activists gathering at houses in Melavassel would congregate in the semi-public area of the porch, seated on beds or chairs, whilst the women served tea and sometimes food before retreating back into the house. The differences between the 'home and the world', therefore, fail to fully replace the opposition between the public and the private. These categories do, however, serve to highlight the differences in socio-cultural organisation that pertain in India. The significance of substituting the word 'home' for the word 'private' with regard to the Dalits is most apparent when it is applied to near neighbours as well as family. The *cheri*, thus, may be understood to function as a partial extension of the domicile. If we primarily define the term 'home' as 'a realm of security', such an interpretation is certainly justified in a way that the term 'private' is not. Dalit women draw strength, friendship and solidarity from their neighbours, but they can be systematically subjected to violence within the privacy of their own houses. Community links in most *cheris* are given more significance than common neighbourly links since they are reinforced by the ties of caste and kinship (if only fictitious). People are more likely to share interests, relatives or difficulties in such situations. Conceiving of such areas as 'home' spaces, highlights the fact that they are certainly not public in that access is restricted. The 'home', in this definition constitutes a semi-public space between the private lives of individuals and the public life of the street.

Integral to the Dalit struggle is an implicit challenge to hierarchical and gendered space. The colonisation of public spaces during protests and rallies constitutes a demand for equal access and the mobilisation of women activists serves to break down the habitual barriers on female movement. Protests often occur in far away, public places where women are subject to the attention of unfamiliar men. Whilst men and women generally sit apart in such meetings, and women

[10] This spatial division is also a temporal one, which varies with the time, season, and the demands of the labour market (Mitchell 1988: 55).

almost always travel together rather than alone, they are increasingly gaining in confidence. Most Dalit meetings are now addressed by female speakers, who have not only transgressed restrictions on movement, but also have the courage to make themselves heard in public, and predominantly male, space. Space is not merely passive, in other words, it 'is both constructed by and the medium of social relations and processes' (Cope 1996: 185, emphasis in the original). Citizenship movements, therefore, must occupy and reconfigure material public spaces if they are to have an impact. 'Indeed, these movements are premised on the notion that democratic (and certainly revolutionary) politics are impossible without the simultaneous creation and control of material space' (Mitchell 1995: 123).

Social relations, as Massey (1994: 168) observes, 'always have a spatial form'. The spaces occupied by Dalit *cheris* serve as more than just homes and neighbourhoods, they not only constitute sites in which the Dalits can be seen and represented, but also constitute sites where they can be controlled and contained. They are also, increasingly, places within which activism can arise and expand outward into the wider community. Movements need not lose their specificity in this process, since public space represents the 'point of contact between political institutions and collective demands between the functions of government and the representation of conflicts' (Melucci 1996: 221). This recognition of public space as *political* space serves to highlight the interconnectedness of spaces, and the 'topography of power' that links them together (Gupta and Ferguson 1999: 8). It also highlights the fact that space cannot be conceptualised independently of time. Space is created by and through dynamic social relations and is, by its very nature, 'full of power and symbolism, a complex web of relations of domination and subordination, of solidarity and co-operation' (D. Massey 1994: 265).

Dalit, women's, non-Brahmin and Independence movements have all been engaged in struggles to gain entrance to and recognition in public space as political actors (Pandian 1995). 'Here public spaces serve not simply to *surface* particular pre-given behaviours, but become an *active medium* through which new identities are *created or contested*' (Ruddick 1996: 135, emphasis in the original). It is only in public space that specific movements and identities can encounter one another and negotiate with them. Social space, thus, is deeply constitutive of a sense of community—regulations over who is allowed in, who is excluded, and the roles that both the insiders and the outsiders play help to shape a community's perception of itself. In this sense, representations of public space are central to the process of 'other-ing' (Ruddick 1996: 146). Complex societies are splintered into innumerable 'publics' and 'counter-publics', each of which annexe their own areas and arenas of discussion. Without spaces in which these counter-publics can be seen and recognised by other factions, therefore, the 'public' may be 'balkanised' into innumerable 'home territories' (Mitchell 1995: 124).

Public space implies accessibility and the potential to bring people with different values, and opinions into proximity.[11] Imposing limits and controls on spatial use and public social interaction has been one of the principle means by which government administrators and corporate urban planners have attempted to regulate public behaviour (Siegel 1995: 371). The increasing 'privatisation' of public space (though in so different ways), by capital, homeless people and locality-based social movements has created a world in which it is arguable that the 'ideal of an unmediated *political* public space is wholly unrealistic' (Mitchell 1995: 121). Kaviraj (1997c) details how the gradual occupation of Calcutta's parks by the lower classes highlighted the difference between *public* space—open to all citizens and beautifully maintained—and *pablik* space which came to mean areas which were not private property and could, therefore, be encroached. The creation of *pablik* space represents a consequence of democratisation, since the lower classes would have been debarred

[11] In competing definitions of public space, activists promote a vision of a space distinguished by the absence of coercion and the possibility of free interaction and expression. For others, however, public space constitutes a regulated and orderly retreat where properly behaved people can gather without the fear of harassment (Siegel 1995: 371). The first of these visions is a radical affirmation of political space, open to everybody and to all discussion even at the risk of social disorder. The latter is a conservative and monitored notion of space, in which access is limited to people deemed capable of acting responsibly. According to this formulation citizenship is something that is earned, and can be removed if individuals fail to meet their responsibilities. This raises questions about who the 'public' is, and who regulates access to 'public spaces'. 'The metaphorical spaces between the legal and moral meanings of citizenship', as Staeheli and Thompson note, 'set the conditions for debates over which citizens should have access to public space' (1997: 30). Public space here is far removed from the idealistic notions of the emancipated public sphere in which the public governs itself.

from such spaces before, but this invasion of territory ironically resulted in the loss of public space for the 'invaders' as well as the city's other inhabitants.

Many analysts now posit the mass media—with its talk shows and debates—as the space in which contemporary society can replicate the idealised forums of public debate such as the Greek agora. It is certainly true that protest in modern democracies has largely been concerned with initiating public debate (Klimova 2000: 258). In a distorted public sphere, however, access to the media is skewed in favour of the powerful and solutions reached through such debates merely serve to reinforce the status quo. The term 'public service broadcasting' connotes the use of news and information media in the best interests of the public, but control over such media is rarely democratic and not all views can find expression through such channels. Even assuming that the mass media was open to different currents of opinion and social debate, the reach of such media in non-literate or poor regions is such that it would disenfranchise the poorer sectors of society. 'Without the occupation of material space', therefore, 'the kinds of protest that came to a point at Tiananmen … would have remained invisible' (Mitchell 1995: 123).

Social and Spatial Exclusion

Exclusion from society and exclusion from material space are mutually reinforcing; without connections and influence it is hard to get things done, and without land or money it is hard to gain these links. To understand the significance of the Dalit movements and the symbolic importance of the emblems of assertion, therefore, the social roots of protest must first be examined. 'The Untouchables, as very impure servants', Dumont points out, 'are segregated outside the villages proper' (1980: 47). Traditionally they could not use the same wells or enter the same temples, nor could they enter the main village without permission of some kind. Even when summoned to the houses of their upper-caste patrons, they were (and often are) obliged to make their way to the back of the house and call out to the inhabitants to make their presence known. 'Untouchables enter the system', as Deliège puts it, 'in order to accomplish their ritual and economic obligations … they leave it again to go back to their colonies' (1997:119). Any unwarranted incursion into the village proper results in verbal or physical abuse. Even where there is no distinct *cheri*, the divisions between the Dalit residences and those of the other castes are quite apparent and are rigidly enforced. As these divisions have been subjected to challenge a pattern has emerged in which an assertion of equality on behalf of the Dalits is met by fierce repression and social ostracism.

Viralipatti is a small village about 50 km west of Madurai. In 1993, the DLM established a branch here and began educating the minority Dalit population about their rights. Subsequent to this development, the Dalits, who had to perform the menial duties of whitewashing, cleaning and beating drums to announce deaths, demanded the right to enter the temple during the local village festival. They appealed to local government officials, the press and other bodies but met with no success. When they tried to enter the temple forcibly on the 22 May 1993, they were violently repulsed. Subsequent to this, the caste Hindus imposed a social boycott and demanded that the local DLM leader Muthaiyah be handed over to the village committee. When the Dalits refused to cooperate their houses were attacked and men, women and children beaten severely. Similar incidences occurred in Themmavur in 2000 (Athreya and Chandra 2000), Kodankipatti in 1990 and 1999, in Allalaberi in 1990, in Indirapuram, Errampatti and Mudakathan in 1991, in Chinthalapatti and Kunnuvaaran in 1995 (interviews and TTS annual reports 1992–93, 1991–92, 1995–96). The catalogue of casteist abuse exhibits what Mendelsohn and Vicziany (1998: 53) refer to as 'exaggerated revenge'.[12]

Affirmative action programmes and the economic uplift of a section of the Dalit community have rendered the higher castes more jealous of their position. Retaliation against 'uppity' Dalits is rising as the dominant castes attempt to maintain their position. Whereas Dalit movements have sought access to the public realm and political recognition, the increasingly assertive movements of BC groups such as the Thevars and the Vanniyars have been concerned with denying the benefits of full citizenship to the Dalits and of excluding them

---

[12] As seen in Chapter 3, a social boycott means that Dalits are barred from entering high-caste streets or from using common water sources. Local shops and services (for example, Barbers) are told not to serve them and local employers use outside labour. Dalit livestock may also be seized if it wanders onto 'common' land.

from public spaces (cf. Pandian 2000). When I was living in Madurai in 1985, for example, the first Dalit graduate from a village in Madurai District walked home at the end of the term passing through the upper-caste area of his village wearing shoes and trousers. Perceiving this to be a challenge to their authority, BC youths set upon him and beat him to death. Similarly, a Dalit youth was fatally assaulted for accidentally brushing against a Thevar lad in a movie theatre (interviews in SMP Colony, 23 March 1999). In 1995, a young schoolgirl who 'presumed' to use the common drinking receptacle in the classroom, was beaten by her teacher. This latter story only made the news headlines because the ruler used to admonish the child gouged out one of her eyes (Rao 1995).

The intent in each of these cases is apparent. The Dalits are to be kept in their place, which is deemed to be beyond the boundaries of society. Such stories are common, though not all such cases are necessarily violent. Mendelsohn and Vicziany (1998: 41) note the increasing 'compartmentalisation' of Untouchability. In 1972, for instance, in the village of Orathur, Dalits were not allowed to use the common village pond. If they wanted water from the reservoir they had to ask caste Hindus to pour it into their vessels. In an attempt to bring a prosecution the Dalits planned to photograph this practice. The caste Hindus forestalled their action by declaring that the pond was common property for all, but since then 'they see it as polluted and do not use it' (Kadirvelu 1998: 124). Likewise, where Dalits have gained legal admittance into temples and shops, the higher castes have frequently responded by building their own private places of worship or commerce. More insidiously, upper castes have sought to maintain clearly-defined boundaries between themselves and Dalits by retaining aspects of tradition that may no longer apply.

These subtle mechanisms for establishing caste difference were rendered visible when DPI activists made use of my presence to interview BC leaders in Kodankipatti and Lingyapatti. Initially the panchayat president of Kodankipatti was adamant that there was no discrimination in that village:

Murugan: Here we are educated, we know about caste problems and will not instigate them…. In this village when we worship God both SC people and we worship together (interview, 21 March 1999).

Shortly after speaking to Murugan, however, Palani Kumar (refered to as PK in this interview) and I interviewed a BC farmer from the village who presented a marginally different story. He claimed that few Dalits were employed in the village simply because there was no work for them and bemoaned the fact that he had to go into debt to pay his dues for the village festival:

> (P.K.): Do you not have common funds with which to worship the God?
> Valaichami (V): ... we have a tax.
> P.K.: You have a tax? Does everyone get asked to pay this?
> V: Yes, everyone.
> P.K.: Do you collect money from *everyone in this village*?
> V: They collect money from certain people and not from certain others.

The interview continued in this vein and the farmer admitted that not everyone in the village attended festivals. He cited 'tribals' as common absentees, but Palani Kumar continued to press him on the issue of tax:

> Author (H.G.): Do they allow SC people into the temple?
> V: Oh, it's not a big temple—it's very small. During important festivals only the vital people—only the priests and big people stand in the temple—whereas the others all have to stand outside and worship from outside.
> P.K.: Do SCs not join in these festivals.
> V: Oh yes they join in with everyone else.
> P.K.: But they do not get asked for tax?
> V: No, they don't give tax.

In both Kodankipatti and Lingyapatti it emerged that taxes for common village festivals were not collected from Dalits. When asked why this was the respondents said that it was because the Dalits were poor—this was later denied when it was pointed out that poor BCs still had to pay. Finally, Madhiarasan, an accountant from Lingyapatti said:

> If you ask why we do not collect taxes, why we generally collect taxes from everyone but not from them, it is because they do all the work, etc., in the village.

Dalits, in other words, were expected to pay in kind. Given the connotations attached to cash and kind payments (as seen in Chapter 3) in essence Dalits were required to mark themselves off as social inferiors. Indeed, when he was pressed further Madhiarasan insisted that:

> Here, if you change any of the old ways of doing things, problems arise. … If we change this, they will say: 'OK, you have changed this system, now why not change this?' Then things that shouldn't change will be questioned one after the other. Then problems will arise, very big problems. … They will turn around and say: 'so, you came to collect taxes but you don't give us respect.' They will ask for the deity to go to their houses (interview, 21 March 1999).

The exchange recounted here is instructive on several counts. It highlights the limits to the social acceptance of Dalits and the way in which even small markers of difference are invested with significance. For the BC interviewees the issue was clearly one of pride and respect: they had it and did not want to extend this to Dalits.[13] For Palani Kumar, likewise, the question was of the utmost importance. He kept pressing the question to reveal the extent of caste sentiment in the village and highlight the continuing inequalities in rural parts of the state. Caste prejudice is clearly deep-rooted and persistent. Although professional Dalits may be educated, erudite, clean and even vegetarian they are still seen as polluted as a result of their birth.[14] College students frequently spoke of 'good friends' whose houses they had never been invited to, and whose villages they cannot visit. In Kodankipatti, Balasubramaniam insisted that one of his college mates was foremost in the attack on the *cheri,* and that friendships could not survive the transition back to the village.

Women in Kodankipatti spoke movingly of the difficulties and daily insults that they faced. They recounted how caste-Hindus prevented them from gaining access to the common pond (*kanmai*), thus depriving them of their bathing, washing and toilet area. Most rural Dalits use the surrounding bushes and wastelands to relieve themselves

[13] See Pandian (2000) for an account of the social significance of 'respect' for BCs in Tamil Nadu.
[14] When B. Prasad, a Dalit judge in the Allahabad High Court retired, his successor insisted on cleansing the chamber with water from the Ganga before assuming office (Raj 1998: 149).

since facilities are either lacking or of poor quality. This means that villagers, especially women, are only able to go to the toilet in peace after sunset and before sunrise. In times of animosity between castes, the threat of sexual violence makes the experience even more uncomfortable. The use of wastelands or common property to build shanty-towns, or to go to the toilet may be said to 'privatise' the area in the sense that it becomes a place for 'private activities'. By prohibiting Dalits from this land, however, the higher castes are able to assert their power and claim the use of 'public' space for themselves. Prohibitions on access to common space in this manner invest the most private acts of ablution and defecation with political significance and all the attendant effects on self-esteem and dignity that this entails. The Dalits of Kodankipatti were, to all intents and purposes, reduced to inhabiting the small area of land around their houses. The struggle for social equality, in other words, is materially manifested in the access to and restrictions imposed upon land and space.

This became more apparent when the Dalits of Kodankipatti challenged their confinement and tried to show a film in the 'public' square of the village. The move started off a train of disputes that resulted in their precipitous flight from the village three months later. Goss (1996) observes the essential ambivalence of marketplaces as public spaces. They are restricted spaces, and yet at the same time they present spaces for politics and debate. This ambivalence was reflected in the dispute between the Dalits of Kodankipatti and the Kounders who form the dominant caste in the village. A week after they were prevented from screening a film, the Dalits protested about the weekly market that is held in the same venue. Given that it was held on public space, the Dalits argued, 'we should have been consulted and we should receive a share of the profits'. By asserting their right to a share of the proceeds the Dalits were claiming the village square as public space. Their demands were rejected by a dominant caste that used its monopoly on the sources of employment, provisions and space to exclude the Dalits. The fact that the challenge was made at all, however, illustrates Pandian's assertion that the BCs no 'longer exercise ideological hegemony over the Dalits in Tamil Nadu' (2000: 501).

'Public space', as Mitchell puts it, 'is always and inescapably a product of social negotiation and contest' (1996a: 131). The process of negotiation, however, does not occur between equals. The peace

committees that were organised, by the local government administration, to facilitate discussion between the opposing factions in
Kodankipatti may have provided a space for the exchange of ideas,
but they could not compel either side to act in good faith. 'Tight and
reasonable boundaries have to be drawn around public space' as
Mitchell notes, 'to retain it as a place open for public political activity'
(1996b: 153). The inability of the government to provide a framework
within which a solution could be agreed upon and enforced in
Kodankipatti and elsewhere places these spaces for negotiation under
threat. The basic issues involved are questions of control over space
and the power to determine access and usage of that space. 'The
exercise and maintenance of these sets of power relations', as Cope
observes, 'occur across space, through space, and require the use of
space as an element of control, opportunity and regulation' (1996:
187).

State, Movement and Caste in the Production of Locality

Metaphorically situated beyond the four *varnas*, Tamil Dalits are
usually physically located beyond the boundaries of the main village
or *oor*. Often deprived of a paved approach road or other modern
amenities such as electricity, piped water, toilets, hospitals or schools,
cheris play an important part in moulding the consciousness, expectations and opinions of their inhabitants. Reprimands, ostracism and
occasional beatings are administered by locally-dominant castes to
ensure that Dalit children learn the limits within which they must
remain. When Dalits recall their own awakening in consciousness,
they invariably refer back to some childhood episode in which they
were reproved for transgressing the bounds of acceptability, which
are often spatially demarcated. Typical of these was Palanivelu
Swamy, the SC/ST State Secretary of the BJP, who recounted several
stories about his realisation of caste consciousness:

> During the rainy season I was wearing some expensive new
> *chappals*. On my way home through the *oor*, a pot was overflowing
> at the tap so I moved it aside in order to wash my feet. When the
> lady who owned the pot returned she immediately slapped me.
> Having hit me she said: 'Why you dog! *Harijan* dog, parai dog! You

deign to come here with shoes on your feet and wash your feet here? Go to the pond and wash them you *****'. Saying which she hit me again. But the tap water was not 'good water' (purified) it was 'salt water', and whoever comes there can use it. I was 13 at that stage and somewhat mature so I would not have washed my feet otherwise. So, the reason why she hit me was that a *Harijan* boy had come wearing *chappals*, there was no wrongdoing on my part (interview, 10 April 1999).

He also recounted punishments for other minor transgressions of village rules. Despite the constitutional provisions against untouchability, caste-based social segregation is rigidly enforced by means of such low-key, day-to-day interventions. Indeed, it is in and through such practices that caste identities are formed. Such altercations are less common in the city, partly because communities are segregated already. Consequently, it may take longer for a caste consciousness to be established. Edwin, born and bred in Madurai, recalls that his first realisation of being an 'other' came in his first year in high-school, when all those receiving scholarships had to stand up. Although the criteria of the award were not announced the implication was that the recipient was from a low caste.

Similar issues of social exclusion and access faced rural Dalits, are perpetuated in the residential patterns of urban India.[15] While the issues of dependency and access to resources are not so prominent in cities, due to the availability of caste-neutral jobs, urban areas tend to be segregated on the basis of caste.[16] Bensman and Vidich (1995: 197) suggest that urban communities are voluntary in nature and

---

[15] Dalit '*bastis*', or slums, are often sited on land that has been 'encroached'; that is, public land that has been illegally occupied by the inhabitants. The rows of make-shift cardboard, corrugated iron and plastic sheeting huts are precarious abodes, subject to the multiple pressures of state clean up drives, police corruption and the forces of nature. Squatter settlements occasionally have the protection of local political parties, but their location is often susceptible to flooding, sited near rubbish tips, or under high voltage electricity pylons. The impermanent nature of the materials used in the construction process render such slums at great risk of fire, flood or high winds and rainstorms (Kannan 2000; Shiri 1998). The recurrent complaint of the Dalits in such areas is poverty.

[16] Having said this, in 1987–88, 33.4 per cent of the total population were below the poverty line whereas the percentage of SCs under the poverty line was 44.7 per cent. Source: Eighth Five-Year Plan, 1992–97 cited in *Thamukku* (1999: 4).

based on choice of dwelling, but there are powerful incentives and sanctions that determine such segregation and only by shrouding their origins are Dalits able to inhabit other areas. Vincent and Rosy, for instance, lived in the vicinity of one of the main cinemas in the heart of Madurai with their three children. Vincent was an artist in a nearby workshop and the children went to school locally. There was nothing to suggest that they were any different from their neighbours. Whilst this was a Dalit Christian family the posters of the Thevar *Peravai* in the surrounding streets identified the predominant caste constituency of the locality. 'We cannot say who we are', the family insisted, 'or we would not be able to live here' (interview, 20 August 1999). Dalits coming to the city for the first time gravitate towards those areas where their relatives live and are put off by the display of casteist political posters in other areas.

They may also experience difficulty in renting rooms from non-Dalit landlords who are wary of the reaction of others in the neighbourhood and often ask for recommendation letters as a means of screening residents. The family of who I speak had intimated that they were Nadars and kept themselves largely to themselves, but it is telling that they have subsequently moved out of the area. Urban neighbourhoods, thus, often create areas of intimate interaction whilst limiting contact with outsiders. The relationship between the neighbourhood and the space around it is perhaps best captured by the idiom of the inside–outside. Within a locality neighbours form bonds and relationships based on real or fictive kinship. They exchange goods, information, services and gossip in a day-to-day sense—borrowing flour or small amounts of money, looking after children, fetching water and so on. Where such bonds are not forged, as in the example discussed here, the neighbourhood can become an oppressive and fearful place to be.

The ties internal to such localities are evinced not only by the sense of community within the area, but in different codes of dress and other conventions of self-presentation. Dalit movement activists, thus, would wear *lungis* (informal waist-cloths) and T-shirts within the 'home', but would insist upon smarter attire before they entered public space. The notion of a 'home space' between the private and the public realms highlights the sense of belonging and security that are offered by such spaces. The democratic state, with its processes of participation, freedom of expression and association and the provision of human rights, does provide possibilities for meaningful social change. The continuing salience of caste in social and political life, however, should caution us against too facile an association of the alterations that are evident in the public sphere, with the more complex and contracted processes of change in the negotiation of public space on a local level.[17] Rather than deducing the existence of a liberal sphere of social relations from the fact of legislative change, we must attempt an 'ascending analysis of power, starting ... from its infinitesimal mechanisms' (Foucault 1983: 308, emphasis in the original).[18]

Continuing discrimination means that local movements often coalesce around immediate issues to do with living conditions: the demand for more land or permanent housing, demands for the provision of certain amenities and demands for legal recognition.[19] Such protest is, perforce, directed at the state and highlights the role of the government in the construction and mediation of public space. At a minimal level, slums and estates often declare allegiance to one particular party or candidate who they look to for protection and assistance. At election time, the candidates travel round the more established settlements making promises and canvassing for votes. The demands for urban services, the regularisation of land and the provision of jobs are some of the main ways through which politicians are able to establish patron–client networks. Such attention is sporadic and is concentrated around the moment of an election, but the semi-official recognition accorded to a settlement by the visit of a candidate may sanction the continued occupation of space and also serves to assimilate Dalit slums into the public sphere. Similarly, official promises of resettlement and re-housing for those whose homes are bull-dozed or swept away in floods symbolise the squatters' recognition as citizens who are entitled to residential space in the city. Even if these promises are subsequently forgotten, protestors seek the acceptance that they signal.

---

[17] I follow Mitchell here in declaring that the public sphere 'in Habermas' sense is a universal, abstract realm in which democracy occurs. The materiality of this sphere is, so to speak, immaterial to its functioning' (1995: 117).

[18] One of the primary criticisms of Habermas is that he neglects the significance of marginal forms of public discourse and activity, which are often in conflict with the bourgeois public sphere (Thompson 1994: 91).

[19] According to MIDS Working Paper 134: 30.9 per cent of SC households have electricity, as opposed to 61.3 per cent of non-SC households. 26.8 per cent of non-SC households have sanitation, whereas only 9.8 per cent of SC houses do. (*Thamukku* 1999: 2).

More permanently, the state is involved in providing housing for the SCs. Such constructions are seen not only as a resource— especially by the homeless street-dwellers who aspire towards more permanent dwellings—but also as a means of regulation and control. The sites selected for such houses are frequently undesirable or outside the city and the main areas of employment. The housing boards in the heart of the city tend to be reserved for those engaged in 'municipal work' (cleaning, sweeping and scavenging) and occu- pancy is predicated on at least one member of the family remaining in council employment. As such, the housing blocks constitute both an opportunity and a limitation, and serve to re-forge a link between employment and caste. Dalit movement orators frequently turn their critical gaze on the houses provided for them by the government. They see them as reproducing the very inequalities that they are trying to eradicate. If such developments were really intended to advance the uplift of the Dalits they argue, they would not be built with sloped roofs that prevent the addition of another storey. The typical 'Dalit house' has one room constructed from concrete with a little toilet at the back. The door is usually a sheet of cast iron that makes the houses unbearably hot in the daytime, but relatively cool at night. There are no open windows, only patterned grids that look out onto similar constructions. In other words, the government persists in the construction of colonies, rather than creating spaces for the free interaction of all castes and communities.

Neighbourhoods, according to Appadurai (1995: 215), are ideally the 'stages for their own self-production', and yet the ideological commitments of a ruling party frequently induce them to engage in the construction of localities. The samathuvarpuram (equality village) project is just such an enterprise. Hailing the scheme as a giant leap forward in the fight against caste, the Government of Tamil Nadu accelerated the construction of samathuvarpurams across the state (although reports in early 2001 suggested that the DMK had aban- doned the scheme). Built along similar lines to the Dalit colonies, these villages are peopled by members of different castes, with the intention of producing a truly casteless society. The imposition, from above, of these mixed-caste villages, attempts to by-pass the gradual processes required to breakdown caste prejudice. Without spaces and incentives for interaction to enable different caste members to question their feelings of distrust and hostility, however, the villages can only provide houses for individuals—they cannot foster a sense of community. The scheme has, therefore, been criticised for being little more than window-dressing. The projects do constitute an attempt to break the caste-based segregation of society, but they highlight the difficulties involved in any attempt to impose a sense of equality and unity. 'Liberty is a practice', as Foucault insists (1993: 162). Material and legal changes, in other words, can never guarantee liberty or equality.

The problem inherent in the state's attempt to create the space for a casteless society is that it ignores the multiple processes of negotiation and discussion that go into the production of a locality. 'The work of producing neighbourhoods—life-worlds constituted by relatively stable associations, by relatively known and shared histories, and by collectively traversed and legible spaces and places—is often at odds with the projects of the nation-state' (Appadurai 1995: 215). To expect community feeling to emerge from mere proximity is misguided. The people who enter a samathuvarpuram are not isolated individuals. Each has been shaped by their social upbringing, which they do not leave behind at the gates of the settlement. The transformation of this mixed residential space into a meaningful place would require a 'conscious moment' to bring people together. Architecture can only produce positive effects, as Foucault argues, 'when the liberating intentions of the architect coincide with the real practice of the people' (1993: 163). The fissures that have appeared in the walls of the samathuvarpuram houses are symbolic of the fragility of the scheme that neglects the root causes of caste conflict (Illangovan 2000a).

The flags, painted boards and posters that adorn the walls of Dalit residential areas, by contrast, pay testimony to the upsurge in Dalit movement activity and emphasise the fragility of the status quo. The assertive images of wild cats and weaponry testify to Dalit rejections of established society and threaten imminent disorder unless there is social change. The process that Cohen (1985) refers to as the 'symbolic construction of community' is certainly central to the work of the DPI and other movements. The emblems of competing movements and parties offer people multiple ways of imagining and positioning themselves in society. 'Spatiality', according to Soja, situates life in an active arena. 'To be alive is to participate in the social production of space, to shape and be shaped by a constantly evolving spatiality which constitutes and concretizes social action and relationships' (1985: 90). Spaces and places are not fixed or immutable in any sense. Everyday social relations create space and are also structured by it. When members of the Ambedkar People's Movement walked down 'high-caste' streets with their shoes on in the 1970s, they were not only challenging the dominance of the local caste landlords, they were establishing a claim to physical space and their rights as members of a democratic polity. The importance of spatial location is reflected in the emphasis that movements give to the term '*cheri*' as they attempt to forge an 'imagined community' of '*cheri* people' to fight against caste.

Lefebvre distinguished between *representational* spaces (social, lived space, space in use) and *representations* of space (planned, imposed, controlled space) (1991: 45). Spaces usually start as the latter, such as the innumerable housing blocks and colonies con-structed for the Dalits by the local and state governments, and become the first as people move in, add makeshift extensions and inhabit the place. This transition of spaces into places, as Appadurai notes, usually 'requires a conscious moment'—such as a house-warming ceremony—'which may subsequently be remembered as relatively routine' (1995: 209). The production of locality, however, is not a 'once-and-for-all' process, but must be constantly renewed and revised to match the changing nature of its constituency. Rituals that contribute to a sense of community are especially salient in this process. 'Insofar as neighbourhoods are imagined, produced and maintained against some sort of ground (social, material, environ-mental) they also require and produce contexts, against which their own intelligibility takes shape' (Appadurai 1995: 209).

Many Dalits in rural Tamil Nadu still live in outlying settlements and Dalit movements refer to urban slums and estates as *cheris* in a rhetorical assertion of continuing inequality. One of the most prominently cited reasons for Dalit protest is the perceived repression of an imagined community of *cheri*-dwellers. Such rhetoric estab-lishes a link between the contemporary experience of social exclusion and older forms of inequality. The *cheri* construct is not only important as a reminder of common exclusion, however, since the relative social homogeneity of such areas in caste terms means that they can be cast as havens of security and strength in a caste-dominated society. The *cheri*, as we have seen, effectively operates as an extension of the domicile in a politicised distinction between the home and the world. This notion of a home space in turn renders it necessary to delineate clear boundaries between the inside and the outside. Across Tamil Nadu, therefore, Dalit movements have sought to establish territories precisely through a process of boundary marking and guarding.

The dynamic nature of social space is evident in the way that movements have succeeded in re-fashioning Dalit settlements. The open assertion of allegiance to a movement and the aggressive imagery of the murals have served to re-cast *cheris* as centres of resistance and social change. Of course, it is not just Dalit movements that are attempting to refashion *cheris* and their inhabitants. The democratic state, in its avowed commitment to eradicate caste discrimination, is also concerned with projects of social reform as we have seen. The organic nature of social movement constructions—where *cheri*-dwellers alter their identity and the space in which they live over a period of time and in association with a wider project—however, contrasts dramatically with state-led versions of an alternative society. In what follows it is not the conditions of life that I want to focus on so much as the means by which social space is contested, constructed and endowed with significance by movement action.

Flying the Flag: The Assertion of Political Space

The multiple markers of political association with which I opened this chapter highlight the contested nature of public space. A Dalit movement's claims to territory, in other words, are not passively accepted. They are questioned, contested, endorsed or ignored by the residents and must be constantly renewed and re-asserted.[20] The Dalit community is not only divided by caste, but also along gender, class and age lines. A Dalit élite has prospered, but they are commonly accused of neglecting the 'community' as a whole and of being content with carving out a niche for themselves and their families, often retiring to plush housing and safer neighbourhoods. By contrast to the mobility strategies of the élite, Dalit movements are fundamentally concerned with gaining *equal* access to public space for all. This struggle is carried forward on a number of different

[20] Anandhi (2000) and Pandian (2000) rightly highlight the significance of these symbolic aspects within the Dalit struggle.

levels. On the one hand, there is the physical occupation of material space by protestors engaged in meetings, hunger-fasts, rallies and road-blockades.[21] This is a political assertion of citizenship and the right to protest.

On the other hand, there is the symbolic or cultural approach involving the construction of Ambedkar statues, the naming of residential areas as 'Ambedkar *Nagar*', the raising of movement flags, the celebration of Ambedkar's birthday, the publication of Dalit magazines and the production of Dalit art festivals. More subtle expressions of this determination for public recognition are witnessed in the choice of names such as Ambedkar for Dalit children, a determination to do well in school and the use of Western clothes that have no caste connotations. Each of these ventures is an attempt to realise the metaphorical spaces provided in the public sphere, and an attempt to register their existence and protest in everyday public consciousness. The TTS, for example, has long had a bookshop that sells books on and by Dalits, but it is located within a private institution. It was with a great sense of achievement, therefore, that the convenor of the Dalit Resource Centre, Alex, opened a bookshop, *Ezhuthu* (Letters), in a complex in the city centre. The bookshop was devoted to the sale of Dalit books and novels, and established Dalit literature on the map of the city. Such incursions into public space are significant in the struggle for social inclusion.

By far the most common manifestation of this concern with marking public space, however, is the erection of movement insignia. The emblems of political and social organisations are legion in India—every fan club devoted to a film star, for example, has a flag. It is not the emblems that matter, therefore, but the prominence accorded to them, the meanings they hold and their relative ability to maintain or enhance their visibility. The significance of aesthetics cannot be ignored. Hence, fading paint on a board indicates decline, whereas glossier images are suggestive of a movement's ascendance.

---

[21] As far as I am aware, the route-ing of Dalit rallies does not pose the difficulties associated with Hindu/Muslim demonstrations. The Dalit movements are seen as politically sensitive, rather than communally problematic. Huge numbers of police are present, therefore, and permission for rallies is often denied but that is to do with more vaguely defined 'law and order' problems.

In 1999, movement activists in Melavassel claimed that the political parties were 'only there for show' and that their popularity derived more from the patronage they were able to dispense than from political conviction. The secrecy of the ballot renders such claims hard to verify but informal conversations with people from different organisations in the estate served to confirm the primacy of the DPI.

An accident in 2002 afforded an opportunity to tentatively assess the validity of this impression. A lorry crashed through the boundary wall by the main entrance destroying the 'halls' of the AIADMK, the DMK, the Communist Party and the DPI—all of whom have a presence within Melavassel—as well as knocking down the DPI board. This gave the differing parties in Melavassel a chance to renegotiate the division of space and stake out their claims to dominance in the locality. In the event the entire section of the reconstructed wall was daubed in the colours of the DPI and proclaimed the area's allegiance to Thirumavalavan. I do not wish to suggest that the political opinions of a locality can be so obviously read off its graffiti, but 'appearances *are* important', as Bourdieu states, 'the concessions of *politeness* always contain *political* concessions' (cited in Scott 1985: 283, emphasis in the original).

Social movements and political parties, thus, are critically involved in the construction of 'home spaces' like Melavassel. The relational and political nature of movement activity is illustrated by the very symbols that mark its presence in an area. Flagpoles, colours, posters and paintings constitute 'part of a "twilight zone of communication", an outlet for often deeply felt but rarely articulated sentiments and attitudes' (Ley and Cybriwsky 1974: 492). In the functioning of a movement or a party, such symbols play an important role in marking off a defended neighbourhood. Dalits in Madurai cited deterrence as one of the primary reasons for joining an aggressive movement like the DPI. Time and again they would point to the flag of their movement as the object that stood between them and violent retaliation on the part of aggressors. This function is only possible because the emblems of the movements are widely recognised. They serve to identify an outpost of a much larger, socially imagined community that will intervene on behalf of its members. Even where these communities are literally *imagined*, as when the movement is little more than a banner, the movement insignia suggests a wider membership. This outward orientation militates against the division of society into independent enclaves from which they emerge only at great risk. 'Public social movements', as Mitchell puts it, 'understand that they must create spaces for representation' (1995: 124).

Consequently, the induction of a locality into a movement or party is symbolised by the flag-raising ceremony. This obscures the processes by which people choose to affiliate themselves to a movement by attending various meetings, speaking to activists and reading papers and journals. It also neglects the painstaking leg-work of key activists who visit areas that have expressed an interest in joining the movement, explain what it stands for, answer questions and get a sense of any problems that need to be resolved. These activists also have to canvass for support and collect money or recruit workers to have a board painted or a flag-pole erected. A site must then be chosen on the periphery of the locality where these emblems can be directed outwards and mark the boundaries of movement influence. The flag-raising marks the culmination of this process and constitutes a joyous affirmation of allegiance. A general meeting is advertised amongst movement members and the public announcing the occasion. On the given day a series of speeches culminates in the leader of the movement unveiling the colours or raising the flag.

Whether the majority of people in a given place support the movement or not, the unveiling of colours marks that area off as an outpost of the given group. As such, planting the flag requires at least the tacit consent of the residents. This is especially the case in rural areas, where such acts of resistance can have severe repercussions. In a very real sense the banners act to re-fashion the self-identity and outward image of a community. Raising the flag of an established party suggests a degree of conformity, political connections and a concomitant conservatism. The tricolour of the DPI, by contrast, suggests radicalism, rejection of hierarchy and desire for change. Ideally the ceremony is a time for celebration. Residents of Melavassel still remember the day of their flag-raising ceremony in 1997. Dhanam, the 20-year-old sister of Palani Kumar, recalled the excitement that the occasion generated: 'There were so many people that we completely blocked off the road for two hours or something, and then Annan [Thirumavalavan] came into Melavassel and visited each house and met the people' (interview, 3 July 1999).

The importance of face-to-face contact with movement leaders cannot be emphasised enough. Perhaps the most symbolic act of an area's induction into a movement is the leader's perambulation through the locality to meet with the people. I say 'symbolic' advisedly, because the leader rarely stays long enough to really get to know the inhabitants. Going to people's houses, asking them about their concerns and partaking of their hospitality are all means by which the leaders of Dalit movements emphasise their commitment and inscribe themselves in the hearts and minds of their constituents. The leader's visit reinforces the sense of community evoked by movement emblems and gives people a sense that their views are being represented. Supporters and sceptics alike are brought together through these means and the sense of unity projected to the external world is given slightly more credence because everyone in an area has met and listened to the leader of a movement.

The flag-raising ceremony, thus, lays claim to an area, but it is also a performance that brings people together. The party lights, loudspeakers, convoys of followers and paintings or flags are designed not only to cement the adherence of a locality to the movement, but also to broadcast this fact to others. It serves both as a warning and as an invitation. It constitutes a warning in the sense that potential aggressors and political rivals are informed that this area is affiliated to a particular movement which will not stand idly by if they are attacked. The presence of a movement implies the existence of informed cadres who know the legal ropes and have the resources to bring cases before a court or to raise the public profile of an incident. At the same time, however, it is also an invitation in the sense that the material is all directed outwards; other Dalits or other oppressed groups can come to such an area for aid.

This emphasises the importance of material public space as an arena in which different people can communicate with each other. The difference in emphasis between the resistant peasants of Scott's (1985, 1990) work, and the activities of social movements, is that the latter are not content to carve out a small breathing space for themselves within the established social structure. Rather, they demand access to the genuine political spaces of any given society. Dalit movements are not content with defending *cheris* against attacks, they are actively seeking to alter the social conditions that give rise to such oppression. The logic of this enterprise dictates an approach that is geared towards the public at large rather than their community alone. This logic is encapsulated in the pasting of posters on buses. Ley and Cybriwsky note the examples of graffiti artists who spray-paint their images in the heart of opposition territory. They refer to this as a 'conquest of territory', and insist that 'to claim access to an inaccessible location is to make a claim of primacy for oneself' (1974: 494).

Such acts are always performed 'for an audience', however, and it is this aspect that strikes me as being most significant for social movements. The presence of a Dalit poster in the heart of the city, in an upper-caste location, or on the sides of buses travelling around the area, is not so much an expression of the power to claim territory as an assertion of the ability to communicate. Such advertisements not only attract more supporters to an event, but also inform countless onlookers about the issues in question. Public space, as Ruddick insists, is 'the active medium for the construction of new class cultures ... or the place where marginalised identities can be challenged' (1996: 135). These incursions into public space ensure that Dalit resistance is neither muted nor contained. Occupation of public space, as Berman puts it, 'can both compel and empower all these people to see each other, not through a glass darkly, but face to face' (in Ruddick 1996: 134).

As we have seen, the emblems of political parties pronounce their presence in settlements across the state. Mimicking the standards of established institutions or following an established repertoire of action, enables easy recognition but it also highlights the fact that Dalits now have autonomous organisations and their own areas of influence. The boards and flags assert the existence of an alternative. The flag-raising ceremony of a Dalit movement, in this perspective, becomes the conscious moment in which a living space is transformed into a political place. 'As a symbolic violation of the social order, such a movement attracts and will continue to attract attention, to provoke censure and to act ... as the fundamental bearer of significance' (Hebdige 1979: 19). The identity of a slum or *cheri* that has affiliated itself to a Dalit movement is qualitatively different from one that remains unmoved by the struggle. Erecting the emblem of a movement in a place marks the end of obedience (though not necessarily the end of fear) and the beginning of an organised struggle against inequality.

The importance of symbols of assertion is central, therefore, but they do not stand alone and nor can they operate outside a specific context. As well as charting the symbolic construction of community, we need an understanding of the processes and practices that give such signifiers meaning. As with state-sponsored attempts at social transformation, we must look beyond the material indicators of change and ask how the various movements are embedded within communities as well as marking them off from others. The construction of space, it is clear, must be *social* as well as material, must be lived as well as planned. Although most Dalit movements succeed in spanning the divide between rural and urban constituencies, the heartlands of Dalit activity are in urban and semi-urban areas.

Protest, as shown in Chapters 3 and 4, is a risky undertaking and urban environments provide greater degrees of support, security and employment. Added to this are the practical difficulties of communicating with far flung outposts of the movement, especially given the fact that few, if any, DPI members had phone lines or e-mail access. The Liberation Panthers, according to Thirumavalavan, were built on the back of a single pager on which the leader could be reached. Each local ward at least has access to a phone. In one or two instances, a DPI office was established in a rented room, furnished with pictures of Thirumavalavan and Ambedkar and provided with a phone. In the Madurai office, near Anna bus-stand, however, the phone was frequently idle whilst activists collected money for the bills. It was more common for each 'cell' to have an agreement with a phone booth operator. These agreements are common in Tamil Nadu, and it is standard practice for phone operators to inform customers that they have a call. Another factor that conspires to give the movement an urban bias is the urban location of government and media offices where petitions may be handed over, demonstrations held and statements issued.

The DPI is consequently built around core cells in the Dalit populated areas of urban Tamil Nadu. As shown in Chapter 1, despite the established structure of command the various movement areas are linked to each other and to the leadership through a network of informal ties. The most formal aspect of the relationship, during my fieldwork, was the distribution of flyers for protest events. Local leaders/contact people received information of the main meetings through the post and were expected to inform their neighbours and local group. For particularly large demonstrations or shows of force these figures would be leant on to ensure a large turnout. In the run-up to large meetings, therefore, the chain of leadership is activated and district secretaries, city leaders and coordinators make the rounds to drum up support. The further afield from the centres one goes, the looser the links between cells become—until they are delicately maintained by threads of trust, informal visits by members and the occasional notice sent by mail. In such areas, the DPI appears to exist more as a supportive concept and symbolic assertion of resistance than as a meaningful movement. It is to the cities that we must turn, therefore, to understand the workings of the movement before we can trace its wider operation.

Melavassel: The Movement in Context

As a stronghold of the movement in the centre of Madurai, Melavassel is a good place to start such an examination. Whilst the estate is architecturally similar to countless others in urban India, its social composition has rendered it an important site for the work of Dalit movements. Whilst the locality in itself fosters interaction and a sense of community among the residents, the movements have mediated the relations between Melavassel and those outside. Events—such as a riot in 1995 in which residents protested against the arrest of a DPI speaker—have, in effect, redefined the boundaries, and the socio-political significance, of the estate. Here, I wish to explore the processes by which these redefinitions of social space were and are accomplished. *Thideer Nagar* or Melavassel is a housing estate for municipal employees in the centre of Madurai, adjacent to the central bus-stand.[22] In examining the operations of the movement in relation to this specific locality I hope to present a clearer picture of the spatial bases and practices of the movement.

Despite the fact that most residents are government workers, the nature of their occupations—cleaning, sweeping, rubbish collection—means that the inhabitants are all Dalits. The estate consists mainly of crumbling three-storey buildings clustered around paved open spaces. The flats are not extraordinary or distinct from other such units save that many of them are in a state of acute dilapidation. Even in this respect, Melavassel is not much different from other cheap housing. The estate is bounded by three walls, abutting onto the main road into town, the Thiruvalur coach stand and a rough

---

[22] *Thideer Nagar* refers to the official name of the housing site, whereas Melavassel (which means west gate) is the most used term and refers to the location of the locality.

area of open land. Along the remaining boundary of the estate runs a thick, black and stinking river of open sewage. Make-shift cattle byres and some mud and coconut matting houses line its banks and the stench and the mosquitoes seem unbearable to most visitors. The flats abutting the sewer are in the worst condition, with rising damp making the electrical connections highly dangerous and with shelves and balcony walls in a state of near collapse. When one person died, after a balcony wall collapsed under their weight there was talk of re-housing the occupants. As is often the case, however, the relocation plans proposed moving the inhabitants outside the city and further away from shops and jobs and so people campaigned to remain in *situ*.[23]

All the inhabitants of Melavassel are Dalits but most of them derive more narrowly from the Arundadhiar (Chakkiliyar) or Paraiyar communities, since few other castes are prepared to engage in municipal cleaning work. Although most government jobs are in high demand due to the conditions and pay, Dalits still constitute the vast majority of those at this bottom end of the employment scale. Workers and activists alike often argue that this work helps account for the high incidence of alcoholism amongst Dalit men, but people here at least have a regular income and a house to live in and the wives of drunken workers contest such suggestions with vehemence. To reside in the quarters one member of the resident's family must work for the corporation. People may be asked to leave after they retire unless a member of their family succeeds them in corporation employment. In lieu of rent Rs 200 is subtracted from each worker's salary. Those who cannot get a place in the quarters are given an additional Rs 200 in their salary, but given the cost of commercial rents this is far from adequate.[24] Within the compound it is clear that many people sub-let flats or parts of their flats in order to raise extra income.

Melavassel is a prime example of an 'urban enclave' or neighbourhood. Due to the caste constituency of its residents it is known as a Dalit 'colony' and it reproduces, in many ways, the

---

[23] There is a fund for repair works extracted from the resident's rent, but residents insist that this fund is never used. They suggest that it is siphoned off by corrupt middle-men.

[24] Rents for similar dwellings in the commercial sector could range from Rs 500 up to Rs 1,500 depending on the location of the flat.

traditional seclusion of the (ex) Untouchable community. The population of Melavassel is fairly stable. Most of the people living in the colony came from surrounding villages around 30 years ago. Many like Palani Kumar have lived there all their lives and see little prospect of moving out unless they are forced to leave. Several people moved in to Melavassel whilst I was there, either due to marriage or to stay with relatives whilst they established themselves in work and sought a different place to stay. There is now a broad generational divide between the older (45 +) generation who have close links and family in rural Tamil Nadu, and a younger, urbanised group for whom Madurai is home. Whilst the younger generation may maintain links with relatives in rural areas, they are more likely to forge bonds of friendship with residents of other *cheris* in the city. Movement members, especially, have forged links with groups throughout the city and frequently visited each other.

Melavassel mirrors the endemic divisions amongst Tamil Dalits. During elections the estate was decked out in the banners of all the main parties in a visual affirmation of heterogeneity and each party had booths outside the main entrance canvassing for votes. Also, alongside the DPI, there is a branch of the Tamizhaga Arundhadiar Youth Front (TAYF).[25] Despite the fact that one is largely a Paraiyar movement and the other mostly Chakkiliyar, relations between the two were amicable. There were even reports of marriages between the two castes, but the differing movements highlight that Melavassel is far from homogeneous. Furthermore, people perform different jobs and earn differing amounts. The majority of the inhabitants are municipal employees at the lowest end of the scale—sweepers and cleaners. The pay that they receive is reasonable, between Rs 2000 and Rs 4000 a month, but the conditions that they work in are difficult. A significant number of inhabitants perform similar tasks, but are not municipal employees. Rag and bone merchants, paper-pickers and self-employed cleaners or scavengers are preponderant in the houses leading into the estate and tricycles piled high with

[25] One of the archways into Melavassel was painted with the emblems and name of the TAYF. This board was getting old and the paint was somewhat faded in a visual representation of the movement's decline. When I visited Madurai again in 2002, however, the board had been repainted and the fortunes of the TAYF were said to be on the up since its electoral merger with the Bahujan Samaj Party.

re-cycled waste often blocked the main approach. Each of the houses nearest the entrance has a backyard which is used to house livestock or store the gathered materials. In the multi-storey buildings occupations vary. There are teachers, sales representatives, auto-drivers and shop assistants. They leave the estate to work all round the city, but rarely move out to other dwellings. Many housewives seek to supplement the household wage through petty vending. As a result of this diversity some of the flats are well furnished and have modern conveniences like fridges and televisions, but others are more or less bare. The less well-off occupy the buildings abutting the open sewer which are in the worst condition.

The open spaces planned by the architects for the heart of the building complex have become the site of rubbish heaps, flea markets, public toilets and livestock. Cattle and goats foul the streets and can be found in some of the blocks of flats, and anyone with anything to sell sets up a stall to hawk home-made *dosai* (rice pancakes), rice and lentils, or cheap sweets, trinkets and fruit. The area is, in every sense a contradiction of the 'bourgeois sense of what it meant for a space to be a modern city', and the governing conventions, and paternalistic state regulations have been inverted to create the 'loose disorder' of a village (Kaviraj 1997a: 84). This inversion is functional, however, in the sense that it provides a sense of community, cheap food, affordable commodities and, in the case of livestock, added income for the inhabitants.[26] People gather in this area to talk, children run about and play in the space and a crèche has been established. Non-residents view Melavassel with disregard; what they fail to appreciate is the functional nature of the apparent disorder.

Melavassel is not only delineated by the walls surrounding it, in other words, but also by the stigma attached to its inhabitants. The stigma is not completely a result of 'traditional' antipathies and caste sentiment, because Melavassel residents have a particular and unsavoury reputation in the present day too. When I first began my fieldwork I was attracted to the striking images of Dalit movement activity in the area but was warned against going into the locality by friends. Indeed, on my first visit to Melavassel I was greeted by

---

[26] Such spaces constitute what Foucault refers to as a *heterotopia*: an 'actually lived and socially created spatiality, concrete and abstract at the same time, the habitus of social practices' (Soja 1993[1989]: 143).

a group of men, some of whom were the worse for drink who asserted their willingness to engage in violence for their leader in a show of bravado intended to impress the vitality of the movement upon me:

> Truly it can be said that Tamil Nadu could not withstand the backlash if Thirumavalavan was arrested. Now we are prepared to fight. In each house there is an *aruval* (machete/scythe) this long for men and a smaller hook for women. We have conducted struggles against high caste Hindus and the police and we are not afraid of anyone (Perumal, DPI activist, 8 March 1999).

Riots and drunken brawls have given the area a reputation for violence but many more are put off by the squalor of some parts of the estate. The common depictions of lower-class Dalits cast them as idle, dirty, ignorant and violent. The poorly maintained, squalid and unhygienic appearance of the estate confirms, at first sight, the accusations of reproving reformers that the 'Dalits do not help themselves'. The discursive constructions of Melavassel serve both to deter outsiders from entering, but also to create a sense of unity amongst the inhabitants.[27] The surrounding walls, thus, are merely the concrete representations of social narratives that present Melavassel as a coherent and unsavoury locality. In this regard it is typical of the way in which Dalit estates or slums are perceived and represented. It is in the context of such communities, and in the face of such (mis)representations of them, that Dalit movements are seeking to reshape social space.

The earlier description of Melavassel as a 'home space', and the prominence of the DPI, should not, however, deceive us into thinking that it was an arena of intimate interaction for all residents. The estate was, as we have seen, divided along multiple fault-lines. Furthermore, there were personal quarrels and disagreements, family feuds and mutual indifference between many residents. The residents were certainly not united in their support for the DPI. Many of the older inhabitants especially regarded the movement as too radical, as giving the locality an unsavoury image or as attracting trouble. Melavassel may still be regarded as a movement stronghold, however,

---

[27] For example, I was more readily accepted by inhabitants when I pointed out that my friend's grandparents lived in one of the flats and, afterwards, when I had made friends with the residents.

for a multiplicity of reasons. First, the movement did have many adherents in the estate even though most were peripheral members who turned up for occasional meetings rather than being full-time activists. Second, a key group of committed activists, centred round Palani Kumar, were deeply involved in movement activity. In combination with the central location of the estate this meant that the locality frequently played host to movement members and leaders. Following the earlier discussion, however, perhaps the most important factor is the fact that the movement had inscribed itself onto the physical space of the estate and into the social imaginings of Melavassel. The public and publicist visual signifiers established a metonymical relationship between the movement and the locality to such a degree that, as we have seen, strangers approached the estate in the expectation that they would receive assistance.

The DPI had gained prominence in the estate due to the activities of a core group of young men. They had been attracted by the rhetorical radicalism of the movement and attended several meetings in other parts of the city. As they became more and more involved with the DPI they sought to persuade others of its supremacy. Palani Kumar, for instance, recalls being taken along to meet Thirumavalavan by members of this group. The activists also held meetings and speeches in the locality. At one such event in 1995 an altercation with an off-duty policeman led to the arrest of Palani Kumar. Rather than abandon him to his fate, the movement members gathered a crowd together, marched to the police station and demolished an outside wall in their demands for his release. The papers described the incident as a riot that emphasised the unruly nature of the estate, but for the residents it was a moment in which internal differences were overcome. Palani Kumar and others like him joined the movement at this time rather than being put off by it. By the time that the flag-raising ceremony occurred, therefore, the movement was recognised as a force in the locality and had an active following.

Movement allegiance cannot be sustained by such dramatic events, however, and the DPI had also filtered into the day-to-day activities of the estate. The auto-rickshaw drivers by the main entrance had erected a board proclaiming this to be the 'Ambedkar Auto-Stand'. The drivers often joined in movement related conversations and their auto-rickshaws were the transport of choice for members. It was also habitual for people to drop by Palani Kumar's house to chat about issues or simply socialise. The conversations ranged over many unrelated topics, but the choice of venue and the pattern of interaction had been established by the DPI. Where the movement is strong and well organised it has set up tuition centres for Dalit school children. This has happened in SMP Colony on the outskirts of Madurai and in some satellite villages, but Melavassel had yet to provide such facilities. The local DPI leaders did, however, act as a first port of call for minor disputes. Legal cases are discussed, and papers filled out, by members who have acquired a modicum of legal knowledge by fighting cases on behalf of the movement. Palani Kumar was frequently called upon to write letters of complaint or accompany people to the courts or police station. This is partly a function of his education but primarily an indication that he knows the ropes. Activists of the DPI throughout the state play this role and serve to mediate between institutions (usually the state) and individuals.

It was also reported by several people that the DPI held informal courts or mediation services. Rather than turning family quarrels or neighbourhood disputes into police cases these are brought to the local organiser of the DPI who sits in judgement, hears both sides, and seeks to reconcile the two parties. Such mediation was reasonably commonplace, but it was further asserted that the movement sometimes fines wrongdoers and appropriates the money for the movement. Palani Kumar was certainly presented with problems of this nature and his word was listened to, but I was never in a position to witness the imposition of fines or other punishments. From time to time the police themselves send petty cases to local leaders to be resolved without acrimony and the DPI in Melavassel had sufficient social standing to take them on board. This is not a feature of the movement per se—since other organisations fulfil a similar function elsewhere (Dietrich, personal communication)—but it is an indication of the movement's assimilation into the fabric of the estate. Palani Kumar says that 'people in Melavassel bring their problems to me and I give "honest judgements". The people there listen to me and heed my judgement (*kattupaadu*)'.

The social component of movement activity extends to more personal matters too, as politics permeates Tamil society. The DPI, therefore, undertakes all the social responsibilities and duties of the more established parties. The names of prominent members are emblazoned on the guest-lists of movement weddings and leaders are asked to grace various family and social functions with their presence. The result is that such celebrations ultimately resemble movement meetings rather than weddings, house-warmings or engagements. The posters that habitually display the names of a bride and groom, for example, give prominence to pictures of Ambedkar or the leader of the DPI and the invited guests are supplemented by members who turn up to see their leaders rather than the happy couple. It is this concern with publicising the movement and broadcasting its presence in an area that we must return to as the most significant aspect of a Dalit movement's re-creation of locality. Melavassel constitutes a DPI stronghold for all the stated reasons, but it is the physical and visible markers of belonging that best capture the significance of space for Dalit movements and their attempts to reshape it.

Perhaps the most striking example of this comes from the inhabitants of 'Jansi Rani Complex' in the heart of Madurai, who do not have proper homes to live in. Makeshift tents on the pavement provide shelter, the river is their bathroom and the concourse of a Hindu shrine provides their meeting space. Working as rag and bone merchants, or as self-employed cleaners of drains they eke out a living on the road. The walls of the shrine where they gather, however, have been painted with the images of the DPI: Ambedkar stares out at the dismal scene and ranged alongside him are likenesses of Thirumavalavan and a panther. 'They are there as a security measure', Alagar, a middle-aged man, slightly the worse for drink, insists. 'To guard against people or against police raids that come at night to drag us away' (interview, 23 March 1999). The residents here do not refer to the mural as a protective charm, but they emphasise the power behind the painting. As Sekhar, a good-looking youngster in his early 20s who has lived in Jansi Rani Complex all his life, says, 'it is only after joining this movement that we can be here undisturbed. Before, there were countless caste clashes and continuous police harassment, but now if he (Thirumavalavan) raises his hand Madurai District will be destroyed' (interview, 23 March 1999).

Melavassel may be a presented as a Dalit 'ghetto', therefore, but it is far from being isolated. Time and again the flags, statues and posters of the DPI were referred to as both a deterrent and an indication that a community does not stand alone. 'There are forty cheris in Madurai depending on SMP colony', as one DPI activist in a Madurai suburb put it, 'and SMP colony is dependent on 40 cheris' (interview, 23 March 1999). Each branch of the movement in Madurai, thus, is perceived as part of a wider network of people who are linked by shared ideals, common fears and ties of friendship cemented at each successive meeting in the city. These branches thus constitute 'pockets of solidarity'. The 'assertive or aggressive graffiti' that are markers of resistance, however, 'represent more than attitudes. They are dispositions to behaviour, and as such impress a bolder outline on the fuzzy transition between perception and action' (Ley and Cybriwsky 1974: 505). The domination of a neighbourhood by one organisation can inspire participation in movement activity, but it can also result in the creation of a counter-community and may lead to violence (Bensman and Vidich 1995: 198). Declaring allegiance to a movement does not necessarily generate security.

Contested Space: Exclusion, Envy and Violence

Assertive slogans resound through the speeches and literature of many Dalit movements exhorting their followers to 'return a blow for a blow'. 'Spring into action, make your enemies tremble', declaims one Liberation Panther catch-phrase, 'plan for the morrow and arise with courage. Escape your fears and set out with resolve [repeated], fall upon your foes like a bolt of thunder [repeated]'. 'If you kill one of us', Sathai 'Bomb' Baikiaraj exclaims, 'we will kill four of you!' Such slogans reflect both the attitudes of a younger more radical generation as well as constituting an inducement to action. The riots in Bodi in 1993 (cf. Alm 1996: 116) were partly set off because the upper castes felt threatened by the violence of the Dalit chants. At some DPI meetings it was apparent that several of those in attendance were bored by the speeches and wanted to resort to direct action. The assertion–action ratio, however, was blurred by the reaction of the other castes to the symbols of Dalit consciousness.

It was often hard to tell whether movement membership predisposed Dalits to assertive action, or whether the mere presence of banners incited the wrath of the dominant castes and led them to initiate confrontation. A flag of defiance without a movement behind it is like a red rag to a bull in areas where caste tensions are already high. The marking of public or private space, is a poor substitute for its occupation and maintenance, and events are a poor substitute for the process of building a movement. 'The DPI is only here in name', the villagers of Vadianpatti complained, and the inhabitants of Allalaberi said that their needs were neglected in the absence of the DLM. In the face of upper-caste aggression, the Dalits of Kodankipatti were unable to defend their claims to autonomy and they fled their village when attacked, leaving the flagpole of the DPI to be uprooted and cast into the village well. Six miles down the road, however, their brethren in Muduvarpatti gave them asylum and afforded them protection from further violence. When the aggressors from Kodankipatti ventured into the latter village, they met with fierce and violent resistance. Movement emblems exist as little more than hollow banners that are meaningless until they are acted upon.[28] 'Establishing the territory generates security', as Ley and Cybriwsky note, 'maintaining or embellishing it guarantees status' (1974: 505).

Movement symbols lay claim to space. When the members of a BC organisation attempted to paste posters in SMP Colony, therefore, the DPI youth of the area challenged them and a clash ensued. Similar sentiments were in play when the arrest of Palani Kumar sparked off the Melavassel 'riot'. The colours of a given movement, thus, are directed against oppressors as well as sympathisers. The concern with space, however, often also slips into an attempt to mark out a territory. Movement markers, thus, also warn other organisations to stay clear.[29] We should consequently be wary of seeing the mere presence of a movement as an indication of community cohesion.

[28] When asked how the movement could protect areas in which the Dalits formed a minority, Thirumavalavan pointed to Muduvarpatti as an example. 'If you ask how the minority areas will receive protection', he said, 'it is when the surrounding and adjacent areas organise. When those people form organisations then the minorities will be protected' (interview, 3 November 1999).

[29] Given the problems associated with movements based upon exclusive identities, I would follow Chandhoke in criticising some of the more utopian advocates of 'civil society'. 'Far from being a realm of solidarity and warm personalised interaction, [civil society] is itself a fragmented, divided and a hierarchically structured realm' (2001: 19). In the aftermath of the wave of Hindutva, the agitations that followed the government's adoption of the Mandal Commission's proposals and the massacre in Melavalavu, 'we can hardly accept Putnam's assumption that social associations function to further civic engagement' (2001: 17). Although Putnam (1993) qualifies many of his assertions he pays insufficient attention to the fissures inherent within civil society itself. Social capital, as Chandhoke notes, is not a panacea. Rather it is highly context dependent and does not benefit all in equal measure. The examples of farmer's movements (well summarised in Corbridge and Harriss 2000) and upper-caste networks (as detailed in Jeffrey 2000) indicate that certain associations are exclusive and particular in their scope.

When I visited the village of Melavalavu in April 1999, for example, there was little to mark the spot as an important site in the Dalit struggle. A few tattered posters advertising past protests clung to the walls, but there were none of the usual indicators of conscious assertion. Speaking to the youth of the village it was apparent that the barren nature of the space reflected the reality. None of them was involved in movement activity and the fear of the events of 1997 was still patent. At the time, news of the massacre had galvanised Dalit movements across India.[30] On the first anniversary of the killings, a public meeting had been held in the village, but no sign of this activism was evident in Melavalavu itself.

I returned to the village on the occasion of the second anniversary of the massacre. In the interim, the DPI had erected a flagpole on a plinth of seven steps, a headstone had been constructed by the graves of the fallen and colourful murals depicting Murugesan, Ambedkar and a panther adorned the walls. Melavalavu had been transformed into a site of resistance, but the process was mechanical rather than organic. The striking visual assertions of social change did not reflect the conscientisation of the local residents. Spaces that have such social centrality, as Hetherington observes, 'are likely also to be what we may call spaces of occasion, in which the values and political views of a group might be expressed and around which identities are ... performed' (1998: 108). Over the course of the day, those assembled were addressed by many Dalit leaders in the state, but the emphasis was on the Liberation Panthers. By occupying the symbolic space of the village the DPI had appropriated the territory for itself and asserted itself as the legitimate guardian of Murugesan's memory. 'The creation of symbolic places is not given in the stars but painstakingly nurtured and fought over precisely because of the hold that place can have over the imaginary.... Materiality, representation and imagination are not separate worlds' (Harvey 1996: 322). By identifying the space with the movement, the DPI was attempting to annex the space to the exclusion of others.

Such exclusivity may help in the process of identity construction

---

[30] The massacre is dealt with in other chapters. The panchayat president of Melavalavu, Murugesan, and five others (one follower was killed later) were pulled from a bus in broad daylight and executed by a Thevar mob. See Appendix for a more detailed version.

and in maintaining a strong commitment to the Liberation Panthers, but it is often counter-productive to the aims of the movement. Disputes over space and the right to represent a community are common and are one of the reasons for continuing disunity amongst Dalits. Issues of this nature are usually confined to criticism of other movements and the approach that they adopt. Although few movements have the time or resources to campaign actively for new recruits and areas, the defection of an area from one movement to another is trumpeted as a success. Consequently, it is rare for many movements to coexist within a single locale—although there may be many within close proximity. At this level conflict is latent and usually avoided and the members of all movements pull together in times of crisis. There is a tendency, however, to associate Dalit movements with caste constituencies. Boundaries of this nature are deep-rooted and more emotive than those drawn along the lines of strategy or ideology.

In March 1999, the emphasis accorded to such differences led to bloodshed between Pallars and Paraiyars in the village of Pudhupatti in the south-central district of Virudhunagar. The emotive importance of symbolic space is highlighted in this case, where a seemingly insignificant quarrel over the siting and size of a flagpole led to the deaths of five people and in the burning down of several huts.[31] Petty squabbles and arguments between the two communities are endemic, especially in liquor shops, but the identification of the two castes with separate organisations heightened the sense of antagonism. The Pallars identified themselves with the PT, whereas the Paraiyars had recently switched allegiance from the caste-based Paraiyar Peravai (PP) to the Liberation Panthers. The caste connotations of the riots may be less significant than the fact of inter-movement competition, but the rhetoric of caste is more likely to inflame passions, and it was in caste terms that the incident was described to me (Arseervardam, interview, 28 March 1999).

The immediate trigger of the violence was a dispute over the erection of a large flagpole by the PT, one of the supports of which rested up against the DPI statue of Ambedkar. The DPI resented this,

---

[31] Pandian (2000: 514) puts the number of huts burned in this incident at 80. In his account, five Paraiyars were killed and 80 Pallar huts razed to the ground. Arseervadam told a different tale which may say more about the importance of saving face than of what actually happened.

claiming that they had wanted to embellish the statue by constructing a dome above it, they therefore asked for the support to be removed. When this request was ignored, DPI activists tore the supporting bar down themselves. Heated words were exchanged, but the problem seemed to be negotiable. The next day, however, a DPI activist was confronted, beaten and then burnt alive. Reprisals followed and a riot ensued that has soured the relations between the two communities. In Madurai, DPI activists portrayed the event as a dispute between an established Dalit party and themselves. They claimed that the violence would show that the DPI was strong and there to stay and would thus enable the two groups to work together (interview in Melavassel, 28 March 1999).

Such analysis is seductive, yet it obscures the dangers of organising along caste lines and viewing violence as the primary means of emancipation. It also blinds us to the fact that five people died in this incident. Inter-movement competition is almost inevitable, but it is exacerbated by the appeal to caste. Indeed the conflict erupted once more the following June, when six Pallars were killed. Caste-based appeals re-emphasise the divisions that the term 'Dalit' attempts to overcome, and they preclude the possibility of a Dalit coalition. The move towards caste-based entities is counter-productive in spatial terms as well since it minimises the strength of the appeal to *cheri*-dwellers and splinters neighbourhoods rather than uniting them in common courses of action. Many Dalit activists subscribed to the view that 'unity is forged in crisis' and the antipathy of upper castes and the establishment to the rise of independent Dalit movements is such that crises are endemic. The internecine feuding between Dalit castes and movements, however, has precluded the emergence of a united Dalit movement and also dissuaded potential members.

Individual movements have cooperated and acted in unison from time to time, but it should be stressed that Dalit unity in Tamil Nadu has been both sporadic and short-lived. It is worth emphasising some of the moments of cohesion, however, to point towards possible futures. In Chapter 8, I will argue that some incidents are so momentous as to erase past differences and change the parameters of the struggle. The massacres in Melavalavu and Tirunelveli were events which captured the fears and demands of the Dalit community and re-asserted the importance of unity in adversity. They confirmed Dalit fears about the violence of the upper castes and the precarious nature of their right to public space. If a panchayat president from the ruling party of the state could be murdered with impunity, then who was safe from the retaliation of the dominant caste? In this context it is obvious that the movements cannot be compared to the urban gangs of 'street corner society'. Gangs engage in similar processes of marking territory, but the *defence* of space is merely one concern of the Dalit movements. More importantly they are an attempt to realise and protect the right of Dalits to *enter* public space.

Movements and NGOs are vital to the assertion and protection of a sphere of public interaction and politics. As seen in Chapter 2, however, they cannot function independently or wholly in opposition to the state. 'Despite the constitutional guarantees of the right to association and freedom of expression', as Karat insists, 'in practice the fundamental rights of ordinary citizens are severely circumscribed. It is only the continuous democratic activity relying on mass mobilisation that has to some extent succeeded in expanding the rights of citizens and breaching the monopoly of privileges vested in those who control wealth and power in society' (2000: 113–14). Without recurrent sorties into public space to voice grievances and demand justice, the rights to association and expression are rendered meaningless, yet it is the state that can facilitate the effective functioning of these rights. Without state intervention or acts of rebellion the public sphere remains a hollow shell.

It is often 'only by being "violent" that excluded groups have gained access to the public spaces of democracy', as Mitchell notes, 'and it is precisely this 'violence' that has forced the liberalisation of public space laws' (1996b: 156). Civil society in such instances becomes '*a site for struggle* between the forces that uphold power equations and those that battle these equations in an attempt to further the democratic project' (Chandhoke 2001: 19, emphasis in the original). When the Liberation Panthers courted arrest in Perambalur (see Chapter 8), they consciously echoed the civil disobedience campaigns of the Indian nationalist movement. Dalit movements frequently point out that the non-violence of the nationalist struggle has been mythologised. Without protest, they argue, Independence and citizenship would have remained mere chimeras. 'For women, African Americans, all manner of ethnic groups, workers and progressive activists, the fight to claim the streets, parks, court houses, and other public spaces of the city is precisely the fight to claim their rights as members of the polity, as citizens who have both the duty and the right to reshape social, economic, and political life' (Mitchell 1996b: 172). The earlier example of recidivist, caste-based movements should remind us that not all social movements are necessarily progressive, but the thrust of the argument remains the same. Public space constitutes a material place or site within and from which political activity flows, it is only through an occupation of such spaces that the aims of protest can be made visible and, thus, negotiable.

Conclusion: Power, Place and Protest

'Public space' denotes those areas that are held in common and have habitually been used as places for gathering and the communication of political ideas and social exchange. Public spaces are sites for the creation and negotiation of identities and ideologies. Exclusions in and from public space have frequently been used to foreclose possibilities for certain groups and enhance those of others. In this chapter I have tried to chart the spatiality of political protest. Without access to public space, it is clear, protest remains a privatised issue of conscience and it can be ignored. Individual Dalit villagers who refuse to perform the demeaning tasks that are habitually demanded of them can be socially boycotted, ostracised and ignored. Only when the Dalits as a community unite in their refusal to undergo such humiliation does meaningful change become a possibility. Without recourse to public space the public may become 'balkanised' into communities of mutual distrust. By protesting in and for public space Dalit movements assert their status as members of the 'public' and demand recognition as citizens. The next chapter charts the struggles by Dalit women to extend the democratic import of Dalit protest and challenge the Dalit movements to match up to their rhetoric. The norms that confine women to a subordinate place within the home are questioned as Dalit women articulate their grievances in public space.

Challenges to public space are mounted in different ways by higher-caste movements that refuse to recognise Dalit rights, by patriarchal conventions that confine women to the home and by the state's reluctance to grant permits for demonstrations or its enact-ment of anti-terrorist laws. The use and availability of public space is also constrained by the encroachment of the homeless onto sidewalks and by the commercialisation of real estate. In the face of these multiple challenges, people's movements assert their right to protest and express themselves publicly, since it is only through public articulation of alternatives that issues of citizenship and democracy can be negotiated and contested. Space, as D. Massey notes, is socially constructed, but 'the social is spatially constructed too' (1994: 254). The spatial organisation of a given society, in other words, influences the way it works. The caste-based segregation of Indian cities and villages has not disappeared and it continues to inform political and social activity. Dalits often speak of being 'imprisoned within *cheris*' and of the immutability of *cheris*. '*Cheris* do not change' was a common rhetorical flourish designed to highlight the continuing subordination and poverty of most Dalits. As the foregoing discussion illustrates, however, the assertion of immutability is in itself merely an exhortation to continue the work of political and social movements that have effected such significant changes already. 'The ability of people to confound the established spatial orders, either through physical movement or through their own conceptual and political acts of re-imagination', as Gupta and Ferguson put it, 'means that space and place can never be 'given', and that the process of their socio-political construction must always be considered' (1999: 17).

6

DALIT WOMEN AND DALIT MOVEMENTS: AGENCY, AUTONOMY AND ACTIVISM

Singularly positioned at the bottom of India's caste, class and gender hierarchies, largely uneducated and consistently paid less than their male counterparts, Dalit women make up the majority of landless labourers and scavengers, as well as a significant percentage of the women forced into prostitution in rural areas or sold into urban brothels (Human Rights Watch 1999: 166).

Introduction: Autonomy and the North/South Divide

Dalit women are frequently referred to as the 'oppressed of the oppressed'. A recurrent debate in any Dalit women's forum is whether they are primarily exploited by caste or gender. The answer to this question influences their mode of organisation. Those that emphasise caste domination call for anti-caste movements, constituted of all members of the lower castes fighting for a more egalitarian society. Those that perceive their subordination in gender terms, however, are more likely to seek cross-class and -caste alliances of women to resist the patriarchal structures of power. This chapter examines the position of Dalit women in Tamil Nadu, and in the movements for change, and draws out the conflicting strands of women's activism. Bela Malik (1999: 323) argues that whilst women in general suffer from oppression on the basis of gender, upper-caste women discriminate against Dalits on the basis of caste. In this context, a purely Dalit women's platform seems natural. Though I partly agree with this sentiment, especially because theoretical feminism has rarely been adequately sensitive to the context of caste oppression, this

should not be allowed to obscure the prevalence of sexual discrimination. Dalit movements undoubtedly draw strength from the participation and leadership of their women and the systematic adoption
of 'women's rights issues' would strengthen the ideological consistency of the struggle for a more equal society.

To fully comprehend the position of Dalit women in Tamil Nadu
it is worth reviewing the radical ideological legacy of Periyar. Tamil
Nadu figures prominently as a 'success story' of fertility decline, partly
due to the history of Periyar's Self-Respect Movement (SRM) which
insisted upon the equality and autonomy of women. Whilst a
prominent strand of Tamil culture portrays motherhood as next to
Godliness, Periyar 'disinvested the reproductive role of women within
the endogamous/monogamous family of its religious aura and linked
it with this-worldly dynamics' (Anandhi 1998: 155). Marriage was
thus cast as an extension of property relations and the means by
which heirs are produced. Where Brahminical patriarchy sought to
control women's sexuality, because the purity of caste was contingent
upon it (Geetha 1998b: 319, 329), the SRM viewed contraception
as a means for women to exercise control over their bodies and thus
free themselves from male domination (Anandhi 1998: 153).[1] Self-
respecters challenged the patriarchal culture which not only absolved
men from housework but 'denied women the dignity of being workers
since society held that work was the mark of being a man' (Geetha
1998a: WS12). The SRM not only demanded equal pay for both
sexes, but also raised the question of wages for housework (ibid.).

These questions were practically addressed in the institution of the
self-respect marriage, in which individual choice was privileged above
social or familial preference. This ritual was secular, in that it
dispensed with the requirement for priests, and it also encouraged
cross-caste alliances and widow remarriage, and demanded reciprocity. The implications were immense. 'With women deemed free to
marry whomsoever they wished to, the integrity of caste too stood
challenged, since caste identity, centred in the woman's body and
consecrated through strategies of control and discipline, could now
be exchanged for one that the woman wished to create for herself'
(Geetha 1998a: WS12). Periyar's theoretical critique of caste was

---

[1] The ability of Tamil women to make 'reasoned decisions about fertility', A. Sen
argues, is an important factor in the state's fertility decline (in Ravindran 1999:
WS-34).

incisive, but its real significance lies in the fact that it continues to inform the world views and actions of some Tamil women today. The emancipatory potential of his ideology was reinforced in a meeting with Kathrine, a Dravida Kazhagam activist, in Melavassel. I was introduced to her in a friend's flat where she was ensconced on the only chair in the room. She spoke boldly about the need to escape the patriarchal aspects of society and emphasised that she was not wearing a *thali* (marriage thread that must not be removed) because she saw it as a symbol of oppression. Pandiyammal, the women's wing leader of the DPI in Madurai held similar views:

> If a husband dies young, when the wife is still twenty something she does not lose her beauty, but she is told not to wear the *pottu*, flowers or colourful saris, which she has worn since childhood. I think that this is misguided, therefore I do not approve of tying the *thali*—why not use rings instead? I would speak against all this ...'good time, bad time' nonsense. Surely all days given by God are good? (interview, 28 March 1999).

This shows that Periyar's ideals are still current, but his more radical suggestions are increasingly sidelined. Kathrine, for example, was respected but viewed as a bit of an oddity. Contemporary political parties in Tamil Nadu lay claim to the legacy of the SRM, but Periyar's ideals—especially with regard to women—have been compromised or neglected. Self-respect marriages are still legal and the state provides financial incentives for cross-caste weddings, but women's rights remain largely rhetorical and their status is arguably declining. This chapter briefly charts the debates surrounding the question of female autonomy, before considering the position of Dalit women in Tamil Nadu today.

Portrayals of women's lives in South Asia frequently present them as the passive subjects of an oppressive social structure and it is important to highlight the very real structural constraints that women have to overcome. Across India property and inheritance rights favour males, and it is the men who receive the benefits of education and the freedoms of association and movement.[2] From a very young age, girls are prepared for marriage. Fear of threats to their chastity before

---

[2] On property rights see Agarwal (1994). See Geetha (1998b: 320) for the male monopolisation of public space. Kapadia (1995: 13–26) and Daniel (1980: 69) deal with the inferior *status* of women in Tamil culture. On differences between north and south India see Dyson and Moore (1983).

marriage and obedience to their husband thereafter, confines women largely to the domestic sphere (Sharma 1980: 218). In the northern states this commonly takes the form of social seclusion within the home (purdah). 'The world beyond the domestic arena is basically male space' (Jeffery et al. 1989: 23). Socio-cultural norms enforce the belief that women should be subordinate to their male kinsmen. This gender hierarchy is manifest in the patterns of social interaction whereby women always serve their men food before eating themselves, stand up when their husband enters a room, or make sure to sit on a lower level.

Men are seen as the breadwinners and providers who have the right to make the final decision on any matter. Land is generally held in the man's name and is passed down from father to son (Agarwal 1994: 2). The patriarchal nature of Indian culture is highlighted by the ritual and social roles assigned to men. Even where a family has no sons, for example, it has to be a male relative who performs the death rites or presides at marriage ceremonies. As Kapadia (1995: 24) notes, these obligations are often only obtained by ceding half the inheritance of the sonless family to the nearest male relative. The inferiority of women to men is accepted in all castes but there are differences in the degree to which this is the case. Differences in region, caste and class significantly affect the status of women, and these need to be considered. In a seminal article, Dyson and Moore (1983) depict kinship patterns across India in a series of ideal types that serve to highlight the regional disparities. In part their article is inspired by the work of Miller (1981: 15) who catalogued the existence of a 'culture against females' in north India through an analysis of sex ratios, infant mortality rates and fertility figures.

Broadly speaking, Dyson and Moore conclude that states in southern and eastern India evince lower marital fertility, a later age of marriage, lower infant mortality and relatively low sex ratios as compared to the north (1983: 42). Their explanations of this highlight the socio-economic and cultural factors that characterise the different systems. In the north, marriage rules are exogamic, which means that women marry out of the families and villages that they are familiar with into an alien setting (Miller 1981: 14). Due to this, parents expect little assistance from their married daughters. This helps to explain why women do not generally inherit property or participate in waged labour. By contrast, marriage patterns in the south encourage cross-cousin matrimony and affinal relations are as strong as patrilineal ones. The practice of bride-wealth is more common, therefore, and 'women sometimes inherit and, or, transfer property rights' (Dyson and Moore 1983: 44). The key question is not whether women have a legal entitlement to land, but whether they can exercise control over it. Yet women are less rigidly controlled in these states and they frequently engage in waged work outside the domestic sphere. Obviously such generalisations are a caricature that do not do justice to the complexity on the ground, but it seems safe to conclude with Karve that the 'South represents ... greater freedom for women' (in Dyson and Moore 1983: 45).

The differences outlined here have given rise to a debate over the relative autonomy of women in India. Individual autonomy involves having the 'freedom to determine one's own action and behaviour' (*Collins English Dictionary*). It is clear that the normal residential and cultural patterns of family life in India greatly reduce the scope of female autonomy, particularly in areas where women are confined to the domestic sphere. It is, as we have seen, the male householder who is expected to make the decisions and the money. Women frequently criticise this state of affairs, but it can be counter-productive to do so, since obedient wives can hope for lifelong economic support from their husbands, and also avoid abuse (Jeffery and Jeffery 1996: 18).[3] Girls are not usually consulted about their marriages beforehand. In north India, cultural practices serve to limit the contact between a woman and her natal village. Indeed, after the marriage and the costs incurred during that ceremony, many parents regard their work as complete. This, combined with norms of seclusion and prohibitions on work, makes it difficult for women to establish personal links in the nuptial home and they may be rendered socially powerless—at least until they have children and a daughter-in-law themselves (Wadley 1980a: 27). This isolation is most apparent in cases of dowry-related abuse, when a young bride is victimised by her in-laws for having provided too little by way of dowry.[4]

---

[3] Subadra (1999: WS28), notes that many women suffer from a 'deep and inescapable sense of dependency' since they have 'no option' in the matter.
[4] The abuse of a young bride because she has brought insufficient dowry can result in murder or suicide. These killings are referred to as 'dowry deaths' and occur across India (de Souza 1980). The Statistical Handbook of Tamil Nadu 1999 notes that the 196 dowry deaths in Tamil Nadu in 1998 constituted 4 per cent of recorded crimes in that year. Given that Tamils used to pay a bride-price

In the south, east and amongst the lower castes by contrast, not only has it been customary to provide a bride-price, but the bride often marries into a close or related family.[5] The advantages of this arrangement were highlighted by Subadra's study of domestic violence in Chennai. She found that the 'parents of the respondent had been the most consistent primary source of support' (1999: WS-33). In such marriages women are not only in closer proximity to their natal homes but a woman maintains her status and a degree of independence due to the equal social standing of the two families (Kapadia 1995: 54). The significance of caste differences were highlighted by Nesamani, an independent-minded Dalit Christian woman in Madurai:

> Viji *Akka* here is a Thevar, a higher caste from the village. She knows that I'm from an SC caste but still she was insistent that I visit her village. Women there are kept so much in line! If a man comes in they have to stand up and show respect—I could never do that. Or if a higher caste man comes along they say 'get up, get up, *Ayya* is coming'! They are really downtrodden, but this feeling is so ingrained that when my brothers—both much younger than her— come in, she will get off the chair and sit on the floor or something (Nesamani, interview, 21 March 1999).

Nesamani is not a village woman nor is she a typical urban Dalit, but her comments serve to cast the differences in caste expectations into relief. Part of the reason for the greater worth accorded to women in the south and east stems from the fact that women play a far bigger role in agricultural production in these areas.[6] Miller (1981: 110) maintains that the higher demand for female labour in rice-producing areas, as opposed to areas where wheat is grown, is a significant factor in the regional variations in gender discrimination.[7]

---

for their wives in recognition of their value to the household, this is a worrying development indicating a decline in the status of women.

[5] For more detail on this see: Good (1981), Cohn (1990) and Agarwal (1994).

[6] On female participation in production see: Wadley (1980c: 161), Miller (1981: 14), Dyson and Moore (1983: 47) and Ravindran (1999: WS34).

[7] Whilst attractive, this thesis has been subject to questioning by several authors. Miller herself notes several exceptions to this rule within India such as West Bengal. Adopting a more nuanced argument, Miller quotes Winzeler to

The fact that women are an integral part of the production process in south India, according to Miller (1981), means that they are not seen as a liability to their parents like they are in the north. Indeed, birth ceremonies and payments to midwives indicate that daughters are often welcomed in the south of India (Wadley 1980c: 161). 'Female child labor is a crucial aspect of the Pallar domestic economy', as Kapadia observes. 'Homes with daughters count themselves lucky because this frees the Pallar mother for wage work' (1995: 200). The gendered division of labour within the household, however, means that women suffer more as a result of the lack of piped water, fuel stocks and sanitation facilities. Fetching water, gathering kindling and cooking on a wood stove are all labour intensive. Dalit men rarely assist women in such household tasks, though attitudes are gradually changing. The prevalence of women in the labour market in the south means that domestic chores are often in addition to paid employment during the day. The low earnings of unskilled Dalit males means that the women take on agricultural or domestic service jobs 'out of sheer economic necessity' (Caplan 1985: 177).

There is a caste/class differential in the proportion of women from a social category who enter into paid employment.[8] In general, as Dyson and Moore (1983: 56) note, the higher castes in the south more closely replicate the social dynamics of the northern system and women from these castes are withdrawn from the labour market, or confine themselves to ritually neutral jobs. By contrast, women from un-propertied or impoverished groups across India consistently participate in wage work.[9] On one hand, the experience of wage labour renders Dalit, lower caste and poor women far more independent of their men than their higher caste counterparts, but this relative

insist that: 'in order to make causal inferences about wet rice cultivation it would seem necessary to specify a number of intervening variables including kinship patterns, population density and, perhaps, cultural traditions' (cited in Miller 1981: 110). Having said this, the significance of female labour to rice production in the south of India has appeared to influence cultural attitudes towards female labour.

[8] 'The women among the Scheduled Castes have a role in all economic and income generation activities, as well as social functions (89.1 percent) and ritual matters (89.5 per cent). But they have generally a lower status and only a few have decision making powers' (Singh 1993: 7).

[9] See also Chapter 4 on the 'feminisation' of agrarian labour.

perspective may obscure continuing discrimination. Having an independent source of income does not necessarily equate to an increase in status or decision-making power (Agarwal 1994: 44). Indeed, participation in the labour market substantially increases their workload and reduces their leisure time.

Their presence in the employment market may accord Dalit women a degree of monetary independence that is not available to the higher-caste women, but it has rendered them extremely vulnerable to exploitation. They are often required to act as the breadwinner as well as housekeeper. When combined with the much-cited incidence of alcoholism amongst poorer men in India, the burden of responsibility is placed firmly onto women's shoulders.[10] Dalit women are less subject to notions of purity and pollution, but this has not resulted in any great degree of liberation for them. Often, the clearest manifestation of this relative independence is the fact that Dalit women are expected to work during menstruation, until the late stages of pregnancy (almost up to childbirth) and are expected to resume work almost immediately after giving birth due to a common misconception that women's agricultural labour is not particularly 'hard work'. 'The Dalit man, while he suffers from caste oppression is not willing to let go of the dominance that this system has given him for being a man' (Rani 1998: WS23). Gender inequality is mediated by caste considerations too and, wherever possible, women are withdrawn from the workforce since it is an indication of low social status for the women of a caste to go to work. Consequently, the withdrawal of BC women from work has resulted in a greater demand for 'Untouchable' labour (Mencher 1988: 101).

Dalit women, according to K. Pawde (1994: 154), are more conscious of their legal rights because of the relative autonomy that their employment affords them. Speaking about the BC (Kounder) panchayat council in her village, Suganthi highlighted this consciousness: 'When a loan for a cow (a government scheme to help the Dalits become more self sufficient) or some other loan arrived, they would never inform us about this. Now we have got to a point where we ask if the loan has come and chase up applications' (interview, 20 March 1999). This independence and knowledge of rights, however,

---

[10] The endemic nature of alcoholism is widely reported: Daniel (1980: 81), Caplan (1985: 10), Berreman (1993: 380), Agarwal (1994: 26), Kapadia (1995: 199) and Ravindran (1999: WS41).

is rarely evident in any depth and consciousness about government programmes remains immaterial so long as these rights are not realised. Addressing a conference on Dalit women's rights, Vasanthi Devi summed up the main issue: 'Farming and agriculture are in your hands, but is the land in your hands? No caste, religion or class gives land into women's hands' (speech, Madurai, 10 April 1999).

Continuing Inequality and the Gender Gap

The quote from Devi highlights the problematic debate about the merits and demerits of a 'women's' as opposed to a 'Dalit' movement. The lack of land, it is noted, is an issue that affects all women, but the appeal to the tillers of the soil can only refer to Dalit or poor BC women since upper-caste women do not work the land. 'An analysis of the dalits solely in view of caste ... may', as Mohanty insists, 'in the absence of its location in relation to other social contradictions such as the ones relating to land restrictions, gender inequality, etc., turn out to be a limited exercise' (1998: 72). As women's movements in Chennai found, it makes little sense to agitate for rights when basic needs have not been met (Caplan 1985: 211). Many Dalit women and children forfeit an education either to save expense or because their income-generating capacity is required. Thus they are trapped in a vicious circle, since education is increasingly a major determinant of employment options. The will of Tamil Dalit women to improve their lot is evinced in their increasing levels of literacy (the figure is still a pitiably low 35 per cent [Government of Tamil Nadu 2002). 'The downward displacement of ignominious roles and obligations from men to women in Harijan households', however, 'indicates the uneven participation of women in social mobility' (Mosse 1994: 86).

This disparity in social mobility has recently been emphasised by the experience of Dalit women panchayat presidents. At the first Tamil Nadu Women Panchayat President's Convention, there was consensus that the women had come 'a long way from merely slogging it out at home and remaining subservient to men without being able to take any decision' (Krishnakumar 2000: 98). There was also recognition of the innumerable obstacles that were placed in the way of the women, especially if they happened to be Dalit. Male relatives frequently tried to dominate and elected male members refused to cooperate. Lack of education hampered women from dealing with files and finances and this could render them dependent on literate male members of the council or office-workers (ibid.).[11] Whilst poverty and a lack of education obviously serve to curtail female autonomy it should be noted that there are far greater threats to women's status.

In a footnote to their article on 'Kinship Structure and Female Autonomy', Dyson and Moore (1983: 56) noted that upwardly-mobile sections of society across the south were increasingly adopting the characteristics of the north Indian model. This, they warned, would result in a decline of female status and they cited Srinivas as insisting that 'Sanskritisation results in harshness towards women' (1983: 56). In a forceful article Berreman (1993: 370) deplores this trend towards sanskritisation. Gender hierarchies, he observes, are strongest among the 'sanskritised, traditional segments of Hindu society', and weakest among tribal communities, the urbanised and 'modern' élite and the lowest castes and classes. Citing his work amongst the Paharis in the far north of India, he details the aspects of female autonomy that used to apply in that society. Pahari women were customarily able to officiate as shamans, they had the freedom to divorce and re-marry and a bride-price was paid for them. Much of this picture applies equally to Dalit women in Tamil Nadu. As little as 15 years ago, respondents asserted, it was customary for Dalit groups to pay a bride price. Since the 1950s, however, there has been an encroachment of Brahminical practices such as 'dowry marriages, widow celibacy, male only initiation of divorce' and similar customs which 'subordinate and endanger women' (Berreman 1993: 373; see also Ravindran 1999: WS38). Sankar, in his mid-40s, summed up the rapid nature of this change:

> When my father got married he had to pay a bride-price while bringing his wife back home. By the time I was married, however,

---

[11] C. Mathew, a Christian Dalit and school teacher in his late 60s has a history of activism and is involved in the Village Community Development Society in Tindivanam. He recalls that the training they provided 'enabled 25 Dalit women to be elected in the panchayat elections, but the benefits of the post were enjoyed by their husbands. The women themselves suffer from social disdain—indeed, any socially active Dalit woman is labelled as a prostitute' (interview, 19 January 1999). cf Pai (2001: 649).

the system had changed dramatically and it was I who received goods in the form of dowry (interview, 5 December 1998).

That this is a 'culture against females' (Miller 1981: 15) is evident in the number of female infanticides (FI) across the country. The records of primary health care centres show an average of 'around 3,000 cases of FI occur in a year in Tamil Nadu. This amounts to between one-sixth to one-fifth of all female infant deaths in the state' (Athreya and Chunkath 2000: 4345). Patriarchal relations within the household also condition the distribution of child-care. As Harriss-White (1999: 312) observes, girls are increasingly discriminated against in access to nutrition and education. This shows a marked shift from Wadley's assertion that women in the south generally live longer and are more valued than their north Indian counterparts (1980c: 161). As Berreman (1993: 370–71) observes, gender discrimination is at its harshest among the lower sectors of society when they are striving for upward mobility through the symbolic emulation of upper-caste norms. In such circumstances, the women have neither the material prosperity nor the social status that helps to alleviate the lot of upper-caste women. In this situation, he observes, female autonomy may be enhanced by the process of secularisation, or through the efforts of ethnic, tribal or low-caste social movements (Berreman 1993: 389).

Dalit women continue to be the first to suffer: both at the hands of those desiring to humble Dalit men and at the hands of desperate or alcoholic husbands. In the emerging rural industries, for instance, women's labour is exploited within the family or by the small-scale firms that deny them the opportunity to unite (Gopal 1999: WS17; Nihila 1999: WS24). 'Women rarely manage economic enterprises', as Harriss-White states, 'and more rarely own business property' (1996: 246), and yet they are responsible for accomplishing much of the essential labour of the household. Research throughout India shows the persistence of wage-based gender discrimination in the form of large differences in pay, even when the job in question is the same. As Dalit women are becoming increasingly prominent in residents' and political organisations, and are making their voices heard, it is impossible to ignore the cross-cutting matrices of domination which constitute contemporary Dalit identity.

There is, therefore, an imperative to adopt a gendered perspective in order to challenge the assumptions of conventional economics:

a) '...[T]he household is an undifferentiated unit in which members share common preferences' (Agarwal 1998: A2). Men and women frequently emphasise different priorities and goals and the 'home' is often the site of violence as a means of social control (Subadra 1999).

b) Income spending patterns within the household are uniform. The contention here is that income in women's hands more commonly benefits the family in general. As Mencher concluded: 'The proportion of income contributed by wage-earning women to the household is far higher than that of their earning husbands' (1985: 365, cf. 1988: 99, 109).

c) '...[W]omen's class can be derived simply from the family's property status and class position' (Agarwal 1998), whereas property laws and wage differentials commonly discriminate against women.

d) '[T]he process of intra-household dynamics and allocations' are unproblematic (Agarwal 1998: A2).

Lay versions of such analysis were not hard to find amongst Dalit women in Tamil Nadu. But the clearest articulation of the need for a gender perspective came from Madhivanan of the Working Peasant's Movement (WPM). More than any other social movement, the WPM had sought to integrate the concerns and demands of both male and female activists into its demands:

> Now I work for eight hours and I get Rs 60. My wife works for those same eight hours, but she only gets Rs 30. Of the Rs 60 I get for my eight hours only Rs 30 is spent on household expenses. But of the Rs 30 a woman gets exactly Rs 30 is spent on the home and the children and for other necessary items. So if women get the salary that men do, the whole family could develop and grow better. This is the reason why we make the demand for an 'equal coolie' [wage]' a central one ...This is a demand at all meetings and protests (interview, 28 September 1999).

Women and Social Action

The increasing participation of women in panchayats and social movements reflects a growing rejection of their subservient status and a demand for more autonomy. These sentiments have led women panchayat chiefs to tackle vital problems that affect women on a daily basis: ending the sale of illicit liquor, ensuring the provision of clean water and enforcing the minimum wage (Krishnakumar 2000: 98–99). More commonly, women are not in positions of responsibility and must resort to other means to make their opinions heard. Dalit women, thus, feature prominently in the forefront of many demonstration marches and protests by Dalit movements. Given the cumulative nature of the discrimination that they face, such activism is to be expected. Indeed, Tanner (1995) suggests that the group-based nature of women's agricultural work helps to explain their greater capacity for collective action. Such sweeping explanations, however, cannot capture the diverse motivations underlying the participation of Dalit women in protest activity and it is worth considering the views of the women themselves.

The women in Kodankipatti typified the consciousness shown, and the struggles faced, by Dalit women across the state. They were determined to have their say and when the tape I was recording on ran out, they hunted round and produced an old film cassette for me to use. 'We hope, through you, to get the true story through to people in positions of influence' Malligai averred. They spoke of taunts and threats that they faced as a matter of course and of difficulties in negotiating access to common resources: 'Before we had a well here if we had to go into the *oor* for water then we really struggled for sustenance. When we went there they'd ask, "*Paiyarchi* could you find nowhere else to get water? What makes you think you can come here?" And they would fight to prevent us getting any water' (Shanthi). 'We have only the land on which we live and ourselves', Arulmozhi stated, 'otherwise nothing in this village is ours or available to us'. Despite this, she went on to insist that they desperately wanted to educate their children and achieve a situation where they could be at ease. 'They say we got independence in 1947 from you, from the white people', Arulmozhi continued, 'but they (higher castes) are the only ones who gained independence and they seek to suppress us just as much as your lot did'.

Such powerlessness and lack of resources amongst people living in constant fear of attack would be presumed to give rise to passivity and fatalism: a grudging acceptance of the status quo and a disinclination to rock the boat. Instead the women spoke of trying to achieve their rights by any available means. 'If you return a blow for a blow', Chellamma opined, 'the grinding stone (*ammi kullu*) will shift'. I asked if it was possible for them to fight back in the village but Tamilarisi said no: 'We lack the resources and economics'. Further on in the interview, however, having detailed the difficulties they faced in getting loans, in securing government sanctioned grants or in using the local shops, Chellamma summed up the prevailing mood: 'Instead of living like this and dying one by one we'd be better off attacking them (higher castes) or dying in the attempt. Here we had thought that we did not want any radicalism or militancy. From now on we should not live in fear. If we do so they will squeeze us dry. "The determined have no fear"' (group interview, 20 March 1999). In their grievances, their vision of a better future and their determination to resist, these women emphasise the degree of consciousness of, but also the discrimination against, Dalit women. It is important to stress that—as labourers, housekeepers and mothers—women feel the brunt of any oppression, whether they are the direct or the indirect targets of any given incident.

Social boycotts deprive them of labour and often force children to stay at home and make it harder for them to obtain potable water. Hostility between castes renders women vulnerable if they have to use the fields to relieve themselves, work for other castes or stay at home whilst their men work elsewhere. The threat and fear of rape and sexual harassment is ever present. Dalit women suffer daily indignities in the form of verbal abuse and exploitation in the work place. As a result of these inequities, Dalit women, such as Dhanam (see introduction) and those interviewed here, articulate a sense of justice and a desire for a more equal society. For most women the imperative for change is felt particularly keenly in the pervasive sense of fear and vulnerability experienced by rural women. In 1999, the Women's Wing of the Dalit People's Front, thus, called for Dalit women to be armed for self-protection—a call that was taken up by other movements. Female Dalit consciousness is particularly high, however, because of the more mundane forms of caste discrimination that punctuate daily life: The prohibition on using certain water sources, unfair treatment in shops, harassment from money-lenders, taunting from men of other castes and so on—a litany of everyday indignities and obstacles that occasion frustration and anger.

In other words, there are powerful factors that incline Dalit women towards protest, but there are equally compelling reasons to render them socially inactive. In the first instance, their disproportionate share of the domestic workload results in a 'lack of time' (Caplan 1985: 34). The benefits of social activism are rarely instantaneous, but the costs of protest are immediately apparent. To get to protest meetings or dharnas, one must give up a day's work, possibly find travel expenses and face potential arrest. Child-care is a further complication, as is the risk of inciting the higher castes in one's neighbourhood. The general attitude was summed up in the earlier quote from Kannimma, an agricultural labourer from Chidambaram District, who emphasised the fact that she was losing a day's wage to protest. Even though she could ill afford to lose a day's wages or the extra expense of attending the rally, she was determined to do so because caste-based discrimination was impinging on her life to such a huge degree.

The patriarchal nature of Tamil households dictates that the women do the cooking, fetch water and collect fuel. Such activities are neglected if a whole day is spent in political activity. Those with servants, as Caplan (1985: 33) notes, are better able to ignore these tasks. However, it is not only poor women who face obstacles to activism, and there are more subtle, structural constraints on women's participation in protest activities. This was made evident at the Centre for Dalit Solidarity Conference in American College, Madurai. The strength of the audience here was dramatically diminished at the stroke of 6 o'clock, as most of the college students departed to catch buses home. 'Otherwise they will not be allowed to come to college tomorrow', the convenor observed (10 April 1999). Such restrictions seldom apply to male students and they constitute a gender-based constraint on skill-acquisition and political participation. The departure of the female students was especially surprising given that the conference was taking place in the campus buildings of their college. Usually Dalit meetings occur on the roadside or in other public spaces.

The gendered geography of social and political space in India acts to confine women to the home. 'Can we stand at a Tea-shop and drink tea?' Viji, a lecturer at the college, asked. 'Can a hard working woman coming back from her work stand at a tea-shop and have a drink? Imagine the reaction! "Look at her! What effrontery! (enna timur)". So who are these spaces for? Certainly not for us!' At social movement gatherings the men and women sit apart, for a woman to go to such a gathering on her own would be inconceivable. If transport is required, then other women must be found to travel in consort for reasons of safety and moral propriety. 'Indeed for women to even participate in group meetings often requires them to challenge and overcome the constraints of social norms, to face the disapproval and wrath of their husbands and other family members' (Agarwal 1994: 43). Whilst some women activists have overcome the cultural barriers to political participation and frequently address meetings attended mostly by males, the majority of women lack the confidence to voice their opinions in such an environment.

Partly in response to this, most movements have a women's wing that is intended to raise issues that pertain to Dalit women and provide a forum in which women can voice their concerns. This division of labour enables the mobilisation of many more women than would otherwise be the case and also brings household issues onto the agenda. Members for such movements are recruited through informal, local support networks, credit unions and friendships. Women's work is more community based and there are more opportunities available to women to gather and debate issues on a daily basis than there are for men. Queues for water, ration shops and so on are places where grievances are felt and solutions discussed. Given the domestic division of labour it is unsurprising that it is the women's wings that highlight the problems faced in ration shops and with money-lenders. 'We are not a separate movement', Pandiyammal of the Tamil Nadu Women's Liberation Movement insisted, 'we are in the Liberation Panther movement and we attend their meetings in groups of one hundred women or so'. The differences between the separate branches of the organisation were evinced, however, when she went on to add, 'we campaign on women's issues too' (interview, 28 March 1999).

'By treating important societal issues such as the collection of fuel, fodder and drinking water as "women's issues"', as Mageli observes, 'these issues become, from a male point of view, issues of low priority' (1997: 4). The work of the women's branches is presented as less urgent than that of the movement 'proper' and issues of importance to women can then be downplayed. Pandiyammal, for instance, said that she *would* speak on matters pertaining to widow re-marriage, the *thali* and the 'nonsense' of auspicious and inauspicious times, but that she had not had the opportunity. Despite the centrality of women's rights in the ideological manifestos of the various Dalit movements it was evident that the women's wings were effectively an after-thought rather than a systematic attempt to raise the voices and profile of Dalit women. On the distaff side, the DPI, for instance, did raise and tackle serious and meaningful issues, but it did not have the prominence or the *modus operandi* of the DPI. Women's wings were more embedded in localities and sought to address immediate concerns and issues.

The women's wings rarely held road-side demonstrations or blockades. Their work was largely confined to the spatial parameters of their participants. Hence there was a focus on credit schemes, on ration shops and on wife-beating or drunkenness. Where the women attempted to reach a wider audience or make a larger point the means of doing so was often to arrange a 'conference' or gathering within a compound. The women's branches only come into their own and attain real public visibility when the main movement is unable to stage protests for fear of repression or when a gathering of women is deemed to be more poignant. After the election violence in Chidambaram, for example, the women's meetings sent out a message that the Dalit community was scared of violence and that innumerable Dalit men had been arrested under the Prevention of Terrorism Act. It was at these meetings that the women's leaders were given a platform, and accorded responsibility.

Whilst women are present in large numbers at the meetings of the main movement, their leaders are rarely accorded the respect and prominence that they deserve. Adline is a graduate and a local leader in the Madurai branch of the Women's Rights Movement (*Penurimai Iyakkam*). She notes that 'Dalit movements as a rule neither respect Dalit women nor use them properly'. Several movements, she points out, have upper-caste women running their women's wings. She cites the instance of the Dalit Liberation Movement (DLM), which approached the PI and asked them to provide legal training for the DLM women. On the programme, however, PI found that 'these women knew more about the law and the implementation of certain Acts than we knew, because they had had practical experience of taking cases to the police and knew far more than we did'.

'They did not need legal training', Adline concluded, 'they needed recognition' (interview, 1 October 1999). They needed to be used in the struggle, but the general perception that Dalit women are uneducated hindered their involvement. Similarly, Thirumavalavan displayed a startling lack of knowledge about the DPI Women's Wing. When asked for a point of contact in Madurai, 'he thought for some time and then mentioned the wife of their legal advisor. She *is* a good woman and she does get involved, but she is neither a Dalit nor a member of the movement. The worst part of the response was that Pandiyammal *Akka* was there when we were speaking—a talented leader of the Women's Wing who has all the required skills—but he didn't mention her' (ibid.).

Waiting in the Wings: Ideological Equality, Actual Inertia

When it was pointed out that all the movements espouse an ideological commitment to the equality of women, Adline was dismissive: 'Of course! Without them there is no protest! They are the bulk of the protestors aren't they?!' (interview, 1 October 1999). While male activists are in favour of women's liberation in principle, as Dietrich (1988: 7) points out, their own lifestyles and expectations are often traditional. As a consequence, their interaction with women activists is coloured by their domestic relationships with mothers, sisters and wives.[12] Daniel (1980: 66) notes the prevalent Tamil belief that males should exercise control over their kinswomen. Certainly, the commitment of many activists is dependent upon having some-one to provide food at home, not to mention their earnings. It would be a mistake, however, to deny that there is a genuine awareness of the need for women's rights in the Dalit movements. At the wedding of the Madurai District organiser Murugan, for example, Thirumavalavan wound up his speech by insisting that 'women are not just wombs, or machines that give birth. They also have desires, wants and dreams, and they also have the fire to fight for a just cause.

---

[12] This 'traditional' approach among the male leaders of the Dalit movements was typified by their approach to political meetings. Standing at the front of the crowd, often on a stage, the senior figures of the movement lectured the crowds in a didactic fashion. Whilst the audience of such speeches comprised members of the movement, the speakers frequently faced away from those ranged behind them and addressed themselves to the street. In the context this was intended to symbolise an attempt to reach out to passers-by and bystanders, and also allowed the press to snap images of the leader during the speech. By contrast, at the women's movement meetings there was more of a participatory emphasis and the leaders faced the audience and interacted with them.

If this is understood, then this family will be based on equal authority with two heads of the household—Murugan and Jayanthi' (16 June 1999).

Though the echoes of the Self-Respect Movement are obvious, it is easy to see this as a cynical appeal to Jayanthi not to hinder Murugan's social activism. 'Tada' Periyasami, the assistant state convenor of the Liberation Panthers, was more explicit: 'If one enters into social activism one can do nothing without the consent of your wife. I know that without my wife's approval I couldn't have become so involved. There are times when I get news of a riot or a caste clash that needs an urgent response. If my wife held me back at that point then the moment will pass and I would be unable to go to the spot, see the riot and face it out.... Households often intend this, they hope that the wife will shackle the lad and calm him down. For example my father wanted to settle me down, since I had joined in a naxalite, a militant group in my student days' (talk, 16 June 1999). Periyasami's comments serve to illustrate the concerns voiced by Dietrich. The notion of equality and women's rights is entwined with an implicit assumption that women will remain behind and mind the home for their activist men.

Whether cynical or not, the liberatory rhetoric and the need to gain a wife's support does help to temper the male chauvinism of the movement activists and raises the consciousness of the Dalit women. Most movements require an internal critique of patriarchy, but it is important to note that the discourse on equality and women's rights does create significant 'spaces within the anti-caste struggle' (Sen 1990). Dalit women, as Rege points out, 'sometimes challenge the patriarchal leadership, making spaces for feminism within the dalit movement' (2000: 494). It is significant that not only do most Dalit movements have a women's wing, but that the Liberation Panthers and the DLM, at least, have cooperated and worked with *Penurimai Iyakkam* on several issues. Furthermore, the experience of social organisation and the provision of networks of female activists, make women more confident in the public sphere. 'Apart from marches, demonstrations and conferences which take place regularly in many places, the day to day organisational efforts in local women's *sanghams* (unions) are therefore of greater importance than their often limited scope suggests. It is these *sanghams* that can deal with issues like drinking, wife-beating, rape, health problems and *balwadis* (nurseries). Such activities are often essential to equip women to be involved in any political process' (Dietrich 1988: 34). The picture is not always so rosy, as Egnor (1980: 27) observes, for women are often culpable in reinforcing the very hierarchies that suppress them. She insists, however, that there remains a strong 'consciousness of solidarity' among Tamil women (1980: 27).

The gender-based separation of movements enables the greater participation of women, and allows household disputes and other local issues to be heard and tackled in a protective environment. 'Women have more responsibilities and household expenditure', Amulakka insisted, 'so they need more help than the men' (interview, 16 March 1999). Amulakka is a middle-aged Dalit woman living in a village 20 miles outside Madurai. She and her husband work on an estate where they manage the coconut groves. She is also the 'accountant' for the DPI Women's Wing in her area because she was educated up to ninth grade in school. 'We saw that all loans available here were for a huge amount of interest, and we questioned why we were forced to use such loan sharks. So, we have started up this union for ourselves. Here in this district we have 15 members. Once a month we contribute Rs 20, which enables us to provide small loans at a low rate of interest' (ibid.). Similar schemes are in evidence in most women's movements, which tend to be closer to ground level than the male equivalents.

The local focus reflects the main issues that exercise the minds of women's wing constituents. Poverty, corruption at the ration shop and the poor quality of ration shop produce, were recurrent themes raised by Dalit women, and were issues that could be (at least partly) addressed at a local level. Pandiyammal spoke of a similar, low-key, credit scheme, but she insisted that their efforts had secured respect for the participants. 'In our area there are no husbands who drink and beat their wives' she claimed (interview, 28 March 1999). Muniamma, an elderly and illiterate flower seller, agreed: 'this movement has given us boldness' she affirmed (interview, 28 March 1999). The notices for women's meetings reflect their core concerns and raise the issues of food, fuel, schooling and loan sharks. In doing so these movements serve to give Dalit women a voice and means of airing their grievances that would not otherwise be available to them. They also provide a forum in which to raise issues of domestic violence and alcoholism and secure some form of mediation.

Conclusion

Dalit movements need to integrate both male and female facets of their organisation if they are to maximise their potential. Whilst the movements continue to be split into gendered halves, the problems of internal patriarchy will remain. Male leaders, as shown in the next chapter, need to know more about their female counterparts and their concerns, and recognise their importance. Were Dalit movements to tackle the issues of excessive drinking, wife-beating and ration shops, they would be able to tap into a wider constituency than they do at present. The popularity of the AIADMK amongst women is in large part due to its policies of prohibition, food subsidies and the mid-day meal scheme for school children (Swamy 1996: 202). 'Money earned outside by men rarely reaches the home', according to Vasanthi Devi. 'The great problem of drink falls hardest on the heads of the women, and until this is eradicated there cannot be true liberation for women' (conference, 10 April 1999). Education, in its broadest sense, is the key to this enterprise, both to make women more confident and assertive, and to encourage men to alter their behaviour.[13]

A change in world view and lifestyle practices, it should be stressed, is neither utopian nor unprecedented. As we have seen, the lower castes had a higher esteem for women, but sanskritisation has resulted in the adoption of higher-caste customs such as dowry. 'We had a more egalitarian, respectful and fair culture but we have changed it' Vasanthi Devi insists. An academic commentator on the Dalit movement, A. Marx, stressed the differences between women when he spoke at the Centre for Dalit Solidarity: 'Dalit women's problems are different from those of others', he said, 'and it is important that we understand this'. Other speakers, however, were less convinced. Nasreen, a university lecturer, and Kameswari, a landless labourer, spoke of sexual and physical abuse within the home and the problems of alcohol abuse. The multiple strands of oppression—caste, class and gender—were presented as intertwined in their

---

[13] In an article on female infanticide, Athreya and Chunkath (2000) stress the importance of education in the attempt to combat the practice, and highlight the successes of a government-funded street theatre programme that raised awareness of the issues involved.

commentaries.[14] The delineation of identities is an act of boundary setting which obscures the multiple identities of individuals who may be Dalits, women, exploited workers and Paraiyars at the same time. Privileging the Dalit/non-Dalit binary, thus, merely downplays the patriarchal structures that Dalits themselves perpetuate. The SRM in Tamil Nadu castigated the nationalist movement for adopting higher-caste norms with regard to women. Periyar's politics sought a free and equal citizenship for diverse (not single) social groups such as BCs, Dalits and women. Dalit movements have continued this tradition in giving women a voice that has frequently been denied them, but as we shall see in the next chapter, the leader-centred nature of most movements is far from egalitarian. It is important, therefore, for these groups to recognise the value and autonomy of Dalit women and to learn the lessons that they teach.

[14] Dalit men highlight the suffering of their women as emphasising the brutality of the upper castes. Karunakaran, an activist from Andhra Pradesh, waxed lyrical; 'Dalit women, beautiful Dalit women, more beautiful than these here (pointing to his relatives), have to suffer with no secure or private bathing facilities. Out in these open spaces they fall prey to the lust of higher-caste men' (interview, 13 October 1999). All too often, however, it is Dalit men who are guilty of sexual violence against women (Geetha 1998b; Subadra 1999).

7

Leaders and Leadership: Movement Organisation and Membership Debates

When people come knocking on my door at midnight I do not get annoyed thinking 'Oh these stupid people'. Rather, I think of my leader—who protests 24 hours a day—a people's leader who eats old kanji *[boiled rice soaked in water] and raw chillies with his followers (Anandan, DPI activist, 23 March 1999).*

Introduction: The Question of Leadership

I had travelled for hours in a rickety bus, asked countless people for directions and walked a couple of kilometres to find the hall, so I was somewhat chagrined when there was nothing happening at the venue. The notice for the event had announced that the programme would start at 9 a.m., and I had arrived around 10. The venue was obviously the right one as the flags of the DLM fluttered on the approach road. There was also a small knot of members who had, like me, assumed that the event would start within at least an hour of the stated time. We were mistaken but at least had each other to speak to. Our conversations were interrupted around 11.30 when a van of movement leaders drew up, ascended the stage and started the speeches that we had all come so far to hear. At least that was what I thought, until my neighbour leaned over and asked if I wanted some tea. 'But', I protested, 'the speeches have begun, do you not want to stay and listen?' His response was as typical as it was instructive: 'This is boring, when *Annan* turns up there will be some interest'. *Annan* (elder brother) is the appellation by which most movement leaders are known to their followers. The fictive kinship it establishes is common in India and all the speakers on stage were addressed as 'elder brother'. Whereas their names would have used to prefix the term, however, the leaders are distinguished from the lesser lights of the organisation by being known simply as 'big brother'. *Annan*, as a form of address on its own could only mean one person.

The DLM is not alone in this respect. When the leader of the Liberation Panthers, R.Thirumavalavan, was indisposed for four months, the attendance at protests dropped, and many meetings, ceremonies and even weddings were postponed. It was not that the movement could not have gone ahead with these programmes, but that the people involved were unwilling to deny themselves a visit by the leader. In short, leaders dominated all the movements which I surveyed and were ubiquitous even in absence as members constantly referred to them, displayed pictures of them or played tapes of the latest speeches. Not all movements were centred round a *single* leader. The Tamilaga Dalit Liberation Movement (TDLM) had deliberately attempted to create a structure that avoided the problems of over-centralisation by forming a leadership committee of five people, all of whom had to ratify any decision. This more participatory structure and ethos was a consequence of, and reaction to, the previous leader's perceived abuse of power. The women's movements, discussed in the previous chapter, also tried to avoid the worst excesses of centralisation though certain leader-figures played key roles.

The issue of leadership, therefore, is a crucial one. Certainly, when questioned why they favoured one movement over others, adherents usually cited the leader. Given this, the number of Dalit movements in Tamil Nadu suggests a wealth of leadership talent. The picture, however, is more complex. It must be stressed that a 'great leader' did not necessarily require great qualities of leadership. Divisions within the SCs mean that belonging to the right caste or sub-caste often carries as much weight as the calibre of the candidate. The attractiveness of a central figure, as Dickey observes, 'is determined more by aspects such as personal nature and even family background than by physical features, although the latter may certainly help' (1993a: 349). I do not wish to suggest that there are no meritorious Dalit leaders in the state, far from it, the intention is to problematise the issue of leadership. Most Dalit movements in Tamil Nadu are centralised around a dominant figure who plays the part of chief decision maker, orator, spokesperson for the movement and hero of the masses. 'Who do you think is the best Dalit leader?', I was frequently asked. Understanding the culture and dynamics of leadership, therefore, is central to understanding contemporary Dalit movements.

'Indian political institutions', as Mageli shows, 'are marked by *factionalism*, dividing but not necessarily breaking up an organisation; *personality focus*, with the leader assuming a powerful position; and *clearly defined hierarchical and authoritarian structures*, with little internal democratic functioning, expressed within a framework of patron-client relationships' (1997: 26, emphasis in the original). Since all social movements are influenced by interaction with the socio-political environment from which they emerge, any analysis of Dalit leadership needs to be placed within this context. In his study of social movements across India, Bonner concludes that the poor have yet to 'shed the inferiority born of centuries of caste oppression and the belief in Karma' (1990: 2). Used as they are to receiving orders, according to de Wit, 'slum people seek to establish personalistic ties and seldom, if ever, do they form associations in relation to ideological commitments' (1996: 51).[1] It is a truism that power creates inequality, so it hardly surprising that 'it is the leadership [of a social movement] which promotes the pursuit of goals, develops strategies and tactics for action, and formulates an ideology' (Melucci 1996: 332).

In Tamil politics party members often identify themselves as subservient disciples in decidedly uneven leader–follower relationships and monarchical values continue to inform political interaction (Price 1996: 43). Frequently the omnipotent leaders are characterised as 'charismatic' figures that attract a personal following. Applying the findings from studies of Tamil politics to Dalit movements could be problematic though, as Deliège found that the Paraiyars evinced a general antipathy to authority *within* the caste. 'The internal organisation of the Paraiyars', he asserts, 'forestalls the development of hierarchy within Paraiyar society itself, by maintaining egalitarian structures' (1997: 33). The Paraiyars are depicted as so segmented

[1] Mines (1994: 79) notes the importance of establishing trust through personalised ties in India. Although he observes that these ties are increasingly being replaced by impersonal contractual relationships, personalised trust and connections are still highly significant determinants of social and economic success.

and jealous of each other, that 'it would take a superior personality to be able to assert himself as a respected leader of all' (ibid.: 40).

Contextualising Charisma

Since the completion of Deliège's fieldwork, the emergence of several coherent Dalit movements have forced a reassessment of these questions. No movements can claim to speak for all Dalits or even all members of a particular caste, but they have succeeded in uniting significant numbers of people. The prominence of the central leaders, and the difficulties in organising the Dalit population, casts them in the light of 'superior personalities' and renders the concept of 'charisma' attractive. 'Charisma', according to Weber, denoted a 'certain quality of an individual personality by virtue of which he is set apart from ordinary men and treated as endowed with supernatural, superhuman or at least specifically exceptional powers or qualities' (1964: 358). These qualities are apparently bestowed on a leader by some supernatural force, and charismatic individuals were seen as 'inspired'. Weber opined that the *Bhakti* tradition had produced a number of 'inspired' Untouchable figures, but the leaders today cannot be said to be charismatic in this sense.

The relationship between a leader and their followers bears a strong resemblance to patron-client ties.[2] 'These alliances', according to Mageli, 'are vertical and imply that political mobilisation takes place when a charismatic leader manages to recruit followers for his cause, rather than when a group of people mobilise because of shared abstract interests' (1997: 27). Widlund's study of Tamil leadership echoes the characterisation of leaders as charismatic, but then

---

[2] Patron–client ties are dyadic relationships, depending to some degree on personal, face to face contact between the patron and the client. They are predicated upon a norm of reciprocity and mutual advantage (Lande 1977). For the poor and weak, in the absence of institutional provisions for the safeguarding of their livelihood, the influential support of the patron is perhaps the most important facet of the alliance. Clients, however, are expected to fulfil their obligations to the patron through the expenditure of labour and effort or through political and social support. Such ties are often relations of affection and loyalty that imitate familial bonds and may be cemented by fictive kinship (Scott 1977).

observes that 'winning elections goes beyond charismatic values. *It's also about mobilising voters, manning booths, keeping the depredations of others in check*' (*Outlook* comment piece, Widlund 2000: 367, emphasis in original). By overemphasising the charismatic aspects of leadership, however, as Melucci rightly notes, 'the nature of the social relationship of leadership tends to become blurred, because one of the terms of the relation, the masses, is annulled as an actor' (1996: 336). The uncritical adoption of the concept of charisma obscures the complexity of leadership relations and negates the conscious activity of followers.

Charismatic leadership describes a specific form of social exchange between the leader and his/her followers resembling that of a messiah and their disciples. Patron–client and movement ties, however, are more open to negotiation. Pitt-Rivers' description of patron–client relationships as 'lop-sided friendships' is particularly apt here, because the links that bind a leader to their followers are not neutral and can often constitute a bond of mutual devotion. It is these relations of reciprocity that distinguish a personal, dyadic alliance from one based on the more formal obligations implied in a contract (Lande 1977: xv). Furthermore, as Weber's (1958) relational account notes, it is followers that endow a leader with political power, prestige and recognition, and the rules of exchange demand an aspect of reciprocity. The conception of charisma as a form of divinely inspired leadership, therefore, can reveal little about the relations that bring actors together. Whilst political institutions in Tamil Nadu exhibit a strong focus on personality, their leaders are not immune to suggestion from below. 'No matter how strong a leader's public image', as Dickey points out, 'voter support can be lost if an opponent provides assistance while the leader ignores voter's needs' (1993a: 352).[3]

Charismatic leadership, in other words, must be analysed within its social context. Indeed, as Boholm argues, 'for a charismatic leader to be able to produce messages which his intended audience will understand and accept, they must be recognised in terms of already familiar cultural presuppositions' (1996b: 12). Leadership, thus, is a negotiated process in which leaders continually seek social

---

[3] In her study of Andhra Pradesh, Robinson notes that participation in the electoral process caused voters to make more demands of their candidates than they had previously done (1988: 259).

legitimacy and sanction. In fact, a large part of a Dalit leader's appeal is that they are 'one of us' and have experienced hardship in their own lives that they have risen above. It is arguable, thus, that they possess charismatic qualities in a Geertzian sense. Geertz (1983) argues that charisma is conferred by virtue of association with cultural values that are at the heart of the society in question. By appropriating the discourses of human rights, the constitution and democratisation, Dalit leaders place themselves at the heart of contemporary Indian politics. More specifically, by articulating the concerns, fears and injustices that confront their constituents, they become central to the aspirations of their followers. Geertz's conceptualisation retains the analytical utility of the term without falling into the popular conception of charisma, which is indistinguishable from personal magnetism. It also helps to explain the fluctuating fortunes of different leaders and the disjunction between the ideal of political equality and the reality of dominant leaders.

The Social Relations of Leadership

Notwithstanding the dominance of leadership figures, much contemporary social movement analysis chooses to focus on group dynamics instead. Indeed, many Western accounts depict 'new social movements' as essentially participatory organisations. Insofar as leadership is discussed, it is presented as a relationship in which the movement members and goals are as likely to shape the leader as the reverse. Such theories are framed in a completely different context and their utility here is open to question. Rather than rejecting them out of hand, though, some of the insights are worth pursuing. For instance, it would certainly be misleading to see Dalit movements as embodied in one central person, because their authority ultimately rests upon their ability to represent their member's interests. As we have seen, reciprocity is essential and most Dalit movements had mechanisms that allowed dissent, and some, such as the Liberation Panthers, had an able secondary leadership. It would also be erroneous to suggest that the role of the leader in Dalit movements is uniform, or that the diverse leaders act according to any preconceived and recognised guidelines. Each leader had his own particular style, approach, and following.

Furthermore, leaders are not hermetically sealed off from movement members who obviously influence leadership style and strategy. The constituents of a movement are the bricks upon and with which the ideology, strategy, cohesion and image of a movement are constructed. The members of any movement have the ultimate sanction of being able to switch allegiance or refrain from political activity. The different approaches of the leaders, thus, are often reflected in the social composition of the movement. Thus, as the Ambedkar People's Movement lost its radicalism, many of its younger members opted to join the Liberation Panthers instead. How much movement positions are dictated by the leadership is hard to assess, but activists assert their commitment to their chosen movement, define themselves accordingly and are protective of its stance. Consequently, as we shall see, when the DPI attempted to alter its position, the leadership met with fierce resistance from its cadres.

It is axiomatic that no one person constitutes a movement since a certain mass is required for it be defined as such. Where this person is not regarded as a prophet, therefore, they will have to take cognisance of the member's opinions. Influence of necessity is a two-way process. 'In reality', as Melucci notes, 'in a complex network of exchanges, influence circulates as a variously distributed resource and becomes also a property of minorities with the ability to assert themselves' (1996: 337). It is possible, however, for one central figure to *symbolise* the organisation that they represent, or to dominate the social imagination about that movement. Such symbolism is a powerful mechanism that serves to link individual and collective action. An admiration for, adulation of or belief in, a central figure can serve to unite disparate individuals around common themes, and ubiquitous references to leaders give cohesion to this 'imagined community' (Anderson 1991 [1983]). The central figures are presented to the public, by the media and the government, as the only known face of the movement and as its only recognised voice.

This focus obscures the organisational dynamics of the movement and also means that movement members themselves gravitate around the leader who can articulate their demands to a wider audience. Meetings at which the leader was present attracted a larger following and, thus, more media coverage. Hence, there is a widespread idea that an event is only worthwhile if the leader is present. Time and again meetings, protests and ceremonies were abandoned or postponed until such time as the leader became available.[4] Mines (1994: 41) refers to such organisations as 'leader-centred groups'. Tamils, he insists, primarily think of the self in relation to others. The individuality of public figures is defined by the 'superiority of leaders over their followers' (ibid.: 40). The leader is thus both the ultimate point of reference and the ultimate source of authority and their position is vested with 'imperative control'. That is: 'The probability that a command within a given specific content will be obeyed by a given group of people' (Weber 1964: 152). The ties binding a member to a leader are not forged of steel, however, and must be constantly renewed. Returning from a lengthy illness, thus, Thirumavalavan attended numerous events to explain his absence and to apologise. A leader's authority, therefore, is tempered by the fact that they 'must circumscribe his or her successes with a reputation for altruism, honesty and commitment to the collective good of the community', in order to avoid accusations of venality (Mines 1994: 42).

Meeting the Leader, Establishing the Movement

Consequently, the ubiquity of recorded speeches, photographs and videotapes, has 'not obviated the need for the personal appearance and the personal favour' (Dickey 1993a: 353). The leaders of the biggest movements reside in Madras, which is far from central geographically but is the centre of political power in Tamil Nadu. When a locality first pledges its allegiance to the movement, however, this affinity is solemnised by a brief visit from the leader. Of course, most leaders are too busy to go around raising flags every time a new area joins the movement. Instead, they wait until a sufficient number of units in one area wish to join, and then the leader spends two to three days in a non-stop tour of that area. On one such flag-raising tour around Ramnad District, the DPI inaugurated several villages into the movement.

Thirumavalavan was due to speak in Emmeneswaram Village at 4 o'clock, but he did not arrive till 10. At 4 o'clock all the local activists piled into two vans and drove out to meet him. The vans were packed

---

[4] At least two weddings in the Madurai area were postponed pending his arrival.

to capacity with youths, many of whom had been drinking. When we met up with the leader's convoy in Manamadurai we formed a group of two cars, two jeeps and four vans. In procession we visited two areas where Thirumavalavan dismounted from his vehicle, raised the flag of the movement and spoke to members. We then drove for a further 40 minutes to a village, where a few speeches were made and another flag raised. Finally we drove back to Emmeneswaram where food was provided for all. Thirumavalavan was allowed some respite before ascending the stage but still nodded off whilst the others talked. He had been on the road since 8 o'clock that morning.

Such contact is crucial to cement the leader's place in people's hearts and minds. The personal intimacy of these occasions reinforces the fictive kinship expressed in the term *Annan* and safeguards leaders from accusations of arrogance. Such appearances ensure that the figurehead of the movement is not only a name in lights but someone whom most members have either met or seen in close proximity. Direct contact with the leaders gives the members a sense of personal recognition and importance and these events are often highlights in an area's collective imagination. As seen in Chapter 5, movement affiliation enables a local populace to redefine their identity. Usually people in a locality contacted a movement after some form of caste discrimination, but meetings could also be prompted by an increase in consciousness. The important point is that they are the ones who make contact. At an early juncture, therefore, they place themselves in a position of weakness with regard to the organisation.

The activists who respond to calls for assistance reinforce this imbalance of power by 'taking classes' which deal with the aims, ideals and history of the movement, usually provide information about Ambedkar and their own leader, and highlight the mutual responsibility of the movement and the members. There is, thus, a pedagogic aspect to movement activism and new recruits expect the movement leadership to guide them through complex socio-political issues. When the local groups are ready to be inducted into the movement, they arrange a meeting. Unless they have been to events elsewhere, the first time they actually meet the leader, of whom they have heard so much about, is during the 'flag-raising ceremony' (*kodi aettru villa*). At such events it is the leader who steps forward to hoist the flag and explain what it represents. The relationship thus established between the leader and the defining symbol of the movement is reinforced by the choreography of the occasion.

There is almost always a stage erected under an awning. The 'big men' or women of the movement are not only elevated physically but also provided with chairs from which they are visible to all. The movement members range themselves in front of the dais seated occasionally on benches, but more frequently on rough blankets, sheets of newspaper, or their *chappals*, as they listen to the speeches that are relayed over loudspeakers. In roadside demonstrations, a semi-circle is formed around the leaders who occupy the most visible places facing outwards. Usually a microphone is installed and each successive orator is close to the leader when talking. Where new branches of the movement are inaugurated, headstones erected or buildings and statues constructed, the process is initiated by a dedication and the name of the leader is etched or painted onto stone plaques or wooden boards that document the visit. 'Each of these', as Dickey notes, 'is a reciprocal event; the presence of the politician, or any respected person, also bestows honour on the ceremony or occasion' (1993a: 350). Hence, there is an obsession with photos that document the presence of members at any such event.

The Experience of Leadership

The significance of personal contact was highlighted by Anandan, from the DPI, who spoke of the difficulties of movement activism— of court cases, violence and of being 'on duty' the whole time. The temptation to give up, he states, is compelling. As the quote at the head of this chapter highlights, however, he insists that his commitment never wavered due to the example and image of his leader (interview, Anandan, 23 March 1999). Those leaders who remain aloof from the people, who do not enter the *cheris*, or dismount from their air-conditioned cars, are mocked and depicted as self-interested individuals out to feather their own nests. A 'good' movement leader is always on call. It was said of Louis XVIII that his life was a public spectacle. The same could be asserted of some movement leaders. When Thirumavalavan has a pee by the roadside, there are some ten to twenty people ranged alongside. When he is washing in the morning messages are relayed through the door, or the newly-acquired mobile phone is passed into the room. When he is in transit the jeep in which he is seated is usually packed to bursting, and is often one in a convoy of crowded vehicles. Furthermore, all the leaders whom I interviewed kept an open house and were frequently inundated by movement members who desired an audience with them. The schedule imposed upon leaders is draining and it was not uncommon to see them dozing off during other's speeches.

The emphasis on experience and on 'being one with the people' places a heavy burden on leaders and also raises the question of what sets them apart from the crowd. They were mostly educated, well versed in law and capable of speaking at length. They are seen as representatives of the people who articulate their woes and aspirations. It was often noted that the most prominent movement leader, Thirumavalavan, is the best orator as well. According to Nambath, the Dalits initially eulogised 'criminal elements who indulged in isolated acts of violence against the oppressor caste for personal ends … But in time the leadership of the community [has] passed on to organisations which systematically and therefore effectively, resisted caste oppression' (*The Hindu*, 25 May 1997). What this has entailed is a class differentiation within the movements, with the more educated sections taking the lead in the struggle. Sathai Baikiaraj, the leader of the All-India Paraiyar Peravai (AIPP), would be an example of the more violent style of leadership. His short, populist and invariably violent speeches meet with rousing applause. Yet even he, who calls himself 'Bomb Baikiaraj', has been forced to take a more muted approach.[5] There is a growing awareness that such isolated action cannot achieve a solution to the issues which Dalit movements are trying to address.

The more popular leaders are those who are educated, articulate and socially respectable. Dr Krishnasamy was a practising cardiologist who gave up his surgery to assume leadership of the PT. Thirumavalavan was a well paid government administrator until he resigned his post to contest the elections. Daniel Gnanasekaran, of

---

[5] Interview with Guruvijay Paraiyar, 10 October 1999: 'We were a violent mob who used to inspire fear in people, but we have reduced that tendency.... Sathai Baikiaraj will turn up and explode bombs if necessary. There is no need for a local riot, but for a serious event, then it serves to identify us. However, if you use bombs like Deepavali crackers then they lose impact'.

the DLM, is an ordained pastor with a BD in Theology. Thirumavalavan emphasised the significance of educated members of the Dalit community and the responsibility that they have to assume. 'It is this white-collar sector alone', he stressed, 'which is the force that can decide the future of the marginalised Dalits. … If government servants do not think about these people or their future, then not only another thousand years, but many thousands of years may pass before these people are able to raise their heads' (speech, 1 December 1999).

This sentiment is not born of middle-class intellectual arrogance; it is an awareness of the poverty of the Dalit masses. Those without the means to eat, it is argued, may partake in—but do not have the means to lead—a social revolution. This approach is problematic and can prompt movements to develop a 'project mentality' that is more concerned with tangible results in the form of houses built, protests held or cases won, than with the empowerment of the people. Organisations involved in relief work for women in Madras, often 'created in them a sense of helplessness and dependency on outsiders' (Mageli 1997: 49). As Kothari argues; 'merely organising the poor' into different activities has little effect. The emphasis must be upon empowering the people socially through the provision of education, public health facilities, housing and environmental enhancement (1995: 73). 'To drag these people out of the mire in which they have been enslaved', Thirumavalavan asserts, 'one needs a clear sighted movement … one with the patience to explain its ideology to the people' (speech, 1 December 1999).

Since the majority of activists stem from the lower sections of society, and many are illiterate, there is often a paternalist aspect to movement work. Although many movement leaders are from the middle classes, the majority of the more educated and affluent activists are involved in NGOs that can pay them for their services. They work *for*, rather than *with*, the Dalit people. The schism that might be expected to develop between movement cadre and the leadership due to the differences in class and education are elided by a strong 'network of affiliation and socialisation' (Melucci 1996: 335). For promising activists, this network functions as a training ground that inculcates the skills of leadership. They are invariably presented with opportunities to speak at meetings and may be asked to handle local issues and recruitment. Palani Kumar, the secretary of Melavassel, made his first speech at the flag-raising ceremony of a village where he had worked to establish the movement. Hesitant at first, he asked for an assessment of his performance and requested me to tape his speech so that he could listen to it later. As he grew in confidence he was granted further openings. Through these processes of socialisation activists can rise through the ranks and serve as a bridge between the locality and the leadership.[6]

Where such links were absent and the distant figures of authority were perceived to be divorced from local concerns and unaccountable to members, the strength of the movement declined. A Dalit leader had to be identified as one of the people. Speeches and ideologies are not in themselves sufficient, for fine words lack significance if people cannot relate to them. The crucial factor here is *experience*. It is seen as vital for the leader themselves to have experienced what it means to be a Dalit. This means that only a Dalit can be a Dalit leader, and also means that they must become one with the people. 'Only by sleeping amongst Dalits and eating with them can we become close to them', as Ravichandran of Marutham Network expressed it. 'But at the same time', he went on, 'many tell of Dalit organisations who speak about Dalit liberation and stay in five star lodges' (interview, 27 September 1999). In an interview with rediff.com, Dr Krishnasamy was asked how he could stay in fine hotels yet campaign for Dalits. He responded that 'your mind has to be attuned to the problems', but elsewhere in the interview he was keen to emphasise the poverty and hardship from which he had emerged (Rediff, 10 November 1998). If you contrast this image with that painted of Thirumavalavan: 'A people's leader who eats old *kanji* and raw chillies with his people', then one has an idea of the sort of leader who people identify with (Anandan, interview, 23 March 1999).[7]

The flip-side of this constant scrutiny is that in many ways the leader must be an entertainer. Movement leaders certainly have to compete with film stars and politicians for people's attention. In Melavassel, pre-school children could identify photographs of 'Thimallan *Annan*' even if they could not as yet pronounce his name. Such public recognition would usually be reserved for the most popular figures of the Tamil film industry, whose faces adorn billboards across the state. Movement occasions often have a festive

[6] Melucci's findings suggest that this is a widespread mode of movement 'socialisation' (1996: 342).

[7] 'Tamils disparage a life lived only for the self', as Mines asserts (1994: 189).

air about them, and a leader's visit is a cause for celebration—often marked by decorated stages, fairy lights and the consumption of alcohol. The speech of the leader is the highlight of such an event and people want to see the person as much as to listen to what is said.[8] 'Touching the leaders, speaking to them, seeing that they are "flesh and blood"', as Cruces and De Rada observe, 'all have an undeniable affective value which is not to be attained through the media' (1996: 118). Movement activists often express their gratitude for the leader's visit by offering gifts. Kertzer refers to such gift giving as a ritual means by which 'people communicate their pledge of clientage to a particular patron' (1988: 31). They are rewarded for their devotion by the public recognition they receive.

'There is a particular intensity of following, a depth of devotion, felt for leaders perceived to be "heroes"', as Dickey observes (1993a: 351). Such adulation is doubtless gratifying, but it carries with it a burden of responsibility. People expect results from their leaders. Not necessarily tangible ones, but at least an indication that the leader is doing his or her best for them, and that their trust is not in vain. One of the ways in which this is judged is in analyses of the leader's comportment and image. A press photograph, for example, depicted Thirumavalavan, Moopanar and Dr Krishnasamy seated alongside each other. The noteworthy feature was that the two major Dalit leaders in Tamil Nadu were sharing a platform together on a common cause, but this was of secondary interest to DPI activists. They were more interested in the fact that Krishnasamy had his trainer clad feet stuck out across the platform, whereas *Annan* (referring to Thirumavalavan in this context) was so neat and decorous. I have no doubt that members of the PT could have given another gloss to the picture, but what it highlights is the significance of image. Dalit leaders are not film style superheroes but their followers come to expect certain modes of behaviour from them.[9] Whilst important, however, the question of leadership cannot be decided on the basis of presentation alone.

---

[8] 'Waiting for the leader's appearance', as Cruces and De Rada note, 'generates a sense of suspense, and his exit induces a sense of closing. This kind of meeting can be deemed to be an authentic ritual event that aims to invest the leader with charisma' (1996: 109).

[9] See also Fearon (1999), who notes that impressions of how the candidate speaks, dresses, expresses and conducts themselves influence people's choice of leader.

The heroic leader is recognised as such in contrast to the perceived corruption and venality of others. Their virtue lies in the fact that they have devoted themselves to work for the good of others, rather than themselves. As Perumal, a DPI activist from Melavassel put it:

> Our leader Thirumavalavan ...20 years ago he bore the brunt of anti-Dalit discrimination, so he decided to dedicate his life to his people. He has a government job, a government job! Rs 10, 000 or so, but that is now in suspension. How old do you think he is? Only 37, but he hasn't married yet, he is still single because he has dedicated himself to the cause (interview, 8 March 1999).

The absolute faith reposed in the leader, however, means that the scope for abuse is huge. Movement members are often highly reflexive about this and examples of 'good and bad leadership' feature prominently in their discussions.

It should be no surprise that those seen as good leaders conform most closely to the conditions outlined here. They are accessible, in touch with the people and good speakers. The increase in Dalit assertion, however, has also fostered a desire for radicalism. The 'softly-softly' approach of the Dalit elder, Vai Balasundaram of the Ambedkar People's Movement (AMI), therefore, has led to an exodus of youth. The AMI was the first major Dalit movement in Tamil Nadu and at its height in the late 1970s 'Vai Ba' was seen as *the* Dalit leader. 'You had to book two or three years in advance if you wanted a meeting' with Vai Ba, as Rajagopalan, a movement activist put it (interview, 11 October 1999). At the time Balasundaram caught the political imagination by resigning as a DMK mayor to fight for the cause. In the 1970s the AMI walked down caste-Hindu streets wearing shoes and smashed up shops that persisted with the two-glass system. They were a radical movement that raised the consciousness of rural Dalits and made the abstract legal prohibitions on caste discrimination more meaningful. Despite this, 'Vai Ba' was never disassociated from party politics—his approach was often legalistic and though bold at the time has lost resonance now. He lost the backing of Rajagopalan when he unilaterally announced his electoral support for Rajiv Gandhi without proper consultation.

As we have seen, the early emphasis on social inclusion has been superseded by a demand for political rights. Today radical speeches are taped and replayed by members who wish to return a hit for a hit rather than resort to the law. As expectations have risen, the demands placed on Dalit leaders have changed and those who have not shifted with the times are being left behind. Regrettably, the significance accorded to representing member's interests and issues frequently translates into the demand that a leader should be from the particular caste that forms the bulk of a movement. There has been an increasing trend towards caste-based mobilisation to the extent that Daniel Gnanasekaran of the DLM spoke of shedding the Dalit label:

> It is the need of the hour. That is the only way to go. I am being forced to become a caste movement. Look *Thambi* [little brother], all movements and parties are organising along caste lines—that is the way it is, that is the sign of these times. It is easy and unproblematic to organise on the basis of caste, but very difficult to call yourself a Dalit (interview, 12 October 1999).

By emphasising the rights and well-being of any one caste community, however, leaders risk severing attachment to an emerging Dalit consciousness and fostering inter-caste rivalries between SCs. Organising on the basis of caste, as the leader of the DLM frankly admitted, is a much easier proposition than the attempt to mobilise disparate individuals against caste per se.[10] The internal solidarity of a caste is cemented by proximity within a locality, endogamous marriage practices and the rhetoric of blood relationship.

Although the leaders of particularistic movements invariably assert their commitment to Dalit rights in general, the immediate objective is to increase the social mobility and cohesion of their own group. Dr Krishnasamy emphasised that the musical notes of diverse instruments may merge to form a symphony and that diverse caste movements could likewise work in harmony on *Dalit* issues (speech, 1 December 1999). More often, the propensity to organise on caste lines has only hampered the cause of Dalit liberation. Putnam asserts that a 'key indicator of civic sociability must be the vibrancy of associational life' (1993: 91), but particularistic movements are constructed in opposition to 'others' who may be Dalits, let alone a higher-caste groups. Furthermore, Mageli (1997: 61) notes the importance of loyalty in Indian organisational behaviour and the

---

[10] See Anandan (*The Hindu*, 24 July 2001) for a critique of 'anti-caste' movements. See Duncan (1999: 36) for an analysis of similar trends in Uttar Pradesh.

difficulties in bridging the gap between different groups. Social capital from such associations, in other words, is not evenly distributed through society but is 'context-dependent' (Chandhoke 2001: 15). Ultimately these movements increase the affinity that members feel towards a leader or caste, rather than towards the common good. This mode of organisation also lends weight to the state's depiction of Dalit movements as casteist institutions that need to be suppressed.

The earlier discussion on charisma should caution us against placing too much emphasis on the leader here. For a start, movements can only cohere around caste sentiments if those sentiments already exist. Leaders alone cannot create caste feeling even though they can exacerbate or help to diminish it. It is abundantly clear that caste concerns continue to inform people's daily lives and that people habitually distinguish themselves from others. The term Dalit has yet to overcome the appeal to more parochial loyalties. The most striking evidence of this in Tamil Nadu is the fact that Ambedkar was often portrayed as a Paraiyar due to the prominence that certain movements have accorded to him. The retreat to caste-specific movements, thus, is as much a reflection of local priorities as a leadership decision. Of more interest are those organisations that have resisted the allure of caste. The DPI refer to themselves as a Dalit organisation and hope to attract followers from all SCs. Others, such as the Devendra Kula Vellallar Union (a Sanskritised epithet for the Pallar community) and the Paraiyar Peravai, however, insist that one must 'put one's own house in order' before uniting.[11]

When asked if he wanted a casteless society, for example, Dr Krishnasamy replied: 'Yes, but not at present' (Rediff, 10 November 1998). The Paraiyar Peravai similarly seek to mobilise a narrower caste category before reaching out to forge horizontal ties. Such organisation is more bottom-up and 'organic' than mobilisation on the basis of wider categories. It is here that the significance of leadership may be seen. As Pudhupatti Aseervadam recalled:

When we first went to meet him [Thirumavalavan] to call him to speak in our area, I knew full well that he was a Paraiyar. We said, 'we are inviting you on behalf of the Paraiyar Peravai and you must

[11] The slogan of the Paraiyar Peravai may be loosely translated as: 'We will build our houses, They can build theirs. On common issues we will unite'.

come and speak to us'. He agreed, but as soon as I said that we would write: 'Thirumavalavan Paraiyar is coming to Speak' on the poster—this was the first time we met, we were trying to build a movement, but not considering this he spoke in a demeaning manner to me—'Do not use any speech except "DALIT". I am not proud to be a Paraiyar, nor am I proud to be a Pallar or a Chakkiliyar, but I am a Dalit. We are enslaved, a downtrodden caste, but I am proud' (interview, 28 March 1999).

The relationship between leader and led is crucial to the survival and success of any movement. What Aseervadam's recollections reveal, however, is the leader's importance in terms of direction, vision and decision making.

The Role of Leadership

The role of movement leadership, as Melucci says, is to define objectives, facilitate action and maintain cohesion (1996: 339–40). The 'fulcrum for leadership action', he insists, 'is the *decision*, that is, the capacity to choose between alternatives and reduce uncertainties' (1996: 340). This does not necessarily mean that the leader is paramount. As Boholm, observes, the leader 'receives political support because he [sic] skilfully draws on a repertoire of current or latent idioms and symbols' (1996c: 163). Becoming a leader, therefore, requires the internalisation of group values. Whilst the leadership may articulate the aims of a movement, in other words, these objectives have to be decided upon in complex, and often contentious, processes of negotiation. A leader's ideals cannot, as the Liberation Panthers realised, be imposed upon an unwilling constituency. Although the leadership was convinced of the need to boycott the elections, for example, Dalits continued to turn out in large numbers to exercise their franchise. This did not mean that the decision to contest the polls in 1999 was a formality, since many of the movement activists had come to perceive themselves as revolutionary actors and they were unwilling to enter the institutions that they had hitherto disdained.[12]

---

[12] One activist at a protest meeting in Vadipatti, for example, insisted that sitting by the road and speaking was a waste of time. 'I came here to sit in the road

The leaders of any movement, thus, are constrained by the views of their members and affected by the position of the population at large. Realising that the election boycott lacked popular appeal convinced the DPI to alter their strategy and yet the move to politics had to be accompanied by assurances that the movement would not lose its radical edge. The TDLM's innovative attempt to create a non-hierarchical and participatory structure has also failed to catch on thus far. In many ways the relationship between the leadership committee of the TDLM and the peripheral members of the movement continues to resemble that of other movements. The mode of organisation, the posters and speeches combine to reinforce the centrality of the leader within a movement. This person-centred mode of organisation is arguably a prominent characteristic of Tamil society.[13] The public image of a person, as we have seen, is fostered in several ways. Price observes that 'superior status and power ... have divine attributes in popular Hinduism' (1989: 571). There is a tendency, therefore, to assign leaders the status of heroes or Gods. The corollary of this position is that members revere and adore leaders rather than seeing them as equals.

This results in a sense of dependency upon, and absolute trust in, the leaders. Leaders were often asked to 'bless' activists' weddings, for example, or to name babies. Leaders are also usually beyond reproach. The Dalits of Allallaberi in Madurai District were turned into refugees after their rejection of the demeaning roles that they were hereditarily forced to perform. The DLM leader worked tirelessly on their behalf and succeeded in relocating them. 'He had blood on his feet from walking here and there on our behalf', as one of the residents put it. Although he had not responded to their requests and pleas for some years now and they were facing problems in their current location, they remained loyal to their 'saviour'. 'We owe it to [Danny] *Annan*, he did so much to help us, we are his followers', as Moses insisted (interview, 16 February 1999). Charity and gift giving by powerful benefactors carry deep-rooted cultural significance, and the ties between leader and follower are often cemented

---

and block traffic'. Having asserted the corruption and pointlessness of institutional politics for so long, it was not easy to convince people of the need to contest the elections.

[13] On this see Rudolph and Rudolph (1967), Mageli (1997), Kohli (1990) and especially Dickey (1993a, 1993b), Mines (1994) and Price (1989).

by acts of patronage.[14] Dalit leaders, however, are rarely in a position to distribute patronage, indeed I only ever saw Thirumavalavan receiving gifts. The pre-eminence of the leader, therefore, depends on their ability to achieve a reputation for commitment, for looking after their members and for getting things done. They are, as Brass observes, 'perceived to have a duty of care for the material interests of followers' (1990: 96).

The adulatory loyalty of activists is not always reciprocated. Movement members are aware of imperfection amongst leaders and are conscious of the problems of autocratic control. The most cited failing of leadership is a lack of accountability. Rajagopalan, as we saw, left the AMI because the leader unilaterally announced an electoral coalition. In the 1999 elections, members of the DLM were outraged by their leaders' decision to support the ruling DMK–BJP combine in the district of Karur, whilst backing the Dalit and minority-based TMC front elsewhere. The reasons that I was given, when I interviewed the leader shortly thereafter, had not been conveyed to the members. The TDLM split off from the DLM, citing this leader's disapproval of local initiatives. 'This movement is our asset. The liberty of the people is our future', Subramaniam of the TDLM explained. 'So for the leader to say, "this is my movement, if you like it stay, otherwise get out", is most unjust' (conversation, 11 October 1999).

The example may be specific, but the sentiment expressed is common. The lack of participation in decision making means that the only way such organisations can be democratic is through a stress upon accountability. This may explain one of the paradoxes involved in being a good leader. On the one hand, they are pivotal to movement organisation, but on the other hand, they must retain a sense that the movement is paramount. Speeches frequently assert that people should not struggle for the leader per se, but for the cause that they espouse. Movement stability is also a recurrent theme in which it is stressed that the leader could be jailed or lose their life but the movement would live on. The contrast between this self-effacement on the one hand, and the deification of the leader on the other is, perhaps, less of a paradox when it is understood in terms

[14] Dickey (1993a: 352), Mines (1994: 42), de Wit (1996: 265) and Subramanian (1999: 287) all comment on this trend.

of the cultural expectations of leadership. The leader is, in effect, saying that they are not involved for their own self-interest.

The emphasis on the movement is a reaffirmation of the issues that are being fought for and a reassertion of the altruism of the leader. It is also a confirmation of the exchange envisioned in movement membership and a public acknowledgement of the dedication of the members. 'We are behind Thirumavalavan *Annan* and he is behind us' as Selvi, a young Dalit woman from Jansi Rani Complex, put it. Her community has no proper houses, recognised jobs or education. They have, however, established a wing of the Liberation Panthers in the shrine where they congregate. They insist that the high profile and radicalism of the DPI has reduced the incidence of police harassment and given them a sense of security (Selvi, Jansi Rani Complex, 22 March 1999). Even in such hero-worship, though, there is the process in which the leader is simultaneously acclaimed and de-emphasised. This is apparent in the following interview with Subramani in Cuddalore:

> You talk as though Thirumavalavan alone was the most important figure, but what has Thirumavalavan himself said? That Thirumavalavan alone is not the DPI! Like me in this organisation there are lakhs of followers who Thirumavalavan has recruited, is recruiting. If Thirumavalavan goes today that is fine—in those lakhs of followers Thirumavalavan remains (interview, 27 April 1999).

We are told, thus, that Thirumavalavan is not the movement because he says so, and because he is present in each of his followers. It is such support that elevates the leader to a position of authority, and it is to acknowledge and retain such support that the rhetoric of self-effacement has arisen. This rhetoric is also functional for the everyday management of the movement. Too exclusive a focus upon the central leader, as we have seen, results in an inability to act in their absence and prompts jealousy amongst subsidiary actors. The prevalence of local conflicts renders such inertia and malcontent fatal to the efficient operation of a movement. No matter how much the presence of the leader increases crowds or is demanded, they cannot be everywhere at once. 'The leader', therefore, 'must facilitate the division and articulation of tasks and make the best possible use of the different talents available to the movement' (Melucci 1996: 339).

Bridging the Gap: The Leader and the Locality

Melucci's emphasis on the role of the leader here is somewhat contradictory given his assertion that 'leaders of movements cannot rely on an institutional structure' (1996: 334). Social movements are said to be distinguished from party structures by not having a clearly defined hierarchy of command. A structure of secondary leadership is required for even the most centralised movements, however, to bridge the gap between the movement and the leader. District and local secretaries are often installed to manage the local organisation on a semi-autonomous basis. Lack of office management, communications, transport and resource infrastructure, as Thirumavalavan observes, precludes Dalit leaders from being instantaneously in touch, or in control, of a given situation (interview, 3 November 1999). Although this would appear to forestall the emergence of a highly centralised leadership, the leader, as we have seen, is very much a presence even when absent.

The reverse is also the case, in that some leaders take a keen interest in the local running of a movement even in their absence. One of the reasons for the T/DLM split was that the absent leader allegedly complained that they were not referring their decisions to him:

> From February to December 1997 we held certain protests and meetings using the names of local leaders ...we were accused of running things without consulting the leadership, but we were taking up local issues as well as general ones....[The leader] questioned us about this saying: 'Am I your leader or the people in this area?' We said that you and the movement are one and the same, the response to which was: 'Then you should not do anything in this constituency without consulting me....This is my movement' he declared. We said 'this is a people's movement, working for the people. It is not an individual's movement'. We said that none of us had saved a single penny due to our activism. This movement is our asset (Subramaniam, 11 October 1999).

Irrespective of the rights and wrongs of this case, it points to a tension between local and regional leadership. Ideally the local cadre should have a level of autonomy that enables them to respond to issues of immediate concern, but they were frequently dependent on the leader, both as an advisor and as an authority whose word would be accepted by all. Dilemmas, such as the wording for a poster of protest, were often referred to the leader who had the final say on any issue.

It is clear, however, that everyday aspects of the movement must continue without the leader and consequently most movements have at least attempted to institute structures of secondary leadership. Some movements do have accepted secondary leaders and the DPI boasts that Thirumavalavan need not visit the northern districts of the state, since the movement's general secretary is so well regarded there. The DPI, as we have seen, had a central committee of 28 and a 'united state committee' of over 100 local leaders. The precise role of each figure and their relationship to other authorities, however, was not clearly spelled out. In acknowledgement of this a rule book was said to be in the offing, but during my fieldwork the structure of command was only apparent to leaders themselves and often seemed to break down. The voluntary nature of activism and the lack of resources have tended to render these hierarchies fluid and unpredictable.

The lack of infrastructure and overriding reliance upon a central figure often impinged upon the smooth running of the movement. On several occasions, for example, the orator of the Liberation Panthers was unable to attend meetings even though his name had been printed on the notice, because he had not been informed in advance or he lacked the necessary bus fare (personal communication). 'Firebrand' Murugan, so termed due to the fiery character of his oratory, worked as a construction labourer when not involved in movement work. On several occasions his speeches displayed a lack of knowledge about the intentions of the leadership.[15] Another factor detrimental to movement operation was the feeling of inadequacy occasioned by the pre-eminence of the leader. No matter how carefully the authority figure managed relations with local leaders there was a palpable sense that only the leader mattered. At numerous meetings, for example, supporters would listen with rapt

[15] In the run up to the election, 'Firebrand Murugan's lack of information was especially noticeable. For several speeches before the DPI aligned with the Third Front he castigated the DMK, AIADMK and the TMC. When he later supported 'Moopanar Aiyah', therefore, he had some explaining to do.

attention during the peroration of the movement's luminary, but would switch off otherwise:

> The hall, barely half full, listened half-heartedly to the village and area representatives, but the degree of respect which they were accorded was symbolised by the interruption of the first speech by the district secretary who lectured the audience on their inattention: 'What have you come here for if you just want to talk? Look! One of you has got his back turned to the speaker! What is being said is important, this is what you have come here for so please pay attention!' (from my fieldnotes, 9 January 1999).

This headmasterly rebuke would be redundant during a leader's speech. Similarly, whilst members might question the decisions and actions of local figures they usually accept the authority of the president unquestioningly. In such circumstances, it is very difficult to establish a clear structure of command. Secondary organisers can only gain 'promotion', as it were, by gaining popularity with the people and can only gain real authority by breaking away and forming their own movements. As well as responding to the demands of the people, therefore, movement presidents have the difficult task of trying to keep secondary figures on board. Even though he was fulsome in his praise of Thirumavalavan and got on well with him, for example, Kannadasan—the Madurai city coordinator of the DPI—grabbed hold of me once and demanded that I take a photo of him and other members and not just of 'MGR'.

Unless sufficient power is devolved downwards, therefore, Dalit movements are likely to be trapped in the perennial cycle of mobilisation and schism that seems to affect so many movements and parties across India. Part of the reason for this is that the focus on the leader is so extreme that it can easily be portrayed as self-aggrandisement when relations are strained. Indeed, it was this accusation that Periyasami, Joint General Secretary of the DPI, levelled at Thirumavalavan when he left. This was despite the fact that Periyasami above all other figures had had opportunities to stand alone and make a name for himself when he was selected to contest the 1999 elections from Perambalur. Part of the problem is that the movements lack the resources to publicise the secondary figures and the press focus almost completely on the central leader. The movement is not embodied in the leader, as we saw earlier, but it is symbolised by him/her and new recruits or ardent activists direct themselves towards them.

There are other factors involved in the fragility of movement organisations, however, and the frequency with which movements splinter may be partly due to the contradictory pulls of radicalism and institutionalisation. It is also augmented by the fact that there are no flows of patronage or distinct party offices with which to reward committed activists. The leader's ability to marshal the talent at his/ her disposal may be crucial, therefore, but it is influenced by factors such as funding, communications infrastructure and the political situation. Apart from the difficulties this leads to with leadership structures, it also forecloses other options. Talented crews of folk artists were available, for instance, and would have been invaluable in spreading the message of the organisation to a largely illiterate population. The prevalence of atrocities and caste conflicts however, rendered the movements predominantly reactive during my stay in 1999. Instead, it was the NGO groups, which have better resources, which organised Dalit art festivals and cultural programmes.

The constraints imposed upon movement organisation mean that it is incumbent upon the leaders to maximise the availability of resources by interacting with other parties (Lipsky 1970: 168). Regardless of the movement's internal structure, the prominent public image of the leader necessitates their presence in all negotiations with other bodies. Members of the secondary leadership may become conspicuous enough to negotiate with other institutions on a local level, but the significance of the leader remains undiminished because neither the wider society nor the media reflect the prominence that secondary figures may receive within the movement. It is the leader, therefore, (or the leadership committee) that has to assess which organisations are acceptable as allies and what sort of relationship to enter into with them. They must though, as we have seen, always bear in mind the reactions of the activists.

When Thirumavalavan went to meet Jayalalitha shortly before the 1999 elections, for example, the press reported that he had entered into an alliance with the AIADMK. Over time the leader could have persuaded the activists of the wisdom of this move, but to move straight from a radical boycott of the electoral process to an alliance with a corrupt and autocratic party was unacceptable. Whether the press was mistaken or not, the furore that erupted within the movement caused DPI leaders to issue swift disclaimers. For months thereafter they denied the reports in movement meetings. The leaders may be in the best position to assess the options open to the movement, because they are frequently in possession of information that is not available to the members. To act on this without first engaging in a process of negotiation within the movement, however, leads to disaffection amongst the ranks. At stake for members of the movement are questions of identity and self-image. As we have seen, DPI activists, resented the transition to electoral participation because this was seen as compromising the objectives of social and political change for short-term expediency.

The 'decision', thus, is evidently the pivotal role of leadership. The brevity of the term, however, serves to conceal the complexity of the processes involved. Extensive consultations with movement members and the leaders of other institutions are required before any major decision can be made. In its simplest manifestation, the leader may be called upon to clarify the wording of a document and settle local differences. For more deep-rooted issues, however, the leader's position has to be justified and 'sold' to the membership. Far from the original definition of charismatic leadership, therefore, Dalit leaders are not perceived to be infallible. Where the leader fails to sell a decision to the activists a schism in the movement may, as the DLM and DPI discovered, result. The reduction of uncertainty, therefore, must be negotiated rather than dictated. Once a decision has been made it must be explained, elaborated upon and presented to the constituents. If it is unclear how a movement benefits from a particular decision the immediate question becomes what is in it for the leader?

'Suitcase politics' is the contemptuous phrase by which people in India denote unprincipled alliances in which money is believed to have changed hands. Such charges are difficult either to validate or disprove and so the onus falls on the leaders to account for their actions. It was to escape such charges of mendicancy that the Dalit movements refused to extend unconditional support to the TMC Front in the 1999 elections. Instead they insisted that any political settlement must be premised upon the Dalit groups experiencing a 'share of power'. The alteration in strategy was significant enough for the Dalit movements to adopt a proactive approach to convince their members of the propriety of the alliance. 'Election cassettes' of songs and speeches were produced and widely distributed, countless speeches were made and innumerable villages visited. Accusations of venality are common and DPI activists certainly felt an initial sense of betrayal. Unless decisions are explained for the benefit of the members, it is clear, they can foster a sense of compromise that weakens morale.

Leaders Gone Astray

Betrayal need not result from external influences, but may occur within a movement itself. The loyalty reposed in the leader means that the members always place themselves in danger of misrepresentation or abuse. The rhetoric of self-effacement affirms the leader's commitment to the people and to the wider cause, but there is always the danger that they will become corrupt or that they will abandon an issue. Taking money to support an established political party was frequently alleged and always condemned. It was the crime that 'other' leaders committed. Where movement leaders did secure political alliances without consultation, as we have seen, this led to disaffection and defections. There were also, however, cases of betrayal on a more basic level. In a collector's office, for example, when the leaders of a movement (which will remain anonymous) sought the release of 45 members who had been arrested at a demonstration, they were apparently offered a choice: 'Hand yourselves over for arrest and we will release the others'. The leader in question opted to remain at liberty and fight for the release of the members from without the prison walls. One of his regional facilitators, however, pointed out that ordinary members were more likely to receive harsh treatment and urged a change of mind. When the decision stood, the facilitator asserted, 'I lost all faith in the leader of the movement'.

A similar tale was recounted in which a leader accepted some money to fight a court case. A member of his movement had been defrauded of several thousand rupees by a higher-caste person. Having taken out a case to get the money returned, the leader allegedly capitulated to lawyers and agreed to settle out of court. The activist, thus, had lost not only the initial sum of money, but also the cash that he put up to fight the case. The leaders in question have not had the opportunity to respond to the allegations and the point here is not to castigate certain movements and endorse others.

What these examples highlight is the position of inferiority from which movement members operate. Those let down by their chosen leader can and do switch allegiances to another, but the relationship between the two is so uneven that there is very often no other means of redress.[16]

There are, however, more patent examples of 'bad leadership'. Manakadavu, a rural village in south west Tamil Nadu, was beset by caste clashes after Dalits in the village challenged the continuing practice of Untouchability (most obviously the two-glass system) there. Dalit leaders rallied to the cause and it was documented in various newspapers and magazines. Six months on from the initial event, however, I visited Manakadavu and found that the solidarity suggested in the early reports was lacking. In the initial enthusiasm of challenging the caste structures in their location the Dalits were united. At the time of my visit, however, they were disheartened. Various Dalit movements had promised to help in the struggle, but the leaders of the DLM, the PT and the TAYF had all abandoned the village due to disputes between themselves (interview with villagers, 18 October 1999). Dr Krishnasamy of the PT defended himself against this charge, declaring that his movement could not intervene where others had entered the fray already. He also stressed that the Chakkiliyar people needed to organise amongst themselves rather than depend upon the muscle of movements built elsewhere (interview, 1 December 1999). The DLM and TAYF are primarily drawn from this category, but they fell out with each other. The result not only highlighted divisions in the Dalit community, but also left the villagers of Manakadavu without organisational support at the time when they most needed it. The betrayal of this community is another indication of how organisational jealousy and concerns about territory hinder Dalit emancipation.

Having experienced such abuse of trust, the TDLM attempted to establish a more participatory and accountable organisational structure. As we have seen, the democratising impulse that prompted this leadership experiment has yet to filter down to the grass roots. The

---

[16] It is not my intention here to make judgements as to which movements were 'better' than others, which leaders were corrupt and which activists were 'most' committed. I have included these examples of malpractice to highlight the problems associated with over centralisation, and the difficulties of activism, rather than to discredit any one movement.

leadership committee of the TDLM continues to replicate the relationship between the leaders and the members (particularly women) that the other movements display. It will be interesting in the future to assess whether this experiment can withstand the gradual expansion of the movement and the need for greater efficiency in organisation and decision making. The participatory emphasis of the movement was evident in the annual general body meeting in October, as were its failings. Although the group sat around in a circle on the floor, and everyone was invited to contribute, it was apparent that some were more equal than others. Only one of the 25 people present was a woman and she was a supplicant rather than an activist. The participatory emphasis of the movement has yet to be extended to the institution of a women's wing and the experiment in participatory leadership can hardly be said to be complete.

There is, however, an alternative mode of organisation that aspires to prefigure a more egalitarian society. This is most evident in the women's organisations that campaign on the Dalit issue. In the aftermath of the violence in Chidambaram constituency, the Women's Struggle Committee organised several protest meetings. Their approach is similar to that of the male equivalent, but without the overwhelming focus upon one central individual. This is not because there are no prominent leaders in the women's movements or that they are not as forceful and articulate as their male counterparts, but they do have a different approach. The leader's speeches are usually short and specific and are part of the process rather than the climax. Gabrielle Dietrich, who is both a leader of the Women's Rights Movement (Penurimai Iyakkam) in Madurai, and an academic, explained that this approach corresponds to ideological beliefs about equality and participation. She also stressed, however, that none of the women's leaders were interested in being 'this big figure' (discussion, 27 October 1997). Women's organisations such as the PI, as Mageli notes, are 'less elitist than male associations because they allowed for more democratic ways of interaction and decision making than is common in Indian political practice' (1997: 12). Certainly the women activists were more proactive in terms of making up slogans and chanting phrases which the leaders subsequently took up.

Despite the ideals, many women's groups retained hierarchical structures in practice and the difference between educated leaders and non-educated followers mirrored the composition of male movements. This was emphasised in the meeting in Cuddalore to protest against the poll violence in Chidambaram. When the *dharna* leaders went into the collector's office to present their demands, some poor, elderly ladies sitting on the ground nearby asked: 'What's the point of this? He won't listen—what have they done so far? Who have they arrested? We ought to sit in the road and take action!' Another woman who was a victim of the violence was similarly unimpressed. She questioned why the leaders were going in and insisted that 'we women should be going!' (25 October 1999). The leadership style of women's movements *was* more participatory and tied to the everyday experiences and concerns of the participants, therefore, but this inclusive emphasis had its limits.

In addition, women have tended to mirror the SCs' political segmentation, often forming separate 'women's wings' (*makila ani*) rather than establishing independent movements. In the relationship between the male and female wings of a movement, the women are seen as peripheral to the 'movement proper'. Many of the women's leaders, as Dietrich notes, face sexist discrimination at home as well as being disregarded by the movement. The patriarchal division of household labour, as discussed in the previous chapter, renders it extremely difficult for women who have to do the cooking and look after the children to become movement activists (personal communication, 27 October 1997). Despite this many of the women's leaders are highly skilled and inspirational. One such figure is Pandiyammal, the DPI secretary in Keerathurai, but as seen in Chapter 6, her contribution was not always recognised by the male leaders. The rhetoric of women's liberation is ever present, but it is all too often belied in practice and sometimes seemed to be more a token gesture than anything else. One incident serves to encapsulate this trend: During a WPM hunger fast in Myaladuthurai, the majority of protestors were women but the speakers were all men. In recognition of this Sangari, an agricultural labourer and activist, was called out of the crowd to give a speech.

> She was not expecting to talk but she made a fiery speech which the women listened to appreciatively. She was cut short, however, by one of the [male] organisers telling her to 'finish, finish, finish' in a low voice behind her back (fieldnote, 29 September 1999).

Stronger and more active women's movements or the integration of the male and female wings of a movement could make a significant

he Dalit struggle. By raising the issue of leadership and
al nature of most movements they could contribute to
cratisation.

1clusion: The Democratic Imperative

ngency' and 'new leadership' approaches represent two
.ttempts to assess the importance of leadership. The former
hasises the situation from which a leader emerges, and the latter
.s the need for direction (including charismatic leadership)
(Bryman 1992: 1). The significance of the contingency approach is
seen here. The new leadership stress on the need for vision highlights
a necessary but by no means determining aspect of leadership in any
struggle. Whilst personal ability, behaviour, adjustment to a situation
and insight are undeniably important in choosing a leader, they do
not seem to explain the form of leadership which is most prevalent
in the social movements under question. In explaining the structural
dominance of Dalit leaders an analysis of the specific political culture
has proved to be most fruitful. From this perspective, Dalit movements may be opposed to the social *system* that oppresses them, but
they remain entangled in the *structures* of that society. These
structures are hierarchical, male-dominated, and revolve around the
idolised individuality of 'big men'.

If it is true that 'a leader attracts a following by the benefits that
he provides' (Mines 1994: 57), then the preponderance of leader-
centred organisations is perhaps inevitable. A participatory emphasis
is the antithesis of the patron–client links that are predicated upon
inequality and several factors conspire to perpetuate the existence
of 'big men': First, the persistence of marked inequalities. Second,
the relative absence of firm, impersonal guarantees of security,
position and livelihood renders people dependent on patrons. Finally
the inability of kinship to serve as an effective means of advancement
(for the Dalits in particular) results in a search for alternative means
of getting ahead. The power asymmetry upon which such relationships are based precludes their swift dissolution and inhibits the
formation of autonomous and participatory organisations. A chronic
disability of Dalit movements is a lack of resources which has
hindered the attempt to escape the traditional caste-based ties of

dependency and acquire a sense of supra-local issue-oriented politics. It is arguable that leader-centred organisations have been able to give Dalits a voice and thus speeded up this process. The emergence of 'big men' from within the community has allowed Dalits to erode local structures of power. In reaction to this process the locally dominant castes have resorted to what Hall (1977) terms 'repressive clientelism'. Threats, violence, rape and murder, have marked a coercive response to increasing Dalit agency. Given the precarious nature of the situation, the prevalence of leader-focussed groups should not be surprising. Dyadic relationships of this nature, as Powell (1977: 147) rightly notes, are a form of 'anxiety reduction behaviour'.

As Dalit struggles transcend their social origins and extend into the political arena they have to apply their critique of the political process to their own organisations. It is vital, therefore, for the Dalit movements to confront the question of internal democracy and implement democratic decision making and dispute solving procedures within their own ranks. If the Dalit movements are not to compromise the principles that led them into politics, they must also attempt to reform the institutions that they have now joined. If Dalit movements metamorphose into corrupt, power-seeking and opportunist political parties, then the disaffection of their members could find a more violent outlet. These themes are addressed in the following section on the 1999 Lok Sabha Elections, when the centrality and power of the DPI leadership came under particular scrutiny. The following chapter will focus on the experience of the Liberation Panthers in 1999 in order to highlight the issues involved. Contemporary Dalit leaders in Tamil Nadu are inspiring, often selfless and dedicated and committed to the vision of a more egalitarian society. The crowds that they mobilise into action, and the numbers of people whose grievances they articulate, are a testimony to their work. The instances of betrayal, the sidelining of 'women's issues' and the envy and neglect of secondary figures, however, highlight the failings of leader-centred movements. 'There can not be a democracy without a revolution', as Ungo paraphrased Rosa Luxemberg as saying, 'neither can there be a revolution without democracy' (in Castañeda 1993: 377).

8

THE MOVE TO POLITICS: THE INSTITUTIONAL SELF-TRANSFORMATION OF THE LIBERATION PANTHERS

The Liberation Panthers are under the military control of Thirumavalavan—at his insistence and to keep the peace we are here on a hunger fast today. ...But if this government keeps oppressing us thousands and thousands of youngsters are prepared to come forward and turn this land into a battlefield. We will block roads, we will chop trees and burn buses (Chella Pandian, 12 September 1999).

Introduction: Institutional Self-Transformation

In 1999, the Liberation Panthers abandoned their boycott of democratic procedures and decided to contest the elections. In this transition they followed the development trajectory of all the main contenders in Tamil politics who have moved from social movement activity into party politics. The prior transformations of the Dravidian parties, the PMK and the PT have established what Offe (1990: 250) terms 'an institutional learning process'. His contention is that social movements are transitory expressions of dissatisfaction with the limitations of 'normal politics' and demands for the inclusion of marginal groups into the mainstream. Extrapolating trends from his analysis of the Green Party of the erstwhile West Germany, Offe delineates a tentative 'stage model of the institutional dilemmas, ambiguities and crises that are typically encountered by these new movements' (1990: 235).

In the process of institutionalisation, according to this model, movements generally go through three stages. The 'take-off' phase of movement politics is radical and idealist. The rhetoric employed is absolute, permitting of no compromise, and change is expected to be imminent. This phase is also the high-point of movement mobilisation as people are caught up in the initial enthusiasm. This involvement is hard to sustain, however, and lack of achievement or partial concessions by the state cause membership to decline and participation to dwindle. The movement goes through a period of 'stagnation', therefore, during which it is forced to restructure itself, become more organised and seek resources with which to continue the struggle. At this juncture, the opportunities afforded by alliances with established parties render a gradual transformation to the institutional modes of 'normal politics' highly attractive, if not imperative. The phase of institutionalisation marks the culmination of movement activity and the initiation of political negotiation. Whilst Offe's model offers useful insights into the macro processes of institutionalisation, the transition on the ground is obviously too complex to be captured by a general model. In what follows I shall outline the DPI's transition from a movement to a political party, which will point to the applicability of Offe's findings as well as highlight the specificity of the Dalit movements.

This section perhaps requires justification. Electoral analysis usually focuses on results, which are said to reflect the popular will. Showing that a party gained a large percentage of the votes in a given election is crucial to leaders, who need to stress the legitimacy and popularity of their programmes. In India, such analysis is frequently broken down to reveal the religious or caste composition of the results. There is an assumption that social groups constitute 'vote-banks' that enter an election with the interests of their group at heart. This tendency is apparent in Tamil Nadu where the two most politically organised castes, the Vanniyars in the north and the Thevars in the south, are said to determine the outcome in many constituencies. Candidates are often chosen on the basis of caste and voters are assumed to favour their own people. The Dalits are somewhat excluded from these calculations as they are commonly presented as 'disunited' and 'easily bought off', but there is a legal requirement to field Dalit candidates in certain constituencies and so they cannot be ignored. Furthermore, insomuch as any community may be described in those terms, the rise of Dalit movements in the state has arguably resulted in the constitution of a 'Dalit vote-bank'.

In what follows, I do not present an analysis of figures and statistics depicting Dalit voting patterns, but focus on the cultural understandings that underpin democracy. By drawing on interviews, observations and speeches, this chapter and the next argue that the results do not tell the whole story. Before we assess the elections, however, we need to disentangle the web of processes, events and decisions that led the Liberation Panthers to abandon their electoral boycott. At the heart of this move was a critique of contemporary politics and a rejection of the hegemony of the two Dravidian parties. Understanding this process of transition, and the way that it was articulated, is vital if we are to grasp the significance of the 1999 elections. In these chapters I focus on the Liberation Panthers, but the arguments have a wider relevance. They are not the only, or even the first, Dalit movement to stand for election. The election of Dr Krishnasamy to the Legislative Assembly in 1996, on behalf of the PT, may be pointed to as a precedent. I shall argue, however, that the events leading up to the elections in 1999 marked a significant turning point in Tamil politics.

Identity Politics

Social movement theorists have recently attempted a synthesis of existing approaches to the study of group action. The move away from a dichotomy between 'cultural' and 'structural' approaches is necessary if we are to fully grasp the complex processes of movement formation and operation. This move enables us to examine the strategies adopted by social movements as more than just opportunist reactions to the opening or closing of the political economic opportunity structure. Few scholars have focused on the choice of tactics or strategy, but these are rarely decisions about which protestors are indifferent. *Actions* express the moral visions and political identities of protestors as well as ideologies (Benford and Hunt 1995: 95). Movement strategies, in other words, help to define identity. In speaking of identity here, we can define it as 'the process by which social actors recognise themselves—and are recognised by other actors—as part of broader groupings' (Della Porta and Diani 1999: 85). It is on this basis that actors achieve a sense of who they are and what they stand for. Identities, thus, are 'sources of meaning for the actors themselves' (Castells 1997: 7). Whilst personal identities are constructed to give meaning to an individual's own experiences and development, 'collective identity consists of perceptions of group distinctiveness, boundaries and interests' (Jasper 1997: 86).

In south India, group identity has often been privileged above that of the individual and the good of the whole (or at least a part of it) has been prioritised over self-interest. This is perhaps most obvious in the institutions for marriage, where arranged matches, often within the extended family, are preferred to individual choice. The bounds of caste now extend beyond the immediate locality, however, and, as with other communities, they are to a large extent 'imagined'. Furthermore, movement identity may be distinguished from that of an ascribed group because it is only constructed, activated and sustained through interaction (Foweraker 1995: 4). Movement identity, thus, is critical in explaining how structural inequality is transformed into an active desire for social change. This process of identity formation, according to Melucci, 'involves cognitive definitions concerning the ends, means, and field of action' (1995: 44). Action strategies are crucial to group cohesion, therefore, and they can either reinforce or challenge these patterns of identity.

The Liberation Panthers whom I encountered early in 1999 saw themselves as 'radical actors' who were not bought off by the 'grand election carnivals' that provide political institutions with legitimacy. They boasted of the 'radical election boycott', which they had conducted for over 10 years. To distinguish their actions from the apathy of others, the DPI had a policy of spoiling ballot papers. In the 1991 elections, they wrote 'none of you are honest, so none will have our votes' on their ballot slips, before casting their 'vote'. A similar message was supposedly substituted for each successive election, but it is difficult to determine the efficacy of this policy. The rejection of political democracy mirrored disillusionment with the legal means of protest. Many members expressed their preference for road-blocks, rail-blocks and retaliation. Of many slogans expressing their willingness to leave the path of legal protest the most popular was the threat to return a blow for a blow. They spoke of being prepared to break the law if necessary and of having *aruvals* (sickles) in every house. When they recalled past protests, or how they would commandeer train carriages to attend meetings in Chennai, it was obvious that they had a sense of empowerment, of the power of protest. Who they were was articulated in what they did and their speeches and interviews are replete with references to themselves as a *restrained force* of revolutionary capacity that could, and would, explode if certain changes were not effected.

Recounting respondents' perspectives on the electoral boycott is instructive in contextualising the movement. Early in my fieldwork, movement members were unquestionably proud of belonging to a radical organisation. I interviewed Kamaraj from Muduvarpatti in March 1999, for example, and he said that the PT was not doing a bad job. When asked if he had voted for PT, however, he replied: 'No, for the past three or so years we have not voted—we spoil ballot papers and write a message on them' (interview, 15 March 1999). His account is telling on a number of counts. He had been in the movement for three years and these years were associated with a boycott. Kamaraj's comments suggest that the practice of spoiling ballots was routine, and indeed he had had the opportunity to 'vote' in three elections between 1996 and 1999. The rationale behind the boycott was apparent to all movement members. There was an abiding impression of the government as casteist and biased, and a widespread perception of politicians as corrupt, self-serving and avaricious. Subramani from Cuddalore summed up the prevalent position:

> If you rear a calf with pigs, then the calf too will eat shit. That is why we reject politics. We can protest and gain from that—we can fight the governments from the outside. If the calf joins the piglets then the two become one and you cannot distinguish between them— both fall into the gutter. No matter who it is this will happen—be it Thirumavalavan or anybody else. Ambedkar said: 'if he entered politics he would not see his own people'—apart from seeking to advance themselves they will do nothing for their community. It is due to this that *Annan* has yet to enter politics. *Even if he does, not all those who are members of the DPI organisation will go with him* (*Subramani*, 27 April 1999).

In other words, movement members had constructed an image of themselves as rebellious and independent actors who were not tempted by the siren calls of political ambition or patronage. They saw themselves as occupying a moral high ground from which they sought to intervene for the good of the entire society. In adopting the methods of democratic contest, therefore, the Liberation Panthers were altering the very identity of the movement.

The notion that a movement encompasses a range of members who differ in terms of commitment and radicalism is an established one (Krishna 1996: 252; Slater 1985b: 6). A distinction between radicals and moderates was apparent in the DPI and never more so than when they were debating whether to abandon their boycott. I have spoken elsewhere of the centrality and authority of movement leaders in Tamil Nadu, but never was Thirumavalavan's leadership challenged so much as in this decision. The DPI's leadership committee met several times and local members entered into heated debates on the issue. 'The identity of a protestor', as Jasper puts it, 'may be that of someone who attends rallies and marches, or somebody who sabotages corporate labs. ... These are quite distinct identities, and there is no reason to think that it is easy to switch from one to another' (1997: 246). One inebriated DPI member interrupted the speakers at a rally in Vadipatti shouting: 'I didn't come here to listen to you spouting off, I came here to block the road!!' Chandra Bose of the TIP echoed the feelings of many DPI members when he insisted that: 'Today those in office are caste fanatics who are combining to marginalise us. To think that one Dalit leader assuming office could provide a solution for us is a false and foolish hope' (1 December 1999).

Given the trenchant critiques of parliamentary democracy, the continuing calls for separate electorates and the near universal disdain with which Dalit activists viewed politicians, the move to politics was never going to be smooth. Ultimately the democrats won the argument and the DPI decided to participate, yet the stance they adopted was not a ringing endorsement of democracy. It was presented as a change in procedure not policy; a strategic decision that could be reversed at any point. 'It is to prevent our direct enemies from harvesting our votes that we have taken the practical decision to cast our votes', Thirumavalavan told members at a wedding reception. 'This is a procedural step (*nadumurai*)', he assured them, 'not a change in policy (*kortpaadu*), it is a tactic (*uthi*)' (Madurai, 16 June 1999). In the months preceding the elections, Thirumavalavan embarked on a tour of movement branches throughout the state explaining the change in policy, urging members to cooperate and emphasising that this was not a decision taken by him alone. Indeed, he stressed the contested nature of the transition as a means of asserting that all the issues had been debated and all perspectives considered. This campaign of information implicitly recognised that there was more at stake than a mere procedural alteration. The existence of a collective actor is usually 'taken for granted' but it is, in fact, 'the product of highly differentiated social processes, action orientations, elements of structure, and motivation' (Melucci 1988: 246). The DPI's move to politics, therefore, highlights important issues, choices and constraints faced by Dalit movements today.

The Rules of the Game

'National strategies'—what Tilly (1986) terms 'the existing reper-toire'—according to Kriesi, 'set the informal and formal rules of the game for the conflict between new social movements and their adversaries' (quoted in Della Porta and Diani 1999: 202). To attract recruits and mobilise protestors, it is arguable that social movements need to follow a policy of limited innovation. Protest movements may call for a more equal society but they usually contain internal structures and relationships of power, which appear to contradict this goal. The Dalit movements' reliance on central, male leaders and their reluctance to take up gender issues are a case in point. To recruit new members, activists need to utilise established institutions and cultural resources. Following one's ideological imperatives too far or too fast may preclude the levels of mobilisation necessary to chal-lenge oppressive social structures. A movement needs to be recognised by others if it is not to be marginalised as 'deviant'. The Dalit movements, thus, are articulated in a cultural form that reflects established socio-political institutions.

The danger of such analysis is that it may justify the perpetuation of inequalities within a movement and delay internal reform. Dalit movements contain frequent references to equality, especially gender equality, to keep those who desire more radical change on board. But the liberatory impulse of these assertions is diluted by the language of 'priorities' in which challenging caste becomes more important than addressing other inequalities. Movement speeches are replete with such contradictions. The concept of *limited innovation* enables us to understand the apparent conservatism of social movement action, when compared to the radicalism of their programmes.[1] It gives an indication of how and why Dalit movements

---

[1] Lipsky (1970: 4), Jasper (1997: 35) and Della Porta and Diani (1999: 156) note how protest is constrained both by protest constituents and the political opportunity structure.

can campaign for human rights and dignity on the one hand, whilst turning a blind eye to patriarchal abuses on the other. The PI (Women's Rights Movement) leaders cited an instance in which a DPI member had got a young Dalit girl pregnant, but then abandoned her. Movement leaders could have influenced the youth to return, the PI insisted, but they failed to cooperate. Eventually a DPI Women's Wing leader took an interest in the case.

Silence on 'moral' issues such as the commonly noted negative habits of Dalit men—smoking, drinking, gambling and wife-beating— may also be understood in these terms.[2] It was common for several members at meetings to be drunk. In fact, as we have seen, the presence of the leader was often seen as an occasion for celebration. A puritanical condemnation of these practices would have conformed to the movement's general emphasis on self-respect and self-determination, and would certainly have been welcomed by Dalit women, but such an innovation may have had the effect of alienating many of the more active and vocal male members. This fear of going too far too fast is intricately bound up with the choice of strategy to be pursued. Political and cultural norms permit radical, and often violent, talk, but they condemn the resort to violence itself. Movement speeches, therefore, frequently raised the prospect of violence and armed struggle in a calculated rhetoric of 'restrained force'. Such assertions are not confined to the DPI, indeed one of the most forceful accounts of this position was articulated by V. Balasundaram of the AMI:

> Tomorrow if we said the word, heads would roll, lakhs of people would be killed if we ordered it—because so many people are ready to take up the struggle. Of that there can be no doubt. At the same time, blood for blood, and revenge killings are a morass that we do not want to descend into (30 June 1999).

The primary difference between this and DPI statements, as the quote at the head of the chapter shows, is that the latter emphasise the significance of their own leader. Such assertions simultaneously speak up the strength of the movement and the patience and moral leadership of their convenor:

---

[2] De Wit (1996: 172–73) notes how excessive drinking amongst male slum dwellers is frequently explained by reference to the nature of their work, insecurity and the conditions in which they live. As he points out, however, women who coexist in these conditions rarely resort to drink.

If our *Annan*, Thirumavalavan, said, if our leader said 'have an
aruval in every house', then [pauses]—but we are heeding his
words and remaining quiet and patient. If he said 'take up your
aruvals' and we took them up and came out, you know, then the
nation would descend into chaos (Sekhar, 22 March 1999).

The assertion is that Dalits are capable of devastating violence,
but that they remain patient and law-abiding. If a couple of buses
are burnt, the message is, be thankful that we did not bring the state
to a halt. A *rhetorical* emphasis on passive resistance would have
been counter-productive and displeased the activists. Gandhian
methods have enriched the repertoire of protest in India, but it is one
of the great ironies that his example is eschewed in favour of role-
models from America and South Africa, because Dalit activists
regard Gandhi as having betrayed them. Innovation in *strategy*,
however, is limited by the fear of alienating 'ordinary' people, upon
whose support the movement ultimately depends. 'Protest constituents limit the options of protest leaders at the same time that the
leader influences their perception of the strategies and rhetoric which
they will support' (Lipsky 1970: 4). This was certainly the case with
the DPI but the story was complicated by the fact that protest
constituents are divided into those who are already committed and
those who are potential members. In trying not to alienate either
grouping the rhetoric of the movement became further removed from
its actions. The speeches sent out a message to activists that 'nothing
has changed' whilst choosing to engage in fasts rather than road
blockades intimated that the movement was a peaceful and democratic organisation.

The 'rules of the game' in Tamil Nadu set the context within which
Dalit movements operate. The differences between Tamil Dalit
movements and those in the north of India owe much to the processes
of political development in the different states. Positive discrimination
in favour of the BCs has a much longer history in the state, where
the Justice Party introduced such measures in the 1920s.[3] The history
of non-Brahmin and Dravidian movement agitation has theoretically
ensured a polity that is more responsive to the demands for social

---

[3] When India erupted into protest following V.P. Singh's decision to implement
the findings of the Mandal Commission in 1991, therefore, Tamil Nadu remained
largely unaffected.

justice. 'Modern Tamil Politics', as Washbrook puts it, 'is dominated by the rise to power at state level of a "Dravidian" movement whose ideology has been committed to the destruction of the caste system' (1989: 207). As shown in Chapter 2, the protest repertoire of the Self-Respect and Dravidian movements, in their demands for recognition of the Tamil language and the Tamil state is familiar today—black flag demonstrations, road-blocks, picketing and protest meetings. 'Movement and counter-movement tend to imitate each other', as Della Porta and Diani note, 'reciprocally adapting particular tactics' (1999: 213). Despite the history of the Indian nationalist movement, the points of reference for Tamil movements largely remain confined to the state (cf. Deliège 1997: 13).

Such parochialism is beginning to open itself up to a conception of India that extends beyond the border of the state, but it is still within the bounds of this social construct that we need to understand the struggles of Tamil Dalits. Although movement activists were conversant with the work of Dalit movements elsewhere, though references to Ambedkar were ubiquitous, and whilst Thirumavalavan and others travelled to Durban for the UN conference on racism, the primary political referent here is the legacy of Dravidianism. 'Firebrand' Murugan, therefore, described Thirumavalavan as a *Tamil*-born leader of the sons of the soil. The five principle ideals of the DPI include an aspiration to 'nurture a Tamil nation undivided by caste or religion' (Thirumavalavan, 18 July 1999). Through such statements the DPI claim for themselves the mantle of Periyar and the egalitarian ideals of the Dravida Kazhagam. The DMK, as Anandhi points out, sought to establish 'Tamilness' as the pre-eminent source of identity for Tamilians. 'In constituting the collective identity of the masses as Tamil identity, as a distinctive cultural and historic entity, North India and Hindu India became the cultural "other"' (1994: 63). It is to this legacy that Thirumavalavan referred when responding to the controversy surrounding the Congress leader:

> If Sonia (Gandhi) is a foreigner, then Vajpayee too is an alien according to Karunanidhi's ideology. This same Karunanidhi stood on a stage and said: 'The Aryans are those who came in through the Khyber Pass. They are cattle grazers these Aryans, they came from central Asia and Iran these Aryans. What business do these lowly Aryans have in Tamil Nadu?' (13 July 1999).

'The *Dravida Munetra Kazhagam's* hold over Tamil political life and culture owes much to its rhetoric of Tamilness' (Rajadurai and Geetha 1996: 551). The Dravidian movement succeeded in prioritising the question of cultural identity to such an extent that anti-Brahminism and the agitation against the imposition of Hindi into schools continue to resonate in Tamil politics. The hegemonic influence of the Dravidian parties is such that even to move away from a perception of the Brahmins as the real enemy has required the construction of a new political discourse. 'The *Dravida Kazhagam* and the Dravidian parties' according to 'Tada' Periyasami, 'have fooled people for 50 years into thinking that the Brahmins are responsible for the caste system. ... By pin-pointing this one enemy, they have been able to cast all blame on the Brahmins for their own gain' (interview, 3 November 1999).

In the past two decades, however, Dalit movements have increasingly distanced themselves from the party-political successors of the DK. The reason for this transformation in attitudes has been a growing realisation of the limitations of existing political and economic programmes. According to Ravichandran, Convenor of the Marutham Network:

> Those who fought so hard to overthrow the domination of the Brahmins have taken on board the caste scriptures and structure in turn. It is the middle caste people who have most land they want to protect this land. They want to protect land rights, so that is why they have to accept the caste system; to ensure that owners remain owners, the slaves remain slaves and untouchables remain untouchable (interview, 27 July 1999).

Indeed, despite their egalitarian rhetoric, neither the DMK nor the AIADMK had radical economic policies. Their 'socialism', as Rajadurai and Geetha explain, 'was but a modern version of benign feudal patrimony where the lord and the slave, the alms-giver and the alms taker are part of a moral universe in which charity is often emphasised at the expense of justice' (1996: 563). These webs of patronage assume the form of clientelism, defined by Banck as the 'dispensing of public resources (or the promise to do so) by political power holders/ seekers and their respective parties, in exchange for votes and other forms of political support' (1986: 522). Resources are extended to the impoverished Dalit population through the mediation of brokers, who are usually party members (de Wit 1996: 17). During the elections each Dalit estate or *cheri* played host to successive political parties that tried to woo the Dalit vote with promises and rewarded their workers with money or food and drink. It is little surprise, therefore, that Dalit movements have only recently been able to challenge the system. 'The Dravidian parties are one of the main causes for the lack of Dalit consciousness in Tamil Nadu', Mathivanan, a leader of the Working Peasant's Movement, insisted. 'They organised Dalits into their parties giving them petty concessions, and so kept them appeased' (interview, 29 September 1999). As Palani Kumar put it:

> Politicians will do anything for power—the Dalits have no say, no influence in government, they are mere pawns. They have been coolie workers for political parties because they were made so by the Dravidian parties (interview, 12 September 1999).

The 'betrayal of Dravidian ideals' is a constant theme through which Dalit movements fulfil the dual function of criticising the government on its own terms and establishing their own legitimacy. This is achieved by projecting their protest as the continuation of 'past political movements whose struggles have long since been vindicated as just' (Rochon in Della Porta and Diani: 1999: 184). Other means of legitimisation include 'grievance extension', whereby activists cast their particular struggle as part of a wider project (Jasper 1997: 273). Dalit movements thus, employ the language of 'human rights' to insist that their struggle has universal resonance and they compare themselves to other protests that are widely regarded as legitimate. The struggle against apartheid is often referred to and imprisoned comrades are likened to Nelson Mandela. The implication is that ultimately their cause will triumph and the oppressors will be brought to justice. Such images have become vital for morale in recent years as the Dravidian parties have increasingly come to regard Dalit movements as a challenge to their monopoly on state power. Given that Dalit votes, until recently, were seen as easily bought, whereas BC groups were perceived to be more organised and conscious of their interests, it is little surprise that politicians targeted the latter groups for support. They are also the communities that stand to lose most by, and are most resistant to, Dalit advancement. Challenges to the hegemony of the Dravidian parties have arguably made these organisations less responsive to Dalit demands. Thus, 'in the past few years the DMK has been anti-Dalit' (Mathivanan, interview, 29 September 1999).

The Politics of Social Protest

Jenkins asserts that there are three main reasons for discussing the state when analysing social movements. First, 'social movements are inherently political' because they are based on demands for social change. As the state retains the *legitimate* monopoly over the use of violence, social movements require some recognition from the state in order to survive. 'Second, the state organises the political environment within which social movements operate'. The structure of opportunities and constraints affects the course of action chosen by a movement. 'Third, social movements constitute a claim for political representation' (1995: 16/17). The state certainly needs to be factored into the analysis and constituted a constant referent for Dalit protest. The AMI, for example, utilised the opportunities for legal redress in challenging practices of Untouchability. They accepted that the democratic state—'with its participatory processes at all levels, its legal system, its freedom of expression, and the right to protest and organise pressure groups and people's movements—*provides genuine spaces and possibilities for liberation*' (Bangalore Social Action Trust 1998: 130). Given these opportunities the reasons for the emergence of radical protest groups require as much explanation as their subsequent move into political competition.

'For the majority of Indian citizens', Gupta argues, 'the most immediate context for encountering the state is provided by the relationship with government bureaucracies at the local level' (1995: 378). The state 'is a distinct set of institutions that has the authority to make the rules which govern society. It has, in the words of Max Weber, a "monopoly on legitimate violence" within a specific territory' (Marshall 1994: 507). This definition is inapt in India, where the coercive power of the higher castes is legitimated by reference to Hindu texts and social custom. In democratic India, the state has arrogated the right to punish such infringements of its supremacy, but the institutions of the state are not impermeable to caste influence.[4] Gupta focuses on the ways in which the state and other institutions 'come to be imagined' and discursively constructed (1995: 376). The multiplicity of institutions within the state, he argues, mean that it cannot be viewed as a unitary entity even though it is portrayed as such. Gupta's conception of the relationship between the state and society is useful for an understanding of the Dalit movements' attempt to challenge the hegemonic configurations of power whilst working with existing political institutions. For many Dalits the state is a vital resource in terms of government houses, jobs, college places and ration cards.

Dalit movements, therefore, often accept the legitimacy of the *state*, which they see as providing them with the means to effect social change, whilst challenging the commitment of the governing party and the police. The Dravidian parties constantly hold out the prospect of social change and new schemes to eradicate untouchability are frequently launched. In September 1997, for instance, the Chief Minister Karunanidhi vowed to abolish untouchability and announced grants and gratuities for inter-caste marriages that included a Dalit member (*The Hindu*, 1 September 1997. See Chapter 5 for other schemes). Dalit activists concede that many of the downtrodden have received state benefits, but they argue that the governing parties have become increasingly antagonistic. Interviews and speeches were laden with accusations against the police, the 'casteist' PMK and the Dravidian parties:

> If we do not exercise our right to vote in the state or general elections our immediate enemies are the ones to gain. They attain power and office and then they continue their hegemony through means of the police. Due to this domination, in Melavalavu the murder of our comrade Murugesan and his followers took place with the knowledge of the police....Countless examples could follow. The group clash in Madurai in 1997 saw three statues of revolutionary Ambedkar destroyed with the knowledge and under the observance of the police. What is the reason for this? The caste domination of government power! The DMK and ADMK hegemony has enabled the state infrastructure to be used to oppress us and prevent us from rising, but our immediate enemies instantaneously get access to benefits using their political power and muscle.

[4] See Jeffrey (2000: 1019) for an excellent ethnography of upper-caste influence and domination.

That is why keeping caste and communalism out of government should be our first priority (Thirumavalavan, 16 June 1999).

Such sentiments are not confined to the DPI, and echoes may be heard in every Dalit movement across the state:

No matter what atrocities are committed against Dalits the courts disregard witnesses and take no action in our favour—think of Kodiyankulam, Chidambaram, Melavalavu. Even if we open a case, the courts are not there for us, the police are not for our people, parliamentary democracy itself has not been for our people hitherto (Ravichandran, 27 September 1999).

Each successive protest meeting highlighted another atrocity, each more gruesome than the last and many alleging the connivance of a casteist police force. Murders were registered as suicides and those protesting against atrocities were as likely, if not more, to be arrested as the perpetrators themselves. The common theme was the political control of the police and the anti-Dalit nature of the main parties. As Saktivel put it:

They say that this is a democratic country, a nation of the people, a nation which provides for freedom of speech and expression— but we are unable to stick up posters and we cannot speak freely on a platform.[5] ...The DMK and ADMK say that they want to eradicate caste and casteists—they say we are doing this and that but our huts are still being burnt, our houses still smashed up (18 July 1999).

Social movements are said to result from the 'inadequacies of the institutions of interest mediation' (Scott 1991: 9–10). This argument is borne out in Tamil Nadu where non-Brahmins, Other Backward Castes, Dalits and Women have organised successively to press their demands for political recognition. The quotes provided here certainly

[5] Somandan, an assistant regional leader, and other Working Peasant's Movement members such as Illangellian reported that that they had been taken in for police questioning because they had put up posters in support of the DPI and condemning the PMK (interviews, 28 September 1999). With regard to speaking on a platform—when Thirumavalavan addressed a TMC rally in the run up to the September elections he was pelted with stones by local Thevar gangs and forced to curtail his speech.

indicate the degree to which Dalit movements had lost faith in political processes in 1999. The 'inadequacy' of the state, it is worth stressing, may be as much a discursive construct as an objective fact, since the perception of institutional performance is highly subjective (Fine 1995: 130; Kaase 1990: 95). In Chidambaram, for example, all the candidates were Dalits, but their perceptions of the state were worlds apart. These discursive constructions of the state are as important in assessing the 'failure' of the state as more common and material indices of government performance (Gupta 1995: 589). The Liberation Panthers maintain that Dalits will only be properly represented when they gain separate electorates and are able to choose their own candidates. They portray the Dalits who stand on behalf of other parties as 'puppets' or as poor children who are rendered disabled so that they can beg for money with which to line the pockets of their 'patron'. This metaphor is highly resonant in India and it rejects the élite conception of Untouchables as unable to represent themselves.[6]

In the discursive constructs of the Dalit movements the government is certainly an oppressor. The police are often accused of abuses and are frequently described as the main enemy of the Dalits. Whether the actions of the police are autonomous of the ruling party or not is hard to ascertain, but in recent years the 'exercise of power has become increasingly cynical' (Desrochers 1991: 8). Under the pretext of 'terrorist threats' governments have been able to introduce draconian laws, which are increasingly used against protestors (ibid., Amnesty International ASA 20/12/98). One such piece of legislation is the Goondas Act. 'In the past year alone', Thirumavalavan told members at a day-long meeting in Madurai, 'Karunanidhi has jailed 46 members of the Liberation Panthers under the Goondas Act. Who is a Goonda? What does the Goondas Act say? Those brewing illicit liquor, those preparing intoxicating drugs, those inciting violence against people, those working as pimps' (13 July 1999). Thirumavalavan here uses his knowledge of the law to counter the state version of events and to render power visible. Other anti-terrorist acts have also been passed and used to suppress protest.

---

[6] Metaphor is a crucial means of 'making power visible'. An apt metaphor may succeed in reversing dominant discourses in a way that facts and figures are unable to do. The response accorded to this picture of Dalit politicians showed that it was accepted as accurate by most of those present. See Melucci (1988) for a more detailed discussion of this.

One of the most widely used provisions is the ability to make 'preventative' arrests. These provisions were drawn up in response to, and are often targeted at, Muslim 'terrorists', but as the DPI have grown in popularity, the government has become increasingly wary of their activities and has tried to minimise their impact. A consequence of this has been increasing interaction between Muslim and Dalit groups under the umbrella of 'minority rights':

> *Cheri* people are suffering, minorities, the Muslims are also suffering. Karunanidhi is the one who pleased Vajpayee. Karunanidhi is the one who introduced the PODA (Prevention of Disorder Act). To put Vajpayee at ease, he invented a character called 'Ayisha', and saying 'we are looking for Ayisha, we are looking for Ayisha', they lifted the veils of Muslim girls and harassed them under Karunanidhi. That is why in the history of Tamil Nadu, the Muslim people who had supported the DMK for 40 or 50 years, for the first time have aligned themselves against Karunanidhi (Thirumavalavan, 13 July 1999).

The salience of common oppression in fostering mutual action was emphasised in references to the treatment of the DPI. 'For a district meeting', Thirumavalavan declaimed, 'he (Karunanidhi) arrests members across the entire state! In Tamil Nadu to date, no government has ever carried out such blatant oppression of an organisation' (Madurai, speech, 13 July 1999).

Despite their increasing popularity, Dalit movements recognise that the politics of numbers will count against them in most instances and the likelihood of attaining power by contesting state elections is minimal. In this situation, the electoral boycott is truly a 'weapon of the weak'; it requires few resources, yet it is a powerful form of moral protest that denies the legitimacy of the political process. Abandoning the boycott and contesting the elections was hard, not only because they stood little chance of winning, but also because it implied a tacit acceptance of the legitimacy of political institutions. The material attractions of political engagement are manifold and readily apparent. An alliance with an established party potentially provides access to resources, a much wider constituency and an important source of support to counter police repression. In this light the move to politics in an unproblematic one. We have seen, however, that the identity of the movement was based on its opposition to the 'corrupt and casteist' political establishment. No party was immune from criticism and none were deemed to be innocent or praiseworthy with regard to Dalit rights. Contesting the elections, therefore, had to be justified to a sceptical audience. So what led the Liberation Panthers to enter the political arena?

The Move to Politics

Seated outside his residence in a Chennai housing block, and surrounded by the hangers-on who stayed with him and acted as 'body-guards', Thirumavalavan spelt out exactly why they had taken this decision. The litany of causes was familiar to me, as it must have been to all present, from the series of speeches delivered across the state to inform members of the change in 'procedure' and convince them that it was required. The fundamental reason for the alteration was quite simply the lack of impact; most people continued to vote anyway. The grand election carnivals are attractive and exciting times, politicians seek you out and party activists distribute largesse and promises of more if they come to power. By failing to direct the voting of sympathisers and by withholding the votes of activists, therefore, the boycott unwittingly often profited the parties who were most antithetical to the concerns of the movement. Not only were caste-based parties elected, they could depict the DPI as undemocratic. This put pressure on the state to clamp down on them, legitimised such repression and further alienated the people from the movement. The feelings invested in the boycott, however, meant that the movement did not immediately make the transition to contesting the elections. 'Who to vote for is the secondary question', Thirumavalavan insisted, 'but who not to vote for is the primary question' (interview, 3 November 1999). In this light, the decision appears to have been a purely pragmatic and defensive move, its objectives were not too far removed from those of the boycott, but there were other factors that deserve closer examination.

'No movement which is divorced from the masses can achieve victory', Thirumavalavan told the National Campaign on Dalit Human Rights. He recalled how he was recurrently surprised by the attitudes of the people. 'Somebody said "go to the people and they will teach you a lesson". Only after I went to the people did I understand this. It is not only in the revolutionary struggle that we have to take up arms. We must also take up the arms of parliamentary democracy—this is what the people said' (speech, 1 December 1999). As Varshney points out: 'Unless we assume short-sightedness, the subaltern seem to think that democracy is working for them' (cited in Corbridge and Harriss 2000: 269). Talking to Dalits, activists and non-activists alike, this statement rings true. The rejection of democratic politics was never popular amongst the wider, non-activist constituency of Dalit movements who wished their particular leader to enter politics to give them a voice and a source of patronage. It is telling that the majority of Dalit movements in the state were avowedly parliamentarian and sought to gain a mandate through the electoral process. Shri Rangan Prakash of the RPI was scathing about the DPI boycott. He questioned how many people *actually* boycotted the polls and said that DPI cadres had worked for other Dalit candidates in previous elections. He also pointed out that even if all Dalits spoiled their ballots 'someone is going to win'. He insisted that the Liberation Panthers should 'meet the people and progress in a democratic manner':

> As far as I am concerned we can only find a solution through politics. That is, in terms of movements there are lots of people in this constituency. This mass of people will only accept us if we stand as a political party (27 April 1999).

Entering the elections, thus, brought the DPI more in line with other movements and the majority of Dalit voters. In relation to the American Civil Rights Movement, Lipsky noted the 'basic problem of overcoming the inhibitions of the people who may be angry at the conditions but are politically unradical or possess some social stakes' (1970: 189). This problem is compounded in Tamil Nadu where the clientelist state offers tangible rewards to those who vote. Individual participation in movements is driven by a variety of motivations and expectations that may be as attractive as tangible material benefits. Such benefits include a sense of doing the right thing, a sense of purpose, a desire to appear in the papers or a hope for love or friendship. The assertion that intangible rewards will be insufficient to *sustain* levels of mobilisation, however, appears to be justified (Lipsky 1970: 165). Social movements are ill-equipped to deal with the passage of time, according to Offe. He insists that movements thrive where they have rights to protest, dramatic events that inspire a reaction and 'the spontaneous motivation of relevant sections of the population', all of which may be withdrawn from the movement (1990: 238). Substantial concessions by the government can also render a movement the 'victim of its own partial success' (ibid.). The state can present itself as responsive to movement demands thereby reducing the urgency of calls to arms and presenting movement radicals as violent extremists who are not prepared to negotiate (Krishna 1996: 241).

Social movements seek to mobilise as many protestors as possible to maximise their impact. The rhetoric required to maintain commitment amongst activists, however, may alienate potential supporters or provoke repressive counter-movements. A movement's ability to articulate its own identity, therefore, is constrained by the knowledge that the recognition of others is vital to the process of identity formation. The assertion of a positive identity can always be contested. The assertion that Dalit drummers are comparable to Bharatnatyam dancers, for example, is meaningless whilst they are still required to play at funerals and weddings for little or no remuneration. 'The ability to impose negative and stigmatised definitions of the identity of other groups, constitutes, effectively, a fundamental mechanism of social domination' (Della Porta and Diani 1999: 92). The media is crucial to get the movement's message across to a wider public. Jasper goes so far as to assert that there would be no 'movement identity without ratification from the news media' (1997: 288). Given that only the more established Dalit movements receive any coverage at all I would dispute the essentialism inherent in this claim, but the significance of the media is undeniable.[7]

The number of people engaging in protest is a tiny proportion of the population. Consequently, most people's perceptions of the movement are filtered through the news media. Whilst often critical of media coverage, movement activists were also acutely aware of it. Magazines featuring interviews with Dalit leaders certainly found an avid readership in the movement members. One problem of continuing the boycott was that the media portrayed the DPI as extremists, so their moral argument was often reversed. Conflicting

---

[7] Kaase (1990: 95), Rucht (1990: 160) and Castells (1997: 106) have all done work on the significance of the media for social movements.

definitions of identity are not necessarily equal. The state and media are in a privileged position to marginalise the movement and the Liberation Panthers lack the communications infrastructure to contest these dominant definitions.[8] Karunanidhi, the then chief minister, owns newspaper and television networks through which he was able to disseminate his ideas and present himself as a champion of the Dalits. Abandoning the boycott, therefore, affirmed the democratic credentials of the DPI and confounded their depiction as militants. Entering the political equation shortly before an election also assured them of coverage. 'When we boycotted the elections', Thirumavalavan points out, 'not even 20,000 people heard Thirumavalavan speak. When I stood in the election, two and a quarter lakh people voted for me and recognised me' (speech, 1 December 1999).

These figures highlight a politically significant shift in support and emphasise the difference that a proactive and high profile campaign can make to public responses. Thirumavalavan highlighted five forces which the DPI wanted to exclude from political office: 'Caste fanatics, communal forces, corrupted forces, opportunists and criminal forces' (interview, 3 November 1999). The Panther's boycott had much greater significance than the removal of their votes from the contest for it allowed these forces to compete for, or buy off, the votes of other Dalits. The number of people who shunned the polls may have been negligible, but the numbers who turned out to vote for an alternative were politically significant. By contesting, the DPI not only harnessed the votes of politically active Dalits who might have been wary of engaging in extra-institutional action, the media coverage and political campaigning gave them access to Dalits who had never voted before. Hindering the political ambitions of opposing forces is vital, Dalit movements insist, because they use the machinery of the state to further oppress the Dalits. By entering the polls, furthermore, Dalit movements ensured that their votes mattered. In the subsequent competition, movement demands had to be addressed in order to garner Dalit votes.

---

[8] Corbridge and Harriss (2000: 204) highlight the partiality of the press in their discussion of the Chunduru massacre in Andhra Pradesh. They note that the media downplayed upper-caste violence and exaggerated the violence of the Dalits.

'Moments of Madness': The Importance of 'Events'

Establishing a sense of threat helps to achieve group cohesion and meetings are very good at doing this. They are also an exercise in propaganda to convince and recruit new members (Cruces and de Rada 1996: 99). To take the speeches of movement ideologues at face value, therefore, would be foolish. The statements of protest groups 'whose primary talents are in dramatising issues', as Lipsky puts it, 'cannot credibly attempt to present data that is considered "objective"' (1970: 175). Movement meetings are also ritualistic— they are 'highly formalised, repetitive clusters of actions, the meanings of which are ... beyond verbal articulation' (Bloch quoted in Boholm 1996b: 2). Collective 'rites' emphasise moral commitments, whip up emotions and reinforce group solidarity. As such, the speech-acts on these occasions are indicative of the values of the group. These values, and the speeches that both shape and reflect them, however, cannot be divorced from the conditions that give rise to them. The relative success of the DPI in the elections cannot be attributed to their mobilisational skills alone.

Merely articulating a sense of oppression does not mean that a group actually is oppressed or that it will act on that basis. Conversely, not all incidents of repression are reported in the media, especially if the group in question lacks social resources. So, if the views expressed at meetings remain confined to the immediate audience, the battle for public opinion will be lost. From this perspective 'big events' and extra-ordinary occurrences stand out in their ability to shape the context of political action. 'Our symbolic universes can change quite suddenly', as Jasper notes. 'Events shock us when they sum up our anxieties, allowing us to name what we feel threatened by' (Jasper 1997: 91). Events can force movements to reassess their positions by emphasising the possibilities and constraints that affect their choice of action or by instilling them with a sense of urgency. Such events, according to Offe (1990: 238), are conducive to *protest*, but two such events stand out as indicative of, or explaining, the DPI's move to politics.

On 12 June 1999, Thirumavalavan broke the ban on holding public meetings in Perambalur. He and 200 others were arrested when they staged a road blockade to 'protest against police violence and bias'. Between the 12 and 13 of June, at least five government-owned buses were pelted with stones and set alight and another five had their windows smashed in as traffic was brought to a halt in several areas. In response to the violence, the papers reported, Thirumavalavan and 120 others were released that afternoon (*Maalai Malar*, 13 June 1999). Though newspapers depicted those engaging in violence as thugs who were to be condemned, the destruction of government buses is an established form of protest that all parties in Tamil Nadu engage in. The decision to defy the ban at that moment in time is instructive. The movement was embroiled in debates about autonomy and many activists were unhappy about the prospect of losing their radical identity. 'The cohesion of relatively powerless groups may be strengthened by militant, ideological leadership which questions the rules of the game and challenges their legitimacy', as Lipsky observes (1970: 165).

For some time, the agenda of the DPI had been set by aggressors, who had rendered protest meetings little more than exercises in condemnation. Those attracted to the movement by its image as a force who returned a blow for a blow, were asking why they were not engaging in revenge attacks (Periyasami, 30 June 1999). In that situation the deliberate courting of arrest, the protests which followed and the subsequent release of the protestors in Perambalur gave members a sense of power. It was presented as a warning to the government of what would happen if patience ran out. At the same time, however, efforts were made to legitimise the event and to retain the moral high ground that is usually the prerogative of the victims of violence. Perambalur was shown to be the last straw, one banning order too far that had convinced them of the need to 'secure this basic right to protest'. 'I did not plan this meeting, or warn people that I might be arrested', Thirumavalavan insisted, 'I turned up on the spot' (speech at a wedding, 16 June 1999). The emphasis on the spontaneity of the event is to insist that the violence was neither orchestrated nor incited. Instead it gives the impression that he was supported by a large number of followers willing to take risks and act in extra-institutional ways to secure their objectives.

Whether the action was taken to this end or not, the show of strength in Perambalur gave the democrats in the DPI the authority to effect a change in movement procedure.

Rhetorical threats of disorder now carried more weight than beforehand. The government, they declared, had tested the waters and 'got a real fright'. Yet, it was as much a case of the DPI testing the waters too. The government was prepared to arrest Thirumavalavan they discovered and even if it was 'forced' to release him again, the media coverage focused on the burnt out buses and 'violent thugs'. The boost to morale gained by the 'victory' can hardly have offset the negative impact on public opinion. Perambalur, therefore, was recast as a show of the political muscle that could be turned against the ruling party in the polls and as an indication that the move to politics would not dampen the militancy of the movement. Months after the event, Thirumavalavan was still drawing on the example to convince members of his radicalism. When he was banned from entering Chidambaram constituency he insisted:

> I do not refrain from going into Chidambaram because I am scared. I do not refrain from going into Chidambaram because I fear arrest. In Perambalur I told everyone who I could, and I even asked Karunanidhi's representative to grant me permission for a 10-minute speech. Then, *because I was not scared*, I broke the ban knowing that I would be arrested. Could Karunanidhi keep me in prison for 12 hours? He couldn't even keep me in for 6! (Thirumavalavan, speech, 5 November 1999).

This speech was made after the election, but it highlights the lingering dissatisfaction within the movement. Activists had complained to me that their leader's speeches had 'lost their spark and fire' and Thirumavalavan here was seeking to regain his authority. Although the DPI was re-cast as a radical party that could revitalise parliament, the move to politics remained contentious, partly because there were no obvious political allies for the movement to endorse. Both Subramanian's (1999: 37) notion of 'organisational pluralism' and the institutional self-transformation model pre-suppose a receptive political environment in which there are possible coalition partners for a movement or at least some institutional provision for political parties.[9] The AIADMK was corrupt, in disarray and had been the first party to afford the BJP a foothold in the state. The communal alliance was presented as the cause for disillusionment with the DMK, so many resented talk of an alliance with the AIADMK. It is unclear

[9] Offe (1990) notes the importance of the provisions in the German system that provide state funding to parties that acquire a certain percentage of the popular vote.

whether DPI leaders were seeking an alliance with the AIADMK or not when they met with Jayalalitha in early August, but the move was met with such anger and dismay that Thirumavalavan spent the next month vociferously denying press reports that had suggested this.

There was, however, no real alternative. Moopanar, the leader of the TMC, had mooted the possibility of a Third Front after falling out with the DMK, but it lacked any political standing. 'A Third Front', as Thirumavalavan insisted, 'is a Karunanidhi Protection Front' (speech, 13 July 1999). The day after this statement the AIADMK clinched a seat sharing deal with the Congress. One of the main reasons for contesting Deliège's (1997: 13) assertion that the Paraiyar's have no sense of the Indian nation, is that Lok Sabha elections have repeatedly shown that voters prefer the regional parties to be allied to a national political party. Lacking this advantage the TMC Front was a weak option with no real standing. The choice appeared to be between supporting the AIADMK or urging Dalits to vote tactically against the DMK–BJP combine. It was at this point of indecision that the events in Tirunelveli occurred. It is easy to over-emphasise the importance of dramatic moments in time, but they are never divorced from other processes and developments that occur in the build-up to, and during, an 'event'. What happened in the space of half-an-hour on the banks of the river Thamiraparani in Nellai (Tirunelveli) on 23 July, however, was instrumental in reconfiguring Tamil politics at least for a few months and possibly for good.

Hundreds of protestors took to the streets in a procession to highlight the plight of tea-estate workers, demand better wage conditions and the release of 652 workers who had been arrested on a similar demonstration in June. The demonstration was led by the TMC, and by Dr Krishnasamy of the PT, which had kept the dispute in the limelight for over a year. The march concluded at the collector's office, where the leaders attempted to present a petition, but the police massed at the gate of the collectorate were reluctant to grant admission to the leaders' jeep. Annoyed by this, the demonstrators took up slogans demanding that their leaders be allowed in. Up until this point the march had been entirely peaceful and nothing had happened to suggest the events which followed.[10] In the words of the

---

[10] I heard various accounts from movement activists but none of them were actually present in Nellai. In what follows, therefore, I shall draw upon the newspaper accounts and articles that they also drew on.

Frontline reporters, 'the Special Action Force men suddenly swung into action, they tried to chase away the demonstrators using force'. The crowd responded by throwing stones and then the police appear to have gone berserk.

In the course of the inquiry into the events, the police suggested that they had been angered by the crowd's harassment of police-women. This, however, can hardly explain the ferocity of their actions. The police started to throw stones back at the crowd and at the vehicle in which the leaders were travelling. They fired shots in the air, used tear gas, and then *lathi-charged* to disperse the crowd, ignoring their own officers who called for restraint.[11] Fleeing from the police charge the demonstrators had few available avenues of escape. The crowd fled onto the dried up riverbed and then into the water. 'The police did not withdraw even at this stage. Some of them jumped into the water and hit on the heads of volunteers with lathis' (Viswanathan and Muthuhar Saquf, *Frontline*, 13 August 1999). Those attempting to rescue people from drowning were not spared neither were journalists covering the event. Forced into the water and under attack by the police on both banks of the river, 17 people, including a small baby, lost their lives and many more were said to be missing.

Confronted by events of such enormity and violence of such ferocity the analytical insights of Crowd Theorists seem attractive. Authors such as Le Bon (1960) perceived there to be a 'psychology of the crowd' that was conducive to violence. This perspective posited 'moments of madness' to be a result of a group mentality in which the attitudes and values of the individual were subsumed and overtaken by the irrationality of the crowd. Canetti (1962) explores similar notions and seeks to explore the psychology and emotions of 'the crowd'. He raises pertinent questions that confront everyone in the wake of violent episodes of this nature:

> But how does a belligerent crowd *form*? What, from one moment to another creates that uncanny coherence? What is it that suddenly moves men to risk their all? The phenomenon is so mysterious that it must be approached with a measure of caution (Canetti: 1962 71).

---

[11] A *lathi* is a wooden cane or truncheon carried by police in India. In a *lathi-charge* this implement is used against protestors or rioters with some force.

Canetti and Le Bon are not alone in seeking to explain crowd violence by reference to notions of 'the crowd'. The caution that Canetti advocates, however, must be extended to the very concept of the 'crowd' as well. To present the massacre in Nellai as a momentary upsurge of destructive violence and to analyse the emotions and psychology of the throngs of activists and police can, at best, only provide limited insights. Rather than casting such events as irrational and, thus, beyond explanation we must interrogate the pre-history of the massacre and enquire about the processes of stereotyping, mutual misunderstanding and contention that occur on a daily basis. It is only in light of such investigations that we can begin to understand the 'madness' that is occasionally manifested in crowd situations. Dr Krishnasamy described the police action as 'pre-planned and politically motivated' and compared the attack to Jallianwallabagh. Whilst not suggesting this, I would contend that it is only in light of the antagonisms that had developed and been inflamed in Tamil Nadu that we can begin to comprehend what happened in Nellai.

The backdrop to the massacre was placed in the foreground shortly afterwards, when the cases against the estate workers arrested in the previous demonstration were hastily withdrawn. Had this action been taken earlier those 17 people, including the wife and child of one of the detainees, need not have died. One significant outcome though, was political. The TMC, which had entered into an electoral alliance with the PT, joined them in a fast on the 31 July to demand that action be taken against the police. Amongst those who took part were several Muslim and Dalit leaders, including Thirumavalavan. A significant fall-out of the massacre, S.Viswanathan noted, 'is a consolidation of the oppressed sectors, particularly Dalits, in Tamil Nadu'. This 'development is seen as having the potential to bring about substantial changes', he adds, 'not only of electoral politics in the state but in the nature of political activism in general and the approach of mainstream political parties to organisations that represent Dalits' aspirations' (*Frontline*, 27 August 1999). Most Dalit movements subscribed to the idea that unity arises in crisis and this proved true in this instance.

The TMC was the state wing of the Congress until it split from its parent body in 1996 when Congress decided to support the AIADMK. In the 1996 state elections, the TMC had profited from an anti-AIADMK wave and had performed very well winning 39 of the 40 seats it contested. Its constituent base is wider than that of the Dalit movements, and includes both Backward and Forward castes. It had never, however, contested the elections independently, without an alliance with either of the Dravidian parties or the Congress. As the established parties reached agreements on seat-sharing and representation it became increasingly clear that the TMC was being isolated. When the DPI, the Bahajun Samaj Party and the RPI joined the TMC–PT Front on 3 August, therefore, it was labelled as a 'Dalit Front'. The lack of proven parties in the alliance was an obvious weakness politically, but it was part of the attraction for the DPI. Four days after joining the front, Thirumavalavan attended a flag-raising ceremony in Virudhunagar to explain the decision. On the day of the massacre itself, the DPI Governing Body had met in the north of the state and determined not to extend their support to any one party. Here, he posed the question: 'Can we still vote for Dravidian Parties after this?'

The Third Front was presented as a real alternative to the two main parties and an opportunity to break the Dravidian domination of Tamil politics. The post-Independence rule of the Congress was resurrected as a golden age in movement speeches and the two Dravidian parties were portrayed as caste-based by comparison. The Front was significant because for the first time Dalit leaders were able to unite and to negotiate their terms: 'If we vote for you', Thirumavalavan is said to have told Moopanar, 'you must vote for us. In future we can only ally with political parties on the basis that we both have a share of power' (speech, 7 August 1999). He asserted that entering the political arena would not dampen their 'warrior spirit' or their determination to fight for liberty. 'To change the monopoly on power we also need to claim a share', appears to be a statement of the obvious. In the context of Dalit struggles, however, the ability to escape dependence and represent themselves is of revolutionary import. In a state where Murugesan, the DMK Melavalavu panchayat president, and five others were murdered for presuming to sit in office above their BC constituents, such a stance has been inconceivable until recently.

Entering democratic politics entails responsibilities as well as rights. The absence of retaliatory violence in the wake of the Nellai atrocity, in this light, was seen as a welcome shift in Dalit politics. The furious debates within the DPI had raised the very real prospects of a split within the movement. Both activists and local leaders were reluctant to realign themselves alongside the tainted parties that they had seen as their duty to oppose. In the run-up to the elections, members and leaders struggling to come to terms with their new role insisted that the decision was not a once and for all transformation. Palani Kumar stressed that the DPI would pull out of any alliance that did not support them. Others pointed to the example of Dr Krishnasamy as showing what a lone voice in Parliament could achieve and 'Firebrand' Murugan asserted that: 'Tomorrow if a *cheri* is burnt or a *cheri* sister raped, then surely these Liberation Panthers will dissolve the Parliament and give up votes to protest' (11 August 1999). Without the events in Nellai, however, it is uncertain whether the transition to politics could have been accomplished so easily. On 16 June, Thirumavalavan addressed those attending the wedding of a movement leader. 'Only when we are united', he said:

> ... will we know our real strength, will we be able to know who we are. Only when we are fully conscious of who we are, will the exercise of votes in the election be meaningful and useful. Due to our awakening, we have brought about a small change in proce- dure ... in future our votes are for us.

The ramifications of this 'procedural change' are redrawing the political map of Tamil Nadu.

Institutionalisation?

The Liberation Panther's transition, from movement to institutional politics, initially appears to follow Offe's model of institutional self- transformation. Adopting the path of parliamentary politics adds impetus to a movement by opening up extra resources, enabling coalitions with others and tapping into the support of sympathisers who will vote but not protest. In this phase, Offe maintains, movements tend to restructure themselves to create formal organ- isations with membership cards, dues, newspapers and structures. The leader-centred nature of most Tamil movements gives them an element of organisation from their very inception, but those move- ments that wish to enter party politics do tend to formalise processes of affiliation. The Bahujan Samaj Party in Uttar Pradesh instituted a policy of 'one rupee, one vote', referring to the membership fee and the political orientation of the organisation. This policy has not been adopted in Tamil Nadu yet, but some movements wanted to. The TDLM issued membership cards to people and the DPI was preparing a rule-book to inform members of the chain of responsibility.

The notion of an institutional learning process is very pertinent, therefore, but the particular chronology of the model is less so. Offe posits a period of stagnation as preceding the move to politics, but the established repertoire of protest in Tamil Nadu suggests a different sequence of transition. Movements have to prove their strength and durability before established parties accept them as coalition partners. As noted in Chapter 2, there is a conscious awareness of this process amongst activists as the following exchange with Palani Kumar indicates:

> Palani Kumar (P.K.): There is no way to change things now without violence. We have tried so hard and so long for a peaceful means to change, but when government is a tool of the dominant castes, the only way to change people is through violence.
> Author (H.G.): Are there no other means—such as the PT's foray into politics?
> P.K.: Puthiya Tamizhagam? How do you think that they got where they are? That was by violent means and protests too! (interview, 20 March 1999).

The institutionalisation of a movement, therefore, is, paradoxically, most likely when extra-institutional activity is at a peak. The movement, according to this model, does not reach a plateau from which there are few means of development. Instead the movement enters party politics at its moment of greatest impact. Each of the major Tamil parties in turn has reached a crescendo of protest activity before being granted grudging admittance to 'normal politics'. The next chapter focuses on the experience of the DPI in the 1999 elections. Merely deciding to contest the polls, it is clear, is insufficient to guarantee the unhindered participation of Dalit voters. Established interests benefited from the political inaction of the Dalit movements and were not prepared to relinquish their power. The compulsions and rewards of institutionalisation are powerful indeed, as Offe shows, and they are not achieved without a struggle.

9

'Voting for Ourselves': Dalit Politics and the 1999 Elections in Tamil Nadu

In Chidambaram Dalit people were prevented from voting for their chosen leader. The thugs of the Dravida Munnetra Kazhagam and the Vanniyar Union attacked Dalits with such impunity that it has become questionable whether India is an Independent or democratic nation. If India is in truth a democratic country, then there are 128 places in Chidambaram constituency that require re-polls. In the face of this violence we are engaged in a peaceful fast to display our faith in democracy.... Even after 52 years of Independence, our people do not have their basic rights, cannot even go to the polls and yet we are called extremists (Saravanan, Puthiya Tamizhagam, 12 September 1999).

Introduction

In electoral terms, the formation of a Third Front, by the TMC and its allies, was an unmitigated failure. The Front, which comprised numerous Dalit and Muslim parties, gave a voice to the minorities but failed to win a single seat in the 1999 Lok Sabha elections in Tamil Nadu. Across the state, the Front was unable to challenge the dominant electoral coalitions that lined up behind the two Dravidian parties. In Chidambaram constituency, however, the leader of the Liberation Panthers came second in a hard-fought contest. Of 732, 994 votes polled, Thirumavalavan received 225, 768 ballots.[1] Speaking at a conference, he gave his assessment of the result:

---

[1] The results for Chidambaram constituency were as follows:

Ponnusamy, E. (PMK):	3,45,331
Thirumavalavan, R (TMC):	2,25,768

Even if I stand in the next election in Chidambaram, I will only get two-and-a-quarter lakh votes. I will not get any more than that. During canvassing I was clear to my comrades: 'the people's consciousness is good, but I cannot believe that we will win. If we are allowed to vote without violence—3 lakh votes, if we have to vote against violent opposition—2 lakh votes'. That is what I predicted, that is what happened. No matter how many times I stand there that is what will happen (speech, 1 December 1999).

This chapter draws on interviews, press reports and independent inquiry findings into the election in Chidambaram constituency to examine the position of Dalit politics in Tamil Nadu. Fundamental to this enquiry are questions about what happens when Dalits challenge their habitual subordination and assert their political rights, how they articulate their political aspirations and changing identity formations, what the response of the state and other castes is and what Dalit movements can learn from this election.

On the day after the first round of the 1999 Lok Sabha elections in Tamil Nadu the national press was positive. 'Voter turnout in the "Vanniyar–belt" was uniformly high', The Hindu reported. There was a suggestion of some malpractice in that, 'Dalits were prevented from voting by some groups in parts of Chidambaram constituency, and they retaliated in areas where their presence was stronger. ... But police said, that the instances were brought to their notice 'within minutes' and they were able to prevent any untoward incidents' (The Hindu, 5 September 1999). The news emerging from eyewitness and independent accounts, however, tells a different story.[2] Palani Kumar and Kamaraj spoke of booths being seized, movement activists

Sumathy, T (INC):	1,50,794
Others	2,412
Total Electorate:	11,10,229
Votes Polled:	7,32,994

Source: The Hindu, 8 October 1999.

These figures are remarkably similar to those of the 2004 poll in which Thirumavalavan registered a slightly higher vote share but still came in second.
[2] I did not observe any of the incidents in Chidambaram personally neither did I travel through the area immediately after the election. This account, therefore, draws heavily upon reports that received wide press coverage and were accepted as independent. Their work was able to cover the area far more comprehensively than I, as a single researcher, could have.

suffering severe violence, huts being burnt and a partisan police force. 'In most of the villages visited in Chidambaram constituency Dalit people had been threatened not to cast their vote on polling day', according to the report by the Independent Initiative team.[3] 'Polling agents belonging to the DPI were attacked and people had been physically attacked, their huts burnt and looted by the upper castes led by the PMK (The Toiler's Party)' (Independent Initiative 1999: 21). Vanniyar thugs had warned Dalits not to cast votes and those Dalits who did try to vote often found that they had been pre-empted. 'I saw with my own eyes', an Arcot Lutheran Church pastor told me; 'At eleven o'clock, when they should have been voting, there was a line of women standing outside the Church telling me that they could not vote', because 'their votes had already been cast' (interview, 26 September 1999).

The seizing of polling booths, denial of voting rights and the use of violence were mostly confined to villages where Dalits were in a minority. In villages where they were dominant there were examples of Dalits engaging in violence against the Vanniyars as well. In Alapakkam, 45 Vanniyar huts were razed to the ground, goods worth Rs 9 lakh were looted and around one hundred Vanniyars were prevented from voting. Similar scenes were witnessed in Kilpoovanikuppam (Independent Initiative 1999: 23). 'Though accusations came from both sides', as an article in the Tamil magazine *Nandan* concluded, 'burned houses and looted goods show that the downtrodden have suffered the most' (Sonamandan 1999: 13). The article cited the People's Union for Civil Liberty's Commission, which stated that at least 50 polling booths had been in the hands of one party and that re-polls should be conducted. Election Commissioner Naresh Gupta insisted that 'only if ballot boxes are seized or ballot papers are torn up will there be a re-poll in Chidambaram'. 'There is also a rule', *Nandan* reminded him, 'that voters should not be threatened, and this regulation has been fully violated' (Sonamandan 1999: 14). Illamvazhudi lay in the government hospital in Cuddalore, his arms and face in plaster after he tried to ward off a petrol bomb.

---

[3] 'Independent Initiative is a public interest organisation headed by Justice V.R. Krishna Iyer, Former Supreme Court Judge' (Independent Initiative 1999: 1). This organisation monitored the poll process in Perambalur and Chidambaram and the findings of their teams give credence to allegations that the contest in Chidambaram was neither free nor fair.

'I can't stand it', he declared, 'they say it is my duty to vote. Is this the price of duty?' (Kaasi 1999: 31).

Paradoxical Marginality: Dalits and the Political Process

A week after the citizens of Chidambaram had turned out in the first phase of the election there was a gathering of a different kind in Madurai.[4] In front of the railway station, a knot of people clustered around a microphone, huddled under an awning that kept the worst of the heat away. Attention was focused on the procession of speakers who stood at the front to denounce what they saw as electoral malpractice and caste prejudice. Throughout the proceedings one theme was recurrent. All present were anxious to point out the restraint of their approach in contrast to the violence of the ruling coalition. 'We have never held hunger fasts before', the assistant state secretary of the DPI, Saktivel, declared. 'I have spoken at road blockades, rail blockades, protests, demonstrations and rallies, but our primary desire today, is to follow a path of non-violence' (Madurai, 12 September 1999). Behind this rhetoric of victimisation, innocence and democratic conviction lay a warning to the state authorities. 'Do not think that we, the Liberation Panthers, are only capable of such quiet modes of protest', Saktivel cautioned. 'We too can burn buses, we too can set huts ablaze, we too can incite violence and we too can disrupt the rule of law in this country—but we believe it is our duty to protect the law' (ibid.). The implication being that the movement's opponents were flouting it.

Deliège has coined the phrase 'paradoxical marginality' to express the 'ambiguity of the untouchables' position which is at the same time inside and outside the system' (1997: 104). Deliège means that Dalits are 'socially excluded but economically indispensable' (1997: 104). It is my contention that the election in Chidambaram exhibits

---

[4] Similar protest fasts were held in towns and cities across the state. These 'common rites serve not only to make these far flung individuals feel part of a larger organisation; they also make the public interpret the actions of the different groups of people as part of the same organisation, the same political group' (Kerzer 1988: 21).

how this 'paradoxical marginality' extends into the political sphere and has defined the position of Dalits in Tamil politics until recently. The SCs constitute 18.5 per cent of the Tamil population, but they are not equally dispersed. In 'reserved' constituencies, such as Chidambaram, they comprise nearly 35 per cent of the electorate.[5] Dalits are indispensable to the process of electoral competition both as voters and because certain seats are reserved for Dalit candidates. Simultaneously, they are excluded from the system, by being denied access to real decision-making power. Since the 1990s, Tamil Dalit movements have tried to move their concerns into the centre of the political process by forming independent parties which truly represent their interests.[6] Democracy is commonly perceived to be the rule of the people, by the people and for the people. 'Even so, "ordinary people" do not rule themselves directly, but through representatives whom they choose through the act of voting' (Boholm 1996b: 8). It is this problematic of representation that has come to dominate Dalit discourse on the political process and explicates the continuing marginality of Dalits in the politics of Tamil Nadu. As they have become more conscious of their rights, and more organised as a

---

[5] The *1961 Census of India, South Arcot District Handbook Vol.1* records the major characteristics and proportions of the caste communities in the area. Vanniyars constitute 32 per cent of the population and the Paraiyars 25 per cent. Most other castes are present only in insignificant numbers. The Karthaka Vellalars comprise 6 per cent of the population, the Idayars 4 per cent, and the Brahmins 1.5 per cent.

The figures for the Paraiyar caste are slightly ambigous since there is also a category of Adi-Dravidars. Adi is a prefix meaning 'original' and the term Adi-Dravidar is a generative term for the 'original Dravidians' or SCs. In my fieldwork, the term was commonly seen to be a term of reference for the Paraiyar caste.

'The Paraiyars', the report concludes, 'form the backbone of the agricultural labour in the District. In rural parts, they are treated as a polluting caste. They usually live in cheris which have separate drinking wells' (*Census of India 1961: Part X-III*, pp. 28–29).

[6] In 1996, Puthiya Tamilagam—a party mostly drawn from the ex-untouchable Pallar caste—contested the Legislative Assembly elections. Dr Krishnasamy was elected as an MLA at this time. The Republican Party of India and the Bahujan Samaj Party have representatives in Tamil Nadu, but they have failed to emulate the success of their northern counterparts. Both of these parties have lost support to the more radical PT and DPI. It will be interesting to see whether the Liberation Panthers can sustain their support now that they have entered the political arena.

community, Dalits are increasingly reluctant to be represented by others. 'For 50 years', Dr Krishnasamy (MLA) stated, 'we have been used by all political parties, duped by them and betrayed by them … Now we are voting for ourselves' (speech, 26 November 1999).

At the Round Table Conference in 1931, Ambedkar argued that the Untouchables would be unable to select candidates who really represented their interests unless they were entitled to vote separately from the rest of the population. When Gandhi went on a 'fast unto death' to condemn this move he presented himself as the representative of Untouchable interests. Separate electorates, he insisted, would drive an irreversible wedge between the Untouchables and the rest of society. Ambedkar finally backed down and the resultant Poona Pact established that there would be constituencies that were reserved for Untouchable *candidates*, but were open to voters of all castes (Joshi 1986: 12; Zelliot 1996: 168). This compromise was based upon the idea of proportionality. Since J.S. Mill many political theorists have assumed an assembly to be representative insofar as it mirrors the composition of the electorate. Pitkin (cited in Manin et al. 1999: 32) challenged this assumption and argued that simply guaranteeing all sectors of society a voice in parliament does not mean that their concerns will be accommodated. It is also questionable whether proportionality can ensure that every group is represented.

Those elected from reserved seats are all, necessarily, Dalits but they are seen (and more importantly, presented) as the pawns of the parties for which they stand. Dalit politicians are commonly seen as unable to speak out against the party line, or as self-interested careerists. Of course there are exceptions to the rule and there is a suggestion that some work 'behind the scenes' to ensure that improvements are made, but representation is an issue precisely 'because politicians have goals, interests and values of their own' (Manin et al. 1999: 29). Dalit movements have consistently insisted that the established political parties do not represent their interests. The significant numbers of people who were prepared to vote for Dalit parties in this election suggests that this perception is widespread. Elections are a useful barometer of the regard in which the representatives of the people are held. They express, in the words of Steven Lukes, 'the symbolic affirmation of the voters' acceptance of the political system and their role within it' (in Spencer 1996: 78). The context, within which such affirmation occurs, however, constrains people's choices.

Reservations, for instance, mean that Dalit 'leaders themselves are badly divided, owing allegiance to different parties. While they frequently express the urgent need of forging a cohesive political organisation of minority groups', as Roy and Sisson observe, 'considerations of their own political career push them into the lap of various political parties' (1990: 28). In effect, therefore, 'the non-Dalits decide which Dalit should win' (Larbeer 1999: 8). For the political process to be considered as legitimate, 'the link between the represented and the representatives must ... be explicated by means of symbols as a morally justified relationship' (Boholm 1996: 8). This has patently failed to happen and most Dalits I spoke to felt that their concerns were not adequately represented. 'In the realm of electoral politics', as Guru states, 'the Dalits argue that they just make a rhetorical appearance in the election manifestos of political parties but never get real representation in terms of access to material, social and cultural resources' (2000: 1). Contemporary Dalit movements, therefore, are engaged in a struggle for political recognition.

Too often, being born into a particular community has been taken as the only valid credential for representing that group, but this claim goes against the perceptions of Dalit voters. 'It cannot be argued that someone's being born in a particular caste or sex or region or religion makes her or his claim automatically valid and authentic', as Guru insists. 'If that were the case, the common Dalits would not have rejected their own leadership in the post-Ambedkar period' (2000: 2). Guru's assertions are somewhat out of alignment with the politics of Tamil Nadu. The rise of 'Dalit power' has followed a different trajectory here than the rest of India, as we have seen. 'When the Dalits (Harijans then) supported the Congress in the fifties and sixties, there was no organisation for them', as N.Kalynasundaram of *The Hindu* put it. 'After the advent of the rule of the Dravidian parties they switched their loyalty from the DMK to the AIADMK because of the influence of MGR, and their votes were taken for granted' (*The Hindu*, 24 August 1999). He goes on to insist that this is no longer the case and that Dalits are starting to vote for themselves.

Guru is right, however, that representation is more than a mechanical exercise. It is rather, the symbolic link between the people and those whom they empower to rule over them. As such, the way in which people perceive their representatives is indicative of the way in which they will perceive political institutions. The derogatory terms in which Dalit politicians are seen extends to the parties that they represent, that are depicted as casteist organisations with no real concern for the downtrodden. As Dalits have organised in defence of their civil rights they have demanded a more meaningful dissolution of social hierarchy and an extension of the political arena. The rhetoric employed by the DPI to explain the transition to politics focused upon Dalit grievances and the state's seeming unwillingness or inability to enforce the stipulations of the constitution. The problem they now faced was to establish themselves as fitting representatives of the people.

'For us, for our people', as Ravichandran of the Village Development Society (VDS) put it, 'if we are to take political power into our hands then we need to identify ourselves. One Krishnasamy has gone (into the Legislative Assembly) and look at the fuss he makes. If there were many representatives like Dr Krishnasamy, or like Thirumavalavan then imagine what it would be like'. Yet so many representatives have gone before, I countered, 'would they really raise their voices much?' 'They would', Ravichandran insisted, 'because they have suffered' (interview, 27 September 1999). Representation, according to this construction, is an ability to identify oneself with (and be recognised by) the constituents by whom one is elected. In contesting the election the DPI made this problematic of representation central to their endeavours. As Kamaraj put it:

> Yes there are hundreds of Dalit MPs in India, but they do not win alone. They win as party people, as politicians. There is no opportunity for Dalit MPs to speak out about Dalit society and problems so we do not need them. We need our own MP who will speak for us! (interview, 10 September 1999).

The Dalits of Chidambaram rallied around Thirumavalavan because he was 'one of us'. Whereas the established political parties had to spend a fortune on people to carry out their electoral work, the Independent Initiative observation team found that most of those working for the DPI were volunteers (Independent Initiative 1999: 2). Activists from all over the state travelled to the constituency to campaign on Thirumavalavan's behalf. 'Whever *Annan* went there were 10, 000 people', Palani Kumar reported. 'We were only allowed two cars, but seven left the guest house and everywhere cars would join in following him round and welcoming him wherever he went' (interview, 10 September 1999). Even non-members proffered their services to canvass during the election. Illangelian, a homeopathic doctor in a neighbouring constituency, was typical. To the approving nods and murmurs of the assembled group he insisted that: 'we have listened to many Thirumavalavan cassettes and speeches, and we have also read news of them in the papers and in magazines ... there is a feeling that we must take part' (interview, 29 September 1999).

In a Geertzian sense, the DPI was endowed with charisma. The enthusiasm that is evident in the quotes from movement supporters found an echo in regional journals and newspapers too: 'Even without speaking', the magazine *Kalki* reported, 'Moopanar is gathering crowds' (*Kalki*, 12 September 1999). The article painted a picture of huge crowds gathering to hear Thirumavalavan. Most of them were Dalit youth from remote villages without facilities, it concluded. The eagerness with which the DPI's campaign was received by the electorate, however, should not blind us to the contradictions that the movement had to confront. Having depicted the political process as unrepresentative, corrupt and conducive to compromise, the DPI had to compete for votes whilst insisting that they would not buy into the system. Contesting the elections, therefore, required more than a shift in the way that politics was articulated, it necessitated a paradigm shift in the way the movement was conducted. Whilst the DPI incorporates a vision of social change, as we have seen, they have predominantly been concerned with the defence of their constitutional rights. 'Political immediacy', as Guru puts it, 'dominates the cognitive map of Dalit politics' (*The Hindu*, 12 January 1999).

Polls, Power and Protest

Della Porta and Diani insist that 'social movements should seek to mobilise the greatest number of demonstrators possible. From this point of view, protest stands in for elections' (1999: 174). Whilst demonstrations obviously indicate a movement's popularity, protest bears significant differences from electoral contests. First, the media coverage is much less likely and second, protests may occur too often for sustained mass participation. To take one or two days off in a year and support the movement in a political show of strength is one thing. It is quite another to give up a couple of days in a month to condemn the abuse of power in a place that is far from home.[7] Kamaraj, who is a committed activist, declared that one meeting per month was as much as he could accommodate whilst working. It was clear that he expected to gain something from each demonstration as he complained after a poorly-attended meeting that he need not have bothered. Small road-side protests lack the sense of empowerment and the gathering of friends that accompany larger protests. Quite often, Dalit movements simply did not have the time or the resources to advertise or organise a mass meeting.

It is also easier to gain police permission to hold a small-scale *dharna*, than a march that may disrupt traffic. Reactive protest demonstrations were usually attended by those directly affected, local activists (both from the movement and from affiliated organisations) who faced pressure to turn up and those who showed up if the leader was present. In Kappaloor, Palani Kumar outlined a model for the escalation of protest. Local villagers had submitted several petitions to the panchayat about the inadequate provision of water to their area. A month had passed since then and they wished to take the matter further. They were advised that the first step should be to stage a demonstration outside the nearby *taluk* office—Palani Kumar said that 10–15 people would be too small and urged them to drag as many people out as possible. If those demands fell on deaf ears they could print a poster of condemnation, take the matter to the district office or block the road. Extra-institutional activity, according to Palani Kumar, may compensate for smaller numbers by engaging in dramatic action to gain public attention (discussion, 30 March 1999). This mode of organisation has the virtue of highlighting the abuses of the higher castes, keeping the movement in the public eye and responding to the grievances of afflicted members. It fails, however, to set an agenda around which a movement can canvass for new recruits.

This mode of operation is challenged by the logistics of electoral competition, which is predicated on the assumption that the candidates will 'go to the people'. Where the DPI was *accessible* to the

[7] The numbers that turned out on the 30 June to mark the second anniversary of the Melavalavu massacre were many times higher than could ever be gathered for a protest meeting in response to more minor incidents.

people before, they now had to gain *access* to, and convince, people that they were the legitimate representatives of their interests. The fact that all the candidates in Chidambaram were Dalits made this task more compelling. 'Elections', as Spencer notes, 'are also dramas of identity and difference, based on the moral affirmation of moral identifications' (1996: 79). The identity of the DPI has been as much imposed by others as defined by the movement itself. Negative portrayals of the movement can lead to it adopting an 'exclusive identity', which tends to 'stress isolation in relation to the outside world' (Della Porta and Diani 1999: 105). The collective 'we' of a movement with such an identity is associated with a particular social group and ideological orientation. On the one hand, this draws a distinction between the movement and the establishment (political parties and press) and on the other, an exclusive collective can more easily be depicted as extremist. Entering the elections required the DPI to adopt a more inclusive and flexible identity that would appeal to a wider audience. By allying with the TMC, they were able to project themselves as being more than a defensive caste organisation.

Although a campaign targeted exclusively at Dalits would have played to the DPI image and strengths, it would have also denied them the chance of winning a seat in the parliamentary elections. The 'practice of electing representatives according to geographical constituencies', as Philips observes, 'suggests that those who are elected are meant to speak for an area or place, the implication being that interests are relatively homogenous within localities' (1991: 63). There are no geographical concentrations that could form the basis of a Dalit constituency. As long as voting is tied to localities, therefore, no Dalit can afford to ignore the other castes represented in the area. To downplay the significance of the Dalit issue, however, would have been to deny the importance of the move to politics. After all, one of the main criticisms levelled against earlier Dalit leaders, was that 'they never tried to establish the self-determination of the Dalits' (Larbeer 1999: 8). The difficulty of deciding what sort of campaign to conduct was compounded by the fact that Thirumavalavan was allied to the TMC rather than completely independent.

Whilst presenting itself as a significant alternative to the two main Dravidian parties therefore, the Front had to be wary of alienating traditional TMC voters. Both in the press and on the ground people saw the election as panning out on caste lines. The three major fronts were broadly representative of different caste constituencies. The

PMK–DMK–BJP combine were seen to represent the interests of the Vanniyar community, the Most Backward Caste group that is dominant in this part of the state. The TMC–PT–DPI alliance was seen as representing the Dalits and minorities. The AIADMK–Congress Front in Chidambaram had no obvious caste basis, but they were dependent upon the BC Thevar vote elsewhere in the state. Obviously the support base of the three fronts was neither so clear cut, nor were they exclusive.

The motives that drive a person to vote are far more complex than this elementary division would suggest. The personal appeal of the candidate, the leader of the party, the alliance with a national party and the policies that they campaign upon can and do influence voting patterns. Consequently, privileging the role of caste in elections may present a distorted picture of the multiple processes at work. There is, however, a sense in which politics has 'simply provided a new ritual idiom in which villagers could express the kinds of divisions that had always existed' (Spencer 1996: 86). A cursory glance through the press coverage of the Tamil elections would confirm the discursive pre-eminence of caste as a means of analysing the prospects and outcomes of the polls. Whilst all three candidates were Dalits, therefore, they were seen to *represent* different castes. This symbolism is apparent in the fact that the PMK and the INC candidates both had to assert their Dalit origins.

That Thirumavalavan was a Dalit required no rhetorical assertion, the problem facing his candidacy was to insist that he would represent others. The difficulty of doing this was made evident in the mundane and crude defacement of party posters. In parts of Chidambaram constituency, the Third Front poster had been selectively smeared with cow dung so that the faces of the two Dalit leaders were obscured. 'A large percentage of the TMC supporters are over 50 years of age', as V. Ganapathi, noted in *The Hindu*. It was, therefore, 'a big question whether they would support the DPI, which came into existence in this part of the state, as a defensive group to stem the influence of the majority Vanniars' (*The Hindu*, 30 August 1999). Given this history, and with the Thevar vote base of the Congress-AIADMK Front largely absent, the contest in Chidambaram effectively became a bi-polar one: Vanniyars against Dalits, the DMK against the TMC and BJP against a 'secular' alternative.

Electoral instability is said to cause established parties to seek new sources of political support and may, therefore, increase the bargaining power of protest groups.[8] It is instructive that the Dalit movements' entry into politics coincided with a period marked by frequent elections that were attended by transformations in electoral alliances. This equation is rendered problematic, however, by the fact that social movements need to show their strength before they are considered worthy of an alliance. Furthermore, such coalitions do not necessarily benefit the protestors as much as the party, since they are rarely in a position of strength when negotiating terms with an established institution. Kamaraj displayed an appreciation of this imbalance when he admitted that:

> The coalition will not stand by us—it is a caste matter. Support will come and go, so we need to go all out for ourselves to get *Annan* there to speak for us (interview, 10 September 1999).

In other words, there is no guarantee of political allegiance, but the important thing is to get into parliament in the first instance. In this regard, as seen in Chapter 2, the past history of successive mobilisation has established a 'repertoire of action'. In accepting violent groups such as the Vanniyar and Thevar Unions into the mainstream, the government acted to legitimate a course of action which the DPI was attempting to emulate in 1999. Whilst the Vanniyar Union, or PMK, had established its democratic credentials through previous electoral victories, however, the members of the DPI had yet to make the transition from agitators to legitimate political representatives.

---

[8] This trend has already become evident in the subsequent electoral pact between the AIADMK and the TMC–DPI combine and the more recent decision by the DPI to join the DMK Front. When in power the AIADMK presided over atrocities against Dalits on a scale that is still resonates in movement rhetoric. In opposition, however, they were willing to condemn state inaction or violence and raise their voices on behalf of the Dalits. The DMK was depicted as the main enemy and as a casteist organisation, until they fell out with the Vanniyar-based PMK. Opposition to the PMK was prioritised over opposition to the DMK–BJP combine. In forging an alliance both the DPI and the DMK have compromised on principles and backtracked on rhetorical assertions that portrayed the other as undemocratic and violent. The 2001 state election results suggest that the established party has suffered more as a consequence of this alliance. In 2004, the DPI and other Dalit parties reverted to a Third Front.

Caste, Identity, and the Election

In its mobilisational phase, the PMK worked with Dalit movements, championed Dalit issues and spoke up on their behalf. P. Subbarayan, a branch manager in the Life Insurance Corporation of India (LIC) recalled an incident where Ramdoss had carried a Dalit body through a village in the face of Vanniyar opposition (interview, 31 March 1999). The PMK gained power in the previous election with the support of many Dalit voters. The PMK candidate 'Dalit' Ezhilmalai had gone on to become health minister and had won plaudits for his work, and the party had worked alongside the Liberation Panthers on various issues. Shri Rangan Prakash of the RPI recalled that many DPI cadres had worked on his behalf in defiance of the election boycott. Had he stood in opposition to Thirumavalavan, the boundaries of caste allegiance may well have been blurred. In a move that surprised many analysts, however, Ezhilmalai was excluded from the first list of PMK candidates to be announced, and was denied the Chidambaram constituency. He resigned in disgust, enabling Dalit parties to claim that the 'real face' of the 'Vanniyar PMK' had been revealed.[9] This was further emphasised by the fact that on the day that the TMC launched its state-wide campaign, BC members of a Thevar organisation hurled stones at the stage when Thirumavalavan was speaking (see *Maalai Marusu, Dinakaran and The Hindu* for 21 August 1999). Scared of an escalation of violence, the TMC urged the Election Commission to enlist the help of the army to maintain the peace (*The Hindu*, 23 August 1999). The chief minister condemned the stone throwing (*The Hindu*, 23 August 1999), but Dalit activists were consistent in pointing the finger of blame at K.Karunanidhi and Dr Ramdoss for waging a campaign against the DPI leader.

Subbarayan claimed that the PMK had become increasingly anti-Dalit as the DPI became more popular in their heartlands. The turning point, apparently, was the huge DPI rally in Cuddalore in 1997 when walls and banners declaimed: 'we will not live in slavery' and 'we will hit back' to which members of the PMK painted replies asserting that 'we will keep you down' and 'if you hit us, we will kill you!'

---

[9] With regard to Ezhilmalai, it is ironic that in the 2001 Assembly elections he contested and won on behalf of the AIADMK and in alliance with the PMK.

(interview, 31 March 1999). Relations between the DPI and the PMK reached a new low during the 1999 elections because the Liberation Panther's were not just intruding upon PMK territory but entering into direct competition with them. In light of the stone throwing and the sidelining of Ezhilmalai, the contest was further polarised on caste lines. 'Vote for someone who has and will represent your interests', the DPI were now able to say, 'or forever abandon the prospect of social change'.

Moopanar described the Third Front as a 'silent revolution' (*The Hindu*, 28 August 1999), but for many Dalits in the rural villages of Chidambaram, it was more akin to a revelation. Dalits in Parengipatti, in Chidambaram constituency 'work either as agricultural labourers for coolie, or in low-grade government jobs'. A group whom I interviewed, after a church service, were aware of the rising conscious-ness of Dalit rights, but displayed a striking ignorance of the wider political scene. Some of them had not even heard of the PT, which highlights the geographical limitations to much Dalit protest. Despite this relative lack of consciousness, the streets and walls of the constituency were festooned with the TMC symbol of the cycle and with the colours and emblems of the DPI in a visual corroboration of reports of extensive campaigning in the area (group discussion, 26 June 1999). For the first time in 50 years of electoral politics, they were presented with a meaningful choice. Dalits were now able to vote for someone who would 'protest for us and speak up for us in Parliament' (ibid.).

The paradoxical marginality of the Dalit movements was some-what masked in 1999 because the Third Front placed them at the centre of its campaign. Indeed, returning from a week of campaigning in Chidambaram, Palani Kumar and Kamaraj insisted that *Annan* stood a great chance of winning. '*Cheri* people who have not voted for 52 years in their reserved constituency, because it was in Vanniyar hands, have now witnessed a huge change. Dalit people told us that they would definitely vote for Thirumavalavan' (interview, 10 Sep-tember 1999). 'Whichever area in Chidambaram you visit, whichever village you go to', Ravichandran asserted, 'the [TMC] symbol of the cycle is present' (interview, 27 September 1999). When I visited the area in the month after the polls, the insignia of the TMC and the DPI were everywhere. Somandam is an assistant regional leader of the WPM in Myaladuthurai. To reach his village it is necessary to wade thigh-deep through a filthy stream and then walk a kilometre or so beyond there. His organisation chose to support Thirumavalavan in the elections because, unlike other party politicians, he was standing 'on behalf of the Dalits' (interview, 28 September 1999).

The high-profile canvassing and the media coverage, however, merely served to paper over the chasms that were evident at ground level. The overriding significance accorded to the question of representation and community interest, by Dalit activists, has its genesis in a radical mistrust of established parties and higher castes. If anything, this election and the state polls in 2001, served to reinforce these notions. To an outside observer in Madurai it was readily apparent that the DPI had not been welcomed into the TMC Front by everyone. Shortly before launching the Third Front, for example, the TMC had a mass rally in the city which was attended by 10,000 or more supporters and the stadium where it was held. When the DPI organised a fast to protest against electoral malpractice in Chidambaram, however, the local TMC candidate, Ram Babu, made a brief appearance with a handful of followers. Admittedly this obscures the levels of organisation that go into planning a mass rally as compared to holding a protest fast, but the meagre show of support mirrored a pattern established during the campaign.

When Thirumavalavan and Moopanar toured the Madurai area the speeches were mobbed by Dalit activists. All DPI activists from Melavassel volunteered to stick up posters, paint walls and drum up supporters. Their excitement was palpable, but it was not matched by the TMC's core constituents. Palani Kumar was delighted: 'Wherever *Annan* went there were 10,000 people, the majority of them Dalit people'. When he joined a group of activists who went to canvass in Chidambaram itself he felt that 'the *cheris* are awakened and conscious and non-Vanniyar castes and Muslims are supporting *Annan* too' (interview, 10 September 1999). The naïve optimism of the committed activist persuaded him that anti-Vanniyar feeling was sufficient to unite OBCs behind the Third Front. Whilst Muslim groups openly extended support to the Front and welcomed the anti-Hindutva stance, there was little sign that large numbers of OBCs felt the same.

In this context, it is worth considering the 2001 Assembly elections briefly.[10] Having dallied with the AIADMK after the 1999 elections,

---

[10] As I was not in India at the time, this account draws on newspaper and other published reports.

the DPI joined the DMK–BJP Front in 2001 so as to be in the camp opposite the PMK. In electoral terms, the DMK combine was routed and its allies suffered from its poor showing. The PT failed to win even one of the ten seats it contested, and though Thirumavalavan emerged victorious in Mangalur, this was the only seat the DPI won of the eight it contested. In the AIADMK Front, the Dalit-based RPI won the seat that it contested but it was said to have profited from the alliance arithmetic rather than consolidated the Dalit vote-base. In sum, the Dalit organisations appear to have been marginal players in the elections. A more detailed analysis of voting trends and opinions, however, paints a different picture. Though the Dalit vote may not have proved decisive, it did significantly influence the outcome of the elections. In a positive sense the Dalits turned out in large numbers to vote for the DMK candidates (Illangovan 2001; Subramanian 2001; Yadav 2001).

More significant in terms of results, was the manner in which members of other castes voted against the 'Dalit-friendly' parties. Even DMK cadres themselves neither campaigned nor voted effec-tively for the PT and the Liberation Panther candidates (Illangovan 2001; Indiresan 2001; Subramanian 2001; Venkatesh 2001). 'The "social aversion" on the part of DMK candidates, mostly belonging to Mukkulathors and other OBCs, to be identified with Dalit leaders and cadres', as Illangovan noted, 'has made the DMK an "untouch-able" among its own rank and file' (*The Hindu*, 14 May 2001). Caste leaders reportedly issued decrees that no caste Hindu should vote for Dalit or Dalit-friendly parties (ibid.). Mendelsohn and Vicziany (1998) spoke of a 'new form of violence' against the Dalits as a means of keeping them in their place. As the Dalit movements have entered the political process such violence has arguably been transferred into the electoral process. 'The DMK's gamble with the Dalit card has failed', as Illangovan concluded, 'thanks to the sharp polarisation of Dalits and non-Dalits, where the party affiliations became irrel-evant' (*The Hindu*, 15 May 2001). Untouchability not only exists, in other words, it has found a new medium of expression.

'Untouchable identity', as Mosse states, 'is not pliable at will. ... The ability to acquire and sustain alternative identities, or to redefine the meaning of symbols of inferiority, depends crucially on having the power and resources to change existing relations of dependence: In short, identity change is caste politics' (Mosse 1996: 2). The issues involved in the election, in other words, were not all symbolic or identity based; politics is not only about moral representations. 'Village politics are all about patronage', as Spencer found in Sri Lanka, 'about getting government jobs and loans' (1996: 87). Indeed, many of the new organisational forms of caste 'are oriented to securing economic benefits, jobs, or special concessions' (Kothari 1997: 68). In this light, voting for a Dalit party could be explained by the hope that this would enable greater access to state resources. It is impossible to dismiss this argument completely because political ties *are* often seen as improving access to tangible resources. This point of itself, however, cannot account for the number of people who turned out to vote. The benefits to be gained are too few for everybody to have access to them. Furthermore, if resources were the main consideration then it would have been a safer bet to support an established party (cf. Prasad and Bechain, *The Hindu*, 4 January 2000). Identity politics, thus, cannot be divorced from the question of power and representation: who controls the resources, and which candidate is likely to represent one's interests.

By refusing to vote as they were told to, by prominently displaying posters of Thirumavalavan and the cycle symbol of the TMC, and by refusing to see themselves as socially subordinate, the Dalits of Chidambaram were explicitly engaging in caste politics. The electoral coalitions in Tamil Nadu are often precarious, with many of the smaller parties keen to ally themselves to the party that is most likely to win. For the Dalits, the creation of a Third Front permitted them to articulate a positive identity that rejected notions of submission and marginality. For the duration of the election, in fact, the Dalits of this area assumed a centre stage position. The success of the new venture would be gauged by the response that Thirumavalavan received. The assertion of political 'we-ness', however, is predicated upon the identification of an 'other'. Dalit social identities are relational; they are defined *in terms* of other groups and structures and *in the terms* of other groups and institutions (Charsley 1996: 13). When Dalits decided to take the responsibility for their own political destiny 'this caused an "allergy" amongst the Vanniyars' (Kamaraj, interview, 10 September 1999). In the face of Dalit assertion, which challenged their social, political and symbolic dominance, Vanniyar groups determined to reassert what they saw as the 'natural order' (cf. Khare 1984: 15).

On statewide television Thirumavalavan broke down in tears. 'Thousands of Dalits have lost their homes and goods', he reported, 'they stand on the street without even the means to buy milk for their babies' (Kaasi 1999: 31). Those in hospitals were mostly Dalit, those on the streets due to the destruction of their houses were the same, but so were those in prisons. The neutrality of the law enforcement authority was questioned once again. Warned well in advance of possible violence they failed to prevent trouble from flaring or arrest the perpetrators. In a damning indictment, Independent Initiative insisted that 'the police and Poll Officers had overlooked their basic duty to protect the human rights of Dalits including their voting rights. They have either been mute witnesses or active agents in perpetrating atrocities on Dalits' (Independent Initiative 1999: 20; Kaasi 1999; Thamukku September–October 1999; Vikest and Maniswaran, 1999). The police, in other words, were accused of *institutionalised casteism*. They were presented as reflecting the prejudices of the castes from which they are drawn. Recent initiatives to introduce officers from other states and, therefore, from castes which are not represented in Tamil Nadu, have been very welcome. Problems arise, however, in the police's tendency to act as the 'servants of the party in power' (Independent Initiative 1999: 21). Certainly, the police force has lost the trust of many Dalits. Events such as those that occurred in Nellai, Chidambaram and Melavalavu have painted a picture of a force that is routinely anti-Dalit. The main issue here is the critical lack of resources and power.

That the Vanniyars in Chidambaram resisted change was no surprise. Had the Third Front merely threatened the hegemony of the AIADMK, its supporters would have faced the resentment of party loyalists. In Chidambaram, however, the issue was further polarised by caste.[11] The Independent Initiative report lent credence to allegations of intimidation and violence by the established parties, it also found that the DMK and AIADMK candidates spent far more on their election campaigns than the TMC candidates and well exceeded the

---

[11] Kannagusabhai, a WPM activist from the neighbouring constituency of Myaladuthurai, insisted that the PMK was a casteist outfit. 'They do not want to see us as humans', he said, 'and no matter what we have done they have not looked on us as humans' (interview, 29 September 1999). Ezhilmalai, by this construction, was depicted as a pawn in the hands of the PMK's political aspirations—utilised so long as he played the game and toed the party line, he was dropped as soon as he became a political player in his own right.

upper limit of Rs 15 lakh stipulated by the Election Commission. Their team was also warned, well ahead of the elections, that there 'was a threat of the Dalits not being able to cast their votes' (ibid.: 3). Before Independence, Dr Ambedkar warned about the difficulties of a 'new life of contradictions'. 'In politics', he cautioned, 'we will be recognising the principle of one man, one vote, one value. In our social and economic life we shall, by reason of our social and economic structure, continue to deny the principle of one man, one value' (in Joshi 1986: 40). In Chidambaram, the playing field was certainly skewed in favour of the dominant castes who, in this instance, can be said to be the BC Vanniyars who are the most populous caste.

Dalits in Tamil Nadu are marginalised physically as well as socially as we saw in Chapter 5. The caste-based segregation renders issues of identification unproblematic, and reinforces the group feelings that are then tapped by political party machines. Discriminatory practices are largely receding today but Dalits are still dependent on the main village (*oor*) for rations, medical assistance and other amenities (cf. Ghosh 1999). This institutionalised inequality has often given the upper castes the means of enforcing their domination. In Chidambaram, the spirit—if not the law—of democratic elections was violated by the location of polling booths in the main *oors*. Those who defied the threats had to brave the intimidating environment of the upper-caste settlement to cast their votes. The Vanniyars did not hesitate to use the imbalance of power in their favour. Drinking water for many Dalit *cheris* was cut off on the day of the election and supply had not been restored even a week after the event. In many areas, subsequent to the poll, Dalits were denied access to much-needed amenities, barred from shops and schools and refused employment by the upper castes (Human Rights Watch Independent Initiative 1999; Thamukku September–October 1999). Valentine, the women's wing leader of the Communist Party reported that even a month after the polls:

> The situation in Chidambaram has not yet returned to normality. In many villages Dalits have been subject to social boycott and are denied work by the higher castes. No action has yet been taken against those who set fire to houses, beat people up and harassed women (Valentine, 25 October 1999).

The DPI and the PMK traded charges about vote-rigging, corruption and the resort to violence, but the problems in Chidambaram were not simply the result of aggressive electoral competition. To present this election as an isolated event would be wrong, but as an event it has served to highlight the continuing significance of caste prejudices in Tamil Nadu.

Affirmative action programmes for the SCs, as we have seen, have made them the subjects of envy amongst BC communities who feel that their position is threatened. There is widespread resentment about constitutional amendments such as the Protection of Civil Rights Act (PCR) and the Prevention of Atrocities Act, which are seen as pandering to the Dalits and open to abuse. I was often told that the Dalits misused the PCR to extort money or favours, by threatening to lodge false cases against caste Hindus. The election in Chidambaram, however, highlights the continuing dependency of the Dalits in terms of vital resources. The violence triggered by Dalit mobility has been facilitated by inequalities in 'money and muscle power' (Independent Initiative 1999). It is a sign of how far Tamil Nadu has come in its attempt to exorcise the 'evil of untouchability', that Dalits were able to contest the election in an independent capacity. In some villages, Dalits hit back and asserted their strength. They were also guilty of electoral malpractice and some of my informants claimed to have voted for *Annan* several times.

These (regrettable) trends indicate the rising confidence and political awareness of the community. The government response, in arresting thousands of Dalit youth as a 'preventative measure' and the social boycotts imposed by locally-dominant castes, reveal the extent to which Dalits are still excluded and lacking in power. The government response was arguably politically motivated rather than caste-based, as no political party would openly support the continuing practice of untouchability. Elite groups are often reluctant to extend the boundaries of the political arena. It is my contention, however, the election reveals the extent to which caste and politics are enmeshed in Tamil Nadu. As the Dalits have established themselves as an organised political force the emphasis has shifted to trying to coopt them as electoral allies rather than address the root causes of caste based discrimination. This process of re-negotiation was apparent in the run up to the 2001 Assembly elections as both main parties competed for the backing of the DPI, but the paramount significance of the politics of caste identity was apparent in the reactions of the rank and file of these parties.

Entering the Mainstream

The DPI are certainly taking steps to broaden their appeal and reach out to other communities, but the most obvious impact of Thirumavalavan's standing for elections in Chidambaram was high- lighted by Ram Babu: 'Because Thirumavalavan stood in the elections things changed. Half the Vanniyars switched over to the opposition. They think that if a Dalit wins they won't be able to sit down on a level' (interview, 12 September 1999). In the short term, at least, it appears that political engagement has served to exacerbate caste tensions and cohesion. More pressing than electoral alliances, from this perspective, is a means of establishing the humanity of the Dalits for the locally-dominant castes. In addressing this problematic Ghosh calls for Dalits to be supported financially as well as in terms of education, to help them escape the ties of dependency (Ghosh 1999). Although this recognises the continuing social oppression of the Dalits, it elides the complexity of the situation.

First, providing more money for the Dalits is no insurance that it will reach them. Second, the cumulative deprivation of the commu- nity cannot be tackled simply by throwing more money at the problem, since even wealthy and educated Dalits face discrimination. Indeed, in the short term at least, this is likely to increase the hostility of BC groups. The provision of reserved seats for the Dalits in local panchayat elections has not proved to be an immediate means of empowerment. 'In several places', as Viswanathan notes, 'Dalit presidents have not been able to hold meetings, because caste Hindu members would not sit down with them at the meetings' (1997: 114). The Dalit quest for equality involves challenging the authority, status and social dominance of those above them in the caste system. By definition, therefore, the process will involve levels of cultural, symbolic, economic and physical violence.

The political path is merely one aspect of that struggle. 'For many Dalits, the election process is an end in itself.... In fact, for under- employed rural and urban masses, the election process brings some immediate sources of income' (Omvedt 1999). Omvedt, thus, rein- troduces the material basis of Dalit subjection and appears to suggest that survival is the core issue for Dalits and getting into office the pre-occupation of Dalit parties. Her points are well taken, but an analysis on the basis of resources alone cannot, as we have seen, account for the numbers of people who turned out to vote for the TMC in 1999. As Prasad and Bachain (2000) insist, 'no Dalit party can compete with the mainstream parties such as the Congress or the BJP in terms of throwing alms to a "hungry" Dalit electorate'. If Omvedt is correct they ask, then how can we account for the rise of autonomous Dalit parties. The BC response to Dalit assertion and the overwhelming support of hitherto apolitical Dalits for Thirumavalavan should highlight that this was more than just another election.

At stake in these elections were questions of self-esteem, self-representation and an assertion of agency. 'In 28th Ward (of Chidambaram constituency) Velliammal, a 62-year-old lady insisted that she would vote for the first time. Vanniyars used to cast votes for all the Dalits, but now they are voting for *Annan*' (Kamaraj, 10 September 1999). After the elections, Dr Krishnasamy suggested that his party could link up with the Liberation Panthers on issues concerning the community as a whole. 'The reasoning was that Dalit leaders should retain the leadership of Dalit campaigns ... and that mainstream political parties should not derive undue political mileage from the struggles of Dalits against caste oppression' (Nambath 1999). Such an appeal emphasises the significance of the rise in Dalit consciousness in Tamil Nadu, but it also runs the risk of further polarising the political field. On the one hand established parties *do* seek to gain mileage from Dalit movements but on the other reinforcing an exclusively Dalit identity could render the upheavals witnessed in the 1999 and 2001 polls endemic.

In the event Krishnasamy's offer was rejected and, as noted earlier, the TMC and the DPI secured an electoral understanding with the AIADMK. This represented a pragmatic acceptance that the Dravidian parties remain hegemonic. The results of three bye-election results in early 2000 and the Assembly elections in 2001, however, suggested that the political benefits of such a move were far from clear cut. In the bye-elections the 'DMK gained from Dalits' apathy to the AIADMK' (*The Hindu*, 29 February 2000). Contrary to the depiction of Dalits as pawns to be manipulated by political parties, or their own leaders, the Dalit electorate refused to endorse a party that they regarded as ideologically opposed to them. In the months preceding the 1999 elections, Thirumavalavan had repeatedly articulated the movement's opposition to the AIADMK and insisted that the atrocities committed under its rule could not be forgiven. On the 5 March

2001, the DPI joined the DMK-led National Democratic Alliance (which included the BJP) for the Assembly elections because the AIADMK's 'secular' Front allied itself with the PMK (Venkatesh 2001). There are powerful political compulsions that make coalitions with established parties attractive, as Omvedt points out, but if Dalit movements are not to be cast as short-term opportunists who use their members to further their own interests an alteration in strategy is required.

Conclusion

'We must be with the people', Thirumavalavan insisted, but 'for the organised Dalits, the absence of an identifiably pro-Dalit front took away much of the interest in the bye-election' in 2000 (Nambath 2000). The election in Chidambaram was about more than political machination and the struggle for political resources. When the Dalit parties campaigned for a 'share of power' they encapsulated the rising political awareness of the Dalit community. Interviews and voter turnout indicated excitement at the prospect of an alternative and determination to vote for an autonomous Dalit candidate. Whilst immediate political considerations may require opportunist electoral alliances, Dalit movements cannot afford to ignore the opinions of their constituents. Having campaigned and voted for a 'share of power' the Dalit electorate may not be prepared to prop up alternate Dravidian parties. Indeed, early in 2002, the DPI suffered a schism because some members of the party were increasingly unhappy with the decisions of the leadership (Palani Kumar, 17 July 2002). Whilst Periyasami opted to found a rival 'Paraiyar' organisation, the elections in 1999 raised the prospect of Dalit unity and of ties with OBCs.

In this light, the 1999 Lok Sabha elections may truly prove to be a turning point in Tamil politics. Sakthidasan is from a remote village in Chidambaram constituency. He spoke of the necessity of entering the political process as the only means by which Dalit leaders could gain more 'respect, attention and power'. The people in this constituency are dependent on other castes for work as agricultural labourers, except for the few that have gained low-grade government jobs. When asked how much faith he had in democracy Sakthidasan was forthright:

We do not have that much faith in democracy, but for the first time a Dalit has stood as a Dalit and we have done our duty by voting for him. Whether he does anything for us or not is the next question, but our votes are for ourselves (Interview, 26 September 1999).

The defining feature of these elections was the prospect of a real alternative to the established parties. The presence of an independent Dalit candidate persuaded many people to vote for the first time and expanded the base of democratic participation. In the concluding chapter, I will argue that this gradual process of democratisation is the most important outcome of the Dalit struggle in Tamil Nadu.

Conclusion

CRITICAL CITIZENS—THE LIBERATION PANTHERS AND DEMOCRATISATION IN INDIA

Creating Citizens: Dalit Movements and Democracy

The second anniversary of the Melavalavu massacre fell on 30 June 1999 and security around the *cheri* was tight. On the road leading out of Madurai some 20 miles away, check points had been set up and vehicles required permits to proceed. The open square of the colony, where the seven 'martyrs' are buried, was transformed beyond recognition. A coconut matting structure sufficiently large to shelter over a thousand people seated cross-legged on the ground had been erected and divided into three main sections: in the first lay the graves of the fallen, covered with flowers with a photograph of each person serving as a tombstone. The main body of the 'hall' was an empty space where activists and onlookers could sit in the shade. Their attention was directed towards the third area where a raised dais was equipped with seats and microphones. Over the course of the day, Dalit leaders from most movements in Tamil Nadu made the pilgrimage to Melavalavu to address the crowds.

Fears about safely meant that a strict time schedule was enforced. Each group arrived in convoy; the leaders paid their respects to the dead, mounted the stage to make their speeches and then drove off before the next contingent arrived. Most of the audience remained constant through the day, but each successive leader brought their own entourage, packed into vans, sitting on the roofs of buses and jeeps and jammed into auto-rickshaws—each vehicle sporting a flag of allegiance. The leaders came and went in swift succession sometimes crossing paths, but were mostly kept apart by the police operation. The message delivered by each leader was specific and had a different emphasis and yet they all chose to be present on this occasion and they all returned to similar themes. Murugesan has been established as a martyr of the *Dalit* struggle in Tamil Nadu and his memory serves as a powerful unifying force in an otherwise disparate cause.

Dalit movements in Tamil Nadu, as we have seen, are riven by the factionalism, personalism, contradictions and particularism that characterise many political parties in India. This should not be surprising given that social movements are always shaped by the political, economic and social context from which they emerge, even as they attempt to alter certain aspects of that world. Despite the divisions that have precluded the emergence of a coherent *Dalit movement*, it would be inaccurate to say that there is no sense of Dalit unity. Although the focus of the book has been the organisation and activists of the Liberation Panthers, the implications of this research have wider relevance. The common thread connecting the various Dalit movements is reflected precisely in the term 'Dalit'. The fact that we can talk about Dalit, as distinct from caste or class, movements serves to emphasise certain distinctive characteristics of the struggle. Despite the contemporary trend towards caste-based organisations that attempt to move away from the term, the diverse movements respond to similar conditions and adopt strategies that conform to an established repertoire of action.

Furthermore, there is a widespread recognition that the diverse ex-untouchable movements are working towards the same ends. Members of the DPI would recognise the leaders of the PT and the TAYF as having common goals even if they take different paths and are in competition for recruits. The significance of occasions like the Melavalavu memorial or Ambedkar's birthday is that it enables the fissiparous Dalit organisations to affirm their shared origins and aspirations for a society free of caste discrimination. This sense of Dalit unity is reinforced by the Ambedkarisation of Tamil movements and the naming of children, streets and houses after Ambedkar. There is, in other words, a convergence of interests. Broadly speaking their demands can be summarised under four headings: The demands for self-esteem, a share of resources, for human rights and for meaningful political participation. Obviously these demands are often interdependent and the denial of one can preclude the attainment of the others. Though they are recurrent themes of the book they are often implicit so it is worth considering them here.

The focus of this review is the implication of these objectives. Self-esteem is perhaps the most difficult to define of the movements' goals. In the context of this study the concept refers to group rather than individual identity but it indicates that the Dalit desire to be treated as equals must coincide with their own efforts and self-belief. The problem is that 'stigma threatens the person stigmatised...' as S.M. Miller notes. 'The stigmatised person experiences the fact of being separated from the rest of society, of being treated as someone different, marginalized, as less than others, as not worthy of everyday exchanges and transactions that make up the community. This experience produces a "spoilt identity", a self-image which is damaged and diminished impeding the autonomous actions of the individual' (in Twine 1994: 97).[1] In the words of S.Martine, a social activist and advocate from Tindivanam, 'you must understand that their instincts and creativity have been killed. He thinks that he is nobody. He has lost his identity. The challenge is to make this lion active, but this will be a slow process' (interview, 18 January 1999).

The oppressed, in other words, are not completely free of the hegemonic world view and may consequently see themselves as lesser beings.[2] They may not perceive their subordination as just or accept the *basis* of their lowly status, but they can see themselves as powerless. This diminishes their capacity for meaningful action and renders them dependent on others. In forming autonomous movements and challenging accepted ways of being in the world, Dalit movements are effectively seeking to foster a sense of group pride and belonging that other caste groups in Tamil Nadu manifestly possess (cf. Pandian 2000). In fighting for self-esteem, the Dalit movements challenge a 'culture of victimhood' and assert that they are capable of becoming 'sovereigns' (G. Dietrich, personal commu-

---

[1] Although Goffman (1970) was the first sociologist to systematically deal with the concept of 'stigma', his seminal work is mostly concerned with social rather than psychological effects. 'Stigma', according to Goffman, refers to 'the situation of the individual who is disqualified from full social acceptance' (1970: 9).

[2] Goffman makes a similar point when he asserts that stigmatised individuals share the norms of the 'normal' people. 'The stigmatized individual tends to hold the same beliefs about identity that we do; this is a pivotal fact' (1970: 17). On being made to feel different or 'other', 'shame becomes a central possibility, arising from the individual's perception of one of his own attributes as being a defiling thing to possess' (Goffman 1970: 18).

nication). Sovereignty here entails the assumption of responsibility for one's own life and the assertion that the Dalits are equal citizens in every sense. Key to this demand is the inversion of past stigmas and the conscious revival of previously denigrated names, arts and customs. Given the subordinate position assigned to Untouchables in Hindu society, the recognition of Dalits as equal citizens will require an alteration in socio-cultural practices as well as political procedure.

Self-esteem and belief are not disembodied attributes. Inequality curtails the options of the poor, thereby limiting their access to socio-political rights and choice. This reduction of opportunity can heighten feelings of powerlessness and inability, thus lowering people's self-perceptions and stunting their aspirations. This is most obviously apparent in the exaggerated body language of subservient Dalits who walk with a stoop, spring to their feet on the approach of a landlord and whip their towels off their shoulders to stand with arms folded and hands clasped. Such submissiveness is the very antithesis of the democratic endeavour and renders it virtually impossible for people to express their political preferences in a free or critical manner. Citizens, in other words, require social resources such as health and education not only to participate in the 'modern' economy, but also to engage effectively in the democratic decision making that can further their own and other people's life projects.[3] Dalits living in cheris and slums, as we have seen, frequently complain of poverty and the denial of basic rights. Where people are concerned about their next meal they are less likely to demand the education, government benefits and social respect that are their due. In villages around Karur, as shown in Chapter 3, Dalits continue to accept overt forms of subordination because they are dependent upon landlords for work. In such circumstances it makes little sense to use the language of citizenship.

The possibility of commuting into a city, however, enabled the villagers of Kodankipatti and Vadianpatti to reject traditional caste work. When combined with the fact that the emerging Dalit middle class forms the resource base for much movement action, it is clear that some redistribution of resources is a pre-requisite for meaningful citizenship (cf. Marshall 1983 [1950]: 249). While Dalits are hindered from finding gainful employment and equal treatment by caste

---

[3] On this line of argument see Marshall (1983: 249), Twine (1994: 105) and Dreze and Sen (1997: ix).

considerations, society will continue to be informed by the discourse of caste identity.[4] Reservations have helped to de-link caste and occupation, but whilst landlessness and poverty correlate with low-caste status, forms of socio-economic coercion delimit the scope of democratic reform. Democracy, in other words, is as much about *social* practice as political systems. A culture of victimhood is perpetuated in conditions of inequality, especially where the paucity of resources coincides with human rights abuses, and it is clear that analyses of democratisation must pay due heed to social and economic structures as well as political institutions and opportunities.

The 'Rights of Man', according to Lefort, 'mark a disentangling of right and power' (1988: 31). In an Indian context, Sethi notes that the diffusion of the language and consciousness of rights means that social relations are no longer 'governed primarily via custom, tradition and obligation' (1998: 414). Dalit movements cannot thus be seen as solely the product of local conflicts. Social movements are often presented as the vanguard in a democratic revolution (Omvedt 1994: 16) and it is certainly impossible to ignore the strands of Dalit activism extending beyond the local area. The importance of national and international links is obvious in the names and strategies of the Liberation Panthers as much as in the language of human rights that they adopt. 'We must', however, 'also recognise that even as power resistance can be 'global', victimage entailed in the violation of human rights ... is uniquely individual; for, power inscribes itself on the body, mind and spirit of individual human beings' (Baxi 1998: 336).

To depict the suffering and struggles of the Tamil Dalits as merely the extension of a universal project does not do justice to the individuals concerned. The promises of the Constitution ring hollow whilst untouchability continues to exist. In his criticism of Marx, Lefort insists that rights are not simply formulaic: 'they both testify to the existence of a new network of human relations and *bring it into existence*' (1988: 32, emphasis added). A consciousness of human rights has certainly percolated through to Dalit movements and shaped their rhetoric and strategies. Yet, rights do not simply filter into social practice; they have to be claimed, fought for and defended. Whilst Lefort points out that the state is not a highly

---

[4] Duncan (1999: 55) and Jenkins (1999: 201) make similar points based on research elsewhere in India.

cohesive formation totally opposed to the spread of human rights, it is not totally committed to them either. Nor is the state divorced from a society that continues to operate along caste lines and reflects a diversity of unequal interests. In this context, the DPI's demand for human rights places them within a wider historical context, and at the forefront of a specific struggle for social justice. Thus, the crucial significance of the DPI's assertion that human rights are not expendable in the quest for stability, economic growth or development, is the implicit avowal that oppression cannot be seen in purely material terms. In this sense, in the words of Norris (1999a), the Liberation Panthers constitute a step towards a more 'critical citizenry' and a culture of questioning rather than passive acceptance.

Mobilisational Pluralism

'Critical citizens', according to Norris, 'are dissatisfied with established authorities and traditional hierarchical institutions, ... feel that existing channels for participation fall short of democratic ideals, and ... want to improve and reform the institutional mechanisms of representative democracy' (1999b: 27). Dalit activists conform to this definition. Like the 'civil disobedients' of Zashin's (1972) study, they begin by addressing people's immediate grievances rather than by seeking power to implement overriding ideological objectives. Unlike revolutionary groups they do not seek to destroy the structures of state power and often see the state as an ally against oppressive elements within civil society. The demand for basic human rights is insufficient, therefore, since the provision of such rights can, and often does, leave the edifice of structural inequality largely intact. The independent state of India supposedly guarantees political rights to all of its citizens, but, as Marx observed, such rights have no meaning in a society that tolerates social and economic inequality. Confidence in, and broad agreement about, political processes and institutions, as Newton (1999: 171) notes, does not necessarily correlate with high levels of *social* trust.

'Equality of status', as Marshall averred, 'is more important than equality of income' (1983: 258). The electorate of Melavalavu panchayat did not challenge the political process or economic structure, but the BCs were not prepared to let an Untouchable represent them. Those who have been accustomed to dominance cannot easily countenance equality with those below them. Arguably the formation of caste-based movements and the support of radical leaders will only exacerbate this social antipathy and mistrust. Inglehart shows that social insecurity often creates a desire for 'strong authority figures to protect one from threatening forces, and breeds an intolerance of cultural change, and of different ethnic groups' (1999: 242). This aptly describes the position of BC groups in Tamil Nadu, but ignores the fact that it is often marginal groups who organise in such fashion. Where identity-based mobilisation is aimed at increasing the political participation of hitherto excluded citizens it may result in major institutional reforms that strengthen democracy rather than weaken it. Civil disobedience is, as Zashin (1972: 1) insists, the last resort of 'basically *allegiant*' citizens (emphasis in the original).

The history of ethnic mobilisation in Tamil Nadu, Subramanian (1999) avers, shows how an active citizenry and a flexible leadership can promote a more tolerant and pluralist democracy. He proceeds to favourably compare Dravidian ideologies to the inflexibility of Hindu nationalism. '*The emergence of organizational pluralism within influential political organizations alone*', according to Subramanian, '*explains the emergence and maintenance of social pluralism*' (1999: 38 emphasis in the original). In the context of Subramanian's other findings this is a puzzling conclusion, especially since, as Jenkins (1995: 19) highlights, it is a critique of plural democracy that social groups gain access to the political process by resorting to extra-institutional action rather than peaceful compromise. My analysis of Dalit movements reflects Subramanian's later assertion that 'popular mobilisation is far more likely to reinforce pluralism than the irresolute actions of governments' (1999: 327). In this sense, the study may be read as a qualified extension of Subramanian's work beyond the 1990s when the dominance of the Dravidian parties has been challenged by hitherto excluded groups. But, as Harriss observes, the assertion that protest mobilisation shaped the emerging Dravidian polity, 'contradicts the notion that 'organisational pluralism' within political institutions explains the emergence of "social pluralism"' (2000: 78).

Subramanian highlights the limitations of the Dravidian parties in terms of land reforms, and the predominantly BC constituency that they draw upon yet he recurrently insists upon the pluralist nature

of Tamil politics. Conversely, he critiques the limited internal pluralism of other ethnic groups and reformist communist parties (1999:
81). From the perspective of countless Dalit, Muslim and MBC
citizens, however, it is clear that the DMK and the AIADMK may also
be described in terms of 'bounded internal pluralism'. As Palani
Kumar put it:

> The Dravidian parties think that they can buy the downtrodden
> people for *coolie* and they use them like this—for sticking up
> posters, shouting slogans, and making up a crowd. They are counted
> as a vote-bank. Dravidian parties maintain this situation, so they
> are the enemies of the downtrodden (speech, 12 September 1999).

Chandhoke also questions whether the Dravidian parties have 'managed to inculcate a democratic spirit among their followers'
(Chandhoke 1999). Given the propensity of AIADMK figures to
prostrate themselves before the leader the 'cadre autonomy' of these
institutions is open to question, and, when Communist and SC
associations are suppressed but Backward Caste groups are accommodated, so too is their commitment to pluralism. Organisational
pluralism, in other words, may be a necessary condition for tolerance
and stability, but it is not sufficient. The prospects for open democracy in Tamil Nadu thus hinge on the acceptance of 'mobilisational'
rather than organisational pluralism. It is through extra-institutional
organisation and protest that the Liberation Panthers and others have
entered the political mainstream. 'There must', therefore, to emphasise
an unstressed conclusion of Subramanian's study, 'be scope for
mobilization inspired by a wide range of visions to ensure that
democratic institutions are sustained'(1999: 80).[5]

It thus seems fair to agree with Norris (1999b: 27) that the
proliferation of extra-institutional mobilisation could point to the
evolution of channels of political participation rather than their
decline. Discontent is often a precursor to apathy, as she points out,
and the turn to social mobilisation should be welcomed as a
consequence. Democratic regimes have an infrastructure for the
incorporation of protest, as Zashin noted, and narrowing this may

---

[5] Given the caste-based polarisation of Tamil society and the dependent nature
of many Dalits, asserting the need for autonomous and assertive mobilisation
is far from being a 'platitude' (Harriss 2000: 78).

result in higher levels of instability than the toleration of discontent. Dalit movements have mobilised to demand their political rights and a voice in decision-making bodies, so granting them a meaningful share of political power will enhance the legitimacy and accountability of the state rather than reduce it. This is especially true when one considers the number of people prepared to vote for Dalit parties in recent elections in Tamil Nadu.

Deepening Democracy

Lefort (1988: 19) describes democracy as the 'dissolution of markers of certainty', but to be effective it is clear that a democratic society must constitute new points of reference. It is a pre-requisite of meaningful democracy that the state is impartial, independent of vested interests and that civil liberties and constitutional rights are upheld. India, as is commonly stated, *is* the world's largest democracy and not only in a formal Schumpeterian sense of the term. India is more than 'a polity that permits the choice between elites by citizens voting in regular and competitive elections' (Karl 1990: 1). Indian citizens are also accorded various civil liberties and the rights to mobilise, protest and campaign freely, which mean that they are able to express and experiment with ideas. What these rights are unable to provide is a level playing field for the articulation of contending programmes. 'Nowhere', as Mugyenyi observes, 'has democracy produced equality' (1988: 189). Equality of opportunity and equality before the law fail to legislate for the heightened disparity of wealth and power.

Citizenship, as Marshall (1983: 249) insisted, consists of three inter-related elements: civil, political *and* social rights. The reservation system attempts to tackle the issues of social rights but the impact of such programmes, whilst meaningful, has been limited. Stipulating that democratic societies should preside over 'socio-economic advances for the majority of the population', in Karl's view, is an ideal that has never been realised (1990: 2). Without reforming the structures of social and economic power, however, the rich or socially dominant are able to influence electoral outcomes disproportionately through media monopolies, social boycotts and the manipulation of marred voting customs (such as offering money and patronage to potential voters). If marginalised groups are to play a meaningful role in democratic politics, electoral legislation and practices need to be improved. Ballot boxes, for instance, should be located in caste neutral areas. Basic services, which are essential to the survival of the poor, must also become rights rather than the largesse of a patrimonial state that can hold out the prospect of patronage to its supporters or dominant landholders who can deny access. Deepening democracy, in other words, must devolve power and redress deep-rooted social inequalities. Democracy 'without bread, freedom of speech and assembly, of association... of political participation', as Baxi points out, '... may be existentially meaningless for its victims' (in Ambrose 1995: 115).

The disenfranchised Dalits of Chidambaram were not only denied their right to vote, they were subject to a social boycott that deprived them of water, work and social amenities such as education. In Myaladuthurai District I attempted to question the validity and utility of violent protest: 'In this democratic country...' I began. 'there is no democracy'. Somandam interjected, 'Tamil Nadu is not a democratic country' (interview, 28 September 1999). When people are denied access to certain jobs (and are over-represented in unskilled and low-paid employment) and barred from certain residential areas, because of their caste status, the efficacy of the liberal democratic state is called into question. When the same people are threatened or told not to vote for certain candidates and see most politicians as corrupt and unrepresentative then its legitimacy is in doubt. Barrington Moore (1966: 354) suggested that liberal democracy was hindering the revolutionary break with the past that India required for economic and social modernisation.[6] Indeed, meaningful social change *has* occurred where state regimes have pursued more proactive politics that emphasised democratic rights over civil liberties.[7]

[6] Numerous other authors likewise observe that the liberal state has not challenged the dominance of the main proprietary classes (Bardhan 1988; Jeffrey 2000; Jenkins 1999; Kohli 1987; Vanaik 1990). See especially, Kohli on the need for a more proactive and interventionist state.
[7] The latter, as Baxi (1998: 338) notes, generally impose restrictions on state power, whereas the former require the state to implement affirmative policies that empower people. Democratic rights go beyond the contested reservation of posts and places for various communities and embrace more basic demands such as delivery of land reform, literacy skills and primary healthcare.

Given the inadequacy of liberal democracy to meet these demands it is hardly surprising that Dalit movements resort to direct action. In fact, such action could be seen as the inevitable disjunction between the promises of the Constitution (given an airing at each election) and the reality on the ground. Social movements play a dual role with regard to the state: 'One role involves constantly exposing the class character, the caste, racial and patriarchal character of the state and seeking to overthrow or replace it. ... The other role of the movements is to steadily reform it by forcing it to implement its own promises' (Mohanty 1998: 75). Over the past two decades, Dalit movements have sought to democratise Tamil society. The Chidambaram voters who asserted that they had voted for the first time in 52 years indicate the Dalit movements' potential to extend the scope of democracy and strengthen civil society. We can, therefore, echo Grzybowski's (1990) conclusion that far from destroying the state, social movements are 'striving to bring about the conditions in which meaningful political democracy can exist' (in Cammack 1994: 189).

Challenging Codes: Caste in Democratic India

The DPI, in one sense, is not 'anti-hegemonic' because its objectives are enshrined in the Constitution and it seeks to ensure that the statutes are properly implemented. Continuing oppression of Dalits, however, shows that whilst the law is a critical means of establishing and reinforcing power, it is by no means the only source of dominance. 'Hegemony refers to power that "naturalises" a social order, an institution, or even everyday practice so that "how things are" seems inevitable and not the consequence of particular historical actors, classes and events' (Hirsch and Lazarus-Black 1994a: 7). The Constitution constituted a challenge to the hegemony of caste structures, but this challenge has not uniformly informed everyday practice. Caste operates at the level both of the state and civil society and must be contested on both levels.[8] This study suggests that

[8] Civil society, as Chandhoke puts it, 'cannot look only to the state, it needs must look inwards, at the power centres within its domain, which may be in complicity with the state, and battle them' (2001: 21).

Dravidian pluralism has been severely curtailed by organised caste groups. It is only the social and political protests of Dalit movements that has kept untouchability on the political agenda and empowered Dalits on a local level.

The Dalits in this study still perceive themselves to be oppressed on the basis of caste and they organise on the basis of that identity to struggle for equality and citizenship. 'Hegemony, once achieved, must be constantly and ceaselessly renewed, re-enacted' (Hall 1988: 54), but once it is contested it comes to be seen merely as an ideology. Deprived of the moral force of social acceptability, those who profit from such ideologies come to rely upon coercion and force to retain their dominance. As Dalits have increasingly challenged their social, political and economic exclusion, therefore, higher-castes have increasingly resorted to repression.[9] Mendelsohn and Vicziany 'suggest that it is precisely the changing character of Untouchable consciousness that lies behind the increased incidence of violence that broke out from the late 1970s' (1998: 76).

The current violence in Tamil Nadu lends credence to this position, for it is increasing Dalit assertion, especially in the last decade, that has led to this situation. To fully comprehend the caste polarisation of contemporary Tamil society, however, this analysis must be complemented by an understanding of BC groups. As Pandian (2000) rightly notes, it is the poorer and 'most backward' sections of the BCs who are the direct adversaries of contemporary Dalit movements. An exaggerated sense of caste identity and pride have been developed in order to re-assert their superiority over Dalit groups who may be economically or educationally better off. There is a deep and wide-spread resentment of the 'special treatment' that Dalits receive which ignores the long history of positive discrimination for BCs in the state. It is partly in context of their assertions of caste identity

[9] Mendelsohn and Vicziany distinguish between 'traditional' and 'new' kinds of anti-Dalit violence. 'Traditional violence' consists of the rape of Dalit women (especially by their higher-caste masters), physical violence and oppression at the hands of the state or the police, and it mainly arose from the 'utter dependence' of the Dalits. Contemporary violence against Dalits, by contrast, may be provoked by their claims to equality, 'by protective measures, or economic advancement' (Mendelsohn and Vicziany 1998: 47). Whilst this crude dichotomy is open to question—the Manusmriti, for example, prescribes a catalogue of punishments for the violation of, or resistance to, caste laws—it does serve to highlight a higher-caste backlash.

that we can understand the trajectory of Dalit movements in Tamil Nadu which have arguably sought to develop a similar sense of group identity and belief.

In Chapter 3 we saw the social significance accorded to notions of pride, honour and dignity and it is around these emotive concepts that Dalit movements are organised. The difference between the mobilisational strategies of the BCs and Dalits is that the latter are at least rhetorically committed to equality for *all*. It is in this light that we can understand why Dalits are increasingly unwilling to accept the status quo and fall into line with the demands of the higher castes despite facing very real threats of violence.[10] Across the state they are cognisant of the perils that potentially attend acts of resistance. Unlike the propensity of some theorists to romanticise resistance (see Abu Lughod 1990), Dalits are fully aware that resistance on one level may catch up with them on another. Maintaining their dignity by refusing degrading jobs, for instance, may lead to a social boycott that deprives them of all forms of employment. It is also clear that different Dalit categories have developed their own responses to the violence and discrimination that they face. Dalit women point to their subordinate status both in the home and in the movement and seek to place 'women's issues' on the agenda, those living in rural areas point out the relative freedom of their urban counterparts and different castes are seen to pursue different strategies for survival with some opting to support the dominant castes.

It is clear that people often resist discrimination from '*inside* the field of power' (Haynes and Prakash 1991: 11, emphasis in the original). The point to stress from this is that Dalits across the state are resisting and challenging the basis of their subordination. This consciousness of equality and determination to renegotiate existing power relations is illustrated in the following example. In December 2000, 2,000 members of the Vanniyar community 'blocked the main streets leading to the Alageeswarar temple, to prevent the proposed march to the temple by Dalits who had been denied entry to the temple for the past several decades' (*The Hindu*, 12 December 2000). The gains to be expected from this show of defiance were, for the most part, intangible. Having managed to worship elsewhere hitherto, it is inconceivable that the temple had suddenly acquired any

---

[10] See Pai (2000) for a similar finding from the northern state of Uttar Pradesh.

particular spiritual significance. It does not have particular political significance, since it is an obscure shrine in a rural area. Neither was the issue an expression of other local grievances, as Dalits in the nearby *cheri*, insisted that 'they had been living peacefully with members of the other community in the village all along' (ibid.). The value of the protest, thus, was primarily symbolic. By entering the sacred space, the Dalits were not only attempting to actualise the legal rulings that opened up any public temple to all, they were asserting their equality.

Their prohibition from entering this space symbolised the fact that they continue to be regarded as ritually impure. It also emphasised the dominance of the Vanniyar caste and their ability to 'lay down the law' locally. The tangible benefits of breaking this convention were virtually non-existent, but it was indicative of the motives of the Dalit movements. The Liberation Panthers, as we have seen, are prepared to engage in struggles to assert their common humanity and dignity and see this as an end in itself. That they do not perceive their deprivation in purely material terms, does not mean that the issue is an immaterial one. The numbers of Vanniyars prepared to flout the law to prevent the march of the Dalits and the number of Dalits prepared to risk the wrath of the locally-dominant caste should testify to that. The Dalits were fully cognisant of the implications of pressing the issue; indeed, on 9 December 2000, they refused to attend a peace committee meeting because they feared that 'the Vanniyas [sic] were armed with deadly weapons' (ibid.).

The costs and dangers of resistance will have been apparent and a litany of recent cases will have weighed on their minds, yet the Dalits were adamant in their demand for temple entry. One of the most important aspects of social movement activity, as Swidler indicates, is the 'public confounding of existing cultural codings' (1995: 25). Whether by demanding access to public spaces or proudly calling themselves by 'Untouchable' caste names or as 'Ambedkar', Dalit activists are engaged in such an enterprise. In villages across Tamil Nadu, Dalits are gaining a consciousness of their rights and their strength in numbers and are refusing to comply with the material and symbolic expressions of their subordination. 'You want us to clean for you, or play music at festivals? Then treat us as equals and pay us well. Otherwise you may find yourselves doing the dirty work yourselves' (composite of interviews with activists). Increasingly even such a statement is seen as too moderate. 'A blow for a blow' (*adi ukku adi*) is the catch-phrase of the DPI, and it exemplifies the determination to stand up and be counted as equal citizens and not lesser humans.

Despite the diverse and particular strands of activism in Tamil Nadu, this shared outlook lends coherence to an emerging Dalit identity. Whilst Pandian (2000) is right that the social and political trajectories of various caste and sub-caste groups require individual research and attention, therefore, it is increasingly meaningful to talk in terms of Dalit politics in the state. Irrespective of their geographic or social background Dalits are beginning to question their exclusion from mainstream institutions and agendas. Whether it is in the establishment of sweet shops that actually serve Dalit children rather than throwing goods at them, the refusal to perform caste jobs (at least not without fair remuneration) or in the resolve to support autonomous Dalit parties and organisations, this determination to be counted is reconfiguring the political map in Tamil Nadu. By insisting on a 'share of power' Dalit movements are asserting their right to shape the political agenda rather than just follow it. In this process they are not simply extending the reach of parliamentary institutions in the state—they are rendering them more accountable and representative.

Reconfiguring Politics: Dalits and the Political Process

It is clear, however, that the achievements to be obtained through the mere fact of political participation are limited. Other political parties can, and do, pursue objectives that are antithetical to those of the DPI and, unless there is a move towards dialogue, democracy can result in the institutionalisation of deep-rooted opposition. Such a situation renders elections a time for the vociferous, and often violent, expression of these differences. The conflict between the PMK and the DPI appears to be developing along these lines. The Panthers are so opposed to the Vanniyar party that they quit the 'secular front' led by the AIADMK in 2001 in order to join the DMK coalition that had hitherto been described as their worst enemy. They have subsequently threatened to desert that Front in turn if the PMK is re-admitted to the fold.

Whilst parties continue to engage in virulent forms of identity politics—premised as much on the vilification of others as the aspiration for a better society—the institutions revitalised by the entry of new political actors are as likely to serve narrow, particularist interests as any other. The DPI frequently condemned the PMK and the BJP for these failings, but unless they moderate their rhetoric to make it more inclusive they are liable to repeat the same mistakes. This highlights the significance of the DPI's determination to avoid being labelled as a caste movement. Dalit movements in Tamil Nadu have the potential to move beyond the caste-based polarisation of politics by stressing their ideological commitments rather than their caste origins. There are some indications that the DPI will follow this route, especially as 'political participation forces people, however imperfectly, to deliberate on the public interest' and take the views of others into account (Twine 1994: 91). The DPI certainly cannot hope to gain electoral success without reaching out to other members of society.

In this sense, 'India's institutions are not only the bedrock of its democracy, providing an ordered process for the politicisation of previously marginalised groups', as Jenkins points out, 'but also ... the means by which democracy's change-resistant tendencies are overcome' (1999: 224). Furthermore, as the movement discovered, the majority of the Dalits still place their faith in the democratic process and—if only for reasons of patronage—they wish to see their leaders in power. In this sense Dalit movements contribute to a more critical civil society and help to render political institutions accountable to it. This is in part because autonomous Dalit movements in the Assembly or Parliament have a more direct relationship with their followers and because those followers have no illusions about political institutions. The threat (or promise) to abandon electoral politics if caste atrocities continue unabated means that the DPI leadership will have to justify themselves to their members in a way that established parties do not have to do. Additionally, the incorporation of hitherto neglected groups is in itself a desirable outcome that will help to expand the political agenda.

A diversity of groups and interests is commonly said to be the marker of a healthy civil society, but one should be wary of such broad claims. Although the diversity of Hinduism contributed to social pluralism in India, for example, the pre-Independence dispersal of power 'was far from egalitarian. Local communities were microcosms of oppression especially for women and untouchables' (Randall 1997: 205). 'Equality', as Putnam states, 'is an essential feature of the civic community' (1993: 105). Whilst legislative and structural changes have altered the conditions that pertained in 'traditional' India, people's movements have been central to the construction of an active and effective civil society. The DPI here has mirrored a pan-Indian trend in which Dalit movements have carved out spaces within which people can articulate alternatives and engage with others in a constructive rather than violent manner.

Civil society, thus, may be described as 'the space of uncoerced human association and also the set of relational networks—formed for the sake of family, faith, interests and ideology—that fill this space' (Walzer in Potter 1997: 4). It is distinct from the state although institutions such as political parties bridge the gap between the two and the boundaries between state and civil society are further blurred by the state's involvement in the production of everyday life (Potter 1997: 4). Some theorists draw a distinction between *civil* and *political* society with the latter referring to 'that arena in which the polity specifically arranges itself for political contestation to gain control over public power and the state apparatus' (Stepan in Haynes 1997: 17). Despite the analytical utility of the distinction, ignoring the interrelated nature of the two spheres downplays the political significance of social action: the fact that the personal often is political. Severing the links between movements and parties, as Blomkvist and Swain (2001) indicate, can jeopardise the development of a healthy political society. One of the strengths of Dalit movements, thus, is that they remain embedded in the communities from which they sprung.

Without such connections and potential avenues to power one can end up with a 'two-tier civil society, with the representative groups of existing or prospective elites inhabiting the top tier and the organisations of the subordinate and marginalised located in the second, lower tier' (Haynes 1997: 174). Similar concerns have led many definitions of civil society to exclude associations that cohere around particularist, especially ethnic, identities which are deemed to weaken social cohesion. Pinkney (1993: 154), however, contends that democracy is more secure if society comprises a greater diversity of groups, regardless of their constituency, because it encourages tolerance. The caveat to this is that some groups are more powerful than others. It is for this reason that contemporary Dalit movements have adopted a more militant approach than their predecessors. It is only when Dalits are regarded as fellow citizens that BC groups may be induced to compromise and ultimately accept them. In entering the political mainstream contemporary Dalit movements have initiated the processes of negotiation and conflict required for such an end.

An achievement of the DPI in this regard is to have expanded the base of democratic contestation and challenged the hegemony of the two Dravidian parties. Although the DPI has subsequently entered into coalitions with both the DMK and the AIADMK it is significant that the movement entered the political process in an alliance that prefigured new political alignments. The TMC-led Third Front in 1999 was a watershed because for the first time Dalit movements were accepted as equal partners. In subsequent elections, the legacy of this process has meant that the DPI and PT were accorded a higher proportion of seats (by their respective allies) than ever before. Should they be reduced to opportunistic alliance hopping, however, then the considerable advantages they could offer will be muted. If they continue to campaign for a share of power and demand a return to the secular and egalitarian ideals of Periyar, however, they will constitute a critical component of Third Front politics. In doing so they will confront the Dravidian parties' hold on power and bolster the left-leaning organisations that have yet to mount an effectual challenge to Dravidian hegemony. If Tamil politics in the 20th century was defined by the non-Brahmin movement, it appears that Dalit and other non-aligned movements have initiated a debate that will enable Tamil politics to escape the bi-partite stagnation of Dravidianism and thus contribute to deepening Indian democracy. Whilst Thirumavalavan and Krishnasamy have constituted lone, autonomous Dalit voices in the Assembly, it is clear that MLA status has leant weight to their pronouncements.

It is too early to judge the impact of the DPI's electoral engagement either for the movement or for Tamil politics. There are some indications of institutionalisation in the formalisation of offices in major cities. It is also apparent that the communications infrastructure that accompanies political success has enabled the DPI to engage in debates and issues that are consistent with their ideals—such as condemnations of the World Trade Organisation (WTO)—that were previously neglected. If this consistency can be employed in relation to political alliances as well as press briefings and protests then the Liberation Panthers may eventually escape the 'untouchable' tag and build cross-caste ties. It is clear, however, that the process will be fraught with obstacles as the continuing rivalry with the PMK shows and the harassment of Dalit panchayat presidents highlights. The Liberation Panthers continues to operate as the critical conscience of the Assembly in much the same manner as before. At present it are best described as a movement with an amplified voice. It remains to be seen if it can make the most of its transition to politics.

Conclusion: From Caste to Citizenship

'Educate, agitate, organise' was Ambedkar's exhortation and movements are beginning to reflect these concerns. Central to all Dalit struggles is the search for independence and equality: the ability to stand alone and be accepted as citizens in the modern democratic state. Education is a pre-requisite of such autonomy. To be a responsible and active citizen one needs to be informed and have a capacity for critical thought. Movements such as the DPI are engaged in consciousness raising, lobbying and pressure tactics in a bid to refashion society, but they are starting to recognise the importance of internal reform. The DPI, thus, is involved in tuition centres and small credit schemes. There are fundamental structural inequalities that conspire to perpetuate the conditions of caste stratification and there is also a lack of political will. Countless places reserved for Dalits remain vacant but reactions to the Mandal Commission indicate the resentment of, and necessity to educate, other communities. It is important to emphasise the marginality and poverty of other social groups especially in the light of the tensions between Dalits and impoverished BCs. One means of starting to address this might be to introduce an economic component into the reservations system. Such a measure could also ensure a more equitable distribution of benefits amongst the Dalit community.

The emergence of a 'Dalit élite' raises the issue of intra-caste inequalities. With regard to women, to caste conflict, to incendiary rhetoric, inter-movement cooperation and internal democracy, the worst enemy of the Dalit movements have often been the movements themselves. 'It is not as if the various movements do not have glaring inadequacies', as Sethi notes, 'they have them in abundance'. Addressing these internal inequalities would put the movements in a better position to forge wider links on issues such as women's rights, poverty and the impact of economic globalisation. As an MLA from 2001–2004, Thirumavalavan intervened on these issues and led campaigns that directly affected the lives of poor people from all categories. It is from such initiatives that Sethi concludes that 'what is heartening is that they represent a mass stirring against the cynical manipulation of the people. A new spirit of questioning is slowly entering our normally passive and apathetic society' (1993: 249). A consequence of this is an increasing challenge to caste itself. In explaining why his movement was part of the 'Caste Eradication Solidarity Front', Chandra Bose was unequivocal:

> Without eradicating caste there can be no solution. Untouchability did not arise of its own accord. It is only because there is caste that there is untouchability.... Now everyone says we need to eradicate untouchability, but that is a fool's errand, that is why we should protest to abolish caste (interview, 23 February 1999).

According to Haynes, the work of action groups in the Third World amounts to 'a "quiet" revolution' even if it is primarily 'defensive in orientation'. People's movements, according to this assessment, 'are making inroads but are still far from overthrowing the old order of poverty and inequality' (Fischer in Haynes 1997: 39). The quote from Chandra Bose, given earlier, neatly captures this uncertainty. Dalit movements are challenging caste from within the field of power which leads to certain contradictions and dilemmas. Thus, movements seek to organise on the basis of caste and at the same time are trying to eradicate it. They desire a more egalitarian society and yet their economic programmes are subordinate to concerns about caste. They attempt to question practices of untouchability, while effectively organising on that. The title of this book reflects this current ambiguity. Although the institutions of citizenship are spreading, citizenship cannot coexist with untouchability.

Democracy is more than just a form of government and the policies that stem from it. It is, as Dewey states, 'primarily a mode of associated living, of conjoint communicated experience' (in Zashin 1972: 55). The shared norms, networks, values and trust that enable coordinated action are referred to as 'social capital' (Putnam 1993:

167). As noted earlier, however, social capital is not evenly distributed in society and the ubiquitous civil associations in India have not eradicated caste discrimination. By mobilising outside mainstream institutions and applying pressure on existing political parties, the DPI and other Dalit movements have opened up Tamil politics to new actors. Their struggle has also forced the hegemonic Dravidian parties to reassess their caste constituencies and revisit the ideal of a society in which people of all castes and classes can work together. Dalit participation in mainstream politics has placed these objectives firmly on the political agenda and the means by which they got there has raised local consciousness across the state. The Dalit struggle, in other words, is not merely concerned with material and political interests, but with refashioning the way in which society is organised and groups relate to each other. In its renegotiation of local hierarchies of power, its rejection of *dharma* and its assertion of equality it constitutes a cultural revolution.

APPENDIX

A Summary of Important Incidents: A Reader's Guide

Although the following events are dealt with extensively at various points in the text, they recur throughout the book to exemplify differing points. Here, therefore, I provide a short summary of the main points for easy reference.

Melavalavu

Melavalavu is a small village in central Tamil Nadu, about 20 miles north of Madurai. In 1997 the panchayat (or local council) was designated as a seat reserved for a member of the SCs. The constituency is mainly populated by the dominant, Thevar, Backward Caste. This community was unhappy with the prospect of a Dalit panchayat president and they attempted to disrupt the local elections. Twice they succeeded in postponing the poll. On the first occasion no Dalit could be found to stand for the position due to the high levels of intimidation. When polling went ahead in the second attempt the ballot boxes were seized and the election nullified. Under police protection and guarantees, Murugesan, a DMK member, was elected on the third poll. The higher caste members of the panchayat refused to cooperate and Murugesan was unable to operate from his official office. He set up a 'panchayat-in-exile' in the Dalit cheri instead. For six months he tried to fulfil the duties of his office against higher-caste opposition. On 30 June 1997, he and several followers travelled to Madurai to meet the Collector to discuss the difficulties of the job. On his return the bus in which he was travelling was stopped on the road between Melavalavu and Melur. A mob wielding sickles and machetes boarded the bus from both portals and dragged Murugesan and his followers off the bus. Six of them were murdered on the road, whilst two escaped across the fields. Later that day, another prominent Dalit was also murdered. Murugesan's head was cut off and cast into a nearby well. The current panchayat president has an armed guard of police, but still faces obstacles to the fulfilment of his position.

Kodankipatti

Kodankipatti is a village about 22 miles west of Madurai. The dominant caste in this village are the Kounders. In 1990, the Dalits in the village refused to perform the demeaning caste jobs that were traditionally demanded of them, such as funeral rites, beating drums at temple festivals and so on. As a result they were first subject to a social boycott that deprived them of work, and then attacked and driven from the village with sticks and stones. Their houses were burned to the ground and many of the Dalits still bear the scars that they received. They were encouraged to return to the village after the government rebuilt their houses with *pucca* tile roofs, plastered walls and also arranged several 'peace committees' where the castes could negotiate their differences. Though they returned to the village the Dalits insist that they were not provided with work any more and so commuted to Madurai to seek alternative employment. In 1999, the uneasy truce was broken by a series of small incidents. First, a number of the Dalits affiliated themselves to the Liberation Panthers. Second, they began to demand certain rights within the village culminating in the demand to be able to show a film in the common square to mark Ambedkar's birthday. The film was disrupted by the higher castes who had not been asked for prior permission. The police were called in but they sided with the higher castes in castigating the Dalits. The next week the Dalits attempted to disrupt a weekly market, claiming that they had not been asked for permission for the square to be used. The government tried to organise some 'peace committees', but negotiations broke down and the Dalits were attacked and chased out of their homes once again. They took refuge six miles away in the DPI stronghold of Muduvarpatti.

Chidambaram

When the DPI abandoned their boycott of the elections and decided to stand in the TMC-led Third Front in the 1999 Lok Sabha polls, Thirumavalavan was given the constituency of Chidambaram. This is situated on the east coast of Tamil Nadu, to the north of the state where the DPI is very strong. After a month of intensive campaigning many Dalit activists believed that Thirumavalavan stood a chance in the election. In the event he came second by a big margin (see footnotes to Chapter 9) but managed to secure some 30 per cent of the vote and to relegate the AIADMK–Congress combine to the third place. The election was most significant not for the result but for the electoral malpractice that the ruling coalition allegedly resorted to. Dalits across the constituency were threatened and warned not to vote and many who went to vote on polling day found that 'their votes had been "cast" already'. There were reports of violence in around 200 villages and social boycotts against the Dalits were said to be in force up to a month after the polling day. Where they were in a majority the Dalits also resorted to violence and electoral malpractice but the Dalits were the chief victims. They were also the community most represented in the prisons. It became apparent that the location of ballot boxes in the higher-caste areas represented a contravention of the spirit—if not the law—of demo-cratic practice. The elections also highlighted the caste-based polarisation of Tamil society since the election was fought on caste lines. In the village of Parengipatti, the symbolic rejection of the Dalit candidates in the election was rendered apparent when cow dung was smeared over the photographs of Dalit candidates. As much as in Melavalavu it was clear that the locally-dominant castes would not countenance the election of an Untouchable in their area. This differentiation between candidates also highlights the failings of the political process in India: Whilst all the candidates in Chidambaram were Dalits, the electorate only saw one as such.

BIBLIOGRAPHY

Books, Chapters in Books and Journal Articles

Abu-Lughod, L. 1990. 'The Romance of Resistance'. *American Ethnologist* 17(1): 41–55.

Adas, M. 1991. 'South Asian Resistance in Comparative Perspective', in D. Haynes and G. Prakash (eds), *Contesting Power*. New Delhi: Oxford University Press (OUP), 290–305.

Agarwal, B. 1994. *A Field of One's Own: Gender and Land Rights in South Asia*. Cambridge: Cambridge University Press (CUP).

———. 1998. 'Disinherited Peasants, Disadvantaged Workers'. *Economic and Political Weekly (EPW)* 33(13): A2–14.

Agnes, F. 1994. 'Women's Movement within a Secular Framework'. *EPW*, 29(19): 1123–27.

Aitken, R. 1999. *Localising Politics*. Leiden: University of Leiden Press.

Alm, B. 1996. 'The State and Caste Conflicts', in N. Jeyaram and S. Saberwal (eds), *Social Conflict*. Oxford: OUP, 113–29.

Ambedkar, B.R. 1989. 'Gandhi and His Fast', in V. Moon (ed.), *Dr Babasaheb Ambedkar: Writings and Speeches, Vol. 5*. Bombay: Government of Maharashtra, Education Department.

Ambrose, B. 1995. *Democratisation and the Protection of Human Rights in Africa*. Westport: Preager.

Amin, S. 1993. 'Social Movements at the Periphery', in P. Wignaraja (ed.), *New Social Movements of the South*, London: Zed Books, 76–100.

Amjad, R. 1989a. (ed.). *To the Gulf and Back*. New Delhi: International Labour Organisation (ILO).

Amjad, R. 1989b. 'Economic Impact of Migration to the Middle East on the Major Asian Sending Countries: An Overview', in R. Amjad (ed.), *To the Gulf and Back*, New Delhi: ILO, 1–27.

Anandhi, S. 1995. *Contending Identities*, Delhi: Indian Social Institute.

———. 1998. 'Reproductive Bodies and Regulated Sexuality', in M. John and J. Nair (eds), *A Question of Silence?* London: Zed Books, 139–66.

———. 2000. *Land to the Dalits: Panchama Land Struggle in Tamilnadu*, Bangalore: Indian Social Institute.

Anderson, B. 1991[1983]. *Imagined Communities*. London: Verso.

Appadurai, A. 1995. 'The Production of Locality', in R. Fardon (ed.), *Counterworks*. London: Routledge, 204–25.

Appavoo, J. 1986. *Folklore for Change*. Madurai: TTS Publications, Tamil Nadu Theological Seminary.

Aronwitz, S. 1986. 'Introduction', in D. Foss and Larkin (eds), *Beyond Revolution*. Massachusetts: Bergen & Garvey, xi–xv.

Ashok Kumar, E. N. 1998. 'Upward Mobility or Class Formation? Samagars of Jenubhavi', in S. Charsley and G. Karanth (eds), *Challenging Untouchability*. London: Sage Publications, 240–62.

Athreya, A. and S. Chunkath. 2000. 'Tackling Female Infanticide'. *EPW* 32(17): 4345–48.

Austin, D. 1994. *Democracy and Violence in India & Sri Lanka*. London: Pinter Press.

Baker, C.J. 1976. *The Politics of South India 1920–1937*. Cambridge: CUP.

Balagopal, K. 1990. 'This Anti-Mandal Mania'. *EPW* 25(40): 2231–34.

Banck, G. 1986. 'Poverty, Politics and the Shaping of Urban Space'. *International Journal of Urban and Regional Research* 10(4): 522–44.

Bandyopadhyaya, N. 1998. 'Agrarian Struggles and Land Reforms in Bengal and West Bengal', in M. Mohanty, P. Mukherji and O. Tornquist (eds), *People's Rights*. New Delhi: Sage Publications, 297–309.

Bardhan, P. 1988. 'Dominant Proprietary Classes', in Kohli (ed.), *India's Democracy: An Analysis of Changing State–Society Relations*. New Jersey: Princeton University Press, 214–24.

———. 1998. *The Political Economy of Development in India*. New Delhi: OUP.

Barnett, M.R. 1976. *The Politics of Cultural Nationalism in South India*. New Jersey: Princeton University Press.

Barnett, S. 1977. 'Identity Choice and Caste Ideology in Contemporary South India', in K. David (ed.), *The New Wind*. The Hague: Mouton Publishers, 393–415.

Basu, A. 1998. 'Conclusion: Reflections on Community Conflicts and the State in India', in A. Basu and A. Kohli (eds), *Community Conflicts and the State in India*. New Delhi: OUP, 239–48.

Basu, A. and A. Kohli. 1998. (eds). *Community Conflicts and the State in India*. New Delhi: OUP.

Basu, D. and R. Sisson. 1986. (eds). *Social & Economic Development in India*. London: Sage Publications.

Baxi, U. 1998. 'The State and Human Rights Movements in India', in M. Mohanty, P. Mukherji and O. Tornquist (eds), *People's Rights*. New Delhi: Sage Publications, 335–52.

Bayly, C.A. 1988. *Indian Society and the Making of the British Empire*. Cambridge: CUP.

Beck, B. 1974. 'The Kin Nucleus in Tamil Folklore', in T. Trautman (ed.), *Kinship and History in South Asia*. Michigan: Ann Arbor, 1–27.

Bellwinkel, M. 1979. 'Objective Appreciation Through Subjective Involvement', in M. Srinivas, A. Shah and E. Ramaswamy (eds), *The Field Worker and the Field*. New Delhi: OUP, 141–51.

Benford, R. and S. Hunt. 1995. 'Dramaturgy and Social Movements', in S. Lyman (ed.), *Social Movements: Critiques, Concepts, Case-Studies*. New York: New York University Press, 84–109.

Bensman, J. and A. Vidich. 1995. 'Race, Ethnicity and New Forms of Urban Community', in P. Kasinitz (ed.), *Metropolis: Center and Symbol of Our Times*. New York: New York University Press, 196–208.

Berreman, G. 1963. *Hindus of the Himalayas*. Berkeley: University of California Press.

———. 1991. 'The Brahminical View of Caste', in D. Gupta (ed.), *Social Stratification*. New Delhi: OUP.

———. 1993. 'Sanskritisation as Female Oppression in India', in B.D. Miller (ed.), *Sex and Gender Hierarchies*. Cambridge: CUP.

Beteille, A. 1967. *Caste, Class and Power*. New Delhi: OUP.

———. 1974. *Studies in Agrarian Social Structure*. New Delhi: OUP.

———. 1986. 'Individualism and Equality'. *Current Anthropology* 29: 121–34.

———. 1991a. 'The Reproduction of Inequality: Occupation, Caste and Family', *Contributions to Indian Sociology* (n.s.) 25(1): 3–28.

———. 1991b. *Society and Politics in India*. New Delhi: OUP.

———. 1996. 'Caste in Contemporary India', in C. Fuller (ed.), *Caste Today*. Cambridge: CUP, 150–79.

Bhaduri, A. 1983. *The Economic Structure of Backward Agriculture*. London: Academic Press.

Bharadwaj, K. 1974. *Production Conditions in Indian Agriculture*. Cambridge: Cambridge University Press.

Blomkvist, H. and A. Swain. 2001. 'Investigating Democracy and Social Capital in India', *EPW* 36(8): 639–43.

Boholm, A. 1996a. (ed.) *Political Ritual*. Gothenburg: IASSA.

———. 1996b. 'Introduction', in A. Boholm (ed.), *Political Ritual*. Gothenburg: IASSA, 1–13.

———. 1996c. 'Political Ritual as Image Making', in A. Boholm (ed.), *Political Ritual*. Gothenburg: IASSA, 158–92.

Bonner, A. 1990. *Averting the Apocalypse*. Durham: Duke University Press.

Bourdieu, P. 1998. *Practical Reason*. Cambridge: Polity.

Brass, P. 1984. *Caste, Faction and Party in Indian Politics*. New Delhi: Chanakya Publications.

———. 1990. *The Politics of India since Independence*. Cambridge: CUP.

———. 1996. *Riots and Pogroms*. Basingstoke: Macmillan.

Bryman, A. 1992. *Charisma and Leadership in Organisations*. London: Sage Publicaitons.

Cammack, P. 1994. 'Democracy and Citizenship in Latin America', in G. Parry and M. Moran (eds), *Democracy and Democratisation*. London: Routledge, 174–95.

Canetti, E. 1962. *Crowds and Power* (translated by Carol Stewart). London: Victor Gollancz.

Caplan, P. 1985. *Class and Gender in India: Women and their Organisations*. New York: Tavistock.

Carter, M. 1996. *Voices from Indenture*. London: Leicester University Press.

Castells, M. 1997. *The Power of Identity*. Oxford: Blackwell.

Casteñeda, J.G. 1993. *Utopia Unarmed: The Latin American Left After the Cold War*. New York: Vintage.

Caute, D. 1970. *Fanon*. London: Fontana.

Cederlöf, G. 1997. *Bonds Lost: Subordination, Conflict and Mobilisation in Rural S. India, c. 1900–1970*. Delhi: Manohar.

Chandhoke, N. 2001. 'The "Civil" and the "Political" in Civil Society'. *Democratization* 8(2): 1–24.

Charsley, S. 1996. '"Untouchable". What is in a Name?' *Journal of the Royal Anthropological Institute* (n.s) 2: 1–23.

Charsley, S. and G. Karanth. 1998. (eds). *Challenging Untouchability*. London: Sage Publications.

Chatterjee, P. 1996. 'The Manifold Uses of Jati', in T. Satyamurthy (ed.), *Region, Religion, Caste, Gender and Culture in Contemporary India*. New Delhi: OUP, 281–92.

Chattopadhyay, M. 2001. 'Waged Labour Arrangements in a West Bengal Village'. *EPW* 36(7): 569–75.

Chowdhry, P. 1998. 'Enforcing Cultural Codes: Gender and Violence in Northern India', in M. John and J. Nair (eds), *A Question of Silence?* London: Zed Books, 332–67.

Cohen, A. 1985. *The Symbolic Construction of Community*. London: Tavistock.

Cohn, B. 1990. *An Anthropologist among the Historians and Other Essays*. New Delhi: OUP.

Comacho, D. 1993. 'Latin America: A Society in Motion', in P. Wignaraja (eds), *New Social Movements of the South*. London, Zed Books, 36–58.

Connery, R. 1968. (ed.). *Urban Riots: Violence and Social Change*. New York: Vintage.

Constable, P. 2000. 'Sitting on the School Verandah: The Ideology and Practice of "Untouchable" Educational Protest in Late 19th Century Western India'. *Indian Economic and Social History Review (IESHR)* 37(4): 383–422.

Cope, M. 1996. 'Weaving the Everyday: Identity, Space and Power in Lawrence, Massachusetts'. *Urban Geography* 17(2): 179–204.

Corbridge, S. and J. Harriss. 2000. *Reinventing India*. Cambridge: Polity.

Cruces, F. and A. De Rada. 1996. 'Symbolic and Political Representation', in A. Boholm (ed.), *Political Ritual*. Gothenburg: IASSA, 94–125.

Dalton, R. and M. Kuechler. 1990. (eds). *Challenging the Political Order*. Cambridge: Polity.

Daniel, E. 1984. *Fluid Signs*. Berkeley: University of California Press.

Daniel, S.B. 1980. 'Marriage in Tamil Culture', in S. Wadley (ed.), *The Powers of Tamil Women*. New York: Syracuse.

Das, I. 1985. 'The Open Letter—to the Inspector General of Registration for Pandit C. Iyothi Das 1892', in T. Kamalanathan (ed.), *SCs Struggle for Emanicipation in South India*. Tirrupatur: Sakkiya Buddhist Association, 10–18.

Dasgupta, J. 1998. 'Community, Authenticity and Autonomy', in A. Basu and A. Kohli (eds), *Community Conflicts and the State in India*. New Delhi: OUP, 183–214.

Datta, R. 1998. 'Public Action, Social Security and Unorganised Sector'. *EPW* 33(22): L2–L5.

de Tocqueville, A. 1994a[1835]. *Democracy in America—Book I*. London: Everyman.

———. 1994b[1840]. *Democracy in America—Book II*. London: Everyman.

De Wit, J.W. 1996. *Poverty, Policy and Politics in Madras Slums*. London: Sage Publications.

Deliége, R. 1992. 'Replication and Consensus: Untouchability, Caste & Ideology in India'. *Man* 27: 155–73.

———. 1997. *The World of the Untouchables: The Paraiyars of Tamilnadu* (translated by D. Philips). Oxford: OUP.

Della Porta, D. 1992. 'Life Histories in the Analysis of Social Movement Activists', in M. Diani and R. Eyerman (eds), *Studying Collective Action*. London: Sage Publications, 168–93.

Della Porta, D. and M. Diani. 1999. *Social Movements: An Introduction*. Oxford: Blackwell.

Desai, A. 1978. (ed.) *Rural Sociology in India*. Bombay: Popular Prakashan.

Desrochers, J. 1991. 'The Role of Social Movements', in J. Desrochers, B. Wielenga and V. Patel (eds), *Social Movements: Towards a Perspective*. Bangalore: The Centre for Social Action, 5–73.

Desrochers, J. B. Wielenga and V. Patel. 1991. *Social Movements: Towards a Perspective*. Bangalore: The Centre for Social Action.

Devasahayam, V. 1992. (ed.). *Dalits and Women: Quest for Humanity*. Madras: Gurukul Lutheran College.

Dews, P. 1984. 'Power and Subjectivity in Foucault'. *New Left Review* 144: 72–79.

Diani, M. and R. Eyerman. 1992a. (eds). *Studying Collective Action.* London: Sage Publications.

———. 1992b. 'The Study of Collective Action: Introductory Remarks', in M. Diani and R. Eyerman (eds), *Studying Collective Action.* London: Sage Publications, 1–21.

Diani, M. 1992. 'Analysing Social Movement Networks', in Diani and Eyerman (eds), *Studying Collective Action.* London: Sage Publications, 107–35.

Dickey, S. 1993a. 'The Politics of Adulation'. *The Journal.of Asian Studies* 52(2): 340–72.

———. 1993b. *Cinema and the Urban Poor in South India.* Cambridge: CUP.

Dietrich, G. 1988. *Women's Movement in India.* Bangalore: Breakthrough Publications.

Dirks, N. 1987. *The Hollow Crown.* Cambridge: CUP.

———. 1989. 'The Invention of Caste: Civil Society in Colonial India', *Social Analysis* 25: 45–52.

———. 1992. 'From Little King to Landlord: Colonial Discourse and Colonial Rule', in N. Dirks (ed.), *Colonialism and Culture.* University of Michigan Press: Ann Arbor, 175–208.

———. 1996. 'Recasting Tamil Society', in C. Fuller (ed.), *Caste Today.* Cambridge: CUP, 263–95.

———. 1997. 'The Invention of Caste', in H. Seneviratne (ed.), *Identity, Consciousness and the Past.* New Delhi: OUP, 120–35.

———. 1997a. (ed.). *Indian Development: Selected Regional Perspectives.* New Delhi: OUP.

Dréze, J. and A. Sen. 1995. (eds). *India: Economic Development and Social Opportunity.* New Delhi: OUP.

———. 1997b. 'Preface' , in J. Dréze and A. Sen (eds), *Indian Development: Selected Regional Perspectives.* New Delhi: OUP, vii–x.

D'Souza, A. 1980. (ed.). *Women in Contemporary India and South Asia.* Delhi: Manohar.

D'Souza, V. 1985. 'Urban Studies', in J. Ferreira (ed.), *Survey Research in Sociology and Social Anthropology.* New Delhi: Satvahan Publications, 139–209.

Dumont K. L. 1980. *Homo Hierarchicus* (2nd ed), translated by L. Dumont, B. Gulati, M. Sainsbury). Chicago: University of Chicago Press.

———. 1997. 'Power and Territory', in S. Kaviraj (ed.), *Politics in India.* New Delhi: OUP, 45–56.

Duncan, I. 1999. 'Dalits and Politics in Rural North India'. *Journal of Peasant Studies* 27(1): 35–60.

Dunn, J. 1999. 'Situating Democratic Political Accountability', in B. Manin, A. Przeworski and S. Stokes (eds), *Democracy, Accountability, and Representation.* Cambridge: CUP, 329–44.

During, S. 1993. (ed.). *The Cultural Studies Reader*. London: Routledge.

Dyson, T. and M. Moore. 1983. 'On Kinship Structure, Female Autonomy and Demographic Behavior in India'. *Population and Development Review* 9(1): 35–60.

Egnor, M. 1980. 'On the Meaning of Sakti to Women in Tamil Nadu', in S. Wadley (ed.), *The Powers of Tamil Women*. New York: Syracuse, 1–34.

Epstein, T. 1962. *Economic Change and Social Change in South India*. Manchester: Manchester University Press.

———. 1973. *South India: Yesterday, Today and Tomorrow*. London: Macmillan.

Escobar, A. 2001. 'Culture Sits in Places: Reflections on Globalisation and Subaltern Strategies of Localisation'. *Political Geography* 20 (2001): 139–174.

Eswaran, M. and A. Kotwal. 1994. *Why Poverty Persists in India*. New Delhi: OUP.

Evers, T. 1985. 'Identity: The Hidden Side of NSMs in Latin America', in D. Slater (ed.), *New Social Movements & the State in Latin America*. Amsterdam: CEDLA, 43–47.

Fanon, F. 1967. *The Wretched of the Earth* (translated by C. Farrington). Harmondsworth: Penguin.

Fearon, J. 1999. 'Electoral Accountability and the Control of Politicians', in B. Manin, A. Przeworski and S. Stokes (eds), *Democracy, Accountability and Representation*. Cambridge: CUP, 55–97.

Fernandes, L. and S. Bhatkal. 1999. *The Fractured Civilisation: Caste Society in the Throes of Change*. Mumbai: Bharatiya Janwadi Aghadi.

Fine, G. 1995. 'Public Narration and Group Culture', in H. Johnston and B. Klandermans (eds), *Social Movements and Culture*. London: UCL, 127–43.

Fitzgerald, T. 1996. 'From Structure to Substance', *Contributions to Indian Sociology* 30(2): 273–88.

Fogel, R.M. 1968. 'Violence as Protest', in R. Connery (ed.), *Urban Riots: Violence and Social Change*. New York: Vintage, 27–44.

Foss, D. and Larkin. R. 1986. *Beyond Revolution: A New Theory of Social Movements*. Massachusetts: Bergen & Garvey.

Foucault, M. 1977. *Discipline and Punish* (translated by A. Sheridan) Harmondsworth: Penguin.

———. 1980. 'Two Lectures', in C. Gordon (ed.), *Power/Knowledge*. London: Harvester Wheatsheaf.

———. 1981. *The History of Sexuality, Vol. 1* (translated by R. Hurley). Harmondsworth: Penguin.

———. 1983. 'Power, Sovereignty and Discipline', in D. Held, J. Anderson, B. Gieben, S. Hall, L. Harris, P. Lewis, N. Parker and B. Turok (eds), *States and Societies*. Oxford: Blackwell, 306–13.

———. 1993. 'Space, Power, Knowledge: Interview with P. Rabinow', in S. During (ed.), *The Cultural Studies Reader*. London: Routledge, 161–69.

Foweraker, J. 1995. *Theorizing Social Movements*. London: Pluto Press.

Francis, C. 1993. 'Organising the Unorganised: The Role of the Voluntary Sector', *Social Action* 43(1): 107–12.

Frankel, F. and M. Rao. 1989 (eds). *Dominance and State Power in Modern India*. New Delhi: OUP.

Fraser, N. 1990. 'Rethinking the Public Sphere'. *Social Text*, 25/26: 56–80.

Freeman, J. 1986. 'The Consciousness of Freedom Among India's Untouchables', in D. Basu and R. Sisson (eds), *Social and Economic Development in India*. London: Sage Publications, 153–71.

Fuchs, S. 1980. *At the Bottom of Indian Society*. New Delhi: Manoharlal.

Fuller, C. (ed.) 1996. *Caste Today*. Cambridge: CUP.

Gallanter, M. 1991. *Competing Equalities: Law and the Backward Classes in India*. Berkeley: University of California Press.

———. 1997. 'Pursuing Equality', in S. Kaviraj (ed.), *Politics in India*. New Delhi: OUP, 187–99.

Geertz, C. 1983. *Local Knowledge*. New York: Basic Books.

Geetha, V. 1998a. 'Periyar, Women and an Ethic of Citizenship'. *EPW* 33(17): WS9–WS15.

———. 1998b. 'On Bodily Love and Hurt', in M. John and J. Nair (eds), *A Question of Silence?* London: Zed Books, 304–31.

Goffman, E. 1970. *Stigma*. Harmondsworth: Pelican Books.

Gokhale, J. 1990. 'The Evolution of a Counter-Ideology: Dalit Consciousness in Maharashtra', in F. Frankel and M. Rao (eds), *Dominance and State Power in India (Vol. I)*. New Delhi: OUP, 212–77.

Good, A. 1981. 'Prescription, Preference and Practice: Marriage Patterns among the Kondaiyankottai Maravar of South India'. *Man* 16(1981): 108–29.

———. 1999. 'The Burning Question: Sacred and Profane Space in a South Indian Temple Town'. *Anthropos* 94(1999): 69–84.

Goss, J. 1996. 'Disquiet on the Waterfront'. *Urban Geography* 17(3): 221–247.

Gopal, M. 1999. 'Disempowered Despite Wage Work'. *EPW* 34(16&17): WS12–WS20.

Gough, K. 1960. 'Caste in a Tanjore Village', in E. Leach (ed.), *Aspects of Caste in South India, Ceylon and North-west Pakistan*. Cambridge: CUP, 11–60.

———. 1978. 'Social Drama in a Tanjore Village', in A.R. Desai (ed.), *Rural Sociology in India*. Bombay: Popular Prakashan, 345–64.

———. 1981. *Rural Society in South-East India*. Cambridge: CUP.

———. 1991. 'Class and Economic Structure in Thanjavur', in D. Gupta (ed.), *Social Stratification*. New Delhi: OUP, 276–87.

Gould, H. 1988. *The Hindu Caste System: Vol. 2: Caste Adaptation in Modernizing Indian Society*. New Delhi: Chanakya Publications.

Guha, R. 1988. 'On Some Aspects of the Historiography of Colonial India', in R. Guha and G. Spivak (eds), *Selected Subaltern Studies*. Oxford: OUP, 37–44.

Guha, R. and G. Spivak. 1988. (eds). *Selected Subaltern Studies*. Oxford: OUP.

Gupta, A. 1995. 'Blurred Boundaries: The Discourse of Corruption, the Culture of Politics, and the Imagined State'. *American Ethnologist* 22(2): 375–402.

Gupta, A. and J. Ferguson. 1999. 'Beyond "Culture": Space, Identity, and the Politics of Difference'. *Cultural Anthropology* 7(1): 6–23.

Gupta, D. 1991. (ed.). *Social Stratification*. New Delhi: OUP.

Guru, G. 1993. 'The Dalit Movement in Mainstream Sociology', *EPW* 28(14): 570–73.

———. 1996. 'Mapping Dalit Politics in India'. *International Dalit Newsletter* 1(3): 6–7.

Habermas, J. 1994. 'The Emergence of the Public Sphere', in A. Giddens, D. Held, D. Husert, S. Loyal, D. Seymour, J. Thompson (eds), *The Polity Reader in Cultural Theory*. Cambridge: Polity, 81–90.

———. 1996. *The Habermas Reader*. W. Outhwaite (ed.). Cambridge: Polity Press.

Hall, A. 1977. 'Patron–Client Relations: Concepts and Terms', in W. Schmidt (ed.), *Friends, Followers and Factions*. Berkeley: University of California Press, 510–12.

Hall, S. 1988. 'The Toad in the Garden', in C. Nelson and L. Grossberg (eds), *Marxism and the Interpretation of Culture*. Basingstoke: MacMillan.

Hansen, T. 1999. *The Saffron Wave*. New Delhi: OUP.

Hardgrave, R. 1979. *Essays in the Political Sociology of South India*. New Delhi: USHA.

Hardgrave R. and S. Kochanek. 1986. *India: Government & Politics in a Developing Nation*. New York: Harcourt, Brace, and Jovanovich.

Harriss, J. 1982. *Capitalism and Peasant Farming*. Oxford: OUP.

———. 2000. 'Successful Populism?' Review Article. *Frontline*, 17 March 2000: 77–78.

Harriss-White, B. 1996. *A Political Economy of Agricultural Markets in South India*. New Delhi: Sage Publications.

———. 1999. 'State, Market, Collective and Household Action in India's Social Sector', in S. Subramanian and B. Harriss-White (eds), *Illfare in India*. New Delhi: Sage Publicaitons, 303–28.

Harriss-White, B. and S. Janakarajan. 1997. 'From Green Revolution to Rural Industrial Revolution in South India', *EPW* 32(25): 1469–77.

Harvey, D. 1988. *Social Justice and the City*. Oxford: Blackwell.

———. 1996. *Justice, Nature and the Geography of Difference*. Oxford: Blackwell.

Haynes, D. and G. Prakash. (eds). 1991. *Contesting Power*. Delhi: OUP.

Haynes, J. 1997. *Democracy and Civil Society in the Third World*. Cambridge: Polity Press.

Hebdige, D. 1979. *Subculture: The Meaning of Style*. London: Routledge.

Hetherington, K. 1998. *Expressions of Identity: Space, Performance, Politics*. London: Sage Publications.

Hirsch, S. and M. Lazarus-Black. 1994a. (eds). *Contested States: Law, Hegemony and Resistance*. London: Routledge.

———. 1994b. 'Performance and Paradox', in S. Hirsch and M. Lazarus-Black (eds), *Contested States*: London: Routledge, 1–31.

Hjejle, B. 1967. 'Slavery and Agricultural Bondage in South India in the 19th Century'. *Scandinavian Econ History Review* 15(1–2): 71–126.

Holmström, M. 1984. *Industry and Inequality: The Social Anthropology of Indian Labour*. Cambridge: CUP.

Huizer, G. and B. Mannheim. 1979. (eds). *The Politics of Anthropology*. The Hague: Mouton Publishers.

Human Rights Watch. 1999. *Broken People*. New York: Human Rights Watch.

Illaiah, K. 1990. 'Reservations: Experience as Framework of Debate'. *EPW* 25(41): 2307–11.

Inden, R. 1990. *Imagining India*. Oxford: Blackwell.

Inglehart, R. 1999. 'Postmodernisation Erodes Respect for Authority, but Increases Support for Democracy', in P. Norris (ed.), *Critical Citizens*. Oxford: OUP, 236–56.

Irschick, E.F. 1969. *Politics and Social Conflict in South India: The Non-Brahman Movement and Tamil Separatism, 1916–1929*. Berkeley: University of California Press.

———. 1986. *Tamil Revivalism in the 1930's*. Madras: Cre-A.

———. 1994. *Dialogue and History*. Berkeley: University of California Press.

Janakarajan, S. and P. Seabright. 1999. 'Subjective and Objective Indicators of Welfare Change Over Time', in S. Subramanian and B. Harriss-White (eds), *Illfare in India*. New Delhi: Sage Publications, 329–49.

Jasper, J. 1997. *The Art of Moral Protest*. Chicago: Chicago University Press.

Jeffrey, R., C.J. Jeffrey and P. Jeffrey. 2001. 'Social and Political Dominance in Western UP: A Response to Sudha Pai'. *Contributions to Indian Sociology* 35(2): 213–36.

Jeffery, P. and R. Jeffery. 1996. *Don't Marry Me to a Plowman*. Boulder: Westview.

Jeffery, P., R. Jeffery and A. Lyon. 1989. *Labour Pains and Labour Power*. London: Zed Books.

Jeffrey, C. 2000. 'Democratisation without Representation?' *Political Geography* 19(2000): 1013–36.

Jenkins, J. and B. Klandermans. 1995 (eds). *The Politics of Social Protest*. Berkeley: University of California Press.

Jenkins, J. 1995. 'Social Movements, Political Representation and the State', in J. Jenkins and Klandermans (eds), *The Politics of Social Protest*. Berkeley: University of California Press, 14–35.

Jenkins, R. 1999. *Democratic Politics and Economic Reform in India*. Cambridge: CUP.

Jeyaranjan, J. and P. Swaminathan. 1999. 'Resilience of Gender Inequities'. *EPW* 34(16&17): WS2–WS11.

John, M. and J. Nair. 1998. (eds). *A Question of Silence? The Sexual Economies of Modern India*. London: Zed Books.

Johnston, H. and B. Klandermans. 1995a. (eds). *Social Movements and Culture*. London: UCL.

——. 1995b. 'The Cultural Analysis of Social Movements', in H. Johnston and B. Klandermans (eds), *Social Movements and Culture*. London: UCL, 3–24.

Joshi, B. 1986. *Untouchable! The Voices of the Dalit Liberation Movement*. London: Zed Books.

Kaase, M. 1990. 'Social Movements and Political Innovation', in R. Dalton and M. Kuechler (eds), *Challenging the Political Order*. Cambridge: Polity, 84–101.

Kakar, S. 1996. *The Colors of Violence*. Chicago: Chicago University Press.

Kamalanathan, T. 1985. (ed.). *SCs Struggle for Emancipation in South India*. Tirrupatur: Sakkiya Buddhist Association.

Kapadia, K. 1995. *Siva and Her Sisters*. Boulder: Westview.

Karanth, G.K. 1997. 'Caste after Fifty Years of Independence', *Review of Development and Change* 2(2): 319–37.

——. 1998. 'Escaping Domination', in S. Charsley and G. Karanth (eds), *Challenging Untouchability*. London: Sage Publications, 312–25.

Karashima, N. 1997. 'The Untouchable in Tamil Inscriptions and Other Historical Sources', in H. Kotani (ed.), *Caste System, Untouchability and the Depressed*. New Delhi: Manohar, 21–30.

Karl, T. 1990. 'Dilemmas of Democratisation in Latin America'. *Comparative Politics* 23(1): 1–17.

Kasinitz, P. 1995. (ed.). *Metropolis: Center and Symbol of Our Times*. New York: New York University Press.

——. 1995. 'Social Relations and Public Places: Introduction', in P. Kasinitz (ed.), *Metropolis: Center and Symbol of Our Times*. New York: New York University Press, 273–79.

Kaul, R. 2001. 'Accessing Primary Education'. *EPW* 36(2): 155–59.

Kaviraj, S. 1997a. (ed.). *Politics in India*. New Delhi: OUP.

——. 1997b. 'On the Construction of Colonial Power', in S. Kaviraj (ed.), *Politics in India*. New Delhi: OUP, 141–58.

——. 1997c. 'Filth and the Public Sphere'. *Public Culture* 10(1): 83–113.

Kazi, S. 1989. 'Domestic Impact of Overseas Migration: Pakistan', in R. Amjad (ed.), *To the Gulf and Back*. New Delhi: ILO, 167–96.

Kertzer, D. 1988. *Ritual, Politics and Power*. New Haven: Yale University Press.

Khare, R.S. 1984. *The Untouchable as Himself*. Cambridge: CUP.

Khilnani, S. 1998. *The Idea of India*. London: Penguin.

Kohli, A. 1987. *The State and Poverty in India*. Cambridge: CUP.

———. 1990. *Democracy and Discontent*. Cambridge: CUP.

———. 1998. 'Can Democracies Accommodate Ethnic Nationalism?', in A. Basu and A. Kohli (eds), *Community Conflicts and the State in India*. New Delhi: OUP, 7–32.

Kolenda, P. 1978. *Caste in Contemporary India*. London: Benjamin Cummings.

Kothari, R. 1997. 'Caste and Modern Politics', in S. Kaviraj (ed.), *Politics in India*. New Delhi: OUP, 57–70.

———. 1995. *Poverty: Human Consciousness and the Amnesia of Development*. London: Zed Books.

———. 1993. 'Masses, Classes, and the State', in P. Wignaraja (ed.), *New Social Movements of the South*. London: Zed Books, 59–77.

———. 1986. 'Masses, Classes, and the State'. *EPW* 21(5): 210–16.

Kothari, S. 1990. 'The Human Rights Movement in India: A Critical Overview'. *Social Action* 40(1): 1–15.

Krishna, S. 1996. 'The Appropriation of Dissent', in T. Satyamurthy (ed.), *Class Formation and Political Transformation in Post-Colonial India*. New Delhi: OUP, 238–57.

Kumar, D. 1965. *Land and Caste in South India*. Cambridge: CUP.

Laclau, E. 1985. 'New Social Movements and the Plurality of the Social', in D. Slater (ed.), *New Social Movements and the State in Latin America*. Amsterdam: CEDLA, 27–42.

Laclau, E. and C. Mouffe. 1985. *Hegemony & Socialist Strategy*. London: Verso.

Lande, C. 1977. 'The Dyadic Basis of Clientelism', in W. Schmidt (ed.), *Friends, Followers and Factions*. Berkeley: University of California Press, xiii–xxxvii.

Le Bon. 1960. *The Crowd: A Study of the Popular Mind*. New York: Viking Press.

Lefort, C. 1988. *Democracy and Political Theory* (translated D. Macey). Cambridge: Polity.

Lefebvre, H. 1991. *The Production of Space*. Oxford: Blackwell.

Lerche, J. 1998. 'Agricultural Labourers, The State and Agrarian Transition in U.P'. *EPW* 33(13): A29–A35.

Lewis, J. 1995. *India's Political Economy*. New Delhi: OUP.

Ley D. and R. Cybriwsky. 1974. 'Urban Graffiti as Territorial Markers', *Annals of the Association of American Geographers* 64(4): 491–505.

Lipsky, M. 1970. *Protest in City Politics: Rent Strikes, Housing and the Power of the Poor*. Chicago: Rand, McNally & Co.

Ludden, D. 1989. *Peasant History in South India*. New Delhi: OUP.

Lynch, O. 1969. *The Politics of Untouchability*. New York: Columbia University Press.

Mageli, E. 1997. *Organising Women's Protest*. London: Curzon.

Mahajan, G. 1995. 'Cultural Embodiment and Histories', in U. Baxi and B. Parekh (eds), *Crisis and Change in Contemporary India*. New Delhi: Sage Publications, 350–69.

Majumdar, M. 1997. 'Lesser Citizens: Social Exclusion of Dalits in Tamil Nadu', *Review of Development and Change* 2(1): 99–121.

——. 1999. 'Exclusion in Education', in S. Subramanian and B. Harriss-White (eds), *Illfare in India*. New Delhi: Sage Publications, 265–99.

Malik, B. 1999. 'Untouchability and Dalit Women's Oppression', *EPW* 34(6): 323–24.

Malloy, J. 1987. *Authoritarians and Democrats*. Pittsburg: University of Pittsburgh Press.

Manin, B., A. Przeworski and S. Stokes. 1999. (eds). *Democracy, Accountability, and Representation*. Cambridge: CUP.

——. 1999a. 'Introduction', in B. Manin, A. Przeworski and S. Stokes (eds), *Democracy, Accountability, and Representation*. Cambridge: CUP, 1–26.

——. 1999b. 'Elections and Representation', in B. Manin, A. Przeworski and S. Stokes (eds), *Democracy, Accountability, and Representation*. Cambridge: CUP, 29–54.

Manor, J. 1990. 'How and Why Liberal Representative Politics Emerged in India'. *Political Studies* 38(1): 20–38.

——. 1997. 'Karnataka: Caste, Class, Dominance and Politics in a Cohesive Society', in S. Kaviraj (ed.), *Politics in India*. New Delhi: OUP, 262–73.

Marshall, T.H. 1983. 'Citizenship and Social Class', in D.Held J. Anderson, B. Gieben, S. Hall, L. Harris, P. Lewis, N. Parker, B. Turok (eds), *States and Societies*. Oxford: Blackwell.

Massey, D. 1994. *Space, Place and Gender*. Cambridge: Polity.

Massey, J. 1994. *Indigenous Peoples*: Dalits. Delhi: ISPCK.

Mathew, J. 1986. *Ideology, Protest and Social Mobility*. Delhi: Inter-India Publishers.

Melucci, A. 1988. 'Social Movements and the Democratization of Everyday Life', in J. Keane (ed.), *Civil Society and the State*. London: Verso, 245–60.

——. 1992. 'Frontier Land: Collective Action Between Actors and Systems', in M. Diani and R. Eyerman (eds), *Studying Collective Action*. London: Sage Publications, 238–58.

——. 1995. 'The Process of Collective Identity', in H. Johnston and Klandermans (eds), *Social Movements and Culture*. London: UCL, 41–63.

Melucci, A. 1996. *Challenging Codes*. Cambridge: CUP.

Mencher, J. 1985. 'Landless Women Agricultural Labourers in India', in *IRRI: Women in Rice Farming*. Aldershot: IRRI.

———. 1988. 'Women's Work and Poverty', in D. Dwyer and J. Bruce (eds), *A Home Divided*. Stanford: Stanford University Press, 99– 119.

———. 1991. 'The Caste System Upside Down', in D. Gupta, (ed.), *Social Stratification*. New Delhi: OUP, 93–109.

Mendelsohn, O. and M. Vicziany. 1998. *The Untouchables*. Cambridge: OUP.

Michael, S.M. 1999a. (ed.). *Untouchable: Dalits in Modern India*. Boulder: Lynne Rienner Publishers.

———. 1999b. 'Dalit Visions of a Just Society', in S.M. Michael (ed.), *Untouchable: Dalits in Modern India*. Boulder: Lynne Rienner Publishers, 25–41.

Miller, B. 1981. *The Endangered Sex*. Ithaca: Cornell.

Mines, M. 1994. *Public Faces, Private Voices*. Berkeley: University of California Press.

Mitchell, D. 1995. 'The End of Public Space? People's Park, Definitions of the Public, and Democracy', *Annals of the Association of American Geographers* 85(1): 108–33.

———. 1996a. 'Introduction: Public Space and the City', *Urban Geography* 17(2): 127–131.

———. 1996b. 'Political Violence, Order and the Legal Construction of Public Space', *Urban Geography* 17(2): 152–78.

Mitchell, T. 1988. *Colonising Egypt*. Berkeley: University of California Press.

Mitra, S.K. and R. Lewis. (eds). 1996. *Subnational Movements in South Asia*. Boulder: Westview Press.

Mitra, S.K and D. Rothermund. (eds). 1997. *Legitimacy and Conflict in South Asia*. Delhi: Manohar.

Mitra, S.K. 1992. *Power, Protest and Participation*. London: Routledge.

———. 1994. 'Caste, Democracy and the Politics of Community Formation in India', in M. Searle-Chatterjee and U. Sharma (eds), *Contextualising Caste*. Oxford: Blackwell, 49–71.

———. 1996a. 'Introduction', in S.K. Mitra and R. Lewis (eds), *Subnational Movements in South Asia*. Boulder: Westview Press, 1–12.

———. 1996b. 'Sub-National Movements in South Asia', in S.K. Mitra and R. Lewis (eds), *Subnational Movements in South Asia*. Boulder: Westview Press, 14–41.

———. 1997. 'Legitimacy, Governance and Political Institutions in India after Independence', in S.K. Mitra and D. Rothermund (eds), *Legitimacy and Conflict in South Asia*. Delhi: Manohar, 17–49.

———. 1999. *Culture and Rationality*. New Delhi: Sage Publications.

Moffatt, M. 1979. *An Untouchable Community in South India*. Princeton: Princeton University Press.

Mohanty, M. 1998. 'Social Movements in Creative Society', in M. Mohanty, P. Mukherji and O. Tornquist (eds), *People's Rights*. New Delhi: Sage Publications, 63–81.

Mohanty. M., P. Mukherji and O. Tornquist. 1998. (eds). *People's Rights*. New Delhi: Sage Publications.

Monshipouri, M. 1995. *Democratisation, Liberalisation and Human Rights in the Third World*. Boulder: Lynne Rienner.

Moore, B. 1966. *Social Origins of Dictatorship and Democracy*. Boston: Beacon Press.

Morkhandikar, R.S. 1990. 'Dilemmas of Dalit Movement in Maharashtra: Unity Moves and After', *EPW* 25(12): 586–90.

Moses, B.C. 1995. 'Struggle for Panchamma Lands: Dalit Assertion in Tamil Nadu', *EPW* 30(5): 247–48.

Mosse, D. 1994. 'Idioms of Subordination and Styles of Protest among Christian and Hindu Harijan Castes in Tamil Nadu', *Contributions to Indian Sociology* 27(1): 67–104.

———. 1996. 'Responding to Subordination': The Politics of Identity Change Among South Indian Untouchable Castes', in J. Campbell and A. Rew (eds), *Identity and Affect: Experiences of Identity in a Globalising World*. London: Pluto Press, 64–104.

Mukherjee, R. 1978. 'Rural Class Structure in West Bengal', in A.R. Desai (ed.), *Rural Sociology in India*. Bombay: Popular Prakashan, 271–90.

Mugyenyi, M. 1988. 'Development First, Democracy Second', in W. Oyugi (ed.), *Democratic Theory and Practice in Africa*. Portsmouth: Heinemann, 178–90.

Mushakoji, K. 1993. 'Foreword', in P. Wignaraja (ed.), *New Social Movements of the South*. London: Zed Books, xi–xiv.

Nagaraj, K. 1999. 'Labour Market Characteristics and Employment Generation Programmes in India', in S. Subramanian and B. Harriss-White (eds), *Illfare in India*. New Delhi: Sage Publications, 73–109.

Nair, P. 1989. 'Incidence, Impact and Implications of Migration to the Middle East from Kerala (India)', in R. Amjad (ed.), *To the Gulf and Back*. New Delhi: ILO, 343–64.

Nandy, A. 1998. *Exiled At Home*. New Delhi: OUP.

Nayyar, D. 1989. 'International Labour Migration from India', in R. Amjad (ed.), *To the Gulf and Back*. New Delhi: ILO, 95–142.

Newton, K. 1999. 'Social and Political Trust in Established Democracies', in P. Norris (ed.), *Critical Citizens: Global Support for Democratic Governance*. Oxford: OUP, 169–87.

Nihila, M. 1999. 'Marginalisation of Women Workers'. *EPW* 34(16&17): WS21–WS27.

Norris, P. 1999a. (ed.). *Critical Citizens: Global Support for Democratic Governance.* Oxford: OUP.

——. 1999b. 'Introduction to the Growth of Critical Citizens', in P. Norris (ed.), *Critical Citizens: Global Support for Democratic Governance.* Oxford: OUP, 1–27.

——. 1999c. 'Conclusions: The Growth of Critical Citizens and its Consequences', in P. Norris (ed.), *Critical Citizens: Global Support for Democratic Governance.* Oxford: OUP, 257–72.

Oberst, R. 1996. 'Youth Militancy and the Rise of Tamil Nationalism', in S.K. Mitra and R. Lewis (eds), *Subnational Movements in South Asia.* Boulder: Westview Press, 140–69.

Offe, C. 1990. 'Reflections on the Institutional Self-Transformation of Movement Politics', in R. Dalton and M. Kuechler (eds), *Challenging the Political Order.* Cambridge: Polity, 232–50.

Oliver, P. 1989. 'Bringing the Crowd Back In: The Nonorganizational Elements of SMs', in L. Kriesberg (ed.), *Research in Social Movements, Conflict and Change, Vol. 11.* Greenwich, Conn.: JAI Press, 1–30.

Olson, M. 1965. *The Logics of Collective Action.* Cambridge, MA: Harvard University Press.

Omvedt, G. 1979. 'On the Participant Study of Women's Movements', in G. Huizer and B. Mannheim (eds), *The Politics of Anthropology.* The Hague: Mouton Publishers, 373–93.

——. 1994. *Dalits and the Democratic Revolution.* New Delhi: Sage Publications.

——. 1995. *Dalit Visions.* Delhi: Orient Longman.

——. 1998. 'Peasants, Dalits and Women', in M. Mohanty, P. Mukherji and O. Tornquist (eds), *People's Rights.* New Delhi: Sage Publications: 223–41.

Oommen, T.K. 1984. 'Sources of Deprivation and Styles of Protest'. *Contributions to Indian Sociology* 18(1): 45–61.

——. 1990. *Protest and Change.* New Delhi: Sage Publications.

——. 1992. 'State Policy & The Socially Deprived in India', in V. Devasahayam (ed.), *Dalits and Women.* Madras: Gurukul Lutheran College, 50–59.

Osella, F and C. Osella. 2000. 'Migration, Money and Masculinity in Kerala'. *Journal of the Royal Anthropological Institute* 6: 2000: 117–33.

O'Toole, M. 1996. 'Epilogue', in S.K. Mitra and R. Lewis (eds), *Subnational Movements in South Asia.* Boulder: Westview Press, 237–46.

Pai, S. 2000. 'New Social and Political Movements of Dalits'. *Contributions to Indian Sociology* 34(2): 189–220.

Pai, S. 2001. 'Social Capital, Panchayats and Grass Roots Democracy'. *EPW* 36(8): 645–54.

Pandian, M.S.S. 1992. *The Image Trap: M.G. Ramachandran in Film and Politics.* New Delhi: Sage Publications.

Pandian, M.S.S. 1994. 'Crisis in DMK'. *EPW* 29(5): 221–23.

———. 1995. 'Beyond Colonial Crumbs: Cambridge School, Identity Politics and Dravidian Movement(s)'. *EPW* 30(7&8): 385–91.

———. 1996. 'Politics of Representation', in T.V. Sathyamurthy (ed.), *Region, Religion, Caste, and Culture in Contemporary India*. New Delhi: OUP, 533–49.

———. 2000. 'Dalit Assertion in Tamilnadu: An Explanatory note'. *Journal of Indian School of Political Economy* 12(3&4): 501–17.

———. 2002. 'One Step outside Modernity: Caste, Identity Politics and Public Sphere'. *EPW* 37(18): 1735–41.

Parish, S. 1996. *Hierarchy and its Discontents*. Philadelphia: Pennsylvania University Press.

Parikh, S. 1998. 'Religion, Reservations and Riots', in A. Basu and A. Kohli (eds), *Community Conflicts and the State in India*. New Delhi: OUP, 33–57.

Parry, G. and M. Moran. 1994. (eds). *Democracy and Democratisation*. London: Routledge.

———. 1994. 'Introduction: Problems of Democracy and Democratisation', in G. Parry and M. Moran (eds), *Democracy and Democratisation*. London: Routledge, 1–17.

Patwardhan, S. 1979. 'Making My Way Through Caste Images', in M. Srinivas, A. Shah and E. Ramaswamy (eds), *The Field Worker and the Field*. New Delhi: OUP, 152–60.

Pawde, K. 1994. 'The Position of Dalit Women in Indian Society', in J. Massey (ed.), *Indigenous Peoples: Dalits*. New Delhi. ISPCK, 143–58.

Philips, A. 1991. *Engendering Democracy*. Cambridge: Polity Press.

Pinkney, R. 1993. *Democracy in the Third World*. Buckingham: Open University Press.

Pitt-Rivers, J. 1961. *The People of the Sierra*. Chicago: University of Chicago Press.

Plotkin, S. 1993. 'Community and Alienation: Enclave Consciousness and Urban Movements', in M. Peter-Smith (ed.), *Breaking Chains: SMs & Collective Action*. New Brunswick: Transaction Publishers.

Potter, D., D. Goldblatt, M. Kiloh and P. Lewis. 1997. (eds). *Democratisation*. Cambridge: Polity Press.

Potter, D. 1997. 'Explaining Democratisation', in D. Potter, D. Goldblatt, M. Kiloh and O. Lewis (eds), *Democratisation*. Cambridge: Polity, 1–40.

Powell, J. 1977. 'Peasant Society and Clientelist Politics', in W. Schmidt (ed.), *Friends, Followers and Factions*. Berkeley: University of California Press, 147–61.

Prakash, G. 1990. *Bonded Histories*. Cambridge: CUP.

Price, P. 1989. 'Kingly Models in Indian Political Behaviour'. *Asian Survey* 29(6): 559–72.

Price, Pamela G. 1996. *Kinship and Political Practice in Colonial India*. Cambridge: CUP.

Putnam, R. 1993. *Making Democracy Work*. Princeton: Princeton University Press.

Racine, J. 1998. 'Introduction'. *Comparative Studies of South Asia, Africa and the Middle East* 18(1): 1–4.

Racine, J. and J. Racine. 1998. 'Dalit Identities and the Dialectics of Oppression and Emancipation' *Comparative Studies of South Asia, Africa and the Middle East* 18(1): 5–20.

Radhakrishnan, P. 1999. 'Caste, Politics and the Reservation Issue', in S. Subramanian and B. Harriss-White (ed.), *Illfare in India*. New Delhi: Sage Publications, 163–95.

Raj, M.C. 1998. 'Paths of Dalit Liberation'. *Integral Liberation* 2(3). A Bangalore Social Action Trust Publication.

Rajadurai, S. and V. Geetha. 1993. 'Dalits and Non-Brahmin Consciousness in Colonial Tamil Nadu'. *EPW* 28(39): 2091–98.

———. 1996. 'DMK Hegemony: The Cultural Limits to Political Consensus'. in T. Satyamurthy (ed.), *Region, Religion, Caste, Gender and Culture in Contemporary India*. New Delhi: OUP, 550–80.

Rajendran, N. 1994. *The National Movement in Tamil Nadu, 1905–14*. New Delhi: OUP.

Rajuladevi, A. 2000. 'Profiles in Poverty: Female Landless Agricultural Labour Households'. *EPW* 35(6): 474–84.

Ram, K. 1991. *Mukkuvar Women*. London: Zed Books.

Ram, N. 1998. 'Dalit Movements in India: A Perspective from Below', in *Indian Journal of Social Work* 59(1): 99–123.

Ramachandran, V. 1990. *Wage Labour and Unfreedom in Agriculture*. Oxford: Clarendon Press.

Ramachandran, V.K. 1997. 'On Kerala's Development Achievements', in J. Drèze and A. Sen (eds), *Indian Development*. New Delhi: OUP, 205–91.

Ramaswamy, S. 1997. *Passions of the Tongue*. Berkeley: University of California Press.

Randall, V. 1997. 'Why have the Political Trajectories of India and China been Different?', in Potter, D. Goldblatt, M. Kiloh and Lewis (eds), *Democratisation*. Cambridge: Polity, 195–218.

Rani, C. S. 1998. 'Dalit Women's Writing in Telegu'. *EPW* 33(17): WS21–WS24.

Rao, M.S.A. 1987. *Social Movements and Social Transformation*. Delhi: Ramesh Jain.

Ravindran, T.K.S. 1999. 'Female Autonomy in Tamil Nadu'. *EPW* 34(16&17): WS34–WS44.

Reddy, M.G. 1990. 'Police and the Weaker Sections of Rural Society'. *Social Action* 40(1): 87–93.

Reiniche, M. 1996. 'The Urban Dynamics of Caste', in C. Fuller (ed.), *Caste Today*. Cambridge: CUP, 124–49.

Rege, S. 2000. '"Real Feminism" and Dalit Women'. *EPW* 35(6): 492–95.

Repetto, R. 1994. *The 'Second India' Revisited*. Washington DC: World Resources Institute.

Robb, P. 1993a. (ed.). *Dalit Movements and the Meanings of Labour in India*. New Delhi: OUP.

———. 1993b. 'Introduction: Meanings of Labour in Indian Social Context', in P. Robb (ed.), *Dalit Movements and the Meanings of Labour*. New Delhi: OUP, 1–67.

Robinson, M. 1988. *Local Politics: The Law of the Fishes*. New Delhi: OUP.

Roy, R. 1990. 'The Political Dilemma of the Scheduled Castes', in R. Roy, and R. Sisson (eds), *Diversity and Dominance in Indian Politics—Vol. II*. New Delhi: Sage Publications, 35–57.

Roy, R. and R. Sisson. 1990. (eds). *Diversity & Dominance in Indian Politics—Vol. II*. New Delhi: Sage Publications.

———. 1990. 'Social Diversity, Partisanship and Public Policy', in R. Roy and R. Sisson (eds), *Diversity and Dominance in Indian Politics—Vol. II*. New Delhi: Sage Publications, 13–31.

Rucht, D. 1990. 'The Strategies and Action Repertoires of New Movements', in R. Dalton and M. Kuechler (eds), *Challenging the Political Order*. Cambridge: Polity, 156–75.

Rucht, D. and Ohlemacher. T. 1992. 'Protest Event Data', in M. Diani and R. Eyerman (eds), *Studying Collective Action*. London: Sage Publications, 76–106.

Ruddick, S. 1996. 'Constructing Difference in Public Spaces', *Urban Geography* 17(2): 132–51.

Rudé, G. 1995. *The Crowd in History*. London: Serif.

Rudolph, L. and S. Rudolph. 1967. *The Modernity of Tradition*. University of Chicago Press.

———. 1987. *In Pursuit of Lakshmi*. Hyderabad: Orient Longman.

Saberwal, S. 1986. *India: The Roots of Crisis*. New Delhi: OUP.

———. 1997. 'On the Diversity of Ruling Traditions', in S. Kaviraj (ed.), *Politics in India*. New Delhi: OUP, 124–40.

Satyamurthy, T. 1996. (ed.). *Region, Religion, Caste, Gender & Culture in Contemporary India*. New Delhi: OUP.

———. 1996. (ed.). *Class Formation and Political Transformation in Post-Colonial India*. New Delhi: OUP.

———. 1997. 'Local Politics, Violence and Panchayati Raj', in S.K. Mitra and D. Rothermund (eds), *Legitimacy and Conflict in South Asia*. Delhi: Manohar, 106–21.

Scharma, B. 1990. *The Report of the Commissioner for SCs & STs: 29th Report: 1987–89*. Faridabad: Government of India Press.

Schmidt, W.S. 1977 (ed.). *Friends, Followers and Factions*. Berkeley: University of California Press.

Scott, A. 1991. *Ideology and Social Movements*. London: Allen & Unwin.

Scott, J. 1977. 'Patron-Client Politics and Political Change in S.E Asia', in W. Schmidt (ed.), *Friends, Followers and Factions*. Berkeley: University of California Press, 123–46.

——. 1985. *Weapons of the Weak*. Berkeley: University of California Press.

——. 1990. *Domination and the Arts of Resistance*. London: Yale University Press.

Searle-Chatterjee, M. and U. Sharma. 1994. (ed.). *Contextualising Caste*. Oxford: Blackwell.

Sebastian, M. 1994. *Liberating the Caged Dalit Panther*. Madras: Emerald Publishers.

Sen, A. 1997. 'Radical Needs and Moderate Reforms', in J. Drèze and A. Sen (eds), *Indian Development*. New Delhi: OUP, 1–32.

Sen, I. 1990. *A Space within the Struggle*. New Delhi: Kali for Women.

Seneviratne, H. 1997(ed.). *Identity, Consciousness and the Past*. New Delhi: OUP.

Sethi, H. 1993. 'Action Groups and the New Politics', in P. Wignaraja (ed.), *NSMs of the South*. London: Zed Books, 230–55.

——. 1998. 'Micro-Struggles, NGOs and the State', in M. Mohanty, P. Mukherji and O. Tornquist (eds), *People's Rights*. Delhi: Sage Publications, 405–20.

Shah, G. 1990. 'Dalit Movements and the Search for Identity'. *Social Action* 40(4): 317–35.

Shariff, A. 1999. *India: Human Development Report*. National Council of Applied Economic Research. New Delhi: OUP.

Sharma, S.K. 1991. 'Social Mobility and Growing Resistance'. *Social Action* 41(1): 64–77.

Sharma, U. 1980. 'Purdah and Public Space', in A de Souza (ed.), *Women in Contemporary India and South Asia*. Delhi: Manohar.

——. 1999. *Caste*. Buckingham: Open University Press.

Shiri, G. 1998. 'Urban Slums: The Tragedy of those Who Sought Escape from Rural Caste-Class Oppression', *Religion & Society* 45(1): 11–36.

Shklar, J. 1991. *American Citizenship: The Quest for Inclusion*. Cambridge, MA: Harvard University Press.

Siegel, F. 1995. 'Reclaiming Our Public Spaces', in P. Kasinitz (ed.), *Metropolis: Center & Symbol of Our Times*. New York: New York University Press, 369–83.

Singh, K. 1993. *The Scheduled Castes*. New Delhi: OUP.

Slater, D. 1985a. (ed.). *New Social Movements and the State in Latin America*. Amsterdam: CEDLA.

Slater, D. 1985b. 'Social Movements and a Recasting of the Political', in D. Slater (ed.), *New Social Movements and the State in Latin America*. Amsterdam: CEDLA, 1–21.

——. 1991. 'New Social Movements and Old Political Questions'. *International Journal of Political Economy* (Spring 1991): 31–60.

Smith, B. 1968. 'The Politics of Protest: How Effective is Violence?', in R. Connery (ed.), *Urban Riots: Violence and Social Change*. New York: Vintage, 115–34.

Smith, R. S. 2000. 'Between Local Tax and Global Statistic: The Census as Local Record'. *Contributions to Indian Sociology* 34(1): 1–35.

Soja, E. 1985. 'The Spatiality of Social Life', in D. Gregory and J. Urry (eds), *Social Relations and Spatial Structures*. New York: St. Martin's Press, 90–127.

——. 1993. 'History: Geography: Modernity', in S. During (ed.), *The Cultural Studies Reader*. London: Routledge, 135–50.

Spencer, J. 1996. 'Democracy as a Cultural System', in A. Boholm (ed.), *Political Ritual*. Gothenburg: IASSA, 78–93.

Srinivas, M. 1962. *Caste in Modern India*. New York: Asia Publishing House.

——. 1984. 'Some Reflections on the Nature of Caste Hierarchy'. *Contribution to Indian Sociology* 18(2): 151–67.

——. 1991. 'Mobility in the Caste System', in D. Gupta (ed.), *Social Stratification*. New Delhi: OUP, 312–25.

Srinivas, M., A. Shah and E. Ramaswamy. 1979a. (eds). *The Field Worker and the Field*. New Delhi: OUP, 152–60.

——. 1979b. 'Introduction', in M. Srinivas, A. Shah and E. Ramaswamy (eds), *The Field Worker and the Field*. New Delhi: OUP, 1–15.

Staeheli, L. and P. Thompson. 1997. 'Citizenship, Community, and Struggles for Public Space', *Professional Geographer* 49(1): 28–38.

Stones, R. 1996. *Sociological Reasoning*. Basingstoke: Macmillan.

Subadra, 1999. 'Violence Against Women: Wife Battering in Chennai'. *EPW* 34(16&17): WS28–WS33.

Subramanian, N. 1999: *Ethnicity and Populist Mobilization*. New Delhi: OUP.

Subramanian, S. and B. Harriss-White. 1999a. (eds). *Illfare in India: Essays on India's Social Sector in Honour of S. Guhan*. New Delhi: Sage Publications.

——. 1999b. 'Introduction', in S. Subramanian and B. Harriss-White (eds), *Illfare in India*. New Delhi: Sage Publications, 17–43.

Sugirtharaj, F. 1990. 'Developing a Common Dalit Ideology', in A. Nirmal (ed.), *Towards a Common Dalit Ideology*. Madras: Gurukul Lutheran College, 19–38.

Suresh, V. 1996. 'The Dalit Movement in India', in T.V. Satyamurthy (ed.), *Region, Religion, Caste, Gender and Culture in Contemporary India*. New Delhi: OUP, 355–87.

Swamy, A. 1998. 'Parties, Political Identities and the Absence of Political Violence in South India', in A. Basu and A. Kohli (eds), *Community Conflicts and the State in India*. New Delhi: OUP, pp108–48.
——. 1996. 'Sense, Sentiment and Populist Coalitions', in S.K. Mitra and Lewis (eds), *Subnational Movements in South Asia*. Boulder: Westview Press, 191–236.
Swidler, A. 1995. 'Cultural Power and Social Movements', in H. Johnston and B. Klandermans (eds), *Social Movements and Culture*. London: UCL, 25–40.
Tambiah, S. 1996. *Levelling Crowds*. Berkeley: University of California Press.
Tanner, C. 1995. 'Class, Caste and Gender in Collective Action'. *Journal of Peasant Studies* 22(4): 672–98.
Tarrow, S. 1990. 'The Phantom at the Opera', in R. Dalton and M. Kuechler (eds), *Challenging the Political Order*. Cambridge: Polity, 271–73.
——. 1998 (1994). *Power in Movement*. Cambridge: CUP.
Taylor, V. and N. Whittier. 1995. 'Analytical Approaches to Social Movement Culture', in H. Johnston and B. Klandermans (eds), *Social Movements and Culture*. London: UCL, 163–87.
Teltumde, A. 2000. 'Theorising the Dalit Movement: A Viewpoint'. *Vikalp Alternatives* 8(1&2): 71–92.
Templeman, D. 1996. *The Northern Nadars of Tamil Nadu*. New Delhi: OUP.
Thompson, E.P. 1991. *Customs in Common*. Harmondsworth: Penguin.
Thompson, J. 1994. 'The Theory of the Public Sphere: A Critical Appraisal', in A. Giddens, D. Held, D. Hubert, S. Loyal, D. Seymour, J. Thompson (eds) *The Polity Reader in Cultural Theory*. Cambridge: Polity, 91–99.
Tilly, C. 1986. *The Contentious French*. Cambridge MA: Harvard University.
Touraine, A. 1981. *The Voice and the Eye*. Cambridge: CUP.
Turner, V. 1975. *Dramas, Fields and Metaphors*. Ithaca: Cornell University Press.
——. 1967. *The Forest of Symbols; Aspects of Ndembu Ritual*. Ithaca, NY: Cornell University Press.
Twine, F. 1994. *Citizenship and Social Rights*. London: Sage Publications.
Unni, J. 1998. 'Non-Agricultural Employment and Poverty in Rural India'. in *EPW* 33(13): A36–A44.
Vanaik, A. 1990. *The Painful Transition*. London: Verso.
Vincentnathan, L. 1993. 'Untouchable Concepts of Person and Society', in *Contributions to Indian Sociology* 27(1): 53–82.
Vincentnathan, S. 1996. 'Caste, Politics and the Panchayat'. *Comparative Studies in Society and History* 38(3): 484–502.

Untouchable Citizens

Viramma, J–L. Racine and J. Racine. 1997. *Viramma: Life of an Untouchable* (translated by W. Hobson) London Verso.

Veltmeyer, H. 1997. 'NSMs in Latin America: The Dynamics of Class and Identity', *The Journal of Peasant Studies* 25(1): 139–69.

Verges, F. 1999. 'Colonizing Citizenship'. *Radical Philosophy* (special issue on Race and Ethnicity) 95(May/June): 3–7.

Wade, R. 1988. *Village Republics: Economic Conditions for Collective Action in South India*. Cambridge: CUP.

Wadley, S (ed.) 1980a. *The Powers of Tamil Women*. New York: Syracuse.

———. 1980b. 'Introduction', in S. Wadley (ed.), *The Powers of Tamil Women*. New York: Syracuse, ix–xix.

———. 1980c. 'The Paradoxical Powers of Tamil Women', in S. Wadley (ed.), *The Powers of Tamil Women*. New York: Syracuse, 153–70.

Washbrook, D. 1976. *The Emergence of Provincial Politics: The Madras Presidency 1870–1920*. Cambridge: CUP.

———. 1989. 'Caste, Class and Dominance in Modern Tamil Nadu' in F. Frankel and M. Rao (eds), *Dominance and State Power in India (Vol. I)*. New Delhi: OUP, 204–64.

———. 1993a. 'Land and Labour in Late 18th Century South India: The Golden Age of the Pariah?', in P. Robb (ed.), *Dalit Movements and the Meanings of Labour*. New Delhi: OUP, 68–86.

———. 1993b. 'The Commercialisation of Agriculture in Colonial India—Production, Subsistence and Reproduction in the "Dry South", c.1870–1930'. *Modern Asian Studies* 28(1): 129.

Weber, M. 1958. *The Religion of India: The Sociology of Hinduism and Buddhism*. New York: The Free Press.

———. 1964. *The Theory of Social and Economic Organisation* (Edited by Talcott Parsons). New York: The Free Press.

Weiner, M. 1997. 'Minority Identities', S. Kaviraj (ed.), *Politics in India*. New Delhi: OUP, 241–53.

Weintraub, J. 1995. 'Varieties and Vicissitudes of Public Space', in P. Kasinitz (ed.), *Metropolis: Center and Symbol of Our Times*. New York. New York University Press, 280–315.

Widlund, I. 2000. *Paths to Power and Patterns of Influence*. Uppsala University: Thesis Publication.

Wignaraja, P. (ed.) 1993. *New Social Movements of the South*. London: Zed Books.

———. 1993. 'Rethinking Development and Democracy', in P. Wignaraja (ed.), *New Social Movements of the South*. London: Zed Books, 4–35.

Wood, J.R. 1990. 'Reservations in Doubt', in R. Roy and R. Sisson (eds), *Diversity and Dominance in Indian Politics—Vol. II*. New Delhi: Sage Publications, 146–69.

Yesumarian, L. 1995. *Dalit Struggle: An Interview with Fr Yesumarian*. Borgia, F (ed.), Robertsonpet: KGF.

Zashin, E. 1972. *Civil Disobedience and Democracy*. New York: The Free Press.
Zelliot, E. 1996. *From Untouchable to Dalit*. New Delhi: Manohar.
Zirakzadeh, C. 1997. *Social Movements in Politics*. London: Longman.

Other Sources

Unpublished Theses:

Jeyaharan, D.J. 1992. *The Concepts and Practices of Purity-Pollution Related to the Situation of Dalits and Women in South Tamil Nadu: An Evaluation of Patterns of Protest*. Master's thesis in social analysis, TTS, Madurai.
Kadirvelu, I. 1998. *People's Control over Common Resources*. Master's thesis in social analysis, TTS, Madurai.
Klimova, S. 2000. *Dis/Agreement: An Enquiry into the Normative Origins of Social Conflict*. Ph.D. thesis, University of Edinburgh.

Websites, Campaign Bulletins and Unnamed Newspaper Reports:

Ambedkar Centre for Justice and Peace. 1998. http://saxakali.com/CommunityLinkups/dalit3.htm.
Amnesty International. Country Report for India:http://www.amnesty.org/ailib/aireport/ar98/asa20.htm.
Bangalore Social Action Trust. 1998. *Integral Liberation* 2(3). R. Sarrao (ed.). A BSA Trust Publication.
Dinakaran. 1999. *More Clashes Between Groups*. Tamil Paper, Correspondent not named, 21 June 1999.
Frontline. 1999. '"Pre-planned & Politically Motivated": An Interview with Dr Krishnasamy'. *Frontline* 16(16): 29 July–13 August.
Government of India, P. Palmanabha. 1984. *Census of India 1981*. Delhi: Indian Administrative Service.
Government of India, A. Muthuswami. 1984. (ed.). *Census of India 1981: Series 20, Tamil Nadu*. New Delhi: GOI Press.
Government of Tamil Nadu. 1999. *Statistical Handbook of Tamil Nadu*. Issued by the Director of Economic and Statistics, Chennai. http://www.tn.gov.in/Default.htm.
Government of Tamil Nadu. 2002. *Statistical Handbook of Tamil Nadu*, Issued by the Director of Economic and Statistics, Chennai. http://www.tn.gov.in/
The Hindu. 1999. 'Untouchability Offences Declining'. Special Correspondent. *The Hindu Newspaper*. 24 January 1999: http://www.indiaserver.com/thehindu/1999ft/01/24/stories/04242232.htm.

The Hindu. 1999. 'Third Front a Silent Revolution: Moopanar'. Special Correspondent. *The Hindu Newspaper:* 28th August 1999.

——. 2000. 'Tension in Village as Dalits Insist on Entering Temple'. Special Correspondent: *The Hindu Newspaper.* 12 December 2000.

——. 2001. 'Opposition Demands PM's Resignation'. Special Correspondent. *The Hindu Newspaper.* 14 March 2001.

——. 2001. '"I have been framed"—Laxman'. Special Correspondent. *The Hindu Newspaper.* 17 March 2001.

Human Rights Watch. 1999. *Journal of Human Rights Watch.* Madurai: Human Rights Watch.

Independent Initiative. 1999. *Report About Elections, Attacks on Dalits, Denial of Voting Right, Bogus Voting.* Published by Independent Initiative under instruction from V.I. Krishna Iyer.

Maalai Malar. 1999. Thirumavalavan Arrested: Government Buses Burnt, Violence in Cuddalore and Perambalur. Tamil Paper, Correspondent not named. 13 June 1999.

Marshall, G. 1994. (ed.). *The Concise Oxford Dictionary of Sociology.* Oxford: OUP.

Thamukku. 1999. *The Newsletter of the Dalit Resource Centre* 1(1&2), September–October 1999, November–December Madurai: TTS: Edited by V. Abraham Ponnudurai.

TTS. 1992. *Annual Report. 1991–1992. Theological Education is a Movement.* TTS: Madurai.

——. 1993. *Annual Report 1992–1993. Ministerial Training: Whose Responsibility is it?* TTS: Madurai.

World Bank. 1997. *India: Achievements and Challenges in Reducing Poverty.* Washington: World Bank.

Statistical Supplements and Discussion Papers:

Gang. I., K. Sen, M-S. Yun November 2002. *Caste, Ethnicity and Poverty in Rural India.* Bonn: Institute for the Study of Labour Discussion Paper.

Rath, N. and S. Konlade. 2000. 'Statistical Supplements'. *Journal of Indian School of Political Economy* 12(3&4): 603–885.

Magazine and Newspaper Articles:

Anandan, T. 2001. 'The Failure of Anti-caste Movements'. *The Hindu Online.* 24 July 2001. http://www.hinduonnet.com/thehindu/2001/07/24/stories/13240611.htm

Athreya, V. and Chandra. 2000. 'The Drumbeats of Oppression'. *Frontline* 17(12), 23 June 2000: 103–5.

Chandhoke, N. 1999. 'Courtailing [sic] Ethnic Conflict'. *The Hindu,* Review Article: 7 March 1999.

Devi, V. 2000. 'A Cry for Justice'. *Frontline* 17(13) 7 July 2000: 48–50.

Ganapathi, V. 1999. 'A Ding-Dong Battle in Perambalur'. *The Hindu* 30 August 1999.

Ghosh, G. 1999. 'Dalit Beating Is A Way of Life Here'. *The Hindu Online*. 30 May 1999. http://www.indiaserver.com/thehindu/1999/o5/30/stories/13300611.htm

Guru, G. 1999. 'A Critical Look At Dalit Activism'. *Hindu Online*. 12 January 1999. http://www.indiaserver.com/thehindu/1999ft/01/12/stories/05122523.htm

———. 2000. 'The Question of Valid Representation'. *Hindu Online*. 25 February 2000. http://www.the-hindu.com/2000/02/25/stories/05252524.htm

Harriss, J. 2000. 'Successful Populism?' *Frontline*, Review Article. 17(5), 4 March 2000: 77–78.

Illangovan, R. 1999. 'Kodankipatti Dalits' Ordeal'. *The Hindu*, Madurai Edition: 07 July.

———. 2000a. 'They Live as "Outcasts" in Samathuvarpuram'. *The Hindu Online*. 18 February 2000. http://www.the-hindu.com/stories/0418223c.htm

———. 2000b. 'Local Body Chief Forced to Live in Exile'. *The Hindu Online*. 18 July 2000. http://www.the-hindu.com/2000/07/19/stories/04192234.htm

———. 2001. 'Dalit Card Cost DMK OBC Vote Bank'. *The Hindu,* 14 May 2001. http://www.hinduonnet.com/thehindu/2001/05/15/stories/04152236.htm

Indiresan, P. 2001. 'The Tamil Nadu Verdict'. *The Hindu*, 25 May 2001. http://www.hinduonnet.com/thehinder/2001/05/25/stories/05252523.htm

Ipriyan and Venkatesh. 1999. 'Moopanar Draws Crowds Even Without Speaking'. *Kalki* (Tamil Journal). 12 September 1999: 4–7.

Kaasi, 1999. 'Chidambaram is Heading to Extremes'. *Nakeeran* (Tamil Journal). 14 September 1999. 12(42): 30–31.

Kannan, R. 2000. 'Slum Dwellers Seek Permanent Solution'. *The Hindu* 17 July 2000.

———. 2001. 'Over 1000 Families in Bonded Labour'. *The Hindu Online*. 3 August 2001. http://www.hinduonnet.com/2001/08/03/04032231.htm.

Karat, P. 2000. 'Distortion of Democracy'. *Frontline* 17(15), 4 August 2000: 113–4.

Krishnakumar, A. 2000. 'Women as Panchayat Heads'. *Frontline* 17(25), 22 December 2000: 98–99.

Larbeer, M. 1999. 'Our Concern'. *Thamukku* editorial. 1(1) pg.8.

Mani, V. R. 1995. 'Centre Seeks Report on the Police Atrocities on Dalits'. *The Sunday Times of India*. 3 December 1995.

Menon, P. 2000. 'Panchayati Raj at Work'. *Frontline* 17(12), 23 June 2000: 118–19.

———. 2001. 'Relief, Delayed or Denied'. *Frontline* 18(4), 2 March 2000: 9–15.

Mukajanga, K. 1997. 'The Politics of the Caste System and the Practice of Untouchability'. The Ambedkar Centre for Peace and Justice.

Muralidharan, S. 2001. 'A Tough Response'. *Frontline* 18(14), 7–20 July 2001: 12–13.

Muthahar, S. 2001. 'PT Threatens Militant Struggle'. *The Hindu Online*. 31 July 2001. http://www.hinduonnet.com/thehindu/2001/07/31/stories/04312236.htm.

Nambath, S. 1999. 'Dalit Consolidation: Setback to PT Efforts'. *Hindu Online*: 14 November 1999. http://www.indiaserver.com/thehindu/1999/11/14/stories/04142239.htm.

———. 2000. 'DMK Gained from Dalits' Apathy to AIADMK'. *Hindu Online*. 29 February 2000. http://www.indiaserver.com/thehindu/2000/02/29/stories/04292231.htm

Omvedt, G. 1999. 'Dalits and Elections II'. *The Hindu*. 6 November 1999 (Madurai).

———. 2001. 'Reservation in the Corporate Sector'. *The Hindu Online*. 1 June 2001. http://www.the-hindu.com/stories/05012524.htm.

Pandiyan, P. 1999. 'Will Panchami Lands Be Reclaimed?' *Nandan* 16–31 October 1999: 38–39.

Prasad, C.B and S. Bechain. S. 2000. 'Where non-Dalit Commentators Err'. *Hindu Online*. 4 January 2000. http://www.indiaserver.com/thehindu/2000/01/04/stories/13040611.htm.

Radhakrishnan, P. 2002. 'The Vanniyar Separatism', *Frontline*, Vol. 19(17), 17–30 August.

Radhakrishnan, R.K. 2000. 'Fresh Encroachments on Cooum'. *The Hindu*. 24 July 2000.

Rao, S. 1995. 'Crime and Punishment: The Story of Dhanam, a Dalit Child'. *Frontline* 12(18): 25–27.

Rajalakshmi, T.K. 2000. 'A Biased Agenda'. *Frontline*, 22 December 2000: 92–93.

———. 2001. 'Castes and Killings'. *Frontline* 18(14), 7–20 July 2001: 38–40.

Sharma, R. 2000. 'Of Human Bondage'. *Frontline* 17(16), 18 August 2000: 45–46.

Sonamandan. 1999. 'Will There Be Re-Polls in Chidambaram?' *Nandan* (Tamil Journal). 16–30 September 1999: 13–14, 36.

Subramanian, T. 2001. 'The Caste of Characters'. *Frontline* 18(4), 2 March 2001: 46–48.

———. 2001a. 'Tamil Nadu's Shame'. *Frontline* 18(14), 7–20 July 2001: 4–12.

Venkatesh, M. 2001. 'DPI Joins DMK-led Front'. *Hindu Online*. 6 March 2001. http://www.indiaserver.com/the-hindu/2001/03/06/stories/04062231.htm.

Vikesh and Maniswaram. 1999. 'If Only He was absent…' *Junior Viketan* (Tamil Journal) 17(75) 19 September 1999: 2–3.

Viswanathan, S. 1995. 'A Village Ruined: In T.N, When the Police Went Beserk'. *Frontline* 14(14): 12(21): 20 October 1995: 40–41.

———. 1997. 'Challenging Casteism'. *Frontline*, 23 July 1997: 111–14.

———. 1998. 'Caste-Based Mobilisation and Violence'. *Frontline* 15(22), 24 October–6 November 1999.

———. 1999a. 'A Consolidation of Forces'. *Frontline* 16(17), 24–27 August 1999.

———. 1999b. 'Police in the Dock'. *Frontline* 16(19), 11–24 September 1999.

Viswanathan, S. and S. Saqaf. 1999. 'The Tirunelveli Massacre'. *Frontline* 16(16), 29 July–13 August 1999.

Yadav, Y. 2001. 'A Matter of Arithmetic'. (With the Centre for the Study of Developing Societies team). *Frontline* 8 June: 113–17.

INDEX

inferiority, inferiority complex,
116, 119, 132, 141, 319
injustice, 72, 135, 246
innovation, 280–81
institutions, institutional network,
politics, 21, 25, 77, 105, 285–
88
institutionalisation process, 79,
84, 265, 273, 274, 301, 342,
345
integration, integrity, 87, 134, 159
interaction, 216
inter-movement competition, 215
internalisation debate, 114–22
intimidation, 24, 349
intra-caste differentiation,
relations, 115, 167
Islam, 81
Iyer, V.R. Krishna, 305n

jajmani system, 149, 172
Jayalalitha, J., 23, 61, 265, 297
Jayanthi, 237
Jayaseelan, N.V., 139
jobocracy, 94
justice, 19, 51, 86, 98, 144, 223,
232, 282, 283
Justice P. Gomathinayagam
Commission of Enquiry, 163
Justice Party, 96, 281

Kallars, dominance, 121
Kamaraj, 31, 32–33, 41–43, 54n,
277, 304, 310, 312, 315, 317
Kambamanikam, S., 142n
Kannadasan, 264
Kappalur, Madurai, Tamil Nadu,
312; caste discrimination,
159–60
Karanai, Chengleput District:
struggle for land, 158
karma, 20, 87n, 116, 120, 243
Karnataka: patron-client relationship; Samagars dominance,
152

Karunakaran, 76
Karunanidhi, K., 23, 81, 82, 133,
282, 286, 288, 289, 293,
296, 316
Karur, 60, 331; agricultural
labourers, 155; Dalits, 161;
DMK–BJP combine, 260
Kashmir: conflicts, 102
Kathrine, 221
Keelathurai, 129, 270
Kilpoovanikuppam, 305
Kilvenmani: labourers massacre,
135n
kinship ties, 55, 89–90, 172,
180, 191, 222, 225n, 241,
244n, 249, 271
knowledge, 92–93
Kodankipatti, Madurai, Tamil
Nadu, 19–20, 34–35, 127,
133, 142–43, 144n, 331,
350; agricultural labourers,
155; Dalits, 131–34, 151,
163, 188–89, 212; divisions,
64; employment, 160;
discrimination against dalits,
185, 187; Naidus and Dalits,
political alliance, 124; taxes,
186; women's consciousness,
231
Kodiyankulam, Tamil Nadu:
violence against Dalits, 162,
163n, 287
Kosuvangundu, Madurai, Tamil
Nadu, 28–29
Kounders, 122, 124, 125, 188,
350
Krishnasamy, 63, 78, 251, 253–
54, 256–57, 268, 297, 299,
301, 307n, 308, 310, 325,
345
Kshatriya, 122

labour, labourers, 88;
casualisation, 161; contractor

ABOUT THE AUTHOR

Hugo Gorringe is Lecturer in Identity, Department of Sociology, University of Edinburgh. He received his doctorate from the University of Edinburgh in 2002.